Figure 1 – Definitions of the Marketing Information System

MIS DEFINITIONS	AUTHORS
Computerized system to provide, in an organized fashion, the flow of information, analytically and operationally, capable of supporting decision-making processes, marketing activities of an organization and all the strategic marketing elements.	Harmon, 2003.
Interacting and continuous structure of people, equipment and procedures to obtain, classify, analyze, assess and distribute necessary and accurate information in a timely manner to the marketing decision makers, whether the information is internal, external or from other markets, which is made necessary, useful and sufficient to serve users.	Kotler & Keller, 2006
A complex interacting structure of people, machines, and procedures to generate, in an orderly and pertinent manner, internal and external information to the organization, used as a base for the decision-making process.	James,1998
Computer planned in a data system whose purpose is to provide a task manager with a continuous flow of information which is relevant to specific decisions in its scope of responsibilities.	Boone & Kurtz, 2007.
Collection of relevant data within a significant goal, whose data composes recommendations which can be stored for future use.	King, 2010.
Quality project to help in the decision-making process, composed of four elements: database (internal reports); marketing intelligence (economy, market, business environment), market research (regular and special occasion/ goal specific); analysis of marketing information (Decision Support System).	Jobber & Fahy, 2006.

Source: Authors, adapted from Ismail (2011, p. 175-178). Mattar *et al.* (2009, p. 100) regard the definition of the MIS by Cox and Good as the most complete, in 1967.

It is a structured and interacting complex of people, machines and procedures whose purpose is to generate an orderly and continuous data flow, collected from internal and external sources of the company, to be used as a base for decision making in areas specifically in charge of marketing.

With no intention of exhausting this subject matter or presenting a broad review of the MIS models, some of them are presented with the purpose of enabling the discussion of this subject matter and obtaining more support for the field research. As for the operational model, Kotlere and Keller (2006) believe that the MIS must feature the following elements: a) the subsystem of internal records, which allows monitoring and analysis of the organization´s performance; b) the subsystem of marketing intelligence, which monitors the many environmental variables and marketing events that influence the business, in which the competitors are included; c) the subsystem of marketing research, which is aimed at the development, collection, analysis and edition of systematic data reports and relevant findings for the resolution of specific marketing problems; d) a subsystem of analysis and support to market decisions – a coordinated set of tools and techniques, software and hardware to assist in the analysis and interpretation of the information. The suggested model is represented by Figure 2 (Kotler, 1998, p. 12)[1]:

Figure 2 – MIS Model by Kotler

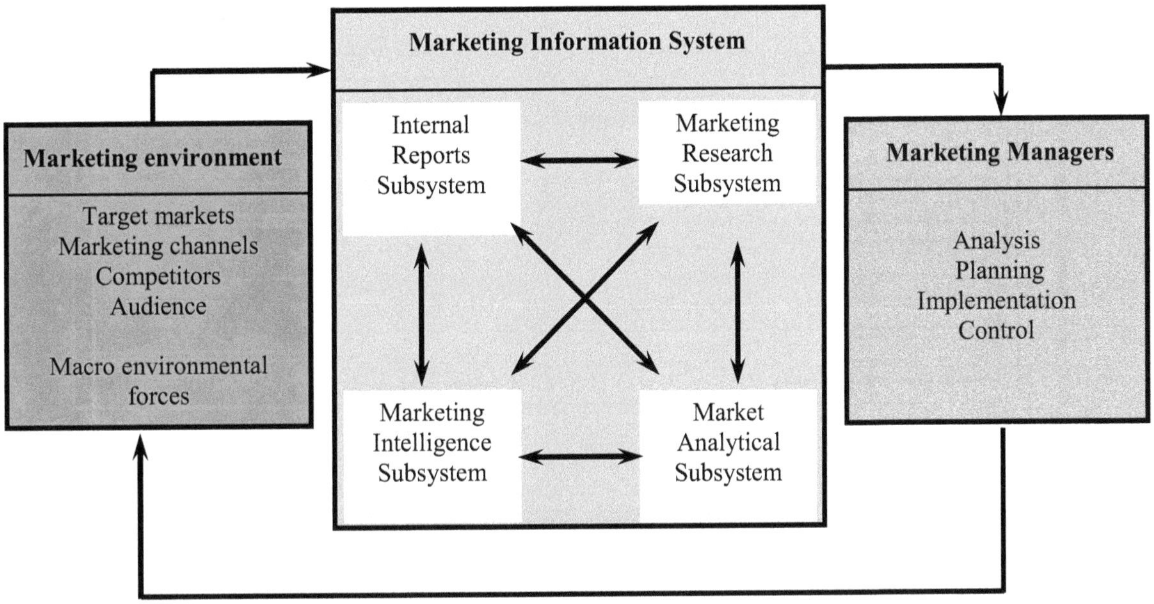

Source: Kotler (1998, p. 12).

Mattar *et al.* (2009) highlight that fact that a generic MIS model must be applied and adapted to the reality of any company as long as it comprehends such activities as joining, processing, disseminating and storing relevant data and information, internal and external to the organization, for marketing decision-making processes.

Thus, the proposed model, as seen in Figure 4, is made up of four subsystems: (1) environmental monitoring system; (2) competitive information systems; (3) internal information systems; (4) marketing research system.

Nevertheless, Mattar *et al.* (2009) add that there is not a standardized MIS model; each company has a particular need for information which corresponds to its expectations, also respecting the management style and/or the culture of the group which manages it.

Figure 3 – MIS Model by Mattar *et al*

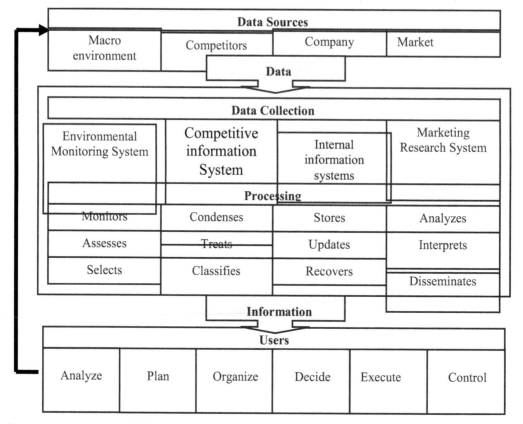

Source: Mattar *et al*. (2009, p.105).

3.   FIELD RESEARCH METHODOLOGY

Allowing for the relevance presented by the literature reviewed regarding the relationship of the MIS with the marketing decision making, the purpose of the field research was defined as the verification of the benefits obtained with the use of the MIS.

For this purpose, the descriptive research was chosen, which was performed by means of a case study, as it refers to a contemporary phenomenon, within a real context, (Vergara, 2004; Yin, 2005). The chosen company for the empirical contribution operates in the clothing retail business, which is viewed as an expressive sector in the Brazilian economy.

Data collection took place by means of personal, individual interviews, with two of the company's executives, based on a semi-structured script, which consisted of questions related to the variables: "use of the MIS" and "benefits provided by the MIS". Such questions were written based on the literature review performed, for the purpose of enabling a confronting and a corresponding analysis. The information obtained was verified and crossed with the information available in the management documents provided by those being researched.

The research was done in February 2009, with two decision makers, in accordance with their roles: one of them from the top management and the other one from the marketing department. Two employees were interviewed for the purpose of reducing biased opinions and personal interests, as it was possible to triangulate the data obtained as well as with the documents provided by the company (Yin, 2005).

Such documents contained specific data on the research variables and data related to the results and their projections, which served as an important indicator for the purposes of the research problem in question, especially regarding the existence of a MIS and the scope and flow of the information generated.

The script was based on the theoretical background described in this paper. The first part of the script attempted to become more familiarized with the company whereas the second part addressed the purpose of the research itself.

The analysis, from the transcription of the answers, which were recorded with the consent of the interviewees, and from the documents provided by them, was descriptive and interpretative, and it attempted to find a correspondence with the theory presented so that the information obtained in the literature review could be reinforced or questioned. (Vergara, 2004; Yin, 2005).

4.   PRESENTATION OF THE RESULTS OF THE FIELD RESEARCH

4.1   Characterization of the business sector of the researched company

According to the Ministry of Development, Industry and Foreign Trade (MDIFT) (2008), by comparing January 2008 with February 2007, the sectors which grew the most in terms of productivity were the ones in transportation equipment (8.1%), machines and equipment (8.3%), leather and shoes (10.7%) and clothing (11.6%).

According to Renner (2009), the fashion retail sector is quite fragmented which allowed the successful development of major department store chains, which increasingly receive investments from foreign groups.

The fragmented market and the search for positioning have made it clear that when it comes to brand consumption, according to Luz (2008), the clothing market is mainly composed of classes A and B, with class A spending 19 times more than the other classes; classes A and B account for the consumption of 57% of the fashion products in Brazil, whereas class C accounts for 31%. Regarding brand consumption, considering the economic expressiveness, Luz (2008) also reveals that the São Paulo Fashion Week [SPFW] event sets in motion around 1.5 billion Brazilian reals.

However, according to a report released by Renner (2009), the increase in the purchasing power of the families in classes C and D have drawn the attention of the retail sector interested in attracting the low-income population. Also, the behavior of the population has been the target of analysis, with the search of a single point of sales, leading to the expansion of the shopping centers and, consequently the presence of department stores.

For the production of items offered for consumption in the fashion market, according to the Ministry of Labor and Employment (MLE), most of the employees who compose the sector are women and the States that hire the most employees in the sector are São Paulo, Santa Catarina and Minas Gerais.

4.2   Characterization of the company

The researched company was founded in the late 40's and its main activity was the sale of textiles. Acquired by a domestic group at the end of the 70's, after restructuring, it started to offer ready-to-wear clothes. Currently, it is among the major fashion retail chains in the country. The quest for better positioning made it, in the 90's, turn its attention to fashion, in international and national trends (the SPFW, for instance). In the same period of time, they introduced quality improvements to its products and the launching of its own brands.

Currently, the company is the second largest chain of department stores in Brazil and it competes with companies that receive foreign investment. Among the domestic ones, it occupies the first position. The group to which it belongs is regarded as the largest group in the making of clothes in Latin America.

The company keeps employees in fashion centers in Europe and in the United States, which enables its collections to be based on the main fashion trends. On average, 120,000 pieces a day are made in their factories, delivered at their own stores by the carrier company that belongs to the group. Advertising campaigns are aimed at the main target audiences of the stores: women aged 25 to 40 years, through television advertisements and specific in-store marketing activities, using information from its customer database.

With the purpose of strengthening the relationship with the active customer, the company offers the store's own card to make financial services available, such as cash withdrawals, personal loans, insurance, home and vehicle assistance, theft and robbery protection, unemployment and home insurance. In Figure 4, it is possible to see other information on the researched company.

Figure 4 – Structure of the Company

Distribution Centers	Natal (State of Rio Grande do Norte) and Guarulhos (State of São Paulo), with 55,000 square meters and 86,000 square meters of living space, respectively.
Operating in	21 Brazilian States and in the Federal District
Head office	São Paulo
Shopping center	Northeastern Region
Number of stores	135 in 2011
Financial services company	17.6 million members in 2010
Total number of meters of the stores	395,636 m^2 square meters
Factories	Northeastern Region - one for the production of plain textile (jeans and shirts), the other for the production of knitwear and shirts.

Departments	Women´s fashion wear; men´s wear, children´s and teenagers´ wear, shoes and home fashion.
Target Audiences	Classes C and D
Number of Employees	38,700 in 2011
Revenue in 2010	R$ 2,6 billion Brazilian reals
Average production in 2009	200 thousand pieces a day

Source: Authors, based on the data collected in the research.

4.2 Description and Analysis of the Researched Variables

4.2.1 Use of the MIS

The company has an Information System (IS) based on the software called SAP (Systems Applications and Products in Data Processing), developed by the German company with the same name. It enables to obtain information and disseminate them throughout the company so that it can be used in its activities. Regarded as slightly complex by the interviewees, it sometimes requires that some information, after being extracted and analyzed, be transferred to the Intranet, which tends to make its use easy by the users. The company´s SAP system is made up of two bases called BW (Business Warehouse); one of them serves the company´s commercial area and the other one serves the remaining areas.

The model can be divided into two blocks: (1) one defined from the user´s profile, who has access only to their department´s information, in order to perform their tasks, as seen in Figure 6, and (2) the other one in which the information presents itself in a disaggregated manner, more complex, and which is worked on with statistical modeling tools. Due to the merging of the Business Intelligence and Information Technology, the Intranet, based on the user´s profile, at the moment, shows some "screens" or accesses under construction, as seen in Figure 5, by the ellipse in white.

Figure 5 – IS model based on the user´s profile.

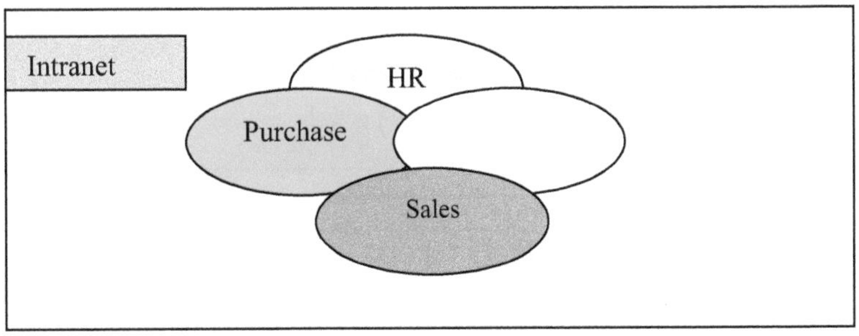

Source: Authors, based upon the company´s Intranet output.

As for the flow and distribution of information, the access is restricted to each department within the company. Each store has only access to its information. The purpose of the restrictions, mentioned by both interviewees, is to keep the information from being passed on to the competition. Due to strategic reasons, the Internal audit alone has full access to all the information and it grants access authorization. However, according to the interviewees, these measures are seen by many users as something unsuitable and complex, which causes delays in the decision-making process, especially in the Marketing area, which needs data that matches the customer´s behavior, regional cultures, sales and other aspects. As for the MIS model, both interviewees stated that the company developed its own model, which meets their needs and features a system of decision-making support and of relationship management with customers and the value chain. In detail, the marketing professional explained that the MIS is an SAP module, accessible to the marketing department, and it has the subsystems of records, marketing research and decision-making support, which enables the use of the statistical modeling.

Therefore, the model developed by the company is the closest to what is proposed by Kotler (1998). Also, as seen in the pertinent literature, the company has an information system structure interconnected with the use of software and the Intranet, which operates in an integrated manner with the MIS for the development of strategies and action plans (Laudon & Laudon, 2004; Cravens & Piercy, 2006; Swartz & Iacobucci, 1999; Hooper, Huff & Thirkell, 2010; Deshpande, 2013).

Nevertheless, by taking into account the fact that the pertinent literature highlights that information must be accessible to all decision makers, the above-mentioned restriction results in certain dissatisfaction from the users, which might hamper the achievement of the benefits suggested by the pertinent literature (Laudon & Laudon, 2004; Hooley, Saunders, & Piercy, 2005; Cravens & Piercy, 2006; Minciotti, 1992; Campomar & Ikeda, 2006; Mattar *et al.*, 2009; Swartz & Iacobucci, 1999; Deshpande, 2013).

4.2.2 Benefits provided by the MIS

The two interviewed managers, when questioned about the benefits the company is provided by the MIS, recognized that there are many of them, but in fact the company only allows to achieve them if they are used with other IS modules, which is not always feasible, due to the above-mentioned access restrictions. The statement is made clear when the interviewees classify in terms of importance the benefits which are solely provided the MIS (Figure 6), whose items were listed based on the literature review.

Figure 6 – Benefits generated from the use of the company´s MIS

Item	RESULTS	BENEFIT OBTAINED		
		High	Average	Low
1	Reduce operational costs		X	
2	Prepare more accurate and timely reports		X	
3	Improve productivity		X	
4	Control Marketing costs	X		
5	Improve internal services performed and offered		X	

Item	RESULTS	BENEFIT OBTAINED		
		High	Average	Low
6	Improve decision-making process		X	
7	Foresee and develop plans		X	
8	Improve the organizational structure			X
9	Promote price and advertising strategies		X	
10	Improve the flexibilization of the changes in environmental factors			X
11	Optimize the provision of services offered to customers.		X	
12	Improve the interaction with their suppliers			X
13	Improve the sales force performance			X
14	Develop staff training programs			X
15	Build a distinctive customer service		X	
16	Identify the target market and concentrate efforts		X	
17	Become familiarized with the competitor´s activities			X
18	Monitor and identify new segments		X	
19	Develop new products/services			X
20	Manage and reduce inventory costs		X	
21	Find new sources of goods			X
22	Strengthen the relationship with consumers		X	
23	Improve the distribution channel control*			
24	Reduce the risk perceived by the customer *			
25	Build advantages in the long run over the competition			X
26	Identify the nature of the services and products offered to the market *			
27	Improvement of the control		X	
28	Improvement in the planning		X	

*N/A / unknown. Source: Authors, developed based upon the data collected from the research.

Both believe that the MIS allows the establishment of the foundation of retail strategies. They also speak highly of the possibility of reducing operational costs, making more accurate reports, improving productivity, controlling marketing costs, improving internal services, improving decision making, developing plans, promoting price and communication strategies, optimizing the services offered to customers, indentifying target markets and new segments and managing inventories.

However, such benefits as improving distribution control, reducing the risks perceived by customers and indentifying the nature of the services and products offered to the market are analyzed in the IS by other sectors and involve Logistics (factory/carrier), Purchasing and Business Intelligence. Even the contribution from the MIS to marketing results needs the monitoring of the responses from campaigns and promotions by the Business Intelligence, particularly due to information access restrictions.

Regarding the development of the main retail strategies, the information obtained contributes to strategic planning and decisions on the lines of products, price setting and store expansion and location.

As to the marketing planning, there is the concern for monitoring needs, satisfaction and customer purchase processes, performed by the Business Intelligence department, which handles the strategic function of supply and provision of information to the managers for decision-making purposes.

With a focus on the customers and maintaining its positioning within the segment in which it operates, the company invests in the integration with the factory in order to gain market and offer fashion with quality and fair prices. This integration is seen as a distinctive element over the competition, a sort of an innovative service added to the customer service. Nevertheless, for the interviewees, the integration store/factory is seen as a distinctive element which tends to enable cost reduction and improvement in price strategies over the competitors.

According to the top management interviewee, based on the analysis of market share: *"Currently, we are the second largest company in this sector, but we have been working to reach the first position soon, and in order to do so the company has worked on the integration between the stores and the group, opening of new stores and refurbishing of the existing ones, consolidation of market share in the Northern and Northeastern regions, increase in the market share in São Paulo and Rio de Janeiro, creation of a financial services company, strengthening of the relationship with customers by means of store cards and focus on innovation, launching of trends and products by means of market research and marketing intelligence, modernization of the manufacturing complex and implementation of information technology for operational and financial management."*

Regarding the interaction of the company with competitors, there is some difficulty obtaining information and, often times, the store´s managers are the ones who visit their competitors and pass information on the Business Intelligence, Commercial, Marketing, and to other operational areas.

With the purpose of meeting market needs and maintaining its positioning, the company believes that observing and analyzing the main events and the demographic trends demand efforts, but which tend to offer more opportunities than difficulties if they are properly explored. Considering the fact that the company has many stores in other States of the country, constant studies are performed in relation to the cultures and customs of each region served, as well as in relation to the main fashion events in each region. This type of analysis is seen as an opportunity to increase sales when associated with meeting seasonal sales demand.

5.   FINAL CONSIDERATIONS

As seen in the statements from the interviewees, the acquisition of new technologies, the acquisition and use of other software and the merging of the IT and BI areas under the same management show the concern of the researched company to significantly invest in IS and in its use in an integrated manner with the MIS and with other company´s databases, which allow analyzing customers, the market and, though poorly, the competition as well.

The close-knit relationship between Marketing, Business Intelligence and Information Technology shows the need for adaptation of the reality and the culture of the company to the use of information. By analyzing the benefits provided by the MIS, it is possible to see the dedication of the company to obtain information about its customers, in order to strengthen their relationship, as well as the search for meeting their customers' needs.

The company uses information more as a support to the risk reduction management in decision making than to the competitive advantage creation, although it is moving in the direction of the use of information as a strategic resource, for the purpose of providing a better performance of the operations and new business opportunities, as it has recently integrated Business Intelligence and Information Technology under the same management.

The search for and creation of a competitive advantage can be maximized if the company uses the MIS effectively, increasing the possibility of profiting from the implemented innovations and from identifying other demands that are not met by its competitors, demands which the company would have conditions to explore (Kotler & Keller, 2006; Gounaris, Panigyrakis & Chatzipanagiotou, 2007; Mattar *et al.*, 2009; Gupta, 2012). The information obtained about customers and the market trends prompted the group to opt for the production of their own products, and, consequently, their distribution by their own stores.

In the company´s business sector, the products have a short life cycle, which challenges it to make speedy and flexible market plannings, where the use of information is essential, in accordance with what the pertinent literature presents (Swartz & Iacobucci, 1999; Sisodia, 1992; Lovelock & Whright, 2005; Levy & Weitz, 2000; Pinto *et al.*, 2006; Minciotti, 1992; Cravens & Piercy, 2006; Kotler & Keller, 2006; Mattar *et al.*, 2009).

Although the information access restrictions, based on the creation of profiles, cause delays in the development of projects and in the definition of plannings, the research permitted to see that the MIS provides the benefits presented in the pertinent literature; however, in order to further enjoy such benefits, there is still the need of its integrated use with the company´s IS.

Within the limitations of this work, the adopted method to perform the field research can be mentioned, as it does not allow for generalizations. However, it is important to highlight that, despite this limitation, the objective established, which is the verification of the benefits obtained with the use of the MIS, was achieved. Another evident limitation is in regards to performing a single case study; it is believed that the possible comparison with other case studies could further clarify the treatment of the flow and distribution of information, which, in this research, was limited to the access based on the creation of user profiles.

As a manner for contributing to further research, the exploration of other variables is recommended, such as the necessary information for decision-making processes and environmental analysis, regarding this research's problem. Also, it is recommended that similar research be done, and also of a quantitative nature in the business sector in question and in other relevant ones, for better assessment of the management of information that the marketing information system provides for creating and maintaining competitiveness, whether due to the scarcity of empirical studies or due to economic representativeness.

REFERENCES

Berhan, E.; Paul, I.; Jan, H. G. (2012). *Marketing information systems and price change decision making:* the case of Ethiopian industries. Germany: LAP Lambert Academic Publishing.

Campomar, M. C., & Ikeda, A. A. (2006). *O planejamento de marketing e a confecção de planos:* dos conceitos a um novo modelo. São Paulo: Saraiva.

Chatzipanagiotou, K.C.; & Coritos, C. D. (2010). A suggested typology of Greek upscale hotels based on their MrKIS: implications for hotels' overall effectiveness. *European Journal of Marketing*, 44 (11/12), 1576-1611.

Cravens, D. W., & Piercy, N. F. (2006). *Strategic marketing.* Columbus: McGraw-Hill.

Deshpande, A. S. (2013). Marketing information system for industrial products. *International Journal of Management & Information Technology*, 3 (1), 71-76.

Gounaris, S. P.; Panigyrakis, G. G.; & Chatzipanagiotou, K. C. (2007). Measuring the effectiveness of marketing information systems: an empirically validated instrument. *Marketing Intelligence & Planning*, 25 (6), 612-631.

Gupta, A. (2012). An overview of information technology in tourism industry. *International Journal Applied Services Marketing*, 1 (1).

Hooley, G. J., Saunders, J. A., & Piercy, N. F. (2005). *Estratégia de marketing e posicionamento competitivo.* São Paulo: Pearson Prentice Hall.

Hooper, V. A.; Huff, S. L.; & Thirkell, C. P. (2010, feb.) The impact of IS-marketing alignment on marketing performance and business performance. *The DATA BASE for Advances in Information Systems*, 41 (1), 36-55.

Ismail, S. T. (2011, jan.) The role of marketing information system on decision making: an applied study on Royal Jordanian Air Lines (RJA). *International Journal of Business and Social Science*, 2 (3), 175-185.

Jaworski, B. J., Macinnis, D. J., & Kohli, A. K. (2002). Generating competitive intelligence in organizations. *Journal of Marketing*, 5 (4), 279- 307.

Karamarko, N. (2010). System of tourist destination management as a Croatian identity. *Tourism & Hospitality Management - Conference Proceedings*, p. 950-966.

Kotler, P. (1998). *Administração de Marketing.* São Paulo: Prentice Hall.

Kotler, P., & Keller, K. L. (2006). *Administração de marketing.* São Paulo: Prentice Hall.

Kubiak, B. F.; & Kowalik, M. F. (2010, dec.). Marketing information systems as a driver of an organization's competitive advantage. *Journal of Internet Banking and Commerce*, 15 (3), 2-10.

Lambin, J. J. (2000). *Marketing estratégico.* Lisboa: McGraw Hill.

Laudon, K. C., & Laudon, J. P. (2001). *Gerenciamento de sistemas de informação.* Rio de Janeiro: LTC.

Laudon, K. C., & Laudon, J. P. (2004). *Sistemas de informação gerenciais:* administrando a empresa digital. São Paulo: Prentice Hall.

Levy, M., & Weitz, B. A. (2000). *Administração de varejo.* São Paulo: Atlas.

Lovelock, C., & Wright, L. (2005). *Serviços:* marketing e gestão. São Paulo: Saraiva.

Luz, M. (2008). *Paulo Borges fala sobre o mercado da moda.* Recuperado em 18 de fevereiro, 2010 de http://simplesmenteelegante.com/?p=1416.

Mattar, F. N., Oliveira B., Motta, S. L. S., & Queiroz, M. J. (2009). *Gestão de produtos, serviços, marcas e mercados:* estratégias e ações para alcançar e manter-se "top of Market". São Paulo: Atlas.

Minciotti, S. A. (1992). *O sistema de informações de marketing como suporte para a adoção do marketing estratégico:* o desenvolvimento de um modelo. Tese de doutorado, Universidade de São Paulo, São Paulo, SP, Brasil.

Ministério do Desenvolvimento, Indústria e Comércio Exterior. (2008). *Encontro nacional de comércio e serviços.* Recuperado em 04 de novembro, 2010, de http://www.desenvolvimento.gov.br/sitio/interna/noticia.php?area=4&noticia=8606.

Ministério do Trabalho e Emprego. (2008). *Revista do trabalho.* Recuperado em 18 de fevereiro, 2010, de http://www.mte.gov.br/revista/edicao2/txt_complementar1.asp.

Pinto F., Marques A., Gago P., & Santos, M. F. Integração da descoberta de conhecimento em bases de dados como suporte a actividades de CRM. (2006, setembro). Anais do Encontro Anual da Associação Nacional de Programas de Pós-Graduação e Pesquisa Em Administração, Salvador, BA, Brasil.

Renner. (2009). *Mercado brasileiro de varejo.* Recuperado em 28 de janeiro, 2010, de http://www.b2i.us/profiles/investor/fullpage.asp?f=1&BzID=1251&to=cp&Nav=0&LangID=3&s=0&ID=3485.

Sisodia, R. S. (1992). Marketing information and decision support systems for services. *The Journal of Services Marketing*, 6 (1), 51-65.

Swartz, T. A., & Iacobucci, D. (Eds). (1999). *Handbook of services marketing & management.* Thousand Oaks: Sage.

Vergara, S. C. (2004). *Projetos e relatórios de pesquisa em administração*. São Paulo: Atlas.

Yin, R. K. (2005). *Estudo de caso:* planejamento e métodos. Porto Alegre: Bookman.

---

[1] The operational theoretical model used in the field research, by graphic representation, as in the illustrated one, was not found in the most recent editions of the work done by the author.

2

USE OF THE RFID TECHNOLOGY TO OVERCOME INEFFICIENCIES IN THE PRODUCTION PROCESS: AN ANALYSIS OF A MICROCOMPUTER COMPANY IN ILHÉUS – BAHIA

Frederico Wergne de Castro Araújo Filho
X. L. Travassos
Paulo S. Figueiredo
Integrated Center of Manufacture and Technology – National Service of Industrial Learning – DR, Salvador, Bahia - Brazil

ABSTRACT

This paper presents a methodology for the integration of RFID technology into microcomputer assembly companies. Such a technology enables inventory control, tracking of parts/products and customer satisfaction. The methodology was developed to identify and evaluate the production process in an assembly company and to apply the process FMEA to evaluate potential faults and propose improvement actions for the use of RFID technology. The methodology was validated in a company from the Pólo de Informática de Ilhéus/BA. In this study, the viability of RFID technology for inventory control and traceability of the product was confirmed. Among the benefits obtained were the reduction of one of the workers from the inventory team, reduction in the costs of substituting a component, and reduction in lead-time.

Keywords: RFID; Process FMEA; Site Survey; Process Automation; Inventory Management

1. INTRODUCTION

According to Whang (2010), Radio-Frequency Identification (RFID) has been hailed as a major innovation to enhance the efficiency of inventory management (Gaukler et al. 2004) and supply chain management (Heinrich 2005). The basic premise

---

Address for correspondence / Endereço para correspondência

Frederico Wergne de Castro Araújo Filho. Integrated Center of Manufacture and Technology – National Service of Industrial Learning – DR. Frederico has an MSc from Senai Cimatec. His research interests are Automating Manufacturing Systems and RFID. Adress: Av. Orlando Gomes 1845 – Piatã, Salvador, Bahia - Brazil, 41650-050.

X. L. Travassos . Federal University of Santa Catarina (UFSC). He finished his PhD at the L'Ecole Centrale de Lyon (France). His research interests are Numerical Modeling and Industrial Engineering. Adress: Rua Presidente Prudente de Moraes, 406, Santo Antônio, 89218-000 - Joinville, SC - Brasil.

Paulo S. Figueiredo. Integrated Center of Manufacture and Technology – National Service of Industrial Learning – DR. Paulo has a Doctoral Degree from Boston University and does research in Operations Management. His research interests include System Dynamics modeling and Product Pipeline Management. Adress: Av. Orlando Gomes 1845 – Piatã, Salvador, Bahia - Brazil, 41650-050.

of RFID is that a radio frequency reader can read as many as 200 tags in a second without the line-of-sight requirement. Near-real-time tracking and tracing capabilities, together with item-level identification through EPC (electronic product code) standard, would allow a host of new improvements in inventory management (Whang, 2010). Among these improvements is increased efficiency by making products available at the right time and in the right place, with a lower operational cost. As a result, numerous manufacturing plants are adopting RFID technology for product tracking purposes, especially within sectors that move multiple parts through their facilities each day (Chow et al. 2006, Kach and Borzabad 2011). According to Stambaugh and Carpenter (2009), RFID systems are rapidly replacing Universal Product Codes (barcodes in many applications). According to Soares *et al.* (2008), inventories are the sectors that can potentially benefit the most from RFID technology. The benefits with its implementation go far beyond the mere change of the technology of automation of data capture. Its main objective is to increase the integration of the entire logistics chain, providing tools that enable tracking and control of the products that circulate in the chain (Fosso Wamba and Chatfield, 2009).

This case study initiates in 2008, motivated by research done in many microcomputer assembly companies of the *Pólo de Informática de Ilhéus/BA*. This group of companies is comprised of 20 assemblers of microcomputers. The raw materials are practically all imported from Asian suppliers (China, South Korea and Thailand, among others) and the companies supply the Brazilian market, specially the north and northeast regions of the country.

The difficulties faced by these companies in managing their inventories of raw materials and finished products, even using barcodes for quick identification during production, were the motivational factor behind this study. These difficulties motivated the development of the methodology of integration presented here.

The most relevant difficulties found in companies of the region are described below:

• Sales of products that did not have all the necessary components as ordered by the client. In such cases, the company frequently substituted the missing component(s) for a component of higher value. This might create a discrepancy between the inventory control system (database) and the actual inventory. RFID may help, in this case, by identifying and tracking all items contained in a product.

• Traceability of components during the phases of assembly – when one component was damaged and was substituted for another one The control of this activity is performed, in most companies, by inspection, i.e. by manually filling a spreadsheet at the end of the working hours, and then inputting the information into the inventory control system (database). Such method was performed in the company being studied.

• Problems while reading the barcodes during the phases of data insertion into the ERP (*Enterprise Resource Planning*) system of the companies. In case there were many metal pieces, the RFID reading was performed with redundancy by means of a portal and a manual reader;

• Manual control of the raw materials inventory.

This research has the objective of evaluating the specific conditions of adoption of an RFID system in a microcomputer assembly company, situated in the *Pólo de Informática de Ilhéus/BA*. The system aims at an adequate return on investment to modernize the company with an up-to-date solution. It is noteworthy that no other company in the region possesses this technology. The actual Internal Rate of Return (IRR) of the project was calculated by Araújo Filho et al. (2013) and its value is 15%.

RFID technology presents some advantages when compared to the barcode technology, previously used in the company. The method used to read the RFID tags enables them to be read at great speed compared to the barcode. The reading of an RFID tag does not depend on the line-of-sight requirement, and it can be reutilized or operated in hazardous environments or environments contaminated by dirt. The reutilization process is simple. It is just necessary to remove the used tags from the items and reattach them to new items.

This paper outlines the activities that were undertaken by a Brazilian microcomputer assembly company while implementing RFID technology. We explore the steps taken by the firm and outline where the company met its expectations or not. The microcomputer industry relies heavily on logistical techniques and inventory management, moving many parts throughout their system, received from multiple suppliers. As such, we believe our analysis can be useful for other firms hoping to use RFID technology to reduce their systematic inefficiencies. The cost of the tag is a problem to be faced, but it is not insurmountable. Tag prices tend to reduce over time and tags can be reutilized.

The innovative side of this research is the creation of a methodology for the integration of the RFID technology into the productive system of a company, to enable the adoption of such technology in companies that aim to increase and improve inventory control and product traceability. It is important to point out that this methodology aims to reduce potential impacts on the structure of the company, in order to facilitate integration. To our knowledge, this is the first methodology that integrates Failure Mode and Effect Analysis (FMEA) into the RFID adoption process. FMEA is used to identify the process failures, which might compromise the integration of the new system with the previous system.

Other benefits inherent to the utilization of this technology were observed: reduction in lead-time, reduction of failures in the process and reduction of defects (since it became possible to identify and trace problems before the product was sent to customers). Such benefits were enabled due to the real time control, the capacity to read many tags at the same time, and the suppression of the manual reading of barcodes.

Furthermore, all the logistic chain to which the company belongs receives benefits, as demonstrated by Fosso Wamba and Chatfield (2009), because with real time inventory control, company suppliers will be able to monitor their inventory and fulfill their clients' needs more precisely.

Therefore, the fundamental question for this study is "will implementing an RFID-based system reduce inefficiencies in the production process of the company in question?"

2. RFID TECHNOLOGY

RFID technology has its origins in the Second World War, with the IFF – Identification Friend-or-Foe identification system, which allowed Allied units to distinguish between Allied and enemy aircraft (Hunt et al. 2007). RFID technology works on the same basic principle. A signal is sent to a tag, which is activated and reflects back the signal (passive system) or transmits its own signal (active system).

According to Pinheiro (2006), the considerable advances of RFID technology are undeniable, however many challenges remain in order to enable its widespread use. These challenges can be perceived by the analysis of applications for the RFID gadgets. For some applications, the technology is reasonably consolidated, while for others there is still a need of new gadgets, security protocols and reductions in the price of tags.

In this section, a literature review is presented, with a list of advantages and disadvantages of RFID technology. Such factors were taken into consideration when the company decided to implement RFID technology.

Advantages of the use of RFID technology

In a multitude of industrial contexts, implementing RFID technology has shown to improve operations, supply chain and logistical systems by reducing forecasting errors and increasing delivery times (Dutta et al. 2007, Kach and Borzabad 2011). The use of RFID technology seems particularly useful within fast moving consumer goods markets, since it allows for real-time visibility of the supply chain (Bottani et al. 2010). Higher material transparency within organizational systems allows for more accurate forecasting, effectively reducing any inefficiencies that may exist within the supply chain (Delen et al. 2007, Kach and Borzabad 2011).

RFID can also be beneficial in managing supply chains. Relying on an increasingly large number of suppliers can make the information flow across all parties difficult. RFID tags and the technology behind them allow for rapid automated item identification without the need of a physical operator, increasing inventory allocation efficiencies. Through the provision of real-time data, RFID technology helps in systematically reducing information gaps across the supply chain. It prevents items from being lost, since they are tracked continuously as they move through the chain, and enables inventory control, since the company knows exactly what is contained in its inventory, in real time (Attaran 2007; Gaukler et al. 2007, Kach and Borzabad 2011).

Disadvantages of the use of RFID technology

RFID technology does not guarantee improved processes across all functions of the supply chain (Wu et al. 2006). Just like any technology, RFID has downsides and risks (Kharif 2005; Taghaboni-Dutta and Velthouse 2006). To begin with, there are costs and capital requirements for implementing the physical technology and software needed for RFID (Ustundag and Tanyas 2009). Justifying the startup costs may be a prohibitive barrier for implementing RFID technology (Kach and Borzabad 2011). Second, there are cases that suggest how RFID may not be so effective and other cases where the implementation of the system was not successful (Kharif 2005). Additionally, lack of timing and technology coordination between suppliers when implementing RFID practices can create problems across the supply streams (Whang 2010). When to implement RFID technology is an important question facing many practitioners and researchers alike (Kach and Borzabad 2011).

In relation to the problem identified in the case study, the main advantages and disadvantages hold the premise that the technology can be implemented; however, it is necessary to identify the process failures, which might compromise the integration with the previous system. This was done by applying FMEA. Therefore, in order to enable the integration process, it is necessary to identify the process failures (listed below in item 3) so that they be evaluated, eliminated or in the worst scenario, minimized. In order to do so, a Failure Mode and Effect Analysis FMEA study was carried out and is presented and explained below. FMEA was one of the first systematic techniques for failure analysis. It was developed by reliability engineers in the 1950s to study problems that might arise from malfunctions of military systems. An FMEA is often the first step of a system reliability study. It involves reviewing as many components, assemblies, and subsystems as possible to identify failure modes, and their causes and effects (Santos and Cabral, 2008).

3. PROCESS FMEA

Among the many tools used for fault analysis (Ishikawa diagram, Fault Tree Analysis, Pareto Chart, 5 Whys, Quality Control story, among others), FMEA was the most adequate for the company, because the use of this methodology shows the process systematically, aggregates more information in the descriptions of the process and identifies causes of faults in the process of microcomputer assembly (Santos and Cabral, 2008). Failure Mode and Effects Analysis (FMEA) was one of the first systematic techniques for failure analysis. It was developed by reliability engineers in the 1950s to study problems that might arise from malfunctions of military systems. An FMEA is often the first step of a system reliability study. It involves reviewing as many components, assemblies, and subsystems as possible to identify failure modes, and their causes and effects. For each component, the failure modes and their resulting effects on the rest of the system are recorded in a specific FMEA worksheet. There are numerous variations of such worksheets. An FMEA is mainly a qualitative analysis

According to Stamatis (2003), the factors, severity, occurrence and detection are calculated by experts according to the scale of values, which in most cases is set from 1 to 10, based on criteria of evaluation defined in common agreement by the team. The RPN (Risk Priority Number) is a measure of risk of a fault in a certain step of the process, and should be used to classify faults and prioritize the actions. Actions are recommended with priority given to those faults that achieved the highest RPN.

Using this concept, a methodology was developed to integrate RFID technology into the supply chain of the microcomputer assembly company, which will be presented below. This methodology has not been tested before. This was the first attempt to systematize it. The methodology can be applied to the other companies in the *Pólo de Informática de Ilhéus*, since no other company possessed RFID technology at the time the study was done. In the global market, there are still many microcomputer companies that still have not made use of RFID technology. These companies could benefit from its many advantages, as listed in section 5.

4. METHODOLOGY

Figure 1 presents the flowchart of the methodology that was developed, detailing each step of the technical viability analysis. It reports the procedures that guided the case study in the company (which will be named XYZ for confidentiality purposes). This company was chosen because it had all the limitations and characteristics of other companies of the region, as mentioned previously.

Even though the methodology contemplates a return on investment analysis, this step will not be presented in this paper for brevity purposes. It is suffice to say that the

Internal Rate of Return (IRR) was 15%, ensuring a large NPV (Net Present Value) for the firm (Araújo Filho et al., 2013). For other papers focusing on economic feasibility, check Balocco et al.(2011) and Jones et al. (2007). The problem of the tag price was minimized by choosing an economically feasible tag and by reutilizing the tags as much as possible.

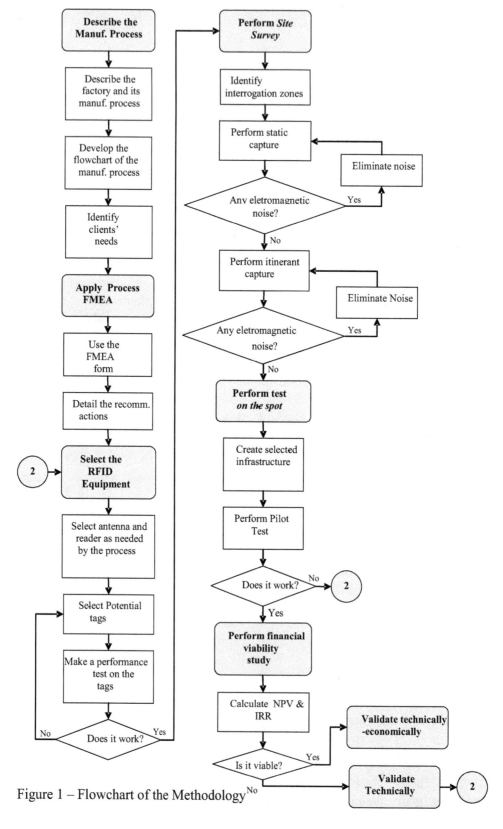

Figure 1 – Flowchart of the Methodology

4.1. Description and evaluation of the process

In this section, a description of the factory of company XYZ will be presented, together with a description of the microcomputer assembly process from the receipt of raw materials to the checkout of finished products.

4.1.1. Description of the Factory

The computer factory was built in 2008 in the *Pólo industrial de Informática* in Ilhéus/BA, with the objective of producing desktop computers and laptops to fulfill the needs of the north and northeast regions of Brazil.

The company has a flexible assembly line, which manufactures 5 desktop models and 1 laptop model. The monthly production of the factory is approximately 12 thousand machines. The factory has a total area of 1134 m^2, with a production area of 895 m^2. Around 200,000 machines will be traced and tracked. For details on costs, please refer to Araujo Filho et al. (2013). We assumed that all the equipment would be tagged.

4.1.2. Description of the Process of Receiving Supplies

The process of receiving supplies is initiated with the arrival of the product in the inventory sector. A worker checks the data on the invoice and the data in the request for parts. After the checking of documents, a physical checking of the products is performed, as well as a checking of the packaging and possible damages caused by transportation. When the new process is initiated, the components will receive an RFID tag when they are first inspected.

All the checking data are registered in the stamp of inspection and acceptance. In case there is no problem with the material, either physical or documental, it is taken into the inventory. If there is a problem, a communication to the Board of Directors of the company is performed, which in turn will decide if the goods will be given back to the supplier or if they will be accepted into the inventory.

After the goods are put into the inventory, barcodes are generated and printed for the components. Just after the printing of barcodes, they are attached to the components and read by an optical reader, so that the information enters the Integrated Enterprise Control System (IECS). Finally, the components are stored in the inventory.

4.1.3. Description of the Process of Computer Assembly

The process of computer assembly is initiated with the generation of a sales order (SO) by the ERP system of the sales team located in the southeast of the country. The inventory manager generates the Production Order (PO) in an ERP system different from the one used by the sales team. Therefore, the factory is obliged to feed the system manually because there is no integration between databases. This was changed radically with the new process. Once the RFID began to be used, the factory fed the system automatically by using new software that was integrated with the existing system.

In case a few items are not in the inventory, they are substituted for equivalent or superior items. In this phase, the barcodes for the power supply unit and for the lot of products (serial number) are generated. The RFID tags will help in this phase because it will be possible to know exactly what is in stock.

After this phase, the PO is printed and taken to the inventory team. The team separates the cases and the power supply units, according to the PO, and the other parts (Motherboard, Hard Disc, Processor and DVD) in the inventory. Once the RFID system is used, all the parts will arrive already with their tags.

The cases and power supply units are taken to the Case Preparation sector (which also attaches the power supply unit). Parallel to this activity, the other parts are checked by the "KIT preparation team". In this stage, the motherboard, processor, cooler and memory are attached. The inspection process uses software to determine the condition of the parts.

After the case is prepared with the power source, the stages of assembly are performed:

- 1st Post: Attach HD, DVD and serial number to the case and attach barcode (BC) of the power supply unit.

- 2nd Post: Attach front part of the case.

- 3rd Post: Connect frontal cables (LEDs, USB, POWER and RESET) on the motherboard.

- 4th Post: Attach KIT to the case and connect power source cable to the motherboard, HD and DVD.

- 5th Post: Tie the power cables with clamps.

- 6th Post: Attach SATA cable to HD and DVD.

- 7th Post: Fasten sides of the case.

- 8th Post: Insert Configuration Label on the side of the case, connect the power cable to outlet and perform a pre-test and setup of the machine (motherboard, processor, memory, DVD, frontal USB). In case the machine is approved, it is made available on the rack for run in. If it is reproved, it is taken to be repaired.

Once the new process is implemented, RFID tags will be attached individually to groups of similar components, as described in section 4.3.3. The tags did perform well with parts made of metal.

After the approval in the assembly line, the machines are made available to run. In this stage, the Operational System (OS) is installed and a fatigue test is performed.

The next step is the final test for the machine. In this test, both hardware and software are tested. In the end of this step the machine is packaged together with a keyboard, loudspeakers, a mouse, manuals, CD of drivers and the label with its serial number is attached to the box. The machine is then put on the pallet.

The pallets are stored in the inventory. When an invoice is generated, the inventory team ties (via barcode [BC] reader) the serial number of the machine to the invoice using the software system provided. As mentioned previously, once the new process begins, RFID tags will be attached to groups of similar components during the initial inspection. The results of the use of RFID tags are discussed in the final section.

4.1.4. Description of the process of Generating an Invoice for a Sales Request

The process of generating an invoice for a sales request initiates with the sales request by the ERP system. The inventory team releases the serial number of the machines, which are on the pallet to compose the amount of machines requested in the sales invoice. After the machines are chosen, the sales invoice is created and the inventory team makes pallets available for removal, by manually checking the invoice numbers with the labels in the machines. Once the new process is initiated, the pallets will receive RFID tags and will be associated to the computers.

4.2. Applying FMEA to the manufacturing Process of the Company

The FMEA form, used for the analysis of the manufacturing process of the company, was developed by a team of four experts (Microelectronics Lab of the Manufacture and Technology Integrated Center - CIMATEC). The most important results of this work were the possibility of evidencing the potential fault modes, their causes and the alternatives to prevent the occurrence of faults. The FMEA form is an established methodology with proven results (Santos and Cabral, 2008; Stamatis, 2003) . The methodology is applied by filling the FMEA form and analyzing it. In order to fill the FMEA form, the team followed the steps explained in section 3.

The improvement actions were focused on the types of operations in which the Risk Priority Number (RPN) was above 125. On the FMEA form, 50 types of operations were identified. Seven of these operations (1, 11, 28, 30, 31, 34 and 43) were the ones with the highest RPN, according to Table 1 below:

ITEM	FUNCTION	POTENTIAL FAULT MODE	POTENTIAL EFFECTS OF FAULTS	SEVERITY	CLASS.	POTENTIAL CAUSE (6M) MECHANISMS	OCURR.	PRESENT PREVENTIVE CONTROL	PRESENT DETECTION CONTROL	DETEC.	RPN
				Table 1 – FMEA Form							
1	Production Order Generation	Unavailable Component in stock	Replacement by component with equivalence higher or lower than SO	5		Raw material control in stock	8	Anual inventory (Manual / BC)	ERP (IECS)	4	160
11	KIT Preparation (motherboard, processor, cooler and RAM Memory)	Reading error in barcodes (BCs) of components	Delay in the KIT release to the assembly line	7		Damaged tag	5	-	Visual Inspection Visual / (ERP) System	5	175
28	Packing	Wrong input of BC tag of the parent serial number on the package	Inconsistent data in the ERP system (Finished product)	7		Improper manual operation	4	-	Visual inspection	5	140

ITEM	FUNCTION	POTENTIAL FAULT MODE	POTENTIAL EFFECTS OF FAULTS	SEVERITY	CLASS.	POTENTIAL CAUSE (6M) MECHANISMS	OCURR.	PRESENT PREVENTIVE CONTROL	PRESENT DETECTION CONTROL	DETEC.	RPN
30	Generation of Invoice	Wrong selection of I/O (mouse, board, speakers, user manual, driver CDs)	Packed machine out of spec. of PO	8		Improper manual operation	4	-	Visual inspection	6	192
31		Input in packing with insufficient number of I/O(mouse, board, speakers, user manual,driver, CDs)	Packed machine out of spec. of PO	8		Improper manual operation	4	-	Visual inspection	6	192
34	Raw material entry	Reading error of BC of parent serial number to set the amount of machines on the invoice	Delay in the release of invoice with the machines	7		Damaged tag	5	-	Visual inspection / (ERP) System	5	175
43	Machine Repair	Reading error of BC of component for insertion in the ERP system (IECS)	Delay in the component release	7		Damaged tag	5	-	Visual inspection / (ERP) System	5	175

Table 1 – FMEA Form

The recommended actions in the FMEA Process are listed below:

1. Real Time Inventory: There were faults due to unavailability of components in the inventory, caused by imprecise control of raw materials. It was found that 30% of the Production Orders were generated by substituting components for others with higher or lower value or grade. It was also found that the inventory of parts and finished products was performed once a year, and demanded 3 days to be executed. This happened because some steps of the inventory checking were performed manually and the results were compared with the values found in the ERP system. Therefore, real time inventory is recommended for the company.

2. Substitution of Barcodes for RFID: During the stages of KIT preparation, packaging, generation of invoice and acquisition of raw materials, a series of faults in the reading of barcodes was found. It happened with both the components and the parent serial number of the machines. It also occurred that a damaged label was attached to the

machine. Because of that, the recommended action is substituting the barcodes (BCs) for RFID tags, because the RFID tag is more resistant to dirt, impact and mechanical friction than the BC label. It is impossible to guarantee that all the tags were adequately read by the equipment, but the error rate of the RFID readers is extremely small according to specifications (less than 1%).

3. Identification of Parts with RFID Tags: Faults were detected in the selection of I/O products (mouse, keyboard, loudspeakers, and also user manual and CDs of drivers) and in the insertion of these parts in the packaging due to wrong manual operation. Therefore, the recommended action is to identify the I/O products with RFID tags and to group them with a RFID tag with the parent serial number of the packaging of the product, via ERP system. Even though the RFID tag may be expensive in relation to the cost of the items, they can be used many times (recycled), so their cost is reduced. The human cost for the process of attaching the tags to the body of the components was not calculated. For a more detailed analysis of the procedures, check Araujo Filho, Travassos and Figueiredo (2013).

4.3. Measurements and tests

In this section, we will explain the steps of the technical viability analysis. The first subsection presents the selection of the RFID equipment. The second subsection presents the analysis performed in the environment to detect electromagnetic noise (site survey), at the points where the RFID equipment were to be installed.

4.3.1. Selection of the Most Adequate RFID Equipment

For the selection of the proper and most adequate RFID equipment, a pre-selection and analysis were performed taking into consideration firstly the technical information of different RFID tags. Reading tests were then performed with the pre-selected list of available tags, antennas and tag readers. We tested most of the components available in the Brazilian market, but we do not show them here for brevity purposes. The tags were put on components, on the computer case and on the packaging box and the tests were performed. The choice of readers and antennas was restricted to the available material in the CIMATEC lab. This equipment had already been tested and proved to be cost efficient and reliable. However, a more detailed analysis was not performed. The choice of tag, however, was performed considering technical and economical criteria. A list of nine tags covering the major types available on the market was analyzed and a series of specifications were considered to enable the choice of the most adequate one, both in terms of performance and in terms of cost. Among such criteria were cost, dimensions, distance for reading, memory size, mounting type, among others. With such criteria in hand, it was possible to determine which tags were a viable alternative for components and for the packaging box. A pre-selection was made. Table 2 presents the kinds of tags that were tested.

Table 2: Choice of RFID Tags

Model	Survivor	Confidex Cruiser	Confidex Corona	Confidex Pino	SteelWave	SteelWave Micro	Ironside	Confidex Halo	ALN-9640
Manufacturer	**CONFIDEX**	**CONFIDEX**	**CONFIDEX**	**CONFIDEX**	**CONFIDEX**	**CONFIDEX**	**CONFIDEX**	**CONFIDEX**	**ALIEN**
Dimensions	224 x 24 x 8 mm	16 x 74 x 0,3 mm	100 x 20,32 x 0,3 mm	75 x 14 x 0,4 mm	45 x 35 x 6 mm	13 x 38 x 3 mm	51,5 x 47,5 x 10 mm	60 x 12 x 14 mm	101,6 x 50,8 x 0,3 mm
Frequency Range	865 – 960 MHz	860 – 960 MHz	860 – 960 MHz	860 – 960 MHz	865 – 869 MHz 902 - 928 MHz	865 - 869 MHz 902 - 928 MHz 952 - 955 MHz	865 – 869 MHz 902 - 928 MHz	865 - 869 MHz 902 - 928 MHz 952 - 955 MHz	840 – 960 MHz
Transmission Protocol	EPC Class 1 Generation 2	EPC Class 1 Generation 2	EPC Class 1 Generation 2 ISSO 18000-6C	EPC Class 1 Generation 2	EPC Class 1 Generation 2	EPC Class 1 Generation 2	EPC Class 1 Generation 2	EPC Class 1 Generation 2 ISO 18000-6C	EPC Class 1 Generation 2 ISO 18000-6C
Distance from Reader	8 - 12 m	4 – 5 m	5 - 9 m	3 – 4 m	4 - 6 m	2,5 m	6 - 7 m	5 - 7 m	4 - 6 m
IC and Memory Size	96-bit EPC Impinj Monza 240-bit EPC NXP G2 + NXP G2XM	96-bit EPC Impinj Monza 240-bit EPC + 512 NXP G2XM	NXP G2XM Up to 240-bit EPC + 512-bit extended user memory	96-bit EPC + 64 bit Impinj Monaco/64 240-bit EPC + 512 NXP G2XM	96-bit EPC Impinj Monza 512-bit EPC NXP G2	Impinj Monza3 96-bit EPC	96-bit EPC Impinj Monza 240-bit EPC + 512 NXP G2XM	96-bit EPC Impinj Monza 240-bit EPC + 512 NXP G2XM	Alien Higgs-3 96-bit EPC
Attachment	Mechanical Adhesive	Adhesive	Mechanical Adhesive	Mechanical	Adhesive	Adhesive	Mechanical Adhesive	Mechanical	Adhesive
Working Temperature	-35°C - +85°C	-35°C - +160°C	-35°C - +200°C	-35°C - +60°C	-20°C - +85°C	-20°C - +85°C	-55°C - +105°C	-35°C - +85°C	-40°C - +70°C
Typical usage	Industrial and Logistics	Tire manufacturing	Industrial solutions	Wood Pallets	Assembly lines and warehouses	Assembly lines and warehouses	Petrochemical industry, automotive and maritime	Metallic surfaces	Document tracking, pallets and boxes
Usage in computer components*	Not viable due to the tag dimensions	Not viable for mettalic surfaces	Not viable due to the tag dimensions	Not viable due to the attachment to the component	Not viable for some components (motherboard, cooler, DVD player, memory)	VIABLE	Not viable for some components (motherboard, cooler, DVD player, memory)	Not viable due to the attachment (clamp)	Not viable for metallic surfaces
Usage in Boxes*	Viable	Viable	Viable	Not viable due to attachment to box	Viable	Viable	Viable	Not viable due to the attachment (clamp)	Viable

Performance tests were done in a sequence. Deavours et al. (2005) recommend a performance test of an RFID tag in order to evaluate the potential success of the RFID system under study. The test consists in adjusting the power of the reader to the maximum position, and making 100 reading attempts with the tag from a fixed distance. In order to simulate other distances, the power of the reader should be attenuated by 0.5dBm for every 100 reading attempts. The rate of response is the number of successful readings divided by the reading trials.

After the pre-selection of tags, such performance tests were done with the *SteelWave Micro* tag for the components (motherboard, HD, DVD, RAM memory, power supply unit and case) and with the *ALN-9640* tag for the packaging box. All these tests were performed in the microelectronics lab. We must admit that results may vary, since the manufacturing environment is slightly different from the microelectronics lab (we tried to mimic the conditions as much as possible). We believe that our choice of tag was the best considering the availability in the market. The tag can be affixed to all parts including the RAM memory.

The fixed distance used for the tests was approximately 70cm +/- 2cm. To ensure more reliability from results, 4 experiments were run for each tag, totaling 10,800 reading attempts. Readings were successful with metal parts and with the closed computer case.

Figure 2 presents the tests performed on the machine's components (motherboard, HD, DVD reader, RAM memory, power supply unit, case and packaging box).

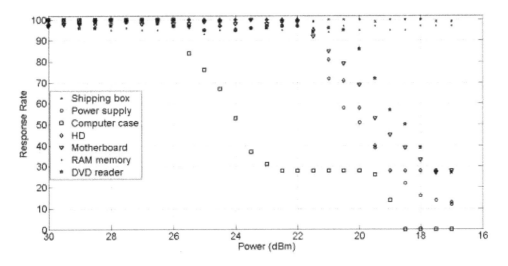

Figure 2 – Performance test on the machine's components

4.3.2. *Site Survey*

According to Sweeney II (2005), in order to perform a site survey it is necessary to follow these steps:

1. **Define the reading places (or areas of inquiry) where the RFID system will be installed.** These locations vary from store to store and require a power outlet and Ethernet connectivity for readers (unless you have players with wireless connectivity). Commonly, the RFID interrogation zones are placed on doors, assembly lines and racks of inventory;

2. **Carry out site survey in local reading respecting all the business process cycle (24h or 48h).** It is usually held on days of normal operation of the company, respecting all hours of operation.

3. **Perform the static capture.** To perform the static capture, you must configure the equipment as follows:

   a. Place the half-wave antenna (attached directly to the tripod) so that the center of the antenna is in the center of the target area;

   b. Connect the antenna to the input port of the spectrum analyzer (via coaxial cable);

c. Connect the laptop to the spectrum analyzer, using an RS-232 connector or Ethernet. If you use a laptop to record data, you must configure the virtual display to record the information every time and save it on your hard disk. Or else, you should shoot/capture the monitor spectrum analyzer every two hours during the normal cycle of operation

d. Set the spectrum analyzer for the operating frequency to be used with the RFID system;

4. **Perform Itinerant Capture.** To perform the itinerant capture, you must configure the equipment as follows:

a. Set the spectrum analyzer exactly the same way as configured in static capturing, except for the voltage source and the antenna that should be mobile;

b. b. If any source of interference is found, its exact location must be identified.

5. **Map the areas of interrogation in the project, locating sources of interference.**

4.3.2.1. Site Survey at XYZ

The site survey was performed in the areas of interrogation, according to Figure 3, on the places where the KIT preparation (Figure 4), generation of invoice (Figure 5) and entry of raw materials occur (Figure 6). For the static capture, images from the spectrum analyzer were recorded every 2 hours in each place, with a cycle of 24 hours (beginning at 08:00 until 08:00 of the next day). However, the last record of each place corresponded to the period between 18:00 of the last day until 8:00 of the following day, because the company did not have any activity after regular working hours. This was performed inside the company.

We identified some areas of frequency spectra of interrogation, but all spectra were outside the working range of the UHF (Ultra High Frequency).For the itinerant capture, no spectrum in the range of 902 to 907.5 MHz and in the range of 915 to 928MHz was recorded by the spectrum analyzer,.

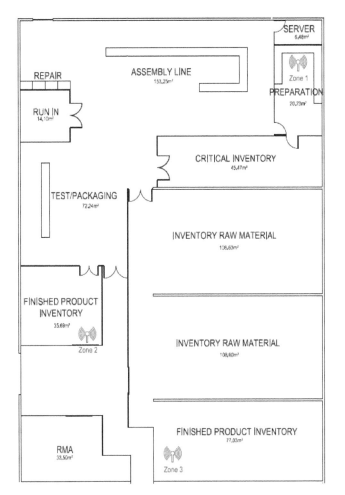

Figure 3 – Static capture zone.

Figure 4 – KIT preparation (Zone 1)

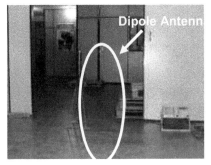

Figure 5 – Invoice issuing (Zone 2)

Figure 6 – Raw material issuing (Zone 3)

4.3.3. Tests in the Product

After the site survey tests, in-place tests were performed. The stages of these tests include:

- **Input of Components:** Through data integration with ERP, the system prompts the user to issue tags for the volumes that comprise a given set / batch of components. Through the information contained in the invoice launched in the ERP system, data will be associated for later traceability. At this point, the components will be credited into the system, releasing them for use if necessary.

- **Inventory:** After proper labeling of RFID tags in the volumes of components, these will be stored as usual.

- **Handling:** With the aid of a RFID Data Collector integrated with the ERP system, the operator will locate the Production Order that lists which components and which amounts must be separated and sent to the production line. At this time, the separate components are read by the RFID Collector and receive the status of Booked, which means that these components can be used at any time.

- **Production:** Through the integration with the ERP system and upon information contained in the Production Order, RFID tags are printed with the necessary information and the Finished Product lot number in question. RFID tags are linked to the Production Order, whose number is also associated with the handling of components, ensuring the association of Finished Goods and Components.

- **Appointment of Production:** All finished products, properly accommodated in a standardized way on a pallet, will go through an RFID portal. At this point, the confirmation of the RFID reading of the finished product will change the status of components used from Debited to Reserved, generating the debt of the component in the inventory system, while a credit of finished product will be held in it.

5.   RESULTS

After the in-place test was performed, the FMEA form was used once again to evaluate the efficiency of the RFID system. The RPN results for the items that were changed are shown below (Table 3):

Table 3 - FMEA Form							
I T EM	RECOMMENDED ACTIONS	RESPONSABILITY FOR THE RECOMMENDED ACTIONS & FOR THE DEADLINES	ACTION TAKEN	S E V E R I D .	O C O R R .	D E T E C .	R P N
1	Perform real-time inventory (RFID tags in the Inventory	CIMATEC/XYX Company jan/11	Validation tests performed	5	5	2	50
11	Replace CBs tags for RFID tags	CIMATEC jan/11	Validation tests	7	5	1	35
28	Replace CBs tags for RFID tags	CIMATEC/XYX Company jan/11	Validation tests performed	7	4	2	56
30	Identify the I / O devices with RFID tags and group them	CIMATEC/XYX Company jan/11	Validation tests performed	8	3	2	48
31	Identify the I / O devices with RFID tags and group them	CIMATEC/ Empresa jan/11	Validation tests performed	8	3	2	48
34	Replace CBs tags for RFID tags	CIMATEC jan/11	Validation tests	7	5	1	35
43	Replace CBs tags for RFID tags	CIMATEC jan/11	Validation tests	7	5	1	35

Table 3 – FMEA Form

These measures enabled the company to attain the following results with the implementation of the methodology for integrating RFID technology in its production system:

- Reduction of one worker in the inventory team due to the substitution of manual reading of barcodes for RFID technology. RFID technology was so efficient in relation to the previous technology (barcode) that the time required to read a pallet in the process of generating an invoice was reduced from ninety seconds to seven seconds on average. These time savings are equivalent to the work of one employee (Araujo Filho, Travassos and Figueiredo, 2013).

- Reduction in the practice of substituting a component for another of higher grade/cost, due to the real time inventory control. This can be measured because the company knows the amount of parts that were substituted in the past.

There were, however, difficulties and challenges in the implementation of the new technology. The different areas of production were arranged in a way that made difficult the installation of the RFID portal, the training of workers demanded a lot of attention and care, and the integration of the RFID system with the ERP system demanded a lot of time.

6. CONCLUSIONS

In this paper, it was evidenced that the methodology for implementation of RFID technology on microcomputer assembly companies was viable. Araujo Filho, Travassos and Figueiredo (2013) determined an internal rate of return of 15%.

It was also observed that the utilization of the FMEA tool for identification and elimination of causes of failure modes in the production process was efficient (Araujo Filho, Travassos and Figueiredo, 2013). The tool details the process systematically and adds more information to the process descriptions. It also identifies the causes of failures in the production process. The difference between the process before and after the FMEA tool being implemented is that the most important failure modes are taken care of, with preventive measures being taken in order to avoid the failures.

Another important point were the technical evaluations performed for tag selection, choice of RFID equipment, analysis of the environment and for detecting electromagnetic noises present in the factory. Such evaluations helped to ensure the technical efficacy of the chosen technology, during in-site tests. A good RFID reading was obtained at all points where data was collected. The technology was so efficient compared with the previous technology (barcodes) that the time required to read a pallet in the process of generating an invoice was reduced from ninety seconds to seven seconds on average.

It is important to point out that there are other significant gains inherent to the use of RFID technology, which are, however, difficult to measure (Araujo Filho, Travassos and Figueiredo, 2013). Such gains are shared by the entire commodity chain, because with real time inventory control the suppliers of this company will be able to monitor the flow of parts and ensure that their customer (the company) will have its needs fulfilled. This real time monitoring between supplier and company is replicated in the remaining links of the chain, which ensures better service quality to the end consumer, and reduction of logistical and operational costs. In such a condition, the component can be tracked from the first supplier to the end consumer (Fosso Wamba and Chatfield, 2009).

There is a need to conduct further research on the RFID supply chain management applications in the microcomputer sector as this area holds a great potential for performance improvements. Additionally, there is a need to conduct more in-depth research into the isolated impact of RFID technology in comparison to the change in management and process redesign that it generates.

One key limitation of this research is the case study approach based on a single case. This paper, however, provides direction for practitioners on how to assess RFID's potential impact in the microcomputer assembly process, from the receiving of supplies to the delivery of final products. This research contributes to our understanding of RFID's potential in intra-organizational supply chain management processes. Hopefully, the experience and lessons learned from this case study can be shared with the readers, and they will be beneficial to those organizations that are contemplating the implementation of RFID systems.

REFERENCES

Araújo Filho, F.W., Travassos, X.L., Figueiredo, P.S. (2013): "Uma Análise De Viabilidade Econômica De Um Sistema RFID Na Cadeia De Suprimentos De Fabricação De Microcomputadores: Há Algum Lucro?" *Gestão da Produção, Operações e Sistemas (Forthcoming)*

Attaran, M. (2007): "RFID: An Enabler of Supply Chain Operations", *Supply Chain Management-an International Journal*, (12:4), pp. 249-257.

Balocco, R., Miragliotta, G., Perego, A., and Tumino, A. (2011): "RFID adoption in the FMCG supply chain: an interpretative framework". *Supply Chain Management: an International Journal*, 16(5), p.299-315.

Bottani, E., R. Montanari and A. Volpi (2010): "The Impact of RFID and Epc Network on the Bullwhip Effect in the Italian Fmcg Supply Chain", *International Journal of Production Economics*, (124:2), pp. 426-432.

Chow, H.K.H., K.L. Choy, W.B. Lee and K.C. Lau (2006): "Design of a RFID Case-Based Resource Management System for Warehouse Operations", *Expert Systems with Applications*, (30:4), pp. 561-576.

Delen, D., B.C. Hardgrave and R. Sharda (2007): "RFID for Better Supply-Chain Management through Enhanced Information Visibility", *Production and Operations Management*, (16:5), pp. 613-624.

Dutta, A., H.L. Lee and S.J. Whang (2007): "RFID and Operations Management: Technology, Value, and Incentives", *Production and Operations Management*, (16:5), pp. 646-655.

Deavours, D.D.; Ramakrishnan, K. M.; Syed, A. (2005): "RFID Performance Tag Analysis". Technical Report ITTC-FY2006-TR-40980-01

Fosso Wamba, S. and A. T. Chatfield (2009) "A contingency model for creating value from RFID supply chain network projects in logistics and manufacturing environments," *European Journal of Information Systems*, vol. 18, pp. 615-636.

Gaukler, G.M., R.W. Seifert and W.H. Hausman (2007): "Item-Level RFID in the Retail Supply Chain", *Production and Operations Management*, (16:1), pp. 65-76.

Gaukler, G.M., O. Ozer, W. Hausman (2004). RFID and product progress information: Improved Dynamic ordering policies. Working paper, Stanford University, Stanford, CA.

Heinrich, C. (2005): *RFID and Beyond*. Wiley Publishing, Indianapolis.

Hunt, V.D., Puglia, A. and Puglia, M. (2007): "*RFID: A Guide to Radio Frequency Identification*". John Wiley & Sons, Hoboken, N.J.

Jones, E.C., Riley,M.W., Franca, R., Reigle, S. (2007): "Case Study: The Engineering Economics of RFID in Specialized Manufacturing. *The Engineering Economist*. 52: 285-303.

Kach, A. and Borzabad, A.F. (2011): "Use of RFID Technology to Overcome Inefficiencies in the Supply Chain: An Analysis of Renault's Operations in Iran". *International Journal of Management*, 28: 365-378.

Kharif, O. (2005): "For Many Retailers, RFID Lacks Roi," *Business Week.*

Pinheiro, J. M. S. (2006): "Identificação por Radiofreqüência: Aplicações e Vulnerabilidades da Tecnologia RFID". *Caderno UniFOA*, Volta Redonda, ano 1, n. 2.

Rausand M., Hoylan A. (2004): "*System Reliability Theory, Models, Statistical Methods, and Applications*". Wiley Series in probability and statistics - second edition page 88.

Santos, F.R.S., Cabral, S. (2008): "FMEA and PMBOK Applied To Project Risk Management", *Journal of Information Systems and Technology Management*, vol.5, No.2, pp. 347-364.

Soares, R. S. (2008): "O impacto da tecnologia de etiqueta inteligente (RFID) na performance de cadeias de suprimentos – Um estudo no Brasil". *Revista Jovens Pesquisadores*, Ano V, No.9

Stamatis, D.H. (2003) *Failure Mode and Effect Analysis: FMEA from Theory to Execution.* 2nd Ed. ASQ Quality Press, Milwaukee, 2003.

Stambaugh, C.T. and F.W. Carpenter (2009): "Wireless innovation in inventory monitoring and accounting". *Strategic Finance* Vol. 91(6), pp. 35-40.

Sweeney II, P. J. (2005): *RFID for Dummies*. Ed. Wiley Publishing Inc., Indianapolis, Indiana, 409 p.

Taghaboni-Dutta, F. and B. Velthouse (2006): "RFID Technology is Revolutionary: Who Should Be Involved in This Game of Tag?", *Academy of Management Perspectives*, (20:4), pp. 65-78.

Ustundag, A. and M. Tanyas (2009): "The Impacts of Radio Frequency Identification (RFID) Technology on Supply Chain Costs", *Transportation Research Part E-Logistics and Transportation Review*, (45:1), pp. 29-38.

Whang, S. (2010): Timing of RFID Adoption in a Supply Chain. *Management Science*, vol. 56, No. 2, pp. 343-355.

Wu, N.C., M.A. Nystrom, T.R. Lin and H.C. Yu (2006). "Challenges to Global RFID Adoption", *Technovation*, (26:12) pp. 1317-1323.

3

DISCOVERING CITIZENS REACTION TOWARD E-GOVERNMENT: FACTORS IN E-GOVERNMENT ADOPTION

Mohammad Kamel Alomari

College of Business and Economics, Qatar University, Doha, Qatar

ABSTRACT

E-government has been considered as one approach for changing the face of government in the eyes of the citizenry. Therefore, citizens' socialization in relation to their engagement with e-government should be explored. This study argues that citizens played a significant role in determining the success of an e-government project in the Middle Eastern country of Jordan. This paper aims to provide insight and evaluation into the factors that could influence e-government's effective functioning in the Jordanian social community through its interaction with citizens. The study collected data from 356 Jordanian citizens via a survey, to ascertain their understanding of 10 factors that may influence their intention to use e-government services. To investigate the adoption of e-government services in depth, two departments in Jordan were selected: the Jordanian Government's Income and Sales Tax Department (ISTD) and its Driver and Vehicle Licenses Department (DVDL). The factor analysis technique was used to identify the main factors related to e-government services' adoption. The results indicated that trust in the internet, website design, religious beliefs, internet and computer skill confidence, word of mouth, resistance to change, perceived usefulness, relative advantage and complexity are the main factors that should be considered when addressing the topic of e-government services' adoption in Jordan. This study is different from most existing studies on e-government adoption as it empirically investigated the impact of word of mouth (WOM), wasta (favoritism), and resistance to change on e-government adoption. This study highlights the importance of considering the social cohesion of the Jordanian community when exploring factors related to e-government adoption.

Keywords: Technological innovation, e-government, adoption, services, survey, government, citizens, social cohesion

Address for correspondence / Endereço para correspondência

Mohammad Kamel Alomari. College of Business and Economics, Qatar University, Doha, Qatar. Dr. Mohammad Alomari is an assistant professor at Qatar University. He received his PhD in Information Systems from Griffith University researching in the area of E-government adoption.

1.   INTRODUCTION

Governments worldwide are implementing and supporting a variety of electronic initiatives such as e-government, e-commerce and e-business. E-government has been developed by governments to improve the efficiency and effectiveness of internal operations and processes, public communication with the citizenry and engagement in transactional processes with individual and organizational elements (Warkentin et al., 2002). For the purpose of the current research paper, e-government was identified as a

Mechanism through which government services are produced and delivered to citizens utilizing Web-based internet applications.

The government in Jordan is one of the governments that decided to implement e-government. It has introduced e-government as one of the initiatives for creating a knowledge-based society (MoICT, 2006a). In 2006, the Jordanian e-Government Strategy ensured e-government's commitment to a customer-centric approach and considered citizens as a core concern when introducing its public services. Delivering enhanced and faster public service through e-government became one of the Jordanian government's obligations. Yet, it has been demonstrated that the lack of citizen-centricity in the implementation of e-government was one of the main challenges of e-government implementation in Jordan (MoICT, 2006b). Therefore, it is necessary to question whether or not citizens intend to use e-government services and to accept this new form of interaction with the government. Previous research has found that the success of e-government implementation was dependent not only on government support, but also on citizens' willingness to accept and adopt e-government services (Alomari et al., 2012).

Therefore, it was necessary to obtain and evaluate Jordanian citizens' perceptions about e-government as a change in their lives and therefore to clarify their response to government in relation to this new technological initiative. This study has shown that the response consisted of a combination of the following factors that need to be scrutinized when highlighting the topic of e-government services' adoption, particularly in a Middle Eastern country like Jordan: trust in the internet, website design, religious beliefs, internet and computer skill confidence, word of mouth (WOM), resistance to change, Wasta (favoritism), perceived usefulness, relative advantage, complexity.

The paper is organized as follows. First, the paper presents previous research work about e-government adoption. After the research's theoretical framework was delineated, data for this study were collected using a questionnaire and were analyzed using factor analysis: significant findings were then discussed and the study's conclusion was presented. Finally, this paper by collecting new data sets, based on a new sample and new research questions, follows a new approach extending previous research work (Alomari, 2010; Alomari et al., 2010, 2012).

2. BACKGROUND

E-government like other technological innovations such as e-business, e-commerce and internet banking is an internet-driven activity. Moon (2002) declared that "... the idea of e-government followed the private-sector adoption of so-called e-business and e-commerce" (p.425). Fang (2002) stated that: "e-business and e-commerce are subsets of e-government" (p.2) Previous studies on e-government were administered based on analytical and evaluation research conducted in the areas of e-commerce and e-business (Alomari et al., 2012; Carter and Bélanger, 2005; Ebrahim and Irani, 2005; Pons, 2004). On researching e-government in Arab countries, Pons (2004) reported "we believe that the issues involving e-commerce can be applied to e-government in order to predict the concerns and problems of the technology" (p.31). The following paragraphs report on the previous main studies which have explored factors related to the adoption of e-government with indications that the research was steered towards addressing the same factors related to the adoption of other technological innovations including internet banking.

Trust in the internet is one of the main factors highlighted as significant in investigating e-government adoption in both developed and developing countries (Al-Shafi and Weerakkody 2008; Carter and Bélanger 2005; Carter et al., 2011; Chang et al. , 2005). Trust in the internet is often identified as institution-based trust which is "the belief that needed structural conditions are present (e.g. in the internet) to enhance the probability of achieving a successful outcome in an endeavour like e-commerce" (McKnight et al., 2002; p. 339). Warkentin et al. (2002) clarified the prominent relationship between institution-based trust and e-government adoption.

Website design has been endorsed as one of the main factors which assist in explaining e-government adoption (Alomari et al., 2012; Gilbert and Balestrini, 2004). Websites were recognized as the main gateway through which the Jordanian Government could deliver its services and interact online with its citizens (MoICT, 2006a, 2006b). Therefore, well-presented content on government websites was very important. Previous evaluation studies of government websites introduced features and criteria that should be included in their design, such as the availability of e-government websites with clear and organized content (Smith, 2001; Zhang and von Dran, 2000). Gilbert and Balestrini (2004) emphasized the importance of the visual appeal of website design on people's willingness to use e-government services.

Religious beliefs were another factor discussed in the literature with respect to information technology especially after the rapid growth of the internet. This has led to a change in the way that people interact in social communities, from face to face to online interaction. Researchers have therefore been prompted to investigate the internet's impact on societies where traditions, norms and religion play a significant role in people's lives (Alomari et al., 2012; Al-Saggaf, 2004; Hill et al., 1998). In previous studies, researchers have explained the effect of religious views on the usage of information technology in Arabic countries (Al-Saggaf, 2004; Hill et al., 1998; Norton, 2002).

The literature has also indicated that confidence in internet and computer skills was another factor related to e-government adoption. Having the required skills to use the technology is necessary to ensure the success of any technology usage (Dugdale et al., 2005; Pons, 2004). Previous studies have indicated the importance of investigating the influence of individuals' internet and computer skills on their intention to use e-government services (Bélanger and Carter, 2009; Carter and Weerakkody, 2008; Vassilakis et al., 2005).

Word of mouth (WOM), wasta (favoritism), and resistance to change are other factors that should be considered when exploring factors related to e-government adoption by the citizenry. There is a lack of studies in the literature investigating the role of these three factors on technology and e-government adoption. This study therefore will be a useful resource and a valuable addition to the literature about technological and e-government adoption.

Word of mouth has captured the attention of many marketing researchers who have considered WOM to be a commanding medium for publicity (Arndt, 1967; Westbrook, 1987). This paper acknowledges the importance of word of mouth in the electronic context in general and in e-government in particular. Therefore, it is very important to highlight its influence on e-government adoption. In researching WOM with respect to technology adoption, Kim and Prabhakar (2004) conducted a survey-based study which revealed the intermediate influence of WOM on the adoption of internet banking. The current research paper is investigating the impact of word of mouth on another technological innovation that is e-government.

Wasta is one of the underlying characteristics of social life and networks in Arabic countries (Makhoul and Harrison ,2004). "Wasta" is clarified as an Arabic term that indicates the act and person who intercede on behalf of another party or parties (Cunningham and Sarayrah, 1994). On the other hand, Feghali (1997) mentioned that the process of utilizing influence in one's interpersonal network to receive favors is called "wasta". In wasta, people deploy their interpersonal connections in order to obtain advantages that would not otherwise be obtainable. Several studies have been conducted to address the issues of wasta within different contexts (Al Awadhi and Morris, 2009; Makhoul and Harrison, 2004). In the technological context, Al Awadhi and Morris (2009) provided a qualitative focus group-based study that indicated that wasta was one of the significant factors related to e-government adoption in the Middle Eastern country of Kuwait. This study through a quantitative-based survey investigates the "wasta" in relation to the adoption of e-government in another Middle Eastern country, Jordan.

Resistance to change is one of the terms that has been identified and clarified mainly in the managerial and organizational context. This study explains resistance to change from a social perspective as it is explores the factors related to citizens' e-government adoption in the social community of Jordan. Ebbers et al (2007) highlighted the importance of investigating the resistance to e-government innovations. Zander (1950) defined "resistance to change" as: "[b]ehavior which is intended to protect an individual from the effects of real or imagined change" (p. 9). Sathye (1999) proved the necessity of investigating the role of resistance to change in adopting the technological innovation, internet banking, through a survey-based study which examined the factors influencing the adoption of internet banking by Australian consumers.

To sustain a comprehensive understanding of e-government adoption in Jordan, it was necessary to introduce the theoretical framework used in this research paper in the following section.

3.   THEORETICAL FRAMEWORK

This study uses two theoretical frameworks to study factors related to e-government adoption in Jordan: these are the Diffusion of Innovation Theory (DOI) (Rogers, 1983) and the Technology Acceptance Model (TAM) (Davis, 1989). Following is a brief presentation on these theories.

Diffusion of Innovation Theory (DOI)

"Innovation" is an "idea, practice, or object that is perceived as new by an individual or other unit of adoption" (Rogers, 1983, p. 11). Based on the characteristics of innovation, researchers studying the adoption of information technology have utilized the Diffusion of Innovation Theory (DOI) to discuss information technology innovation. According to the DOI, there are five characteristics of successful adoption (Rogers, 1983): relative advantage, complexity, compatibility, triability, observability.

Three among these five characteristics have been found to be consistently significant in technology adoption (Tornatzky and Klein, 1982). These are:

• Relative advantage: "the degree to which an innovation is perceived as better than the idea it supersedes" (Rogers, 1983, p. 213)

• Compatibility: "the degree to which an innovation is perceived as being consistent with the existing values, past experience, and needs of potential adopters" (Rogers, 1983, p. 223)

• Complexity: "the degree to which an innovation is perceived as difficult to understand and use" (Rogers, 1983, p. 230).

Previous research has recognized the importance of relative advantage, compatibility, and complexity in investigating the adoption of different technological innovations including e-government (Carter and Belanger, 2005; Ojha et al., 2009; Schaupp and Carter, 2005; Van Slyke et al., 2004).

Technology Acceptance Model (TAM)

The Technology Acceptance Model (TAM) is an adaptation of the Theory of Reasoned Action which states that actual behavior is influenced by the person's intention to perform such behavior with this intention influenced by one's attitudes and subjective norms (Ajzen and Fishbein, 1972). The TAM asserts that there are two determinants for the consumer's attitudes towards usage intention which are:

• Perceived usefulness (PU): "the degree to which a person believes that using a particular system would enhance his or her job performance" (Davis, 1989)

- Perceived ease of use (PEOU): "the degree to which a person believes that using a particular system would be free of effort" (Davis, 1989).

If technology is relatively easy to use and helpful, this will positively influence the person's attitudes and intention towards using that technology (Davis, 1989). Davis's (1989) model, the TAM, is used to evaluate a user's acceptance of a technology. Previous studies have confirmed the applicability of using the aforementioned constructs to research e-government adoption (Carter and Blanger, 2005; Chang et al., 2005; Hung et al., 2006).

In previous research (Alomari, 2010; Alomari et al., 2012), the above constructs of the DOI and the TAM were used. Based on qualitative and quantitative studies, the authors found that relative advantage, complexity, and PU played a significant role when they investigated the adoption of e-government websites in Jordan. Thus, a modified version of these theories will be examined in this paper by investigating in depth the applicability of the aforementioned constructs to study the adoption of e-government services with the services of two government departments, ISTD and DVLD, selected for study. Based on a quantitative based survey, new data sets with a new sample were collected to conduct the current study. The following section illustrates the method used in this research paper.

4.   METHOD

This section introduces the main demographic characteristics of the sample used and also details of the survey utilized to conduct the study.

Sample

A questionnaire was administered to 356 Jordanian citizens who regularly accessed the internet and who were major users of ISTD and DVLD's services, to obtain their perceptions about e-government adoption. Purposive sampling was used in the current study. This kind of sample is used when the purpose is to gain information from particular target groups (Tashakkori and Teddlie ,2003).

Of the respondents, 64.9% were males and 35.1% were females. Of the sample, 3.9% were less than 20 years old, 36% were in the age group of 20–29 years old, 30.1% were in the age group of 30–39 years old, 21.6% were in the age group of 40–49 years old, and % were over 50 years old. Among respondents, 71.3% resided in urban areas in Jordan, while 27.2% of respondents resided in remote areas. The majority of respondents were generally employees: 33.4% were employees in government services and 37.4% were employed in the private sector. Most of the respondents (52.8%) held a bachelor degree level of education. Internet usage at home and work recorded the highest percentage, 45.5% and 30.9% respectively. Of the respondents, 32.8% used the internet for email and chatting purposes, 5.9% used it for shopping, 22.7% used it for homework or checking educational study results, 41% used it for reading news, and 31.2% used it for obtaining information from government websites and downloading forms. Most of the respondents (48.9%) accessed the internet one to three hours per week. Figure 1 shows a graphical presentation for some demographic characteristics of the current study's participants.

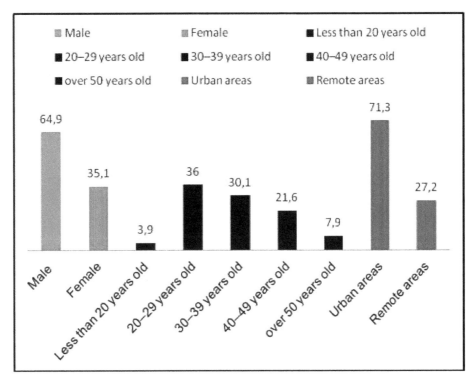

Figure 1: Demographic Characteristics of Survey's Participants

The survey

This study used a survey to determine the factors related to e-government adoption in Jordan. To develop a greater understanding of e-government adoption in Jordan, two survey instruments were designed for the two government departments:

- Income and Sales Tax Department (ISTD)

- Driver and Vehicle Licenses Department (DVDL)

The same item scales were used in the two instruments. The survey consisted of 53 scale items which were designed to examine different factors. The items of some factors were adopted from previous studies (Carter and Bélanger, 2005; Wang, 2003; Alomari et al., 2012; Waddel and Sohal, 1998; Harrison-Walker, 2001; Carter and Bélanger, 2005; van Slyke et al., 2004). Some items were self-developed items with their design based on a literature review and research project conducted by Alomari (2010). These items were reworded to make them more suitable for Jordanian participants.

This study's questionnaire utilized the five-point Likert scale (interval scale from strongly agree to strongly disagree) to measure different scale items. As English is not the first language of Jordan, with most people not fluent in English, the questionnaire was translated into Arabic by an accredited translator. A panel of experienced people then reviewed the translations to ensure accuracy and integrity. A back-translation was also utilized and reviewed to ensure the credibility of the questionnaire after its translation, firstly from English to Arabic and then from Arabic to English. A panel of experienced e-government researchers reviewed and approved the final questionnaire.

5.   RESULTS

This section reports the results of factor analyses undertaken to identify the main factors related to e-government adoption in Jordan. It describes factor analysis and its reliability.

Factor analysis

To first analyse the results of the survey, exploratory factor analysis was conducted for each independent variable and the dependent variable. The 53 items of the Likert scale were subjected to axial components analysis using SPSS version 17.0. Prior to performing axial component analysis, the suitability of data for factor analysis was assessed. Inspection of the correlation matrix revealed the presence of many coefficients of 0.3 and above. The Kaiser–Meyer–Oklin values were above 0.6 for the different constructs, except for wasta (favouritism), and the Bartlett's Test of Sphericity reached statistical significance, supporting the factorability of the correlation matrix. Axial components analysis was conducted with Varimax rotation. The axial factor analysis revealed the presence of 3, 8, 3, 4, 5, 5, 4, 5, 4, and 5 components with eigenvalues exceeding 1 for trust in the internet, website design, belief, internet and computer skill confidence, word of mouth, resistance to change, perceived usefulness, relative advantage, complexity, and e-government adoption, respectively. According to the general rule of thumb, only those factors with eigenvalues greater than 1 should be considered important for analysis purposes (Hair et al., 1998). The screenplot for the aforementioned variables was inspected.

Thus, the variables which showed a strong loading in this study: trust in the internet, website design, religious beliefs, internet and computer skill confidence, word of mouth, resistance to change, perceived usefulness, relative advantage, complexity, e-government adoption. It was decided to eliminate the factor of wasta from any further analysis. Table 1 shows the loading for the different constructs.

Table 1: Factor analysis—citizen data										
	FACTOR LOADING									
ITEM	TRUST_I	WEB	BELIEF	SKILL	WOM	RTC	PU	RA	CX	ADOP
TRUST_I3	.788									

TRUST_I1	.788							
TRUST_I2	.712							
WEB3		.828						
WEB4		.808						
WEB6		.759						
WEB5		.750						
WEB2		.713						
WEB1		.705						
WEB7		.683						
WEB8		.550						
BELIEF3			.951					
BELIEF2			.930					
BELIEF1			.780					
SKILL1				.827				
SKILL4				.821				
SKILL3				.797				
SKILL2				.760				
WOM3					.741			
WOM1					.708			
WOM4					.615			
WOM6					.594			
WOM2					.564			
RTC3						.802		
RTC4						.789		
RTC5						.788		
RTC2						.550		
RTC1						.463		
PU2							.816	
PU1							.709	
PU5							.689	
PU4							.651	
RA5								0.710
RA6								0.670
RA1								0.669
RA2								0.663
RA4								0.647

										.811	
CX3										.811	
CX2										.762	
CX4										.742	
CX1										.688	
ADOP1											.688
ADOP3											.685
ADOP5											.646
ADOP2											.599
ADOP4											.555

Notes: Trust_I = trust in the internet; WEB = website design; BELIEF = religious beliefs; SKILL = internet and computer skill confidence; WOM = word of mouth; RTC = resistance to change; PU = perceived usefulness; RA = relative advantage; CX = complexity; ADOP = adoption

Reliability Analysis

The internal reliability of the main components of factor analysis was evaluated using Cronbach's alpha. Table 2 introduces the major components of the exploratory factor analysis and the reliability analysis.

Table 2 : Reliability analysis of variables		
CONSTRUCT	NUMBER OF ITEMS	CRONBACH'S α
Trust in the internet	3	.807
Website design	8	.899
Religious beliefs	3	.917
Internet and computer skill confidence	4	.879
Word of mouth	5	.783
Resistance to change	5	.804
Perceived usefulness	4	.804
Relative advantage	5	.806
Complexity	4	.838
Adoption	5	.775

6.   DISCUSSION

This section discusses the following significant factors as presented in Table 2: trust in the internet, religious beliefs, website design, internet and computer skill confidence, word of mouth, resistance to change, perceived usefulness, relative advantage and complexity.

The results related to trust in the internet showed that it is essential to incorporate the concerns of citizens in the developing country of Jordan with regard to the privacy and security of their personal details and to consider their willingness to engage with e-government. This study's findings are in the line with previous research conducted by Carter and Bélanger (2005) in the developed country of the USA as trust in the internet showed a strong loading in the factor analysis. This research paper showed the necessity of exploring this factor in relation to e-government adoption in developed and developing countries.

The factor, religious beliefs, was measured using different scale items which described different religious beliefs and views toward the internet, for example, immorality issues and adult themes. Although there is a lack of research on the role of religious beliefs in e-government adoption, the substantial body of research conducted by Alomari et al. (2012) has leveraged a knowledge base in order to explain this role. This paper extends the authors' research by providing an in-depth understanding through the usage of more scale items, such as anti-religious propaganda, to measure religious beliefs.

Website design emerged as a significant component of e-government adoption in Jordan. Different evaluation studies denoted the effect of government websites including adequate features to ensure users' satisfaction (Smith, 2001; Wang et al., 2005). These studies provided a base for the present study in its design of the main scale items for measuring website design: an example of these items is the availability of clear directions for navigating e-government websites. In terms of the factor, internet and computer skill confidence, this study presents the importance of considering the fundamental role of technical skills, that is, internet and computer skills, when researching the factors that influence people's intentions to use e-government services. The varied purposes of using the internet, such as reading news and online shopping, mentioned by survey respondents indicated their different skill levels in interacting with the internet. This study is in line with the literature as it reports on the need to discuss the variation in citizens' technical skill level and their enthusiasm for using e-government services (Belanger and Carter, 2006; Vassilakis et al., 2005).

The nature of the survey respondent population, who were mostly employees, explained the strong loading in the factor analysis in terms of the resistance to change factor. Most of the scale items used to measure this factor reflected the changes that would occur with the introduction of e-government services. Employees would be concerned about different kinds of changes related to e-government as a technological innovation such as losing their jobs as they might be replaced by technology. On the other hand, word of mouth recorded a strong loading in the factor analysis. The way in which this factor was measured showed how people would socialize and network about e-government. Jordan is one of the Arabic societies that are collectivist in nature (Hofstede, 2009). Individuals demonstrate their commitment to and trust in the group to which they belong in different ways, such as when they make decisions about whether or not to use the internet based on the experiences of others whom they trust.

Relative advantage, perceived usefulness and complexity factors were recorded with strong loadings in the factor analysis. The participants were internet-literate and major users of the two government departments (DVLD and ISTD) on which the survey was conducted. This enabled participants to be more capable of assessing how easy it was to understand and use e-government services, how useful these services were when conducting different transactions and to what extent they considered e-government more important than the traditional ways of interacting with the government. In previous research conducted in a developed country, the USA, relative advantage and perceived usefulness were loaded together in the factor analysis and the researchers decided to drop them from further analysis (Carter and Bélanger, 2005). Yet in this research, PU and relative advantage were loaded separately, thus showing the importance of including both constructs to investigate e-government service adoption in developing and Middle Eastern countries like Jordan.

Wasta was the only factor was dropped down from further analysis since it has recorded a weak loading. This might refer to the sample used in this study who was internet literate people. Internet literate people may view the internet as a desirable channel by which to interact with government, as they are more aware of how this kind of interaction could limit wasta.

The discussion and evaluation of the aforementioned factors are necessary to further examine their direct influence on citizens' intentions to use e-government. Further research will determine the direct impact of these factors on e-government adoption.

7.   RESEARCH IMPLICATIONS

This research prompts the government in Jordan on a series of factors that could be used to stimulate a proposal for their promotional campaign about e-government, with word of mouth (WOM) being an example of these factors. To join the two-way live conversation occurring between people about e-government, the government in Jordan needs to design the right promotional campaigns about e-government services. These campaigns could include different themes such as why e-government is important in people's real lives and real success stories about using e-government. These campaigns should clearly address and answer people's different concerns and questions related to e-government. These concerns include the issue of security and privacy in dealing with e-government through different electronic channels and could be addressed by announcing the different strategies and applications being used to secure data. Through the promotional campaigns, different brand communications could be used to ensure access for different categories of society (people who have or who do not access to the internet): these would include traditional advertising (offline media) and technology-based advertising through internet and television.

Social networking applications, such as Facebook and Twitter, are one of the internet based technologies through which the Jordanian government can increase awareness of people about e-government. The government in Jordan should introduce social networking applications as future potential channels to enhance citizenry's interaction with different governmental ministries and agencies.

8.   CONCLUSION

This paper presents a study with a multidimensional theoretical framework which combines a literature review, the Diffusion of Innovation Theory (DOI) and the Technology Acceptance Model (TAM) to identify the main factors related to e-government adoption by the public in Jordan. The study collected data from 356 Jordanian people who had regular access to the internet. Factor analysis was the main analytical technique utilized to identify the factors related to e-government services' adoption. This study has provided an in-depth analysis of e-government adoption by focusing on services provided by two government departments, ISTD and DVDL. The main conclusion is that trust in the internet, religious beliefs, website design, internet and computer skill confidence, word of mouth, resistance to change, perceived usefulness, relative advantage, and complexity are the main factors related to e-government adoption. The research paper has highlighted that the government in Jordan should be sensitive to the dynamics of social and cultural life in Jordan in formulating the response needed from citizens when introducing e-government services as a new channel of interaction with government.

REFERENCES

Ajzen, I. & Fishbein, M. (1972). "Attitudes and Normative Beliefs as Factors Influencing Behavioral Intentions," Journal of Personality and Social Psychology, 21(1), pp.1-9.

AlAwadhi, S., & Morris, A. (2009). "Factors Influencing the Adoption of E-Government Services," Journal of Software, 4 (6), pp. 584-590.

Alomari M.K. (2010). Predictors for Successful E-government Adoption in the Hashemite Kingdom of Jordan: The Deployment of an Empirical Evaluation Based on Citizen- Centric Perspectives, PhD Thesis, Griffith University, Brisbane, Australia.

Alomari, M.K., Sandhu, K. & Woods, P. (2010). "Measuring Social Factors in E-government Adoption in the Hashemite Kingdom of Jordan," International Journal of Digit Society (IJDS), 1 (2), pp.163-172.

Alomari, M.K., Woods, P, & Sandhu, K. (2012). "Predictors for E-government Adoption in Jordan: Deployment of an Empirical Evaluation based on a Citizen-Centric Approach," Information Technology & People, 25 (2), pp.207-234.

Al-Saggaf, Y. (2004). "The Effect of Online Community on Offline Community in Saudi Arabia," The electronic Journal on Information Systems in Developing Countries, 16(2), pp.1-16.

Al-Shafi, S., & Weerakkody, V. 2008. "Adoption of Wireless Internet Parks: An Empirical Study in Qatar". Proceedings of the European and Mediterranean Conference on Information Systems, ISeing Press.

Arndt, J. (1967). "Role of Product-Related Conversations in the Diffusion of a New Product," Journal of Marketing Research, 4 (3), pp.291-295.

Bélanger, F., & Carter, L. (2009). "The Impact of the Digital Divide on e-Government Use," Communications of the ACM, 52 (4), pp.132-135.

Carter, L., & Bélanger, F. (2005). "The Utilization of E-Government Services: Citizen Trust, Innovation and Acceptance Factors," Information Systems Journal, 15(1), pp.5-25.

Carter, L., Shaupp, L. C., Hobbs, J., & Campbell, R. (2011). "The role of security and trust in the adoption of online tax filing. Transforming Government: People, Process and Policy, 5(4), 303-318.

Carter, L., & Weerakkody, V. (2008). "E-Government Adoption: A Cultural Comparison," Information Systems Frontiers, 10(4), pp.473-482.

Chang, I. C., Li, Y.-C., Hung, W.-F., & Hwang, H.-G. (2005). "An Empirical Study on the Impact of Quality Antecedents on Tax Payers' Acceptance of Internet Tax-Filing Systems," Government Information Quarterly, 22(3), pp.389-410.

Cunningham, R. B., & Sarayrah, Y. K. (1994). "Taming Wasta to Achieve Development," Arab Studies Quarterly, 16(3), pp.29-41.

Davis, F.D. (1989). "Perceived Usefulness, Perceived Ease of Use, and User Acceptance of Information Technology". MIS Quarterly, 13(3), pp.319-40.

Dugdale, A., Daly, A., Papandrea, F., & Maley, M. (2005). "Accessing E-Government: Challenges for Citizens and Organizations," International Review of Administrative Sciences, 71(1), pp.109-118.

Ebbers, W. E., & van Dijk, J. A. G. M. (2007). "Resistance and support to electronic government, building a model of innovation". Government Information Quarterly, 24(3), 554-575.

Ebrahim, Z., & Irani, Z. (2005). "E-government Adoption: Architecture and Barriers," Business Process Management Journal, 11(5), pp.589-611.

Fang, Z. (2002). "E-Government in Digital Era: Concept, Practice, and Development," International Journal of The Computer, The Internet and Management, 10(2), pp.1-22.

Feghali, E. (1997). "Arab Cultural Communication Patterns," International Journal of Intercultural Relations, 21(3), pp.345-378.

Gilbert, D., & Balestrini, P. (2004). "Barriers and Benefits in the Adoption of E-Government," The International Journal of Public Sector Management, 17(4), pp.286-301.

Hair, J.F. Jr, Anderson, R.E., Tatham, R.L. & Black, W.C. (1998). Multivariate Data Analysis with Readings. Prentice Hall International, Inc: New Jersey.

Harrison-Walker, L. J. (2001). "The Measurement of Word-Of-Mouth Communication and an Investigation of Service Quality and Customer Commitment as Potential Antecedents," Journal of Service Research: JSR, 4 (1), pp.60-75.

Hill, C. E., Loch, K. D., Straub, D. W., & El-Sheshai, K. (1998). "A Qualitative Assessment of Arab Culture and Information Technology Transfer," Journal of Global Information Management, 6 (3), pp.28-38.

Hofstede, G. (2001). Culture's Consequences: Comparing Values, Behaviors, Institutions, and Organizations Across Nations. Sage Publications: Thousand Oaks, California.

Hofstede, G. (2009). "Geert Hofstede Cultural Dimensions.The Hofstede Centre,"

Hung, S.-Y., Chang, C.-M. & Yu, T.-J. (2006). "Determinants Of User Acceptance Of The E-Government Services: The Case Of Online Tax filing And Payment System," Government Information Quarterly, 23(1), pp.97-122.

Kim, K. & Prabhakar, B. (2000). "Initial Trust, Perceived Risk, and the Adoption of Internet Banking," Proceedings of the 21st international conference on Information systems, AIS Electronic Library.

Makhoul, J., & Harrison, L. (2004). "Intercessory Wasta and Village Development in Lebanon," Arab Studies Quarterly, 26(3), pp.25-41.

McKnight, D.H., Choudhury, V. & Kacmar, C. (2002). "Developing and Validating Trust Measures for E-Commerce: An Integrative Typology," Information Systems Research, 13(3), pp.334-59.

MoICT (2006a). "E-readiness Assessment of the Hashemite Kingdom of Jordan,"

MoICT (2006b). "Jordan E-government Program: E-government Strategy,"

Moon, M. J. (2002). "The Evolution of E-Government among Municipalities: Rhetoric or Reality?," Public Administration Review, 62(4), pp.424-433.

Norton, L. (2002). "The Expanding Universe: Internet Adoption in the Arab Region,"

Ojha, A., Sahu, G. P., & Gupta, M. P. (2009). "Antecedents of Paperless Income Tax Filing by Young Professionals in India: An Exploratory Study," Transforming Government: People, Process and Policy, 3(1), pp.65-90.

Pons, A. (2004). "E-government for Arab countries," Journal of Global Information Technology Management, 7(1), pp.30-46.

Rogers, E.M. (1983). Diffusion of Innovations. The Free Press: New York.

Sathye, M. (1999). "Adoption of Internet Banking By Australian Consumers: An Empirical Investigation," International Journal of Bank Marketing, 17 (7), pp.324-334.

Schaupp, L.C. & Carter, L. (2005). "E-voting: from apathy to adoption," The Journal of Enterprise Information Management Science, 18(5), pp.586-601.

Smith, A.G. (2001). "Applying Evaluation Criteria to New Zealand Government Websites," International Journal of Information Management, 21(2), pp.137-49.

Tashakkori, A., Teddlie , C. (2003). Handbook of Mixed Methods in Social and Behavioral Research. Sage: Thousand Oaks.

Waddell, D., & Sohal, A. S. (1998). "Measuring Resistance to Change: An Instrument and Its Application" (Working Paper 62/98), Monash University, Caulfield East, Victoria.

Wang, Y.-S. (2003). "The Adoption of Electronic Tax Filing Systems: An Empirical Study," Government Information Quarterly, 20(4), pp.333-352.

Warkentin, M., Gefen, D., Pavlou, P.A. & Rose, G.M. (2002). "Encouraging Citizen Adoption of E-Government by Building Trust," Electronic Markets, 12(3), pp.157-62.

Westbrook, R. A. (1987). "Product/Consumption-Based Affective Responses and Postpurchase Processes," Journal of Marketing Research, 24(3), pp.258-270.

Van Slyke, C., Belanger, F., & Comunale, C. L. (2004). "Adopting Business -To-Consumer Electronic Commerce: The Effects of Trust and Perceived Innovation Characteristics," The Data Base for Advances in Information Systems, 35(2), pp.32-49.

Vassilakis, C., Lepouras, G., Fraser, J., Haston, S., & Georgiadis, P. (2005). "Barriers to Electronic Service Development," e-Service Journal, 4(1), pp.41-63.

Zander, A. F. (1950). "Resistance to Change-Its Analysis and Prevention," Advanced Management, 4(5), pp.9-11.

Zhang, P. & von Dran, G.M. (2000). "Satisfiers and Dissatisfiers: A Two-Factor Model for Website Design and Evaluation," Journal of the American Society for Information Science, 51(14), pp.1253-68.

USING THE BSC FOR STRATEGIC PLANNING OF IT (INFORMATION TECHNOLOGY) IN BRAZILIAN ORGANIZATIONS

Adriano Olímpio Tonelli
Instituto Federal de Educação, Ciência e Tecnologia de Minas Gerais, Formiga, MG, Brasil
Paulo Henrique de Souza Bermejo
André Luiz Zambalde
Universidade Federal de Lavras, Lavras/MG, Brasil

ABSTRACT

This paper presents a method that integrates Balanced Scorecard (BSC) concepts and IT strategic planning (ITSP) processes. The resulting method was applied in two organizations in order to verify contributions of Balanced Scorecard regarding the identified ITSP problems. The development of this work was realized in qualitative, exploratory research based on two case studies. The results show that the use of BSC contributed directly to work with IT strategic planning challenges and involved middle management, multifunctional teams, and top management support, all beyond IT boundaries.

Keywords: information technology strategic planning; balanced scorecard; information system management; IT strategic management; IT strategic alignment.

Address for correspondence / Endereço para correspondência

Adriano Olímpio Tonelli, Professor do Instituto Federal de Educação, Ciência e Tecnologia de Minas gerais, doutorando em Administração pela Universidade Federal de Lavras (UFLA). Possui mestrado em Administração, graduação em Ciência da Computação e MBA em Governança de TI, pela UFLA. Atua em atividades de pesquisa nas áreas de sistemas de informação, inovação, desenvolvimento de software e gestão estratégica de TI.

Paulo Henrique S. Bermejo, professor adjunto do Departamento de Ciência da Computação da Universidade Federal de Lavras (UFLA). Formado na área de computação, Paulo Henrique realizou pós-doutorado na Universidade de Bentley (EUA), e doutorado em Engenharia e Gestão do Conhecimento pela Universidade Federal de Santa Catarina. Atua em atividades de pesquisa e ensino nas páreas de sistemas de informação, inovação e gestão estratégica de TI.

André Luiz Zambalde, Professor Associado da Universidade Federal de Lavras-MG (UFLA), nos Departamentos de Ciência da Computação e Administração. É Engenheiro de Telecomunicações (INATEL-MG 1984). Pós-graduado em Administração (UFLA-MG 1989), Mestre em Eletrônica (UNIFEI-MG 1991), Doutor em Engenharia de Sistemas e Computação (COPPE/UFRJ 2000), com Pos-Doutorado em Ciência da Computação (UFMG-MG 2005) e Estatística e Gestão da Informação (UNINOVA - Portugal PT 2010).

1. INTRODUCTION

The strategic use of IT resources has recently attracted increased interest from researchers and organizations. Information technology (IT) has been established in the business world as a fundamental factor for corporate strategy development and realization (Gutierrez & Serrano, 2008). However, ensuring that IT investments and initiatives deliver better performance and value to corporate strategies has become the main challenge for IT and business executives (Gutierrez & Serrano, 2008; Lee & Bai, 2003).

Based on this tendency in information technology in organizations, researchers (Grover & Segars, 2005; Lederer & Salmela, 1996; Lutchen, 2004; Mentzas, 1997; Min, Suh, & Kim, 1999) have proposed and applied IT strategic planning methods. The adoption of ITSP methods and techniques has provided many benefits for organizations. These methods and techniques provide ways to develop a planning structure, improve the relationships between business and IT, support an identification of risks and threats, and allow strategies for evaluation and review (Cerpa & Verner, 1998). ITSP methods are essential for aligning IT and organizational strategies in a way that enhances competitive advantages, creates market opportunities, provides direction, and concentrates efforts (Boar, 1994; Lee & Pai, 2003; Newkirk, L., & Srinivasan, 2003; Pai, 2006). However, in practice, promoting the effectiveness of IT strategic planning has been a major challenge to executives (Bechor, Neumann, Zviran, Chanan, & 2010;(Lee & Bai, 2003). As a result, IT strategic planning processes have faced many problems. According to Boar (1994), IT has historically made strategic plans that are either completely or partially devoid of respect within these business goals or with general organizational contexts. Previous surveys have found that more than half of all ITSP-involved stakeholders are not satisfied with the results (Bechor, et al., 2010).

The proliferation of the web and internet as business platforms, the outsourcing of IT resources and services, service-oriented architectures, cloud computing, and IT pervasiveness tend to expand ITSP development activities, which then creates new challenges to IT strategic planning (Grover & Segars, 2005).

Many other challenges and deficiencies associated with ITSP development have been identified in the literature. Major challenges associated with IT strategic planning include stiffness of the applied methods (Lederer & Salmela, 1996; Salmela & Spil, 2002), difficulty in applying complex methodology (Grover & Segars, 2005; Lederer & Sethi, 2003; Salmela & Spil, 2002; Segars & Grover, 1998), a lack of support from top management on ITSP execution and IT strategic implementation (Lederer & Sethi, 2003), excessive focus on IT functions inside specific aspects (Heckman, 2003), appropriated involvement of middle-level managers (Heckman, 2003), low participation of multifunctional teams (Earl, 2003; Huang & Hu, 2007), distance and low relationship levels between formulation process (planning) and strategies implementation (Broady-Preston & Hayward, 1998; Lederer & Sethi, 2003; Littler, Aisthorpe, Hudson, & Keasey, 2000), and a lack of learning and knowledge emphasis (Bermejo, Tonelli, Brito, & Zambalde, in press; Lederer & Salmela, 1996; Lee & Pai, 2003; Pai, 2006).

As IT departments have faced these challenges to develop the ITSP, Balanced Scorecard (Kaplan & Norton, 1997) has been changing and consolidating as an important tool for strategic management (Kaplan & Norton, 2008), including IT strategy development and implementation (Huang & Hu, 2007; Simon, 2011).

Keyes (2005) highlights that, to promote a better alignment, a BSC must be intimately attached to an IT strategic planning process. This integration must extend beyond the simple capability of balanced scorecard in measuring improvements in IT. Despite the importance attached to ITSP development (Keyes, 2005), the Balanced Scorecard has not been extensively explored in IT strategic planning methods currently available in the literature. Balanced scorecard applications in IT function include BSC utilization as a mechanism to support the implementation of IT strategies (Littler, et al., 2000), promote IT-business strategic alignment and better communication (Huang & Hu, 2007), and conduct IT performance analysis (Velcu, 2010). In addition, other works focus on personalized structure development for IT balanced scorecards (Van Grembergen & De Haes, 2005) and general IT BSC development orientations (Niven, 2002).

Studies that consider Balanced Scorecard application for short-, medium-, and long-term planning, including IT strategy formulations, have not been addressed in the literature. Additionally, in the broader context of ITSP studies, according to Grover and Segars (2005), only a few studies have emphasized questions about how to develop ITSP from a BSC perspective through a defined process, including planning process comprehension and whether it provides satisfactory results for an organization. This work aims to investigate the integration between ITSP and BSC in order to mitigate problems in IT strategic planning initiatives. Of these problems, we highlight the lack of support from top management (Lederer & Sethi, 2003), excessive focus on specific aspects of IT functions (Earl, 2003), the need for ITSP expansion over frontiers (Grover & Segars, 2005), low involvement of middle and top management (Lederer & Sethi, 2003), and infrequent use of multidisciplinary teams (Earl, 2003).

This paper is organized as follows. Section 2 includes the paper's methodology. Section 3 shows the ITSP-BSC method. Section 4 summarizes the results obtained with the application of the proposed method in two organizations and then discusses the findings of this application. Finally, Section 5 describes conclusions, research limitations, and proposals for future works.

2. METHODOLOGY

This study integrates the concepts of Balanced Scorecard (Kaplan & Norton, 1997; Keyes, 2005; Niven, 2002; Van Grembergen & De Haes, 2005) and IT strategic planning (Bechor, et al., 2010; Bermejo, et al., 2012; Boar, 1994; Broady-Preston & Hayward, 1998; Earl, 2003; Grover & Segars, 2005; Lederer & Sethi, 2003; Lee & Bai, 2003; Littler, et al., 2000; Newkirk, et al., 2003; Pai, 2006; Salmela & Spil, 2002; Segars & Grover, 1998). The integration between BSC and ITSP was obtained using a deductive manner (Gimbel, 1968), which resulted in an ITSP-BSC method. This method was used to empirically examine two organizations, and the examination was based on qualitative data collected during the implementation of the proposed method.

Therefore, the research can be characterized as exploratory, based on qualitative and longitudinal data, and conducted within a case study approach (Jung, 2004; Yin, 2005).

The data was collected from a semi-structured questionnaire, participant observation, and focus groups. These activities were performed by student teams from a graduate program of business education who were trained, oriented, and led by the authors.

The selection of the organizations was judgmental (Jung, 2004). The criteria followed the organization's top management interests and their availability in providing conditions for the case study implementation. In addition, we selected organizations that have a prior corporate BSC.

3. THE REFERENCE ITSP METHOD

To develop the proposed method, specific studies about ITSP, IT Governance and Management and Balanced Scorecard were considered. The ITSP studies considered were Boar (1994), Lederer and Salmela (1996), Lutchen (2004), and Bermejo et al. (2012). The ITSP phases proposed by Bermejo et al. (2012) were used as a reference to the structure of the proposed method. This choice was made considering that the method proposed in Bermejo et al. (2012) is aligned with IT Governance features and practices and shows a systematic structure that made possible to incorporate BSC practices in ITSP. In addition, the IT governance framework of Cobit (ITGI, 2007) was utilized.

The proposed method is structured in five phases: (1) IT alignment to business; (2) capacity and performance evaluation; (3) IT strategic planning; (4) IT tactic planning; and (5) ITSP results on socialization and closure.

In phase 1, IT visions and IT goals are defined for the organization. In phase 2, IT performance and capability for addressing the defined IT goals are evaluated. In this phase, the IT resources and critical processes are identified and analyzed. Conducting phases 1 and 2 makes it possible to identify gaps between current IT capabilities and future directions for strategic IT use in the organization. In phase 3, strategic actions are defined to narrow the gaps between current capabilities and future directions. In this phase, performance indicators are also developed to measure the performance of IT strategic actions. In phase 4, IT tactical projects are developed to implement the IT strategic actions defined in phase 3. In this phase, an IT strategic portfolio is developed. Finally, in phase 5, the results are shared with the stakeholders.

BSC application in the ITSP method

The following BSC concepts and practices were incorporated into the previously presented IT strategic planning process: 1) balanced perspectives to translate IT vision into IT goals and indicators; 2) strategic maps to establish cause-and-effect relationships among IT goals; and 3) performance vector indicators and results indicators. Additionally, alternative concepts and perspectives proposed for BSC application for information technology were used. Balanced perspectives developed by Van Grembergen and De Haes (2005) for an IT BSC—corporate contribution, user, operational excellence, and future orientation—were incorporated as an alternative to Kaplan and Norton's (1997) traditional perspectives—financial, customer, internal, and learning and growth. An IT BSC cascade was also incorporated during phase 1 to define the IT BSC aligned with corporate strategies.

Table 1 shows results provided for IT BSC incorporation along method phases.

Table 1. IT BSC evolution through the proposed method

Phase	BSC-related activities incorporated into the ITSP method
1	IT BSC initial development; IT vision and goals definition according to different perspectives in an IT BSC
2	SWOT analysis and analysis of IT critical processes' maturity, based on thematic defined by the balanced perspectives in the IT BSC
3	IT BSC increment; inclusion of strategic actions and performance indicators development
	Strategic maps development: inclusion of cause and effect relations between IT goals and performance vector and result
4	IT BSC increment; inclusion of projects and strategic services development for IT strategic portfolio composition
5	IT BSC release to the organization

During the first phase, activities were carried out in order to develop an initial IT BSC structure. These processes were based on the business goals, corporate BSC, and indicators to translate an IT vision into different relevant perspectives that could then be related by IT. An IT vision is represented in different perspectives. It is presupposed that the use of balanced perspectives to describe IT goals can1) direct ITSP activities over IT frontiers; 2) encourage top management and business unit members' involvement and 3) create the bases for multifunctional teams' development for ITSP conduction. Through the use of balanced perspectives, it is necessary to identify and analyze strategic IT demands from different organization units, including financial and billing issues, customer relationships, and internal processes in order to support continuous business growth and sustainability.

In phase 2, the balanced perspectives defined in phase 1 are used to drive the points to be considered in the evaluation of IT strategic questions, considering aspects inside and outside the organization. It is presupposed that the perspectives incorporated in phase 1 can direct the analysis of IT concerns in different organizational units, thus involving1) top management members to provide information relevant to IT capacity in attending costs, budget, and revenue goals; 2) organizational unit members—IT customers and users—to provide demands for strategic IT support to critical business processes; and

3) IT staff to demand IT internal capacity in terms of staff, IT service delivery, and support. In phase 3, strategic indicators and strategic maps are included in the BSC. In phase 4, an IT portfolio is included. Finally, in phase 5, the IT BSC is released to the organization.

Through the incorporation of strategies and indicators organized on strategic maps, it is presupposed that the proposed method can contribute to a better synergy between IT and other business strategic units. This assumption is based on the potential of strategic maps to establish dependency between IT internal issues (internal perspective), sustainability and capacitating (learning and growing perspective), customers' IT demands (customer perspective), and owners and or shareholders (financial perspective).

4. APPLYING THE PROPOSED METHOD

The method was applied to two organizations from different sectors, one from the pharmaceutical sector and another from the health sector. The empirical results will be presented by summarizing the results of each phase of the method in each organization studied.

Organization Alpha

Organization Alpha operates in the pharmaceutical sector. The organization is 45 years old and has a portfolio of 240 products. In the 2000s, the organization adopted expansion for generic drug lines as the main direction for the business. Based on this vision, the organization's focus turned to the creation of productive expansion, aiming to facilitate the increase of products´ quality.

Phase 1: IT-business alignment. Through the method application in Organization Alpha, it was possible to develop, during phase 1, the IT BSC initial structure with an IT vision related to efficient responsiveness and business growth support.

During phase 1, which involved the strategic committee, commercial director, industrial director, and administrative director, it was possible to define1) the strategic orientation for business expansion aligned to increased quality in the products, and2) specific directions related to planning, production, and quality control. Therefore, production and quality control were defined as the two areas in which IT needed to provide strategic support.

Table 2 illustrates the involvement of stakeholders—top management, strategic areas and IT managers—at the development of the IT BSC initial version, as well as the results obtained from this involvement.

Table 2. Stakeholders' involvement on IT BSC initial version development in Organization Alpha

Event	Stakeholders involved	Results
Startup meeting	IT + top management	Strategic priority: business expansion and increase in quality Strategic areas: planning, production, and quality control
IT vision	Top management + strategic areas + IT	To become a responsive sector to support business expansion.
IT goals	Top management + IT	**Financial perspective:** Efficiency in IT expenditures and support to business expansion and product quality
	Organizational areas + IT	**Customer perspective:** Guarantee responsiveness to production and quality control demands relative to raw material sampling and weighing Improve quality control through IT solutions
	Organizational areas + IT	**Internal perspective:** 4. Optimize IT services delivery and IT infrastructure **Learning and growth perspective:** 5. IT capacitating in strategic competences: production and quality

Based on the IT vision, it was possible to define the IT goals in different balanced scorecard perspectives.

Phase 2: Capacity and performance analysis. Based on the initial BSC structure, the following themes were defined to guide the capacity and performance analysis: 1) cost controlling process (financial perspective); 2) IT services in attending to quality control and production processes (customers' perspective); 3) IT internal organization (internal perspective); 4) IT teams' competence in production process, quality control, and financial management, and 5) top management competence on IT demand identification and analysis (learning and growth perspective).

Table 3 shows a sample of the SWOT analysis conducted in Organization Alpha, considering the main weaknesses found in the data collection process. Due to space limitations, we present only the most representative parts of the SWOT analysis, that is, the problems that need to be overcome in order to strategically direct IT.

Table 3. Synthesis of Organization Alpha SWOT analysis results

Theme	Perspective	Weaknesses	Involvement
Cost control	Financial	Costs allocation is done by IT leader, without alignment with strategic business priority Costs allocation do not reflect IT expansion and flexibility strategic priorities Processes for monitoring costs and returns are absent	Commercial Director Administrative Director Industrial Director IT Manager
Service quality	Customers	Low understanding of how IT can be involved in changes within organizational units Deficiencies in defining priorities for changes according to business strategies Low involvement of customer areas during definitions of scope and quality requirements in IT projects High incidences of rework on projects due to inaccurate scope specification	Quality Manager Planning and Production Manager IT Manager
Internal Organization	Internal	Unclear definition of responsibilities within IT function Reactive approaches in treating IT incidents Lack of information about IT infrastructure due to an ad-hoc configuration management	IT Manager
Competences and communication	Learning and growth	Minimal knowledge of IT relating to strategic priorities for effort directing IT staff lacks clear knowledge of the strategic priorities of the business	IT Manager Quality Manager Planning and Production Manager

Phase 3. IT strategic planning. Considering IT goals to be achieved (phase 1) and major deficiencies of IT to such achievement (phase 2), phase 3 execution defined strategic maps for IT followed by performance actions and indicators.

The IT strategic map for Organization Alpha starts from the learning and growth perspective in order to provide conditions for the proper development and execution of critical processes that will deliver value to the business units. Once effectively and efficiently executed, these processes could ensure responsiveness to production and quality control demands that, in turn, will support top management demands for expansion and cost control.

Figure 1 illustrates the strategic map developed for Organization Alpha.

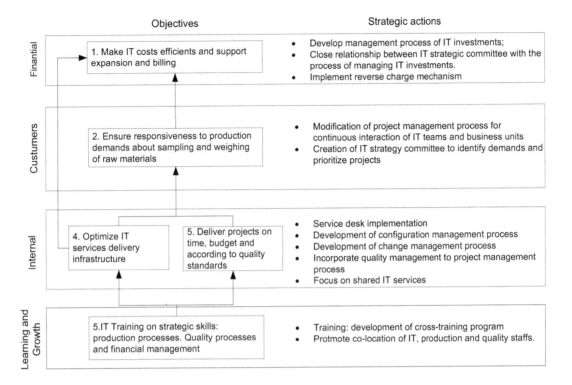

Figure 1. IT strategic map of Alpha Organization

Following the creation of the strategic map, indicators associated with IT goals were developed. Figure 2 illustrates the set of indicators and cause-effect relationship developed in the organization. For confidentiality purposes, we do not include the financial perspective.

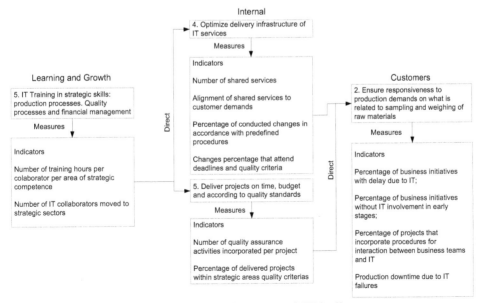

Figure 2. Organization Alpha strategic map and IT indicators

Based on the results obtained in phase 3, synergy between IT and other areas in the organization were identified. In Organization Alpha, synergies were raised between IT function, production and quality sectors, and top management. Table 4 describes the synergies defined in Organization Alpha.

Table 4. Synergies defined on Organization Alpha

Synergy	Description	Related perspective
IT + Production	Joint development of training program	Learning and Growth
	Identification of services that are candidate for shared IT services	Internal
	Composition of IT project team for Production Sector	Customers
	Interaction by strategic committee	Customers
IT + Top Management	Interaction by strategic committee Announcement of new strategic priorities for cost allocation and investments prioritization	Financial

These interaction profiles were considered in phase 4 when projects for tactical plan composition were defined.

Organization Beta

Organization Beta, a fictitious name applied for confidentiality, acts in the private health care sector. Business operations in the organization are strongly regulated by the Health National Agency, especially with regard to pricing, accounting, and how customers' health information is handled.

Phase 1: IT alignment to business. During the execution of phase 1, the following stakeholders were involved: 1) CEO, CFO, and juridical departments, to support definitions in financial perspectives and to make appointments of strategic areas in the organization; 2) general management, exchange and proceedings area, and accounting (customer perspective); and 3) information technology management (internal perspectives and learning and growth). Table 5 illustrates BSC initial development in Organization Beta, considering the involvement of different stakeholders.

Table 5. IT initial BSC in Organization Beta

Event	Involvement	Results
Startup meeting	IT + Top Management	Main focus: Ensure compliance with regulatory requirements in the health sector Prioritize strategic areas for compliance: general management, juridical sector, and exchange and authorizing
ITVision	Top Management + Strategic Areas + IT	Ensure conformity of IT with regulations regarding health information protection
IT objectives	Top Management + IT	**Financial perspective:** Minimize financial impacts arising from service interruption and related penalties Reduce financial losses arising from service interruption
	Exchange and Authorizing + IT	**Customers perspectives:** 3. Ensure protection of sensitive information related to authorization of health services and accounting 4. Promote awareness of and training on health information security
	IT + Strategic areas	**Internal perspective:** 5. Ensure, through web services and IT management practices, security in transactions involving health information 6. Ensure continuity of systems that support transactions associated with billing and health information processing 7. Create close ties between human resource management and information security management **Learning and growth perspective:** 8. Improve IT staff competencies associated with IT service delivery. 9. Improve employees' competencies associated within formation security.

Phase 2: Capacity and performance analysis. In this phase, strengths, weaknesses, opportunities, and threats were gathered, and the following issues were considered: 1) treatment of regulations related to health information protection and services continuity (financial perspective); 2) IT services delivered to authentication, authorization and accounting (customers' perspective); 3) relationship between IT areas and human resources on what is relevant to information security issues related to people (customers' perspective); 4) IT internal processes and resources for delivering IT services related to the organization's strategic areas (internal perspective of learning and growth).

Table 6 shows a sample of Organization Beta SWOT analysis results, considering major weaknesses found during data collection.

Table 6. Beta Organization SWOT analysis results synthesis

Theme	Perspective	Weaknesses	Involvement
Compliance treatment	Financial	Low understanding about the current status of the organization´s compliance with legal requirements Weak alignment between top management, IT function, and general management to meet new legal requirements	Executive Director Financial Director Juridical Department
IT services delivery	Customers	Weak interaction between IT function and other organizational units to define IT services levels Lack of mechanisms to monitor IT service delivery to organizational units	Exchange Authorization Accountability
Relationship with HR	Customers	Low understanding of HR management on what information must be protected Essential technical focus of IT regarding information security.	Human Resources
Internal IT process and resources	Internal Learning and growth	IT leadership with essentially technical capacity and weak interdisciplinary competencies Reactive approach in dealing with IT service continuity concerns Low interaction with organizational units and top management to discuss and treat new compliance requirements	Information Technology

Phase 3. IT strategic planning

Based on IT goals to be achieved (phase 1) and on major IT deficiencies identified (phase 2), in phase 3, the strategic map was defined for Organization Beta. The strategic map developed for Organization Beta starts from the learning and growth perspective to create the necessary conditions—staff capabilities and interaction among organizational units—to conduct internal processes with required levels of information security.

Figure 3 shows the strategic map developed on Beta Organization.

Objectives		Strategic actions
Minimize financial impacts arising from regulations non-compliance	Minimize financial losses resulting from interruption of health procedures authorization services	• Develop performance monitoring mechanism in information security and treatment to compliance
	Ensure protection of sensitive information on systems that support authorization, accounting and exchange process;	• Consolidate information security committee : alignment between identification of requirements compliance with HR management and management and processes of IT services • Implementing information security management process in HR
Systems to ensure continuity of transactions involving billing and health information	Ensure, through use of web services and management practices, safety in transactions involving health information;	• Implement service desk and incident management for security and continuity • Implement service level managing process for security and continuity
Develop closer links with management of human resources for information security management		• Creation of information security committee: identification and reporting of compliance requirements for security • Consultancy for training IT teams • Cross-training. • Environment redesign for physical approach of IT with strategic areas.
Training IT staff in service management and IT security	Training of employees in information security procedures.	

Figure 3. IT strategic map of Organization Beta

Following the creation of strategic maps, indicators associated with IT goals were developed. Figure 4 shows the set of indicators and the cause-effect relationship developed in Organization Beta.

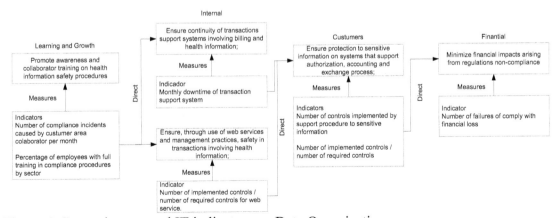

Figure 4. Strategic map and IT indicators on Beta Organization

In phase 3, synergies with different organizational units—juridical, exchange and authorization of health proceedings, human resources, and top management sectors— were observed. Table 7 shows the synergies observed in this phase.

Table 7. Description of synergies defined in Organization Beta

Synergy	Description	Related perspective
IT + Exchange and Authorization	Development of a training program for information security and IT service level management	Learning and growth
	Interaction for compliance requirement impact analysis	Customers
	Development of IT service levels	Internal
IT + Juridical	Identification and analysis of compliance requirements	Customers
IT + HR	Definition and maintenance of information security processes for HR	Customers

As in Organization Alpha, these interaction profiles for Organization Beta were considerate in phase 4, when projects to tactical plan were defined.

5. CONCLUSIONS AND FURTHER RESEARCH

In this paper, we propose a method that integrates IT strategic planning and Balanced Scorecard concepts in order to provide a systematic approach to direct IT in alignment with strategic business priorities.

The application of the proposed method in two organizations showed that the integration between BSC and ITSP can contribute to the expansion of ITSP over IT frontiers and involve both business units and top management. The results show that the definition of balanced perspectives in the method contributed to the identification and involvement of relevant stakeholders that are outside the IT function. Therefore, based on the two case studies, we conclude that the proposed method can be an instrument that contributes to expansion of IT frontiers (Grover & Segars, 2005), and it can mitigate the excessive focus on IT internal aspects and decrease the use of multidisciplinary teams (Earl, 2003).

The main contributions of this study are, through the proposed method, the clarification of how to incorporate the Balanced Scorecard in an IT strategic planning effort. Through a presentation and application of an ITSP method that incorporates balanced scorecard concepts, this work provides guidelines to mitigate common IT strategic planning challenges, such as the expansion of ITSP frontiers and the interaction between IT and other organizational units in the planning process. The two case studies show that the incorporation of BSC provides synergies between different groups (such as Top Management, IT, and Exchange and Authorizing Area) in the development of key activities to strategically direct IT in both organizations. These synergies were possible, in part, due to the need to consider the different perspectives from which IT strategies and actions can be described, including customers, financial, internal processes, and learning and growth.

In this way, this work extends the contributions provided by contributes to Segars and Grover's (2005) with respect to ITSP process definition and comprehending how it can provide satisfactory results. The alignment between BSC and ITSP offers a systematic approach that guides the definition of IT directions in alignment with business units and strategic priorities. The proposed method provides generic guidelines that organizations can use to incorporate balanced scorecard concepts in the ITSP. Then, they can create an environment that is more conductive to the necessary synergies between groups when developing IT strategies that are aligned with the business.

However, the method itself is not a sufficient condition to overcome ITSP challenges. Skilled people, organizational culture, and other factors also exert significant influence and must be investigated in future works.

This study has some natural limitations in terms of study focus. Two organizations were studied; however, these findings cannot be used to generalize the results and conclusions obtained from this study to any other specific organization. Moreover, this work is limited to ITSP development and does not cover implementation from developing strategies outside of the ITSP process. As one aim of this study is to establish an understanding of the applicability of BSC on ITSP, the following future studies are proposed.

Future works can expand the context of the proposed method to other organizations and contexts, aiming to deepen the understanding of balanced scorecard applicability on ITSP. Additionally, future researchers can adopt a quantitative approach to define and test hypotheses about BSC application on ITSP. Finally, future works can evaluate the implementation results of IT strategic plans developed using balanced scorecard concepts. Such studies can be relevant to evaluate the contributions of BSC for approximating IT strategies, implementation, and planning activities.

Acknowledgements

The authors thank the National Council of Technological and Scientific Development (CNPq – Brazil), Coordination for the Improvement of Higher Level Personnel (Capes - Brazil), and the Foundation for Research Support of the State of Minas Gerais (FAPEMIG - Brazil) for the financial support.

A prior version of this paper was presented at the 9th International Conference on Information System and Technology Management (CONTECSI) in 2010 in São Paulo, Brazil. The authors also thank the double-blind reviewers of this conference.

REFERENCES

Bechor, T., Neumann, S., Zviran, M., Chanan, G., & (2010). A contingency model for estimating success of strategic information systems Planning. *Information & Management., 47*(1), 17-29.

Bermejo, P. H. S., Tonelli, A. O., Brito, M., J., & Zambalde, A. L. (2012).Implementation of information technology governance through IT strategic planning. *African Journal of Business Management,* 6: 11179-11189.

Boar, B. H. (1994).*Practical steps for aligning information technology with business strategies: how to achieve a competitive advantage.* New York: John Wiley.

Broady-Preston, J., & Hayward, T. E. (1998).An assessment of the relationship between marketing, information and strategy formulation in the retail banking sector. *International Journal of Information Management, 18*(4), 277-285.

Cerpa, N., & Verner, J. M. (1998). Case study: The effect of IS maturity on information systems strategic planning. *Information & Management, 34*(2), 199-208. .

Earl, M. J. (2003). Approaches to information systems planning. Experiences in strategic information systems planning. In R. D. Galliers & D. E. Leidner (Eds.), *Strategic information management: challenges and strategies in managing information systems* (Third ed.). Burlington: Elsevier.

Gimbel, S. (1968).*Exploring the Scientific Method: Cases and Questions.* London: The University of Chicago Press.

Grover, V., & Segars, A. H. (2005). An empirical evaluation of stages of strategic information systems planning: patterns of process design and effectiveness. *Information & Management, 42*(5), 761-779.

Gutierrez, A., & Serrano, A. (2008). Assessing Strategic, Tactical, and Operational Alignment Factors for SMEs: Alignment Across the Organisation's Value Chain. *International Journal of Value Chain Management, 2*(1), 33-56.

Heckman, R. (2003). Strategic Information Technology Planning and the Line Manager's Role. *Information Systems Management 20*(4), 16-21.

Huang, C., & Hu, Q. (2007).Achieving IT-business strategic alignment via enterprise-wide implementation of balanced scorecards. *Information Systems Management 24*(2), 173-184.

ITGI, I. G. I. (2007).*COBIT 4.1: control objectives, management guidelines, maturity models.* Rolling Meadows: ITGI.

Jung, C. F. (2004). *Metodologia para pesquisa & desenvolvimento aplicada a novas tecnologias, produtos e processos.* Rio de Janeiro: Axcel Books do Brasil.

Kaplan, R. S., & Norton, D. P. (1997). *A estratégia em ação: balanced scorecard* (22th ed.). Rio de Janeiro: Elsevier.

Kaplan, R. S., & Norton, D. P. (2008). *A Execução Premium: A obtenção de vantagem competitiva através do vínculo da estratégia com as operações de negócio*. Rio de Janeiro: Elsevier.

Keyes, J. (2005). *Implementing the IT Balanced Scorecard: Aligning IT with Corporate Strategy*. Boca Raton: Auerbach Publications.

Lederer, A. L., & Salmela, H. (1996).Toward a theory of strategic information systems planning.*Journal of Strategic Information Systems, 5*(3), 237-253.

Lederer, A. L., & Sethi, V. (2003). The Information Systems Planning Process: Meeting the challenges of information systems planning. In R. D. Galliers & L. D. E. (Eds.), *Strategic information management: challenges and strategies in managing information systems* United Kingdom: Elsevier.

Lee, G. G., & Bai, R. J. (2003). Organizational Mechanisms for successful IT/IS strategic planning in the digital era. *Management Decision, 41*(1), 32-42.

Lee, G. G., & Pai, R. J. (2003).Effects of organizational context and inter-group behaviour on the success of strategic information systems planning: an empirical study. *Behaviour and Information Technology, 22*(4), 263-280.

Littler, K., Aisthorpe, P., Hudson, R., & Keasey, K. (2000). A new approach to linking strategy formulation and strategy implementation: an example from the UK banking sector. *International Journal of Information Management, 20*, 411-428.

Lutchen, M. D. (2004). *Managing IT as a business: a survival guide for CEOs*. Hoboken: John Wiley & Sons.

Mentzas, G. (1997). Implementing is an strategy: a team approach. *Long Range Planning, 30*(1), 84-95.

Min, S. K., Suh, E. H., & Kim, S. Y. (1999).An integrated approach toward strategic information systems planning. *Journal of Strategic Information Systems, 8*(4), 373-394.

Newkirk, H. E., L., L. A., & Srinivasan, C. (2003). Strategic information systems planning: too little or too much. *Journal of Strategic Information Systems, 12*(3), 201-228.

Niven, P. (2002). *Balanced Scorecard Step by Step: Maximizing Performance and Maximizing Results*. New York: John Wiley & Sons.

Pai, J. C. (2006). An empirical study of the relationship between knowledge sharing and IS/IT strategic planning (ISSP). . *Management Decision, 44*(1), 105-122.

Salmela, H., & Spil, T. A. M. (2002).Dynamic and emergent information systems strategy formulation and implementation. *International Journal of Information Management, 22*, 441-460.

Segars, A. H., & Grover, V. (1998). Strategic information systems planning success: an investigation of the construct and its measurement. *MIS Quarterly, 22*(2), 139-163.

Simon, P. P. (2011). Design and implementation of the Balanced Scorecard at a university institute. *Measuring Business Excellence, 15*(3), 34 - 45.

Van Grembergen, W., & De Haes, S. (2005). Measuring and Improving IT Governance Through the Balanced Scorecard. *Information Systems Control Journal 2*.

Velcu, O. (2010). Strategic alignment of ERP implementation stages: An empirical investigation. *Information & Management, 47*(3), 158-166.

Yin, R. (2005). *Estudo de caso: planejamento e métodos* (Third ed.). São Paulo: Artmed.

5

ENTERPRISE TECHNOLOGY IN SUPPORT FOR ACCOUNTING INFORMATION SYSTEMS. AN INNOVATION AND PRODUCTIVITY APPROACH

Jose Melchor Medina-Quintero
Alberto Mora
Demian Abrego
Universidad Autonoma de Tamaulipas, Tamaulipas, México

ABSTRACT

Technology and the accounting information systems are implemented in an organization with the aim of improving their efficiency. Companies spend large amounts of money on these tools every year in order to improve their organizational performance. The aim of this research is to determine the influence of SMEs' technological alignment, information management and technological infrastructure on the performance of an institution (innovation and productivity) in which accounting information systems are used. An empirical study is conducted in enterprises belonging to the service, commercial and industrial sectors in Ciudad Victoria, México, with the help of the SmartPLS statistical tool. The results mainly show that technology has helped raise productivity (improvement in administrative activities, in decision-making and in the use of generated information).

Keywords: technological alignment, information management, innovation, AIS, productivity

1. INTRODUCTION

Accounting is the engine that moves an enterprise forward, and helps it face its competitors' efforts, trade agreements, fiscal issues, etc. The accounting's aim is to mirror an enterprise's state, financial statements, and outcomes. Decision makers in a company benefit from this information when they receive it. For example, they can decide what direction they can give to the company or what policies they can develop. Similarly, information related to accounting is also beneficial for enterprise's partners as a good performance of the company can determine the benefits they will obtain from it. The American Institute of Certified Public Accountants in the United States of America has made a call for the need to incorporate the concepts of information technology (IT) into the accounting professionals' knowledge, skills, and abilities (Dillon and Kruck, 2004). They claim that such competencies should be applied

Address for correspondence / Endereço para correspondência

Dr. José-Melchor Medina, Universidad Autónoma de Tamaulipas. Centro Médico y Educativo "Adolfo López Mateos" Cd. Victoria, Tamaulipas. México. ext. 139.

Dr. Alberto Mora, Universidad Autónoma de Tamaulipas, Tamaulipas. México.

Dr. Demian Abrego, Universidad Autónoma de Tamaulipas, Tamaulipas. México.

to the organizational performance improvement efforts. To do so, it is fundamental for organizations to be aware of the importance of the accounting function, otherwise, all the financial information may become an underused resource. However, entrepreneurs often raise questions regarding the IT return on investment, specifically, in Accounting Information Systems (AIS), even though there is evidence of their positive impact on various aspects such as productivity and organizational performance, as they help increase sales levels and have access to more customers and improve the relationship with them, raise efficiency levels in the business processes, and decrease cost, among others.

Scholars have been trying to explain the strategic value of IT capabilities for a long time (Fink, 2011). There is ample evidence of the ways in which IT has been applied in the achievement of enterprises' productivity and in helping them become more competitive globally. This enables them to put their human and economic efforts into the development of new products.

The spread of technology is central to an organization's development and change. According to Gordon and Tarafdar (2007), IT entails information, project management, collaboration, communication, and their involvement helps enterprises improve their ability to innovate, as the technological developments are the result of innovative processes. However, Hevner et al. (2004) sustain that there are insufficient constructs, models, methods and tools to represent accurately the link between business and technology. In this context, many small and medium sized enterprises (SMEs) have aligned technological applications with their business operations, but few have been able to successfully integrate IT into their business units (Chen and Wu, 2011). A concrete example of this is the case of AIS, which has not been exploited for the benefit of an organization's harmonious development.

SMEs play an important role in most countries' economies. However, when compared to large enterprises, SMEs have a more simple structure, fewer specialized tasks, and fewer resources than those of human, financial and material (Feller et al., 2011). Regarding IT, they do not normally have an IT department; they lack project leaders; and formal IT staff training programs do not exist. In other words, they have scarce resources, and according to the resources and capabilities theory, they need different competencies to be able to face the challenges that the scarcity of resources represents.

In addition to the aforementioned, the knowledge age has had an effect on SMEs. For example, IT has an impact on the accounting based performance, which is determined mainly by their knowledge management capacity (Tanriverdi, 2005), as knowledge is considered a strategic resource within the resource based theory. In other words, SMEs should try to make the most of technology which has become more and more accessible thanks to the constant reduction in costs, which in turn facilitates the justification of the acquisition of IT and AIS.

Nevertheless, it is important to mention that most studies that address this topic have been focused on the context of developed countries (Sabherwal et al., 2006; Petter et al., 2008; Ferreira and Cherobim, 2012). Therefore, there is an urgent need to undertake research that is not only limited to those countries. Scholars such as Mahmood and Mannm (2000) have also suggested the need for other scholars to include the experience of other countries as well.

IT and AIS are undoubtedly of paramount importance nowadays. In the Mexican context, little research into the impact of information systems (IS) and their benefits at the organizational level has been conducted; and this study is an attempt to fill that gap in the literature. Therefore, the aim of this paper is to determine the impact of technological alignment, information management and technological infrastructure on the performance of an institution in terms of innovation and productivity with the daily use of an AIS in the

SMEs. To achieve this aim, a research model is tested and examined in SMEs belonging to the service, commercial and manufacturing sectors in Ciudad Victoria, Mexico. Data is collected directly from the participating economic units. Such data is in turn analyzed statistically through the use of SmartPLS, developed by Ringle et al. (2005). The research is based on the review of the literature related to the dependent and independent variables studied. After that, the empirical part of the research is carried out (administration of the questionnaire, its analysis and discussion of the main findings). The conclusions are then drawn and the main contributions to knowledge are outlined.

2. REVIEW OF LITERATURE

2.1. INNOVATION

Innovation affects firms' ability to compete successfully in an increasingly global market (Madrid-Guijarro et al., 2009), as innovation is central to organizations' modernization and transformation (Feller et al., 2011). In this sense, organizations not only need to pay attention to efficiency and productivity, but also they need to promote innovation and their mechanisms to develop it which support knowledge generation, sharing and integration (Albers and Brewer, 2003). These two researchers define innovation as the use of knowledge that offers a new product or service needed by customers. However, the concept of innovation is complex; and from the technological and administrative point of view, it requires time, devotion and investment (Toledo and Zilber, 2012). For Sala-I-Martin et al. (2013), innovation can come through the technological aspect or non-technological knowledge. Basically, the innovation process is connected with the search, experimentation, development and implementation of new products, services, processes, ideas and new organizational approaches. Hsu (2010) summarizes innovation as one new technology idea, application of the existing technology for a new invent and improvement of the existing technology or products. For this paper, innovation occurs when an idea, process, service or product is established in the firm, and it faces competition efficiently.

The impact of innovation on performance (both profitability and growth) is primarily indirect and is instead fueled by IT (Dibrell et al., 2008). During the decade of the 1990's, IT proved to be a particularly powerful innovation tool as it enabled the development of new products and helped improve business processes; but the learning of new creative techniques is an ongoing process within an organization and will result in an improvement of processes, products and methods. This raises the following questions: How to innovate with information technology and AIS in an enterprise? How to gain competitive advantages through AIS? Therefore, those organizations wishing to innovate should cultivate the identification of IT competences (Gordon and Tarafdar, 2007). These same scholars warn that IT and the IS could suffocate creativity and innovation by standardizing, automating and institutionalizing the existing processes and work flows. In the same vein, according to Fink (2011), in order for an enterprise to sustain its competitive advantage, it is essential not to open its resources to imitation or substitution. Similarly, an industry's ability to innovate and gain competitive advantage depends on factors such as R&D stock, human capital, engagement (of products and people) in international business, and market regulations, among others (Apergis et al., 2008).

Innovation is a variable that needs to be promoted within the institutions, regardless of the benefits already gained through such innovation, of the construction of infrastructure, of the reduction of the macroeconomic instability, or of the improvement of the human resources of the population, especially because all these factors seem to run into diminishing returns (Sala-I-Martin et al., 2013). In this context, Mexico is ranked in the 49th position, which has started to become difficult to sustain due to the deceleration of many world economies. In addition to that, there is also the lack of knowledge about the creativity potential to increase the organization's innovative capability; therefore, it is imperative for organizations to incorporate into their hierarchical culture the idea that innovation is important for the institution and stakeholders (Toledo and Zilber, 2012).

Undoubtedly, innovation is a factor that any type of enterprise needs to consider if they are to survive in these changing times. The SMEs are not an exception. This is especially true when there are large amounts of information available generated by AIS which have not been used for the common good in the SMEs. In other words, the SMEs are also required to use the data generated within them, not only to compete, but also to survive. The role that IT and AIS play in helping organizations become innovative is not clear. However, because of the importance of innovation, many scholars have analyzed its roots with the hope of determining what an enterprise should do to become more innovative. No doubt more investment in research and development is needed in order to understand and assess new technology and innovation trends. .

2.2. PRODUCTIVITY

Sala-I-Martin et al. (2008) stated that enterprises will depend to a great extent on their ability to adapt themselves to the existing technologies in order to increase their productivity. For this research, productivity enables enterprises to develop better decision-making processes, more effective information and technology usage and more efficient ways to align the organizational strategies with IT.

In addition, as IT has become more important for enterprises, their executives demand more accountability, which requires the measurement of their productivity. In this context, the brief history of the IT shows that they joined the organizations precisely because they promised the automation of monotonous processes and a reduction of staff costs. In other words, they promised an increase in productivity. Nowadays, managers call into question the little benefit they obtain from the financial, human, time and effort investments they make, including all their risks involved in this process. Badescu and Garcés-Ayerbe (2009) found that while organizations have experienced improvements in the work productivity in a reasonable time, but such improvements do not result from the investment made in IT; even, Robert M. Solow, the Nobel Prize winner in 1987, mentioned that "we see the computer era everywhere except in the productivity statistics". This is so because according to Mahmood et al. (2000) investments in computers will be profitable only if they entail an increase in productivity. Nonetheless, the emergence of the IT productivity paradox came to exacerbate this situation due to the huge investments made, which most of the time are not reflected in the organizational productivity. This situation leads to the conclusion that despite the investments in IT, it fails mainly because there is a lack of acceptance of it on the part of its users, an absence of a systematic planning as well as a lack of managers' participation in it.

With respect to the impact of investments in IT, at organizational productivity levels, positive and significant relationships have been observed and recognized lately, especially with the IS and AIS in particular. This situation is even present in those organizations which have been successful in adopting IS; they are normally looking for ways of improving their business processes, considering the IS as a means of increasing productivity (Feller et al., 2011). In another study, Farrell (2003) also recognizes this co-relation, but framed and justified in highly competitive environments, and therefore, with a high demand for innovations; in such environments, innovation and technology transfer have been found to be statistically significant for productivity gains (Apergis et al., 2008).

Some researchers wonder whether it is possible to maximize IT performance if this is not done simultaneously with the restructuring of organizations; what is not debatable is the fact that investments made in IT may facilitate the complimenting innovations in the economy such as the business processes and the work practices, which leads to an increase in productivity through a cost reduction and quality improvement (Han et al., 2011).

As can be seen, the Productivity variable is very important for small and medium-sized enterprises. AIS may be a source of progress and a generator of organizational productivity if used efficiently. This can be achieved by utilizing all data created through its continuous usage.

2.3. TECHNOLOGICAL ALIGNMENT

The alignment between businesses and IT has been defined by Venkatranman (1989) as the relationship between strategy and performance at the information technology service level, as well as at the business level. Based on this concept, IT professionals and business leaders are constantly in pursuit of their best administrative practices so as to be able to align their business strategies with those of technology (Hammett, 2008). Similarly, Henderson and Venkatraman (1993) suggest that the alignment between IT human skills and IT infrastructure capacity has a positive strategic effect; that is why technology has an important role to play in the strategic planning process for the achievement of objectives and mission (Lewis III, 2009). For his part, Davenport (2000) argues that a combination of strategy, technology, data (relevant), organization, culture, skills and knowledge helps develop the organization's capabilities for the data analysis process. The benefits can be even greater if the focus is on the data obtained from an AIS, as this can be an important measure for the development of the strategies aimed at such technological alignment.

The sharing of knowledge between managers and IS professionals is an important factor for the achievement of alignment between business objectives and those of IT. This is especially the case when the management of an organization's technology has been assigned to the IT department; therefore, there needs to be a strategic alignment between business strategies, IT strategies, IS infrastructure and organizational infrastructure (Henderson and Venkatraman, 1993). To do so, there are certain aspects that need to be taken into consideration for the alignment of business with IT (Onita and Dhaliwal, 2011): scope, governance, availability of resources, competences and process. With the current tendencies of evaluation and fiscal audits, accounting cannot be left out in this context. Unfortunately, organizations have not been able to succeed in maintaining a harmonious relationship between business and IT (Hammett, 2008).

While there is a general agreement among practitioners that the alignment of IT and the businesses is necessary, the pathway to achieve it is not completely clear. This is because business strategies are firstly defined and then operations and support strategies, including the technologies are aligned with them (Feurer et al., 2000). For example, Dibrell et al. (2008) argue that IT initiatives should be aligned with innovation. That is to say, in order to obtain a real integration between IT and business strategy, it is necessary that the very process of establishing the strategy incorporates ingredients of IT just as it does with other functions (commercial, sales, production, and others), and according to Peak et al. (2005), this alignment involves the good use of the decisions of the IT resources for the achievement of strategic objectives of the businesses (anticipation to the future requirements), tactics (location of resources) and operational (efficiency and effectiveness achievement) of the organization; because any change in the strategy and technology potentially results in a change in the value system, in the culture and in the structure of the organization teams (Feurer et al., 2000).

In today's business environment, the alignment of IT with business processes, such as the stakeholders' abilities, constant technological changes, new standards, strategies with competitors, among others is more and more difficult. The integration of IT and IS (which includes AIS) with the enterprise's operations has been widely recognized as a requirement for improving various aspects of an organization.

We need to understand that the alignment of the conduct of the strategic business units within the corporation and the alignment of the organization with IT and then with these units have been a top priority for many managers. Therefore, enterprises need to integrate it into their business plans in order to ensure that they are aligned with their strategy (Galleta and Lederer, 1989) also highlight its important role in the support of management decision making processes. They go on to suggest that SMEs should consider how they can apply IT to other strategic initiatives, such as customer responsiveness, in order to enhance the overall effectiveness of the strategy.

Overall, there are different key factors that contribute to the alignment of organizational strategies with technology in an enterprise. These include their leaders' communication, participation and support in IT, the sharing of knowledge, the clear definition of processes, the technological infrastructure and the integral planning.

After having reviewed the literature on technological alignment, we now proceed to present the hypotheses of our work for this construct. A description of their operationalization is provided in the Method section:

H_1. The technological alignment generated through the use of AIS is a means to innovate in an SME.

H_2. The technological alignment generated through the use of AIS allows SMEs to increase their productivity levels.

2.4. INFORMATION MANAGEMENT

The organizational information processing theory is based on the idea that an organizational adjustment is adequate when the business strategies' information processing requirements are in concordance with the organizational structure's information processing capacity (Jarvenpaa and Ives, 1993). Unfortunately, few SMEs have formally designed their information policies and management (Feller et al., 2011) even though globalization requires the performance of structured and unstructured transactions, and the sharing of information beyond their boundaries.

All enterprises depend on information technology for the accurate and timely management of information. However, many enterprises tend to collect large amounts of data from the entire organization. This raises the following question: Now what do we do with them? According to Oppenheim et al. (2004) information may contribute to the organizational effectiveness. They warn that its impact remains hidden until it is removed or lost. In other words, information makes sense only if someone uses it for something.

Davenport and Prusak (1997) have argued that information plays a role in the facilitation of the exchange process with the value chain as part of its business strategy as its users need it to understand the meaning of the data and virtually, all the stakeholders in the enterprise (operators, executives, etc.) use information to produce more information. Moreover, for enterprises, knowledge management is an essential managerial activity for sustaining competitive advantage in today's information economy (Lin et al., 2012). Nevertheless, knowledge, including information, is also an organizational capability which is a source of a sustainable competitive advantage. As Ray et al. (2005) have stated, those enterprises with a high level of knowledge and information sharing achieve good results in offering services to their customers. In this respect, Davenport (2000) introduces the *data oriented culture* and calls for the need for data analysis, data integrity, data synthesis, complete data and prompt extraction of data. For this reason, AIS are a useful tool for the generation of tangible information which can help create competitive advantages and if treated adequately, they can become a knowledge creation source.

Undoubtedly, information is an intrinsic component in almost all the information activities in every organization to the degree of becoming *transparent*. This is so because it is the means through which people express, represent, communicate and share their knowledge. Marchand et al. (2002) highlight that it is the use of information which has an influence on the creation of business value through four strategic priorities: *i*) Minimizing financial, commercial and operational risks, *ii*) reducing costs of transactions and processes, *iii*) adding value to customers and markets, and *iv*) creating new realities through innovation.

As can be seen, information management is an information technology trend that is having, or will have, a short-term impact on all types of businesses. Therefore, organizations should implement strategies related to information management technologies if they are to increase their effectiveness, competitiveness and their ability to address competition (Lin et al., 2012).

We now proceed to present the hypotheses of our work for this construct. A description of their operationalization is provided in the Method section:

H_3. The information management generated through the use of AIS is a means to innovate in an SME.

H_4. The information management generated through the use of AIS allows SMEs to increase their productivity levels.

2.5. TECHNOLOGICAL INFRASTRUCTURE

Technological infrastructure allows organizations to develop key applications, and to share information related to division and products (Han et al., 2011). It is defined as the group of interrelated capital resources which provide the foundation on which IT applications are built. It is made up of hardware, software and orgware, which support the AIS that record all the commercial activities of an organization. However, standardizing all the IT infrastructure aspects is not recommended since the business units need autonomy to meet their specific technological needs (Tanriverdi, 2005). The sharing of joint objectives, principles, values and language among the talented IT people in the business units is needed.

The majority of the enterprises view the new technologies as instruments to gain certain advantages and many of the times as tools to bring about a change in the business strategies and the institutional corporate processes. In addition, IT infrastructure is positively associated with the duration of the sustainability of the competitive advantage, although it is not eternal. A constant renewal in IT infrastructure is needed as this has become more and more inexpensive and accessible to all organizations.

It has also been noticed that the promises of IT have not been fulfilled, and the so-called productivity paradox has been called into question, especially due to the big investments made by organizations in computers and technology hoping to obtain a substantial profit (Hitt and Brynjolfsson, 1996), to improve performance, best decision making gains competitive advantage and because of the influence it has on the strategy (Davenport, 2000), for the impact it has on the enterprises and for the changes in the businesses' environment. What is surprising about the paradox is that just when the technology adds amazing quantities, it has not been able to respond to the fundamental needs of the enterprise. Imposing a uniform IT strategy and infrastructure through all the business units and centralizing the management of the IT resources may be useful for the central objectives; nevertheless, this can also limit the degree of autonomy and performance of the business (Tanriverdi, 2005).

Similarly, Dibrell et al. (2008) contend that an appropriate use of IT infrastructure may impact positively on innovation, productivity and competitiveness. Yet, some organizations have failed in their attempts, and those enterprises with a high degree of success in the adoption and use of IS were constantly searching for new IT techniques and ways to incorporate them into the organization's business processes (Feller et al., 2011). However, some researchers such as Heo and Han (2003) contradict this claim arguing that IT may lead to an increase in costs and affect management. This study intends to contribute to the debate about these issues.

We now proceed to present the hypotheses of our work for this construct. A description of their operationalization is provided in the Method section:

H_5. Technological infrastructure in the way of AIS is a means to innovate in an SME.

H_6. Technological infrastructure in the way for AIS to allow SMEs to increase their productivity levels.

3. METHOD

Information technology plays a central role in the harmonious development of organizations. Nowadays, it is difficult to conceive an institution without the use of any technology as a means to achieve a certain competitive advantage. In this research in particular, technology is of paramount importance as the literature review carried out in the main research centers and universities in Mexico reveals that there is little, if any, research conducted in this discipline.

The process used to achieve the main objective of the literature review started with a review of the state of the art of the independent variables related to the technological alignment, information management and technological infrastructure. This was followed by a review of the state of the art of the dependent variables related to an organization's performance from an innovation and productivity point of view. The constructs of the independent and dependent variables have been operationalized as follows:

- Independent variables (with the use of the AIS and the information generated through it):

Technological Alignment (aims and achievement of objectives, perception of improvement in the performance of activities, definition of strategies in cooperation with organizations and IT), Information Management (strategic use of information, participation of key staff members in information management, continuous acknowledgement of information processes) and Technological Infrastructure (efficiency in operations, relating processes and persons, forecasting market trends, defending the market position).

- Dependent variables (with the use of AIS and the information generated through it):

Innovation (select the most promising innovations, making the most of the market opportunities, higher level of products and services innovation), and Productivity (perception of activity improvement, information for decision-making, the AIS information is considered as an asset to the organization).

After that, a tentative questionnaire was designed and reviewed by professionals in the field. The instrument was validated by academicians and experts; the next step involved the pre-testing of the instrument, which helped in establishing the validity of the items and their contents. In other words, the administration of pre-tests of the instrument served for improvement purposes, as it requested feedback from the 12 participating enterprises. The results of the pilot test allowed the detection of a few items which did not meet the minimum recommended statistical load. The final version of the instrument was made up of 4 items for the technological alignment section, 3 for information management, 5 for technological infrastructure, 4 for innovation, and 3 for the productivity, in addition to the demographic data section. All of them were assessed in a 5 point Likert scale (Totally Disagree ... Totally Agree), which has more than three values for its measurement as a lower or larger scale will not provide the respondents' discriminating power. The 5 point Likert scale was considered an ideal option since the establishment of acceptable levels of the constructs is critical for any research project. The empirical work was carried out in the central region of the Mexican state of Tamaulipas.

The most recent census conducted by the Mexico's National Institute of Statistics and Geography (INEGI, 2011) shows that there are 5782 SMEs in the state of Tamaulipas (in Mexico, small enterprises are those which have between 11 and 50 employees and medium-sized enterprises are those with a range of 51 and 250 employees). The region under study (Ciudad Victoria) has 636 SMEs. The final version of the instrument was applied to 63 enterprises (10% of the total population). Unfortunately, the participation of entrepreneurs and managers in this kind of studies in this region is still low. Two questionnaires were applied to each of the enterprises, generating 126 completed questionnaires for their analysis. The respondents were those people who make use of AIS such as the finance manager, the top manager, the main accountant, and the accounting staff. All responses would be kept anonymous and confidential. The criterion for the selection of units of analysis was that the organization had a recognized accounting management function through an AIS.

The data analysis was carried out through descriptive and inferential statistics, with the help of the multivariate SmartPLS (it is PLS variation: Partial Least Squares) software package. This along with a re-sampling of 500 sub-samples allowed us to obtain the crossing of variables, correlation matrices, factorial loadings, average variance extracted (AVE), t-statistics, explained variance and standardized coefficient paths. This was done with the purpose of obtaining an answer to the proposed hypotheses. Conclusions are then drawn from the analysis conducted as well as their implications for practice and policy making.

The use of PLS has generated interest among information systems researchers due to the possibility that it offers to model latent constructs under abnormal conditions and with small or medium sized samples (Chin et al., 2003). It is used in a wide variety of disciplines, including economics, political sciences, educational psychology, chemistry and marketing (Fornell and Bookstein, 1982). The aim of the PLS modeling is to predict both latent and manifest dependent variables. Such aim is translated into an attempt to maximize the explained variance (R^2) of the independent variables. This in turn leads to the fact that the estimations of the parameters are based on the capacity to minimize the residual of the endogenous variables (Cepeda and Roldán, 2004).

SmartPLS will serve as a means to validate the model in an integral form. That is to say, the results of this statistical tool will help determine whether the research model has sufficient reliability. Overall, PLS is an adequate means for research in information systems (Roldán and Sánchez-Franco, 2012). To do so, the measurement and structural parameters are estimated simultaneously (analyzed and interpreted in two stages): PLS enabled researchers to assess the *measurement model* (psychometric properties of the scale used to measure a variable), and the estimation of the *structural model* (the strength and direction of the relationships between variables). In addition to that, PLS has few restrictions regarding measurement scales, sample size and residual distributions. Therefore, it is more appropriate to explain complex causal relationships (Chen and Wu, 2011), especially when there is little theoretical information available (Roldán and Sánchez-Franco, 2012).

A. MEASUREMENT MODEL

- Reliability: For the purposes of this research, it is assessed by examining the loadings (λ) or simple correlations. In order for an indicator to be accepted, it needs to possess an equal or greater loading than 0.707 (λ^2, 50% of the explained variance).

- Internal Consistency (Constructs Reliability), it is assessed by a Cronbach's alpha of (0.7). In this case, the statistic proposed by Fornell and Larcker (1981) is used. Based on their research, these authors claim that their 0.707 measure is greater than that of Cronbach's.

- Discriminant Validation: For this assessment, the square root of the AVE is used (Fornell and Larcker, 1981), which should be greater than the shared variance between the construct and the other constructs in the model. The corresponding matrix provides these values.

- Convergent Validity: This assessment was conducted through the AVE; its values should be greater than 0.50, which implies that more than 50% of the construct variance is due to its indicators (Fornell and Larcker, 1981). It can only be applied to reflective indicators (Chin, 1998a).

B. STRUCTURAL MODEL

The structural model assesses the weight and magnitude of the relationships (hypotheses) among the different variables. For this assessment, two basic indexes are used: the explained variance (R^2) and the standardized path coefficients (β). R^2 indicates the explained variance by the construct within the model; it should be equal or greater than 0.1, as lower values, even if they are significant, provide little information, and represent the measure of the predictive power (Roldán and Sánchez-Franco, 2012). The R^2 provides an indication of the predictive ability of the independent variables, as well as the standardized path. β represents the path coefficients, which has been identified in the monogram (SmartPLS figure) with the arrows that link the constructs in the internal model. This coefficient is obtained in the traditional way (as multiple regression). Chin (1998a) suggests that in order for the standardized path coefficients to be considered significant, they should achieve at least a value of 0.2, and ideally be greater than 0.3; in addition to that, Chin (1998b) considers R^2 values of 0.67, 0.33, and 0.19 as substantial, moderate, and weak respectively.

3.1. RESULTS

From the 126 valid questionnaires, the *gender* distribution was 78% woman and 22% men. The *Age* rank was classified into four levels: Up to 20 years old (9%), 21-30 years old (83%), 31-40 years old (4%), 41-50 years old (3%) and 51 or more years old (1%). *Use of the system (weekly)*, five groups came from the sample: 0-10 hours (22%), 11-20 hours (31%), 21-30 hours (21%), 31-40 hours (18%), and 41 or more hours (8%). Regarding educational level: high school (7%), undergraduate (83%), graduate (10%). And finally, the sector to which the participating enterprises belong: service (85%), commercial (12%) and industry (3%).

A. MEASUREMENT MODEL

- Reliability: The indicators present acceptable values, including the 19 reflective indicators (Table 1); the loading factor varies between 0.7079 and 0.9073, surpassing the minimum requirements of 0.707.

- Internal Consistency (Constructs Reliability): Table 1 shows that the internal (composite) reliability is given in this research, surpassing the minimum requirements in the Fornell statistical of 0.707.

- Discriminant Validity: In order to value the discriminant validity (Table 2), the AVE square root was used (the numbers in bold on the diagonal line are the square root of the variance shared between the constructs and their measures). The variables satisfy the necessary condition; thus adequate discriminant validity was achieved.

- Convergent Validity: The convergent validity of the survey measurement was right (Table 1), AVE exceeds in everything the 0.50 (the values are valuating from 0.6071 until 0.8019). Re-sampling was coming out (500) for getting the T-statistic values; the results showed that almost everyone was significant (Table 3).

Table 1. Individual reliability of the reflective indicators' loading and coefficients' convergent validity

Construct Item	Item Loading	Composite Reliability	Cronbach's Alpha	AVE	R^2
Information Management		0.8968	0.8276	0.744	NA
IM_1	0.7962				
IM_2	0.8842				
IM_3	0.9034				
Technological Alignment		0.8837	0.8248	0.6553	NA
Alig_1	0.7651				
Alig_2	0.8130				
Alig_3	0.8308				
Alig_4	0.8275				
Technological Infrastructure		0.8848	0.8392	0.6071	NA
TI_1	0.7956				
TI_2	0.8074				
TI_3	0.7077				
TI_4	0.8662				
TI_5	0.7079				
Innovation		0.9418	0.9177	0.8019	0.345
Inno_1	0.8917				
Inno_2	0.9073				
Inno_3	0.8998				
Inno_4	0.8829				
Productivity		0.8831	0.8003	0.7161	0.522
Prod_1	0.7895				
Prod_2	0.8641				
Prod_3	0.8823				

Table 2. Correlation of variables (discriminant validity)

	IM	Alig	TI	Innov	Prod
IM	**0.8626**				
Alig	0.6316	**0.8095**			
TI	0.5172	0.5700	**0.7791**		
Innov	0.5568	0.4973	0.3380	**0.8955**	
Prod	0.5940	0.6327	0.6060	0.4941	**0.8462**

Note: elements on the diagonal line are the result of the square root of AVE. For the discriminant validity, these values should exceed the inter-construct correlations. IM (Information Management), Alig (Technological Alignment), TI (technological infrastructure), Innov (Innovation) and Prod (Productivity).

B. STRUCTURAL MODEL

Table 3 shows every planning hypothesis; in Figure 1, they are detailed in a graphic form, showing the research model evaluated empirically; they also show that the values obtained are within the ranks of the previous parameters.

Table 3. Summary of SmartPLS results

Hypothesis	Coefficient Path	T-statistic	Remarks
Technological Alignment → Innovation	0.246	2.000 *	Supported
Technological Alignment → Productivity	0.353	3.039 **	Supported
Information Management → Innovation	0.358	2.919 **	Supported
Information Management → Productivity	0.250	2.176 *	Supported
Technological Infrastructure → Innovation	0.014	0.532	Not Supported
Technological Infrastructure → Productivity	0.365	3.343 ***	Supported

Figure 1. Research Model

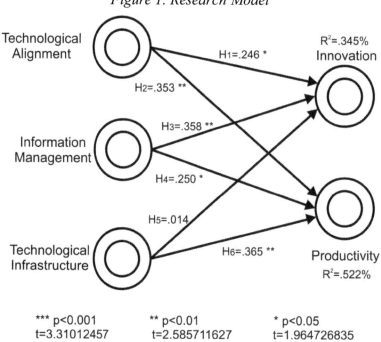

*** p<0.001   ** p<0.01   * p<0.05
t=3.31012457   t=2.585711627   t=1.964726835

The data analysis suggests that all investments in AIS made by the managers has influenced the employees' perception that there has been an increase in productivity. Employees perceive a substantial improvement in the development of activities and processes; this means that the information generated is being used to make more and better decisions. Such information is represented as an additional asset in organizations, which can become a means to information management in the short or medium term. Similarly, it has helped make planning based on organizational needs and IT, in which staff members of both parties participate actively in their best interest and their enterprises´. A close monitoring of market trends is also performed.

With respect to innovation, the results indicate that the SME's attempt to improve their activities and the few innovations (administrative, processes and products/services) they have. However, they make a conservative use of their information. Unfortunately, the technological base in place is not the most adequate or it is not used efficiently for their own benefit.

4. CONCLUSIONS

AIS have become an essential tool in today's businesses. Therefore, organizations continue to invest in these technologies as a measure to improve their performance. The aim of this research is to determine the influence that enterprises' technological infrastructure has on their organizational performance from an innovation and productivity point of view through the daily use of an AIS.

Productivity is one of the main demands from the managers; nevertheless, they may be satisfied as such productivity has been achieved through the daily use of AIS, both to be able to provide information requested by government entities and to generate data to be able to face competition. This is especially true when it comes to the employees' perceptions of the improvement in the activities they perform, information to be able to make more and better decisions and, above all, to create the culture of the importance of an appropriate use of information which can lay the foundations for the discussion about knowledge management. For that reason, the investment made in IT is justified, calling into questioning the productivity paradox, at least for these enterprises under study. However, as has been said, IT and productivity are not everlasting; a constant innovation is needed, which involves further investments in hardware, software and, above all, in people.

Similarly, it is important to point out that, just as productivity, there has been a significant progress in innovation. Nevertheless, such innovation is not necessarily technology related; but the SMEs intend to improve their administrative processes through AIS (their generated data), which in turn is reflected mainly on the products quality/services they commercialize or sell.

Finally, the results show that SME's have inadequate technological infrastructure. However, it is important to make clear that no evidence is available from our research that can explain whether such inadequate technological infrastructure has to do with obsolete technology, inappropriate use, lack of it, little training, among other factors that can account for this users' perception. Likewise, overall, technological infrastructure which includes alignment, information management and technological infrastructure itself do not seem to be of any help for enterprises to be able to efficiently face competition. Therefore, this issue requires special attention on the part of the participating enterprises. It can be argued that these enterprises are facing competition through efficiency in administrative processes, quality service and higher levels of productivity; unfortunately, they appear to be merely responding to market needs, rather than doing it in a systematic way which may result in greater and better benefits for the organization.

5. LIMITATIONS AND FURTHER RESEARCH

This study has some limitations, which must be acknowledged. First, given that research data represents one snapshot in time, the validity of a model can not be established on the basis of a single study. Second, the study was carried out in a specific geographical context of the northeastern region in Mexico, and was focused on one single type of information systems (accounting). Therefore, care needs to be taken when making generalizations of the results. Furthermore, critiques of the cause and effect relationships among the constructs in the model need to be made with caution. For this reason, other researchers should add other IS and IT success factors that can assist in the development of more specific theories in this respect. Such theories might help managers make more informed decisions regarding investment in AIS. This in turn can increase the likeliness of securing a positive impact of investments made in technology.

REFERENCES

Albers, J.A., and S. Brewer, 2003. Knowledge management and the innovation process: The Eco-Innovation Model. *Journal of Knowledge Management Practice*, 4, pp. 1-10

Apergis, N., C. Economidou, and I. Filippidis, 2008. Innovation, technology transfer and labor productivity linkages: Evidence from panel of manufacturing industries. *Review of World Economics*, 144(3), pp. 491-508

Badescu, M., and C. Garcés-Ayerbe, 2009. The impact of information technologies on firm productivity: Empirical evidence from Spain. *Technovation*, 29(2), pp. 122-129

Cepeda, C. y J.L. Roldán, 2004. Aplicando en la Práctica la Técnica PLS en la Administración de Empresas. Congreso de la ACEDE 2004. Septiembre 19, 20 y 21. Murcia, España

Chen, Y.C., and J.H. Wu, 2011. IT management capability and its impact on the performance of a CIO. *Information & Management*, 48, pp. 145-156

Chin, W.W., 1998a. Issues and opinion on Structural Equation Modeling. *MIS Quarterly*, 22(1), pp. vii-xvi

Chin, W.W, 1998b. The partial least squares approach to structural equation modelling. In: Marcoulides, GA. (Ed.), *Modern methods for business research* (pp. 295-336). Nahwah, NJ: Lawrence Erlbaum

Chin, W.W., B. Marcolin, and P. Newsted, 2003. A Partial Least Squares latent variable modeling approach for measuring interaction effects: Results from a Monte Carlo simulation study and an electronic-mail emotion/adoption study. *Information Systems Research*, 14(2), pp. 189-217

Davenport, T. H., 2000. *Mission critical: Realizing the promise of enterprise systems*. Boston, MA: Harvard Business School Press

Davenport, T.H., and L. Prusak, 1997. *Information ecology. Mastering the information and knowledge environment*. Oxford University Press, New York, USA

Dibrell, C., P.S. Davis, and J. Creig, 2008. Fueling innovation through information technology in SMEs. *Journal of Small Business Management,* 46(2), pp. 203-218

Dillon, T.W., and S.E. Kruck, 2004. The emergence of accounting information systems programs. *Management Accounting Quarterly*, 5(3), pp. 29-36

Farrell, D., 2003. The real new economy. *Harvard Business Review*, 81(10), pp. 104-112

Ferreira, R., and A. Cherobim, 2012. Impacts of investments in it on the organizational performance of baking companies of minas gerais state: a multicase study. *Revista de Administração e Contabilidade da Unisinos*, 9(2), pp. 147-161

Feller, J., P. Finnegan, and O. Nilsson, 2011. Open innovation and public administration: transformational typologies and business model impacts. *European Journal of Information Systems*, 20, pp. 358-374

Feurer, R., K. Chaharbaghi, M. Weber, and J. Wargin, 2000. Aligning strategies, processes, and IT: A case study. *IEEE Engineering Management Review*, 17(1), pp. 23-34

Fink, L., 2011. How do IT capabilities create strategic value? Toward greater integration of insights from reductionistic and holistic approaches. *European Journal of Information Systems*, 20, pp. 16-33

Fornell, C., and D.F. Larcker, 1981. Evaluating Structural Equation Models with unobservable variables and measurement error. *Journal of Marketing Research,* 18(1), pp. 39-50

Fornell, C., and F. Bookstein, F., 1982. Two Structural Equation Models: LISREL and PLS Applied to Consumer Exit-Voice Theory. *Journal of Marketing Research*, 19(4), pp. 440-445

Galleta, D., and A.L. Lederer, 1989. Some cautions on the measurement of user information satisfaction. *Decision Sciences*, 20(3), 419-438

Gordon, S.R., and M. Tarafdar, 2007. How do a company's information technology competences influence its ability to innovate? *Journal of Enterprise Information Management*, 20(3), pp. 271-290

Hammett, B.M., 2008. *Corporate startegy and technology alignment factors that contribute to strategy and technology aligment*. Doctoral dissertaion. Capella, University

Han, Ch., Ch. Hsieh, F. Lai, and X. Li, 2011. Information technology investment and manufacturing worker productivity. *Journal of Computer Information Systems*, 52(2), pp. 51-60

Henderson, J., and N. Venkatraman, 1993. Strategic alignment: Leveraging information technology for transforming organizations. *IBM Systems Journal*, 32(1), p. 4-16

Hevner, A.R., S.T. March, and J. Park, 2004. Design science in information systems research. *MIS Quarterly*, 28(1), pp. 75-104

Heo, J., and I. Han, 2003. Performance measure of Information Systems (IS) in evolving computing environments: An empirical Investigation. *Information & Management*, 40(4), pp. 243-256

Hitt, L.M., and E. Brynjolfsson, 1996. Productivity, business profitability, and consumer surplus: Three different measures of information technology value. *MIS Quarterly*, 20(2), pp. 121-142

Hsu, J., 2010. Effectiveness of technology transfer measures in improving SME productivity: An empirical study of Taiwan. *The Journal of American Academy of Business*, 15(2), pp. 206-211

Inegi, 2011. *Directorio Estadístico Nacional de Unidades Económicas (DENUE)*. http://gaia.inegi.org.mx/denue/viewer.html. Consulted: Nov 3, 2013

Jarvenpaa, S.L., and B. Ives, 1993. Organizing for global competition: The fit of information technology. *Decision Science*, 24(3), pp. 547-580

Lewis III, N., 2009. *Identifying critical dimensions that shape the business and information technology alignment process: A case study of a university.* Doctoral Dissertation, Capella University

Lin, Ch., J. Wu, and D.C. Yen, 2012. Exploring barriers to knowledge flow at different knowledge management maturity stages. *Information & Management,* 49, pp. 10-23

Madrid-GUIJARRO, A., D. Garcia, and H. Van Auken, 2009. Barriers to innovation among Spanish manufacturing SMEs. *Journal of Small Business Management,* 47(4), pp. 665-487

Mahmood, M.A., J.M. Burn, L.A. Gemoets, and C. Jacquez, 2000. Variables Affecting Information Technology End-User Satisfaction: A Meta-analysis of the Empirical Literature. *International Journal of Human Computer Studies,* 52(4), pp. 751-771

Marchand, D., W. Kettinger, and J. Rollins, 2002. *Information Orientation: The best link to business performance.* Oxford University Press, USA

Oppenheim, Ch., J. Stenson, and R.M.S. Wilson, 2004. Studies on Information as an Asset III: Views of Information Professionals. *Journal of Information Science,* 30(2), pp. 181-190

Onita, C., and J. Dhaliwal, 2011. Alignment within the corporate IT unit: An analysis of software testing and development. *European Journal of Information Systems,* 20, pp.48-68

Peak, D., Guynes, C.S., and Kroon, 2005. Information technology alignment planning – A case study. *Information & Management,* 42(3), pp. 619-633

Petter, S., W. DeLone, and E. McLean, 2008. Measuring information systems success: models, dimensions, measures, and interrelationships. *European Journal of Information Systems,* 17, pp. 236–263.

Ray, G., W.A. Muhanna, and J.B. Barney, 2005. Information technology and the performance of the customer service process: A resource-based analysis. *MIS Quarterly,* 29(4), pp. 625-652

Ringle, Ch.M., S. Wende, and A. Will, 2005. SmartPLS 2.0 (beta). http://www.smartpls.de. Consulted: May 10, 2013

Roldán, J.L., and M.J. Sánchez-Franco, 2012. Variance-based Structural Equation Modeling: Guidelines for using Partial Least Squares in information systems research. In Mora et al. (ed). *Research Methodologies Innovations and Philosophies in Software Systems Engineering and Information Systems,* pp. 193-221. IGI Global, Hershey: PA

Sala-I-MARTIN, X., J. Blake, M. Drezeniek, T. Geiger, I. Mia, and F. Paua, 2008. The Global Competitiveness Index: Prioritizing the Economic Policy Agenda, In *The Global Competitiveness Report 2008–2009.* Ed. Porter, M., and L. Schwab. World Economic Forum. Switzerland

Sala-I-MARTIN, X., B. Bilbao-Osorio, J. Blanke, R. Crotti, M. Drezeniek, T. Geiger and C. Ko, 2013. The Global Competitiveness Index 2012-2013: Strengthening Recovery by Raising Productivity. In *The Global Competitiveness Report 2012–2013.* Ed. K. Schwab. World Economic Forum. Switzerland

Sabherwal, R., A. Jeyaraj, and C. Chowa, 2006. Information system success: Individual and organizational determinants. *Management Science,* 52(12), pp.1849-1864.

Tanriverdi, H., 2005. Information technology relatedness, knowledge management capability, and performance of multibusiness firms. *MIS Quarterly,* 29(2), pp. 311-334

Toledo, L.A., and M.A. Zilber, 2012. An analysis of the fallacy of taking apart technology and innovation. *Revista de Administração e Inovação,* 9(1), pp. 211-230

Venkatranman, N., 1989. The concept of fit in strategy research: Toward verbal and statistical correspondence. *Academy of Management Review,* 14(2), pp. 423-444

6

THE FUTURE OF AUDIT

Danielle Lombardi
Villanova University, Pennsylvania, United States, USA
Rebecca Bloch
Fairfield University, Connecticut, United States, USA
Miklos Vasarhelyi
Rutgers University, New Jersey, Unites States, USA

ABSTRACT

The purpose of this study is to discuss the current state and future of auditing. Expert consensus is used as a basis to examine the current state of auditing and generate modifications both needed and likely to occur in the audit profession. This study contributes to the literature by using the Delphi method to develop predictions as to the direction of the audit industry and discuss the implications associated with these predictions. If auditors can better understand where the profession stands and where it is headed, then they can better prepare for the future. Some predictions emerging from this study relative to future audit practices include increasing automation of audit procedures, more predictive financial statements, continuous auditing of financial statements and transactions, and an increasingly global perspective regarding audit activities.

Keywords: Audit; Brainstorming; Delphi method; Information systems; Expert panel

1.   INTRODUCTION

The auditing field is at a critical juncture. Independent audits continue to take place annually, whereby associated analysis and reporting routines are based solely on historical data. With the resulting lack of timeliness between data generation and information assurance in this context, it seems that stakeholders would typically not view audited financial statements as being useful for decision-making in the current and

---

Address for correspondence / Endereço para correspondência

Danielle Lombardi, Assistant Professor at the Villanova School of Business, Villanova University, 800 E. Lancaster Ave. Bartley Hall - 3048 Villanova, PA 19085

Rebecca Bloch, Assistant Professor at the Dolan School of Business, Fairfield University, 1073 North Benson Road, Dolan School of Business – 2109, Fairfield, CT 06824

Miklos Vasarhelyi, Professor II KPMG Professor of AIS Director CarLab, RARC room 946 1, Washington Park Newark, NJ 07102 Rutgers University, New Jersey, Unites States, USA

evolving real-time global economy. Given that decision usefulness is a primary criterion for effective financial reporting, the need for a more timely and proactive auditing methodology is apparent. To remain relevant, auditing must take advantage of technological advances and provide assurances that are meaningful to real-time financial statement users.

This study reports on experts' consensus about the current status of the audit profession and forecasts of what the profession might resemble in a decade. Agreement about the present state of the profession was obtained through a brainstorming session and a forecast of the future was generated via the Delphi technique. This study employs a formal methodology to assess the current and future status of the audit profession, and has utility for at least two distinct groups: 1) audit professionals in helping them determine how to best structure their assurance practices, and 2) regulators in anticipating audit regulations that may be needed for audits in a real-time economy.

Audits are performed to provide assurance that financial statements properly follow current accounting standards and accurately reflect the financial position of a company. Historically, this paradigm has been useful to investors and creditors who had little information available beyond the financial statements. However, in recent years, technology has taken the lag out of conducting business such that events may be captured instantaneously, and, in some cases, markets are able to react to the constant updating of real-time information (Vasarhelyi et al. 2010). Thus, the business environment has evolved more rapidly than the audit profession (Eilifsen et al. 2001; Humphrey et al. 2009), and audited accounting information is now in a substantially disadvantaged state relative to other forms of timely information. For example, company news is readily available in the financial press and investors can differentiate between competitors by reading about product quality and other industry information posted by consumer product groups. Most important, much of this information is generated very soon after event occurrence and readily available for online consumption and processing. Auditors must be prepared and properly trained to handle the new challenges associated with collecting, processing, and incorporating new forms and large volumes of data, many of which will likely require the application and understanding of sophisticated technologies. To better clarify and address this matter, this study seeks to determine the current state of auditing and what experts believe the future auditing landscape might resemble.

The study is performed in two discrete stages: 1) a brainstorming exercise is used to determine the current state of the profession, and 2) the Delphi method is employed to obtain predictions concerning the future of auditing. The Delphi method has been suggested as a methodology that provides value and rigor to research in the fields of auditing (Garsombke and Cerrulo 1984), accounting, and accounting information systems (Worrell et al 2013), and it has been found to accurately forecast future events and trends (Bell, 1967, Mehr and Neumann1970, Dalkey and Helmer 1963, Baldwin-Morgan 1993, Holstrum et al. 1986, Brancheau et al.1996; Rowe and Wright 1999). Furthermore, it has been used extensively to predict the direction of specific industries (Melnyk et al. 2009; Ogden et al. 2005; Singh 2005; Chen 2005; Baldwin-Morgan 1993; Cegielski 2008).

The next section provides background literature and the ensuing section explains the methodology. Results and analysis are presented in the third section, and the last section contains the conclusions.

2. BACKGROUND

The literature predicting changes to the audit profession can be divided into those using generic prediction efforts (Hunton and Rose 2010, Holstrum et al. 1988, Elliott 1994, 2002, Violino 2004), and papers using a formal methodology to predict specific aspects of the profession (Baldwin-Morgan 1993), rather than looking at the profession as a whole.

Elliott (1994) emphasized potential opportunities and threats within the auditing profession, specifically noting that information technology provides users with a plethora of information sources beyond the traditional financial statements, and impacts the preparation, audit, and use of financial statements. Elliot's position was that the current audit profession is threatened because audited financial statements are becoming less relevant to users such as investors, creditors, and analysts. However, he also noted that there are opportunities for the auditing profession to evolve by providing a new set of assurances on information acquired via real-time information.

Elliott (2002) recommended that the academic community study the changes needed in the assurance domain to help practitioners prepare for the future. Elliott implied that reliance on information technology (IT) may supersede the need for traditional audited financial statements, and that future users may be decision-makers beyond just investors and creditors. He noted: "Every aspect of the accounting profession is being pervasively affected by advances in information technology".

Violino (2004) discussed trends in IT audits, noting that they are "moving into the mainstream as regulatory compliance, risk management, and information security become higher corporate priorities".

Hunton and Rose (2010) argued that auditors will begin to transition from manually collecting data to managing complex decision support systems, and will thus have to become comfortable with trusting these systems.

3. METHODOLOGY

The methodology applied in this study was originally used at AT&T Bell Laboratories and RAND Corporation (Bell 1967). Two rounds of brainstorming and Delphi were performed during a six-month interval, and contained some variation of expert participation between sessions. The experts in this study had in-depth backgrounds and experience in auditing and accounting, and were considered the first movers and thought leaders of the field by other audit and accounting professionals. Refer to Figure 1 for a description of the experts who participated at both sessions.

First Delphi Panel Members	Second Delphi Panel Members
•Ex-chairman of AICPA and retired partner •President and CEO of a Consulting Company •President and CEO of an Advisory Company •Director of a Consulting Company •Accounting Information Systems Professor •Accounting Professor •Big 4 Partner in Forensics •Big 4 Partner in Audit	•Ex-chairman of AICPA and retired partner •Ex-executive Vice President of AICPA •Director - New Jersey Information Systems Audit and Control Association •Member of Canadian Institute of Chartered Accountants •Database director of a company •Accounting Information Systems Professor •Accounting Professor - Fellow of the Association of Chartered Certified Accountants •Big 4 Partner in Forensics

Figure 1 - The Expert Participants

For a procedural overview of the brainstorming and Delphi methods performed at both sessions, refer to Figure 2 below.

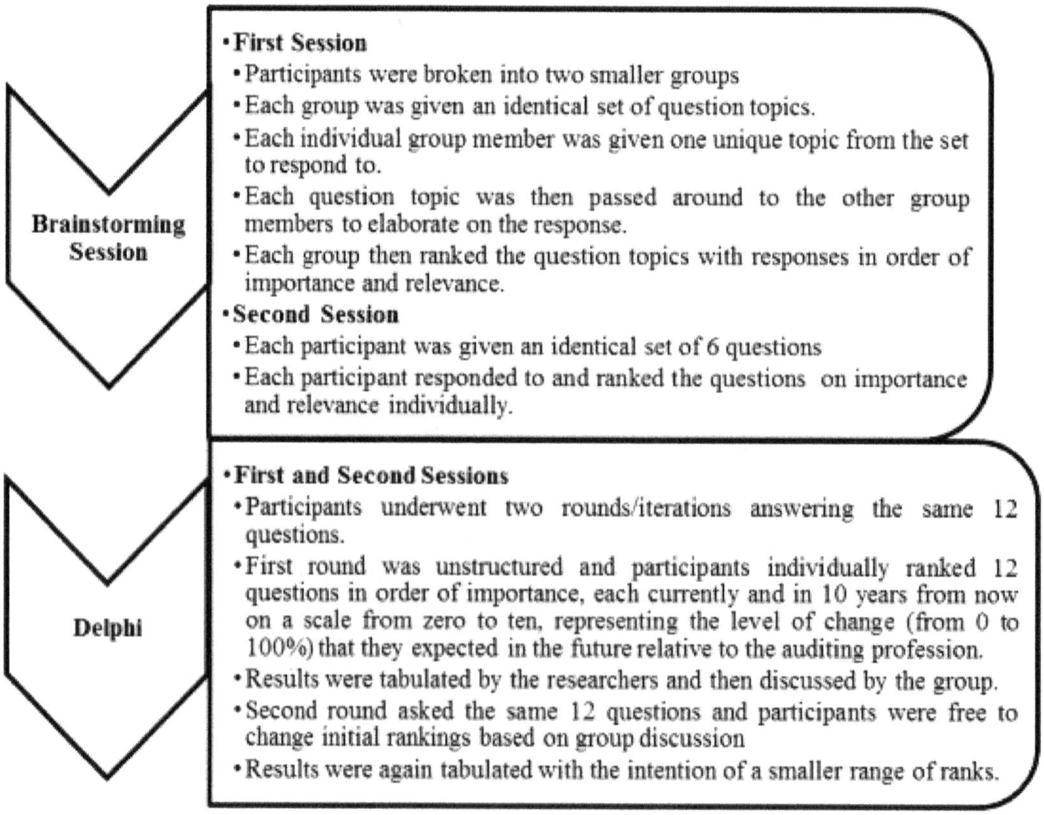

Brainstorming Session

•**First Session**
• Participants were broken into two smaller groups
• Each group was given an identical set of question topics.
• Each individual group member was given one unique topic from the set to respond to.
• Each question topic was then passed around to the other group members to elaborate on the response.
• Each group then ranked the question topics with responses in order of importance and relevance.
•**Second Session**
• Each participant was given an identical set of 6 questions
• Each participant responded to and ranked the questions on importance and relevance individually.

Delphi

•**First and Second Sessions**
• Participants underwent two rounds/iterations answering the same 12 questions.
• First round was unstructured and participants individually ranked 12 questions in order of importance, each currently and in 10 years from now on a scale from zero to ten, representing the level of change (from 0 to 100%) that they expected in the future relative to the auditing profession.
• Results were tabulated by the researchers and then discussed by the group.
• Second round asked the same 12 questions and participants were free to change initial rankings based on group discussion
• Results were again tabulated with the intention of a smaller range of ranks.

Figure 2 - The Overall Methods Used in this Study

Brainstorming Method - The Current State of Audit

The brainstorming sessions used open-ended topics developed by a team of researchers with varied backgrounds in accounting and auditing. See Appendix 1 for brainstorming topics presented at each session.

Delphi Method - The Future of Audit

The Delphi methodology employed multiple questionnaire rounds to obtain response stability (Baldwin-Morgan 1993). Both sessions were recorded and participant discussions were transcribed to allow for a more accurate analysis and quotation of participant responses. Refer to Appendix 2 for questions asked during both Delphi sessions.

4.   RESULTS AND ANALYSIS

The results from both sessions indicate an overall group consensus on both the current state and future of auditing. In addition, responses provided in the brainstorming method closely matched the topics of questions used during the Delphi; which provides methodological validation that the questions used in the Delphi focused on pertinent areas impacting the future of audit.

Brainstorming Method Results - The Current State of Audit

The three major areas highlighted by participants were: the audit model, technology and automation tools, and audit education.

The audit model

The audit model is evolving from traditional audits (i.e. historical data at a cutoff date) to a more continuous audit of the entire business process and associated risks, which enables current business issues to be more adequately addressed. Participants indicated that audits have changed from periodic to continuous, covering a much higher percentage of company data and monitoring of business processes. The real-time economy requires real-time assurance, and continuous auditing provides this assurance through verification and quality control. Continuous monitoring of business processes can identify emerging issues, and possibly lead to non-audit opportunities within companies. Conversely, sampling currently used in the audit process provides assurance on historical data and does not evaluate business processes.

Technology and automation tools

Automation tools, such as decision aids, currently assist auditors in analyses and risk assessments. Furthermore, these tools allow for increased usage of quantitative analyses, such as probability evaluations. As a result of increased audit automation, auditors can now spend more time reviewing analyses and interpreting results rather than performing tasks. Audit automation tools evaluate inherent risks for a particular audit, so the auditor can spend more time reviewing and interpreting analyses (rather than performing tests) and determining the desired course of action. Automated tools currently used also simulate audit procedures to determine if they are robust. Once the simulation procedures have been constructed, they may continually run and the auditor can reconfigure the process at any time. Some of the top technologies used currently in auditing are analytics, data bases, and sampling.

Accounting education

Accounting education has significantly progressed and now incorporates more technology, analytics, fraud detection, risk analysis, forensics, and International Financial Reporting Standards into the classroom. More electives are now available to students, as well as collaboration among courses to cover these very timely topics.

Delphi Method Results - The Future of Audit

Participant responses were examined by the researchers and paraphrased below. The paraphrasing used in this study is selective, and aims to illustrate the tone and tenor of participant discussions. Participant responses from the Delphi indicate that consensus was reached. Overall, the ranges of responses decreased round over round, with an insignificant amount of dissenters among the groups. The questions used in the Delphi sessions are shown in Appendix 2. Questions are grouped by topic to better analyze the questionnaire sessions from both Delphi meetings.

Audit automation, procedures, and judgment (Q1→Q5)

The overall consensus was that auditing is judgmental in nature, and, although automation can support the judgment process, it cannot replace human judgment. P3 said "Technology should reduce the barriers and repetitiveness of time-consuming sampling. We can leverage technology to get greater coverage on some areas than what we currently are doing. However, you never can automate the human judgment component. It is a part of auditing and I don't know that we want that to be automated." The use of automation also varies with company type and size, with larger companies driving the use of technology in their organizations and internal audit departments.

Judgment is also needed in the audit process to ensure that what was recorded by the system appropriately represents the actual occurrence. "I have to be able to change the lens that I am looking through because I know that people will end up sensing a pattern and their behavior will either change or stay consistent with the pattern" (P3). P1 agreed, "The firm is supposed to capture what happens in the real world in their information system. The most important issue for auditors is whether what happened in the real world is reflected in the client's and I don't think this can be 100 percent automated."

"Judgment and expertise" are contingent on each other, meaning expertise is required to make a quality judgment (Mock et al. 1993). Overall, participants foresee auditor judgment in conjunction with automation as essential components of the future audit. "Judgment is something that comes with experience and training. It is driven by the use of technology. Ten years from now, more and more things are going to be automated. For what we use to sit down and analyze there will be different tools to do the analytics so you can use your judgment in a different way" (P4).

To keep up with technology, more frequent auditor training will be needed, which will impose additional costs and the need for staff availability for training. Although newer staff has less experience than veteran staff, they tend to be more up-to-date on technology and software because experienced staff might often not receive the necessary training.

The continuing advancement of technologies is leading to a better evaluation of audit evidence. Auditors will be able to use sensors, biometrics, voice recognition, meta-information exchange, clustering, and expert systems to evaluate clients and analyze relationships among companies. A meta-information exchange will be developed from data to efficiently and effectively examine relationships among similar companies. This includes capabilities to drill down for more detailed information. Through the use of these emergent technologies, data will be delivered straight to auditors' desktops and inconsistencies will be easily identified.

Last, the use of electronic reporting, eXtensible Business Reporting Language (XBRL), may serve to expedite and improve certain audit functions, such as benchmarking and analytical review. XBRL data allows auditors to examine risks across clients in similar industries, resulting in an overall meta-analysis. This information can be provided repetitively and instantly impounded into analytic models. In addition, XBRL allows various levels of data to be tagged and subsequently used in customized reports to analyze and compare different industries and companies. These aggregation techniques allow for the combination of qualitative and quantitative data as well as historical and real-time data for a dynamic assessment including probabilities for fraud or potential error. Furthermore, these techniques allow for a more flexible, customized audit plan and a better audit by exception.

Internal auditors taking over some functions from external auditors (Q6, Q7)

The participants discussed a shift in the role of internal audit resulting from demands of end-users and regulatory bodies. For example, when the Sarbanes-Oxley Act was enacted, companies did not want external auditors doing non-audit-type work that was required by the new regulation. Currently, audit firms are more aggressive about maintaining this work, and some entities are either providing the services for free or steeply discounting them to keep other firms out. It is still unclear to the participants how this will ultimately be handled in the future.

The participants did postulate that the relationship between internal and external audit will evolve in the future so that the roles and responsibilities of internal audit will increase relative to external audit. New internal audit technologies, such as automated controls monitoring, will allow external auditors to place more reliance on the work of internal auditors. Some of this is already in place and being applied by external auditors,; such as internal journal entry analysis and audit assessments provided by internal auditors. If this trend continues, internal audit will ultimately have more responsibility than external audit regarding assurance on the quality of data for low-risk areas. However, high-risk areas must remain the responsibility of external audit because of independence issues. Ultimately, the American Institute of Certified Public Accountants (AICPA) will have to provide updated guidance concerning reliance on internal audit work by external auditors, and internal auditors have to be properly trained to meet these new challenges

Frequency of externally audited financial statements, audit fees, and changing audit platform (Q8, Q9, Q10)

Participants debated the diminishing role of externally audited financial statements and the constant availability of externally audited financial statements due to real-time reporting and continuous reporting. "People are making individual types of decisions whether to invest or not invest, and the type of information they need to make decisions differs. A system designed from scratch would permit them to take a view of the information that's relevant to their decision problem instead of forcing everything into a one size fits all model. Ten years out infrastructure changes would be necessary to change the information paradigm that is in place. The only thing that prevents it from happening now and ten years from now is that the SEC and the AICPA and others have a vested interest in this one size fits all model" (P1).

There were varying opinions from participants regarding the audit fee model. If the same parties responsible for hiring the auditors remain responsible for agreeing and paying the audit fees, a bias will exist for either the company or the audit firm. The auditor will have an incentive to agree with the client in order to increase the likelihood of being fully compensated for current work and retained as the auditor in future engagements. This creates obvious problems relative to auditor independence and objectivity. It was suggested that the PCAOB either take on the responsibility of setting audit fees or handle the process of selecting company auditors in order to assist with ensuring that auditor independence is consistently maintained. This topic also relates to the potential for rolling the audit function into a general management monitoring and control platform. Within this framework, segregation of duties would need to be achieved to better prevent and deter decreased auditor professional skepticism. Furthermore, this would presumably enhance auditor independence and objectivity as well.

The main profile of services provided by large CPA firms in the future will incorporate forensics into the traditional audit, with an increase in revenue from this service. Assurance services will continue, but the nature of assurance will shift to an emphasis on real-time assurance via continuous auditing. Clients will require more risk-based services and wider forms of assurance services.

Utilization of XBRL/GL, (Q11)

There was an initial variation in responses which was mainly due to the lack of knowledge and confusion of XBRL/GL and its intended uses and capabilities. IT education must stem from the classroom, so that students gain the basic knowledge and skills necessary for performing in the field. Educators must account for XBRL/GL by both familiarizing students with the most current standard retrieval methodologies available, and allowing them to discover future tools later on in their careers.

In addition, participants noted that a common data model needs to be created across all ERP systems, so every general ledger ERP system knows the needed fields; such as, payment amount, date, payee, and payer. With the recent mandate from the Securities and Exchange Commission for public companies using XBRL for financial statements, the necessity for learning and training on XBRL/GL exists and needs to be addressed by companies as well as educational institutions.

5.   CONCLUSIONS

Expert consensus was reached relative to both the current state of audit and the future of audit over the next decade.

For a summary of highlights and recommendations resulting from both Delphi sessions, refer to Table 1.

First Session	Second Session
• External auditors will rely more on internal audit work in the future • Although use of automation will increase, judgment and decision-making cannot be automated • The view of many of the topics would vary depending upon the evolution of the financial statements • Audit will be cycled over the year, instead of only at year-end • There is a need for a more global perspective	• Client technology is leading audit procedures • The use of technology depends upon proper safeguards for privacy (i.e. HIPAA) • Automation can be used for more tedious tasks so that auditors can use their expert judgment for more pressing issues

Table 1 - Highlights and Recommendations Provided by Participants from the Delphi Method

Participants agreed that the audit model is currently incorporating continuous audits of business processes, and that auditors are using automation tools such as decision aids and risk assessment tools to assist with their audits. This will continue to evolve over the next decade as meta-analysis information exchanges with drill down capabilities will become more widely used for this purpose. Audit education has progressed and now increasingly incorporates the use of technology as well as offers new electives to help students better prepare for real-world audit. To keep up with technology, additional auditor technology training will be needed, especially for experienced auditors.

Over the next decade, the participants forecasted that technology will continue to be an important part of the audit process, but that it will not take over the judgment that is inherent in the auditing process. Judgment from audit experts will continue to be essential.

The participants also stated that the relationship between internal and external audit will continue to evolve with more responsibility shifting to the internal audit function. However, there was some debate as to whether the traditional audited financial statements will be replaced with more predictive, real-time statements. Although some participants noted that financial statements are competing with other forms of information, others felt that too many regulatory bodies are invested in the traditional model for it to significantly change.

Participant responses during the brainstorming sessions validated the questions posed during the questionnaire rounds. Participants' insights during the brainstorming sessions related to the same areas of audit the Delphi addressed during both sessions.

Overall, results suggest it is not only likely, but necessary that the traditional audit undergoes changes to make it more relevant in this real-time economy. Auditing needs to stay in tune with continuous advancements in the profession in order to effectively meet the needs of the users of information.

REFERENCES

Anderson, U. (2012). Assurance Coordination: Managing the Organization's Assurance Network, presentation, 2/22/12.

Baldwin-Morgan, A. (1993). The impact of expert system audit tools on auditing firms in the year 2001: A Delphi investigation. *Journal of Information Systems, 7*(1), 16-34.

Bell, W. (1967). Technological forecasting - what it is and what it does. *Management Review,56*(8), 64.

Brancheau, J. C., Janz, B.D. & Wetherbe, J.C. (1996). Key issues in information systems management: 1994-95 SIM Delphi results. *MIS Quarterly, 20*(2), 225-242.

Cegielski, C. G. (2008). Toward the development of an interdisciplinary information assurance curriculum: Knowledge domains and skill sets required of information assurance professionals. *Decision Sciences Journal of Innovative Education, 6*(1), 29-49.

Chen, M. (2005). Ethics: An urgent competency in financial education. *Journal of American Academy of Business, Cambridge, 6*(2), 74-79.

Dalkey, N., & Helmer, O. (1963). An experimental application of the Delphi method to the use of experts. *Management Science, 9*(3), 458-467.

Eilifsen, A., Knechel, R. & Wallage, P. (2001). Application of the business risk audit model: A field study. *Accounting Horizons, 15*(3), 193-207.

Elliott, R. K. (1994). The future of audits. *Journal of Accountancy, 178*(3), 74-82.

Elliott, R. K. (1996). Auditing Reborn. *CA Magazine*, 129, 36-8.

Elliott, R. K. (2002). Twenty-first century assurance. *Auditing, 21*(1). 139.

Garsombke, H. & Cerullo, M. (1984): Auditing advanced computer systems, *The EDP Auditors Journal*, 2(1): 1-11.

Holstrum, G.L.; Mock, T. J. & West, R.N. (1986): The impact of technological events and trends on audit evidence in the year 2000: Phase I, Auditing Symposium VIII. *Proceedings of the 1986 Touche Ross-- University of Kansas Symposium on Auditing Problems, Lawrence, KS*: University of Kansas, 125-146.

Holstrum, G. L., T.J. Mock, & West, R.N. (1988). The impact of technology on auditing: Moving into the 21st century. *Institute of Internal Auditors Research Foundation*, Altamonte Springs, Florida.

Humphrey, C., A. Loft, and M. Woods. (2009). The global audit profession and the international financial architecture: Understanding regulatory relationships at a time of financial crisis. *Accounting, Organizations & Society*, 31(6/7), 810-825.

Hunton, J. E., and J.M. Rose. (2010). 21st Century Auditing: Advancing Decision Support Systems to Achieve Continuous Auditing. *Accounting Horizons*, 24(2), 297-312.

Mehr, R. I., and S. Neumann. (1970). Delphi forecasting project. *Journal of Risk & Insurance*, 37(2), 241-246.

Melnyk, S. A., R.R. Lummus, R.J. Vokurka, L.J. Burns, and J. Sandor. (2009). Mapping the future of supply chain management: A Delphi study. *International Journal of Production Research 47*(16): 4629-4653.

Mock, T. J., P.R. Watkins, P. Caster, and K. Pincus. (1993). A review of the audit judgment symposium: 1983-1992. *Auditing 12*(2): 3.

Ogden, J. A., K.J. Petersen, J.R. Carter, and R.M. Monczka. (2005). Supply management strategies for the future: A Delphi study. *Journal of Supply Chain Management: A Global Review of Purchasing & Supply 41*(3): 29-48.

Rowe, G., and G. Wright. (1999). The Delphi technique as a forecasting tool: Issues and analysis. *International Journal of Forecasting 15*(4): 353-375.

Singh, A. J. (2005). Future events and their impact on financial management in the US lodging industry: Delphi study to predict changes in 2007 and 2027. *Journal of Retail & Leisure Property 4*(3): 236-254.

Vasarhelyi, M., R. Teeter, and J.P. Krahel. (2010). Audit Education and the Real-Time Economy. *Issues in Accounting Education 25*(3): 405-423.

Violino, B. (2004). You bought it, now audit. *CFO 20*(8): 17-19.

Worrell, J. L., Di Gangi, P. M., & Bush, A. A. (2013). Exploring the use of the Delphi method in accounting information systems research. *International Journal Of Accounting Information Systems*, *14*(3), 193-208.

APPENDIX 1
QUESTIONS ASKED TO EXPERT PARTICIPANTS DURING THE BRAINSTORMING SESSIONS
First Delphi Meeting's Brainstorming session
Non-audit opportunities (assurance services for CPAs that uses CPA competencies that has expanded the scope of provided services, e.g. provide independent continuous monitoring services)
E-Audit (Ways the audit service has been extended through electronic media e.g. perform large part of the audit remotely through video and voice and desktop sharing)
Audit automation (ways the audit has been automated, e.g. drive most of audit objective by data alarms)
Audit process (ways the way we audit has changed e.g. create automatic pinging)
Second Delphi Meeting's Brainstorming Session
Choose and rank five top technologies – most important to least important –used in audit.
How do you estimate the fee structure/base of billing? Please list issues and trends in what you see as the most important first. Please also specify the cause of any changes that have led to changing the fee structure.
How has the relationship changed between internal audit and external audit?

How has accounting/auditing education changed to satisfy requirements of the new audit environment?

How has the litigation environment changed?

What are the main functions (profiles) of services being provided by the larger CPA firms and how do they interplay?

APPENDIX 2
QUESTIONS ASKED TO EXPERT PARTICIPANTS DURING THE DELPHI SESSIONS

First Delphi Meeting's Questionnaire Session

What percentage of the external audit will be automated?

What percentage of the internal audit will be automated?

What will happen to usage of sampling techniques in auditing?

What will happen to usage of analytic procedures in auditing?

What will happen to audit judgment in auditing?

To what extent will internal auditors take over responsibility for the IT auditing now undertaken by the external auditor?

What is the likelihood that external auditors will offer opinions on financial statements more frequently than once a year?

What is the likelihood that a different model of auditor compensation will become prominent in practice?

What is the likelihood that inside the firm the audit function will be rolled into a general management monitoring and control platform?

What is the likelihood that XBRL-GL will emerge as the common platform for both reporting and assurance?

Assuming that eventually there will be continuous auditing, will there be more frequent reporting?

What is the likelihood that continuous assurance will be synonymous with auditing, as far as audit practice education is concerned?

Second Delphi Meeting's Questionnaire Session

What percentage of the external audit will be automated?

What percentage of the internal audit will be automated?

What will happen to usage of sampling techniques in auditing?

What will happen to usage of analytic procedures in auditing?

What will happen to human audit judgment in auditing?

To what extent will internal auditors take over the responsibility for the IT auditing which is currently undertaken by the external auditor?

To what extent will internal auditors take over the responsibility for financial auditing which is currently undertaken by the external auditor?

What is the likelihood that external auditors will offer opinions on financial statements more frequently?

What is the likelihood that a different model of audit fees will become prominent in practice?

What is the likelihood that inside the firm the audit function will be rolled into a general management monitoring and control platform?

What percentage of companies will utilize XBRL/ GL?

Assuming that eventually there will be some form of continuous auditing, will there be more frequent reporting?

7

THE USEFULNESS OF USER TESTING METHODS IN IDENTIFYING PROBLEMS ON UNIVERSITY WEBSITES

Layla Hasan
Department of Computer Information Systems, Zarqa University, Jordan

ABSTRACT

This paper aims to investigate the usefulness of three user testing methods (observation, and using both quantitative and qualitative data from a post-test questionnaire) in terms of their ability or inability to find specific usability problems on university websites. The results showed that observation was the best method, compared to the other two, in identifying large numbers of major and minor usability problems on university websites. The results also showed that employing qualitative data from a post-test questionnaire was a useful complementary method since this identified additional usability problems that were not identified by the observation method. However, the results showed that the quantitative data from the post-test questionnaire were inaccurate and ineffective in terms of identifying usability problems on such websites.

Keywords: Usefulness, user testing, methods, university websites, usability, comparison

1. INTRODUCTION

The root of usability is in the field of Human Computer Interaction (HCI), which is a broad field related to all the aspects and ways in which people interact with computers (Stone *et al.*, 2005). Humans interact with computers through a user interface. The design of this user interface and, specifically, the usability of the interface is a core area in the field of HCI (Gray and Salzman, 1998). The concept of usability has been defined and measured differently by different authors. For example, Nielsen (2003) stated that usability is not a single attribute; instead, usability is defined in terms of five characteristics: learnability, efficiency, memorability, errors and satisfaction. This definition indicates that usability is defined in terms of a set of attributes or design

Address for correspondence / Endereço para correspondência

Layla Hasan, Department of Computer Information Systems, Zarqa University, Jordan E-mail: l.hasan2@yahoo.co.uk

goals of a system/product. However, the International Standards (ISO 9241-11, 1998) provide a broader definition of usability, stating that: "Usability is the extent to which a product can be used by specified users to achieve specified goals with effectiveness, efficiency and satisfaction in a specified context of use" (ISO 9241-11, 1998).

Usability Evaluation Methods (UEMs) are a set of methods used to evaluate human interaction with a product; they are aimed at identifying issues or areas of improvement in this interaction in order to increase usability (Gray and Salzman, 1998). A variety of usability evaluation methods have been developed to identify usability problems. These methods have been categorized differently by different authors. For example, Hasan *et al.* (2012) categorized usability evaluation methods into three categories in terms of how usability problems were identified: user-based UEMs (which involve real users in the process of identifying usability problems), evaluator-based UEMs (which involve evaluators in the process of identifying usability problems), and tool-based UEMs (which involve the use of software tools and models in the process of identifying usability problems).

The user testing methods (user-based UEMs) aim to record users' performance while interacting with an interface and/or users' preferences or satisfaction with the interface being tested. The most common user-based UEM relates to user testing. The other methods are either variations of a user testing approach or supplementary techniques that could be used with a user testing method. Section two summarizes the most common user-based UEMs.

Earlier research has employed different user testing methods in the evaluation of the usability of university websites, such as observations and/or questionnaires (Tüzün *et al.*, 2013; Chaparro, 2008; Alexander, 2005; Kasli and Aucikurt, 2008; Christoun *et al.*, 2006; Lencastre and Chaves, 2008; Mustafa and Al-Zoua'bi, 2008; Hasan, 2014). The results of these studies were useful in providing an idea regarding common usability problems that were identified on university websites. However, there is a lack of research that compares issues identified by different user testing methods in the evaluation of the usability of university websites in terms of the types of usability problem that can be identified by them.

The aim of this research is to investigate the usefulness of three supplementary user testing methods (employing observation, quantitative data from the post-test questionnaire, and qualitative data from the post-test questionnaire) regarding their ability or inability to identify specific usability problems on university websites.

The specific objectives of this research are:

1. To employ three supplementary user testing methods (observation, quantitative data from post-test questionnaire, and qualitative data from post-test questionnaire) to evaluate the usability of three selected university websites;

2. To illustrate the types of specific usability problem identified by each method;

3. To compare the specific usability problems identified by each method with the other methods; and

4. To provide empirical evidence regarding the usefulness of each of the three methods in evaluating the usability of university websites.

This paper is organized as follows. Section two summarizes user-based usability evaluation methods while section three reviews earlier research that has used user testing methods in the evaluation of the usability of university websites. Section four describes the methods used. Section five outlines the main results and section six discusses the results in the light of the literature. Finally, section seven reviews and presents some conclusions.

2. USER-BASED USABILITY EVALUATION METHODS (UEMs)

This section reviews the most common user testing methods that can be used to evaluate the usability of websites. The effectiveness of the various user evaluation methods is also presented.

a) *User Testing*

The user testing method is "a systematic way of observing actual users trying out a product and collecting information about the specific ways in which the product is easy or difficult for them" (Dumas and Redish, 1999). It is the most important and useful approach since it provides direct information regarding how real users use the interface and it illustrates exactly what problems the users encounter in their interaction (Nielsen and Mack, 1994).

Different supplementary techniques have been suggested for use during a user testing session, such as making different types of observation (*e.g.,* notes, audio, video or interaction log files) to capture users' performance; questionnaires and interviews have also been suggested as ways of collecting data concerning users' satisfaction (Nielsen, 1993; Rogers *et al.*, 2011; Dumas and Redish, 1999; Rubin, 2008). Capturing user performance can be automated using tools such as Camtasia and/or Morae. Camtasia is a screen capture software package, provided by the TechSmith Company, which has proved to be an effective tool for capturing website usability data (Goodwin, 2005). Morae software, also provided by the TechSmith Company, is used to gain a deep understanding of customers' experience through its ability to record user interactions with an application, site, or product (TechSmith, 2014). Morae records desktop activity on the user's computer and makes a camera video of the user. Using TechSmith Corporation's patented Rich Recording Technology, the Morae recorder captures all system events, including the screen, mouse clicks, web page changes, onscreen text, any notes or markers logged by observers and more. Also, Morae can capture the participant's face with a Web cam via a Picture-in-Picture mode.

b) *Think-Aloud Method*

This is a user testing method with a condition: the condition of asking users to think aloud during their interaction with an interface (Lazar, 2006; Nielsen, 1993). Nielsen (1993) indicated that having users verbalize their thoughts using this method offers an understanding of how users view or interpret an interface. However, the Think-Aloud method has some disadvantages related to the fact that the test setting, with an observer and recording equipment, does not represent a natural setting; this therefore will not encourage users to act and talk naturally (van den Haak and de Jong, 2005).

c) *Constructive Interaction (also known as Co-Discovery Learning)*

This method is a think-aloud method with one condition: the condition of having two users (instead of a single user) interacting with an interface together or working together to complete specific tasks (Holzinger, 2005; Nielsen, 1993). The main advantage of employing this technique is that the test situation is much more natural in comparison with the Think-Aloud tests because people are used to verbalizing their thoughts when trying to solve a problem together (Holzinger, 2005; Nielsen, 1993). However, the unnatural settings which are associated with the Think-Aloud method constitute one of the drawbacks of the constructive interaction method.

d) *Questionnaires and Interviews*

Different types of questionnaire (*e.g.,* closed or open) and interviews (*e.g.,* unstructured, semi-structured or structured) are considered useful and simple techniques that collect data regarding users' satisfaction with, or preferences for, a user interface, such as the features and the presentation of websites (Bidgoli, 2004; Rogers *et al.,* 2011; Rubin, 2008). These could be used as supplementary techniques to the user testing method or they could be used alone. However, if these techniques are used alone then they are considered as indirect usability methods because they do not study the user interface directly; instead, they reflect users' opinions about that interface (Holzinger, 2005; Nielsen, 1993). Various satisfaction/usability questionnaires have been found in the literature that can be used as post-test questionnaires for assessing the usability of and/or satisfaction with websites. Examples of common satisfaction/usability questionnaires are:

- **System Usability Scale (SUS):** This is a common, reliable, simple, low-cost usability scale that can be used for global/general assessments of subjective assessments of a system's usability (Brooke, 1996; Sauro, 2011). SUS was developed by the Digital Equipment Corporation and consists of 10 questions that are scored on a 5-point Likert scale on strength of agreement (Tullis and Stetson, 2004). SUS yields a single number representing a composite measure of the overall usability of the system being studied. SUS scores have a range of 0 to 100 (Brooke, 1996). Its ease of administration and scoring makes it a popular choice among usability professionals (Finstad, 2006).

- **Questionnaire for User Interaction Satisfaction (QUIS):** This was developed at the University of Maryland and was designed to evaluate users' satisfaction with different aspects of an interface (Chin *et al.,* 1988). QUIS consists of demographic, overall system satisfaction and interface questions on terminology; screen factors and system feedback; system capabilities and learning factors; as well as questions on system components such as technical manuals, online tutorials, multimedia, voice recognition, virtual environments, Internet access, and software installation (Harper *et al.,* 1997). Each question measures users' perceptions on a 9-point categorical scale. Additional space is provided to allow users to make comments on the interface factors. QUIS is available in two different formats: a long form with 71 questions and a short form with 27 questions. However, Tullis and Stetson (2004) made a modification to the short form to make it appropriate to websites.

They dropped three questions (e.g., "Remembering names and use of commands").

- **Computer System Usability Questionnaire (CSUQ):** This is a short and reliable questionnaire that was developed by IBM (Lewis, 1995). CSUQ is composed of 19 questions. Each question is a statement with a rating on a seven-point scale of "Strongly Disagree" to "Strongly Agree" (Tullis and Stetson, 2004). CSUQ measures three factors: system usefulness, informational quality, and interface quality.

- **Software Usability Measurement Inventory (SUMI):** This was developed by the Human Factors Research Group (Kirakowski and Corbett, 1993). SUMI measures users' attitudes to specific software systems (Kirakowski, 1995). It consists of 50 attitude statements, to each of which the user may respond "agree, don't know, or disagree" and provides an overarching usability rating across five subscales (Veenendall, 1998). The five subscales are: efficiency, effect, helpfulness, control and learnability.

- **End-User Computing Satisfaction Questionnaire (EUCS):** This was developed by Doll and Torzadeh in 1988. EUCS is a short, reliable, valid and easy to administer questionnaire that can be used as a general measure of user satisfaction with all types of applications (Doll and Torkzade, 1988). EUCS has 12 items that measure five components of end-user satisfaction: content, accuracy, format, ease of use, and timeliness. The questionnaire uses a five-point Likert scale.

- **Website Analysis and MeasureMent Inventory (WAMMI):** This is a web analytics service that measures and analyses user satisfaction with a website (Alva *et al.*, 2003). It is the best tool to assess user experience as it relates to the actual experience visitors have of a website (WAMMI, 2014). WAMMI was created by Nigel Claridge and Jurek Kirakowski; it consists of 20 statements, which were selected from a large range of questions about users' experiences with websites. It is based on five factors: attractiveness, controllability, efficiency, helpfulness and learnability.

e) *Eye Tracking*

This is a method which aims to record and observe exactly the paths on a computer screen users follow while using the web (Nielsen and Pernice, 2010). In order to employ this method, special eye tracking equipment is needed to be built into the computer monitor. Also, eye tracking software is required to track the user's screen. This method is useful because it observes normal behavior and can discover exactly what users look at. However, the collected data cannot provide information regarding whether users are happy or confused when they look at certain things on a screen and not at others (Nielsen and Pernice, 2010). Also, the special equipment required to conduct eye tracking method is expensive.

3. LITERATURE REVIEW

This section summarizes earlier research that evaluated the usability of university websites using different types of user-based usability evaluation methods. For example, some studies employed more than one user testing methods, including observation, in the evaluation of the usability of such websites. Examples of such include the study conducted by Tüzün *et al.* (2013) who employed five user testing approaches related to observation, questionnaires, interviews, think-aloud, and eye tracking to evaluate the usability of the registration unit sub-site at Hacettepe University. The results showed that the students experienced several usability problems related to the design of the tested sub-site, including: inappropriate design of pages (e.g. long pages), inappropriate design of the menus, poor organization of the sub-site's data, and inappropriate font size (small).

Chaparro (2008) also employed three user testing methods (observation, questionnaires and interviews) to evaluate the usability of a university portal website. The results showed that the website had several usability problems including: having non-obvious links, inappropriate organization of information on the site, inappropriate use of images (icons), and inappropriate page design (having three different search functions on the same page).

Similarly, Alexander (2005) employed three user testing methods (observation, think-aloud and questionnaire) in an evaluation of the usability of 15 university websites. The results highlighted six usability problems that were found on the websites including: poor information architecture, poor content (*e.g.,* insufficient detail), ineffective internal search function, difficulty using PDF documents, poor page design, and broken links.

Other studies were found in the literature that employed only the questionnaire method in the evaluation of university websites. Kasli and Aucikurt (2008), for example, employed only the questionnaire method and asked 54 students to investigate 132 websites of tourism departments at universities in Turkey. The results shed light on the following usability problems: old information, lack of an internal search function, lack of support for foreign languages, and failure to display important information (*e.g.,* an academic calendar, FAQs and programs).

Christoun *et al.* (2006) also investigated students' overall satisfaction with an academic website with regard to its technology, usability, aesthetics and content using an online questionnaire. The results showed that the website had usability problems related to: ineffective search function and difficulty in finding information.

Similarly, Lencastre and Chaves (2008) employed only the questionnaire method aimed at students in the evaluation of the usability of an educational website used by Master's degree students at Minho University, Portugal. The results showed that in general the website had positive ratings. However, Lencastre and Chaves (2008), unlike the other studies which involved the questionnaire method in the evaluation of the usability of university websites, provided evidence regarding the inaccuracy of the results that were obtained using the questionnaire method. For example, they stated that many respondents via their answers to the questionnaire indicated that there was no online help on the site while in fact it was always there.

Also, the study conducted by Mustafa and Al-Zoua'bi (2008) employed a questionnaire to evaluate the usability of nine Jordanian university websites by 252 students. The results showed that the usability of the tested websites was, in general, good. However, the study of Mustafa and Al-Zoua'bi (2008) provided no details regarding specific types of usability problem that users identified on university sites.

Furthermore, Hasan (2014) asked 237 students to provide ratings for nine Jordanian university websites using usability criteria. The students were also asked to report qualitatively what they liked and disliked regarding the design of the websites. The results showed that the most common weaknesses on the websites included: the design of the sites, the fact that most of the sites were inconsistent in terms of colors and fonts, the Arabic and English language interfaces, the design of the pages, and the lack of support for the Arabic language.

The studies outlined in this section showed that earlier research employed different types of user-based usability evaluation methods in the evaluation of the usability of university websites and proved the usefulness of these methods in highlighting common usability problems that could be found on such websites from the students´ point of view of. The results from those studies outlined above, which employed more than one method in the usability evaluation, stressed the fact that employing more than one user testing method is useful since the methods complement each other and provide a clear picture of usability problems on the tested websites. Unfortunately, these studies did not provide detailed information regarding to what extent the different methods complemented each other in the identification of the usability problems. No examples were offered by these studies regarding common usability problems that were identified by the methods, and/or unique issues that were raised by each of the employed methods. This research aims to address this gap noted in the literature by illustrating the extent to which three supplementary user testing methods (observation, and using both quantitative and qualitative data from the satisfaction questionnaire) complement each other in the evaluation of the usability of university websites. This research provides empirical evidence regarding the specific usability problems that were identified by each of the three methods.

4. METHODOLOGY

In order to employ and compare usability methodologies with regard to university websites, three university websites in Jordan were selected. The selection was based on the results of one of the major international university ranking websites, which is Eduroute (Eduroute, 2011). The three universities, which had the highest rankings provided by Eduroute for the year 2011, were selected as the sample for this research. The universities were: Hashemite University, the University of Jordan, and Yarmouk University. These universities are large public universities offering a variety of disciplines.

To achieve the aim of this research, three common supplementary user testing methods were used. The first related to the observation; different types of observation were used, including the observer taking notes and using Camtasia software, to capture performance data. The second method related to the closed-ended post-test questionnaire, which was designed to collect quantitative data to assess users' satisfaction with the tested sites. The third method related to the open-ended post-test questionnaire, which was designed to collect qualitative data to assess users' satisfaction with the tested sites.

A pre-test questionnaire was developed to gather users' background information. A task scenario was developed for each of the three websites, as shown in Table 1. This included typical tasks for the three university websites that represented their actual use. The typical tasks were derived from an earlier study, which listed types of pages visited frequently by Jordanian students on a university website (Hasan, 2013). For clarity and simplicity throughout this paper, the titles website 1, website 2 and website 3 are used to refer to the University of Jordan's website, the Hashemite University's website, and Yarmouk University's website, respectively.

Table 1: Task scenarios for the three websites

Task No.	Website	Tasks
Task 1	All websites	When will the summer semester for the academic year 2011/2012 start?
Task 2	All websites	What is the subject of the university's latest announcement?
Task 3	All websites	What activities/student clubs are supported by the university?
Task 4	All websites	What services are offered by the university to the students?
Task 5	Website 1	What are the conditions/requirements to transfer from a public university to the University of Jordan?
	Website 2	What are the conditions/requirements to transfer from a public university to Hashemite University?
	Website 3	What are the conditions/requirements to transfer from a public university to Yarmouk University?
Task 6	Website 1	What is the time(s) for the Principles of Management Information Systems course, which will be offered by the Faculty of Business for the summer semester 2011/2012?
	Website 2	What is the time for the Management Information Systems course, which will be offered by the Faculty of Economics and Administrative Sciences for the summer semester 2011/2012?
	Website 3	What is the time for the Knowledge Management course, which will be offered by the Faculty of Economics and Administrative Sciences for the summer semester 2011/2012?
Task 7	All websites	Is there a study plan for the mathematics course at the Bachelor level?
Task 8	Website 1	What is the academic rank of Dr. Mohammad Al-Kilani, who is a member of the Chemistry Department's staff?
	Website 2	What is the academic rank of Dr. Ayman Issa, who is a member of the Chemistry Department's staff?
	Website 3	What is the academic rank of Dr. Ahmad Al Omari, who is a member of the Chemistry Department's staff?

In order to gather quantitative and qualitative data from the students regarding their preferences with the tested websites, three specific post-test questionnaires were developed for the purpose of this research, despite the fact that there are many validated satisfaction/usability scales that are available (for examples the ones mentioned in section 2). This is related to the fact that all of the usability questionnaires reviewed in section 2 were developed to measure the overall usability of a system or to measure general usability issues. Thus, they are not comprehensive enough to determine specific usability issues with educational websites. None of them were developed specifically to evaluate the usability of educational websites. Furthermore, the literature review presented above shows that those questionnaires were not used to evaluate the usability of educational websites. Therefore, none in their current state could adequately assess the usability problems specific to an educational website.

Each user responded to the appropriate post-test questionnaire after interacting with each website. The post-test questionnaires were divided into two sections. The first was designed to collect quantitative data using closed-ended questions (Appendix 1), while the second section was designed to collect qualitative data using open-ended questions. The first section was based on specific criteria for evaluating the usability of educational websites that was proposed in an earlier study (Hasan, 2014). This part of the questionnaire included 25 questions which were scored on a 7-point Likert scale on strength of agreement. The questionnaire was organized into five sections: navigation, architecture/organization, ease of use and communication, design, and content. The navigation section consisted of six questions which assessed whether the site included the main tools (e.g. navigation menu, internal search facility) and links which facilitated the navigation of users through the site, enabling them to reach the required information quickly. The architecture/organization section consisted of two questions. These related to the structure of a site's information which should be divided into logical, clear groups; each group should include related information. The ease of use and communication section consisted of four questions, which related to the cognitive effort required to use a website, and to the existence of basic information which facilitated communications with the university in different ways. The design section consisted of six questions that related to the visual attractiveness of the site's design; the appropriateness of the design of the site's pages; and the appropriateness of the use of images, fonts and colors in the design of the site. Finally, the content section consisted of seven questions which assessed whether the information on the site was up-to-date, sufficient, relevant to user needs, and accurate; and whether a site included the information students required (e.g. information about the university, information about the colleges, and information about the departments).

The second part of the questionnaires included two open-ended questions. The first asked the students to list five features on each site they most preferred, while the second question asked the students to list five features they disliked on each site.

Thirty students were recruited to conduct this research. The students were selected randomly from different faculties at Zarqa University in Jordan where the researcher was working. The students reported that they had not explored the three websites prior to the usability testing. All user testing sessions followed the same procedure. Data were gathered using screen capture software (Camtasia) with four questionnaires and observations of the users working through the tasks. The user session began with the researcher welcoming the user and asking him/her to fill out a pre-test questionnaire in order to obtain information regarding his/her background and experience. Before beginning the tasks related to each website, the user was asked to explore the website for a maximum of 10 minutes. After the exploration, the user was given the tasks for a particular website from the three tested sites. As the user worked on each task, the observer noted the sequence of pages, the time taken to complete each task, and any comments made by the user. After completing the tasks for the tested website, the user was given the post-test questionnaire to fill out in order to get his/her feedback. Then the user took a break before beginning to test the second website. A similar procedure was followed by the user while testing the second and third sites. At the end, the user was thanked. For each session, the order of the three websites that were evaluated was changed so that each website was tested fairly by all the users since, while testing the first website, the user might be slow and unfamiliar with the testing tasks. The user testing methods were deployed between May 2012 and June 2012. No website changes were made by the universities' web designers during this timeframe.

Descriptive analysis was used to analyze data collected from the pre-test questionnaires. The performance data were summarized in two ways: the tasks' timings (in seconds) and the tasks' accuracy. Descriptive statistics were used to obtain the mean time (in seconds) and the standard deviation for each of the eight tasks (Appendix 2). Furthermore, the one-way within subject ANOVA test was employed for each of the eight tasks. The results of this test are presented in Appendix 3. The task accuracy represented the percentage of users who completed each task successfully within the time benchmark. In order to identify the usability problems from the performance data, two steps were used, as suggested by Rubin (2008):

a) Identifying the problematic tasks: all the problematic tasks were considered.

b) Identifying students' problems and conducting a source of error analysis. In order to identify users' problems/obstacles/difficulties with the problematic tasks, and to investigate the usability problems behind these, different sources were examined. These included the in-session observation notes, notes taken from reviewing the ninety Camtasia sessions, and users' comments noted during the test.

Data collected from the post-test questionnaires were used to find evidence of usability problems with the sites. Likert scores were calculated for each statement in section 1 of the post-test questionnaire for each site in order to obtain the results concerning the participants' satisfaction with the sites. A Likert score of 1-3 was regarded as a negative response, 5-7 a positive response, and 4 a neutral one.

Qualitative data obtained from students' responses to the open-ended questions in the post-test questionnaires were taken into account in determining the usability problems. Users' answers were translated into English from Arabic and were then combined for each site; these were grouped under the five categories of the post-test questionnaires and their corresponding sub-categories.

5. RESULTS

This section presents the findings obtained from the analysis of the different user testing methods. The first subsection presents an overview of the users in terms of their characteristics while the second subsection presents the findings from the performance data and observations. The third and fourth subsections present the quantitative and qualitative results obtained from the analysis of the post-test (satisfaction) questionnaires, respectively.

5.1 Participants' Characteristics

The participant students comprised 16 males and 14 females. They were in general experienced computer and web users; 97% had more than three years of computer experience and 63% had used the Internet for more than three years. The students were also frequent users of the website of their university; 97% of them had used their university's website.

5.2 Performance Data and Observation

The summary of the performance data is presented in Appendix 2 and Table 2. Appendix 2 presents the mean time in seconds and the standard deviation for each task. Table 2 presents the levels of accuracy for each task across the three websites. It shows that all the tasks were problematic; no task was performed successfully by all the students on any of the three websites. This indicates that it was difficult for the students to perform the typical tasks on the three websites. However, Table 2 shows that the tasks' accuracy varied for each website. A one-way within-subjects ANOVA test showed that the time spent performing the majority (six) of the eight tasks was significantly different for the three sites. Appendix 3 shows the results of the ANOVA test for each task.

Table 2: Task accuracy

Task	Accuracy Score		
	Website 1	Website 2	Website 3
Task 1	73%	13%	87%
Task 2	93%	67%	93%
Task 3	30%	10%	60%
Task 4	13%	43%	63%
Task 5	83%	73%	83%
Task 6	13%	57%	63%
Task 7	10%	10%	80%
Task 8	7%	7%	83%

The observation notes, the notes generated from reviewing the 90 Camtasia files, and users' comments from the user testing were summarized in terms of tasks. This observation summary presents a snapshot of each task and highlights the critical incidents that occurred during each task across the sites. These incidents represent potential problems with users' interactions with the sites. Using the observation summary, a large number of usability problems were identified on each website for each task. Similar problems in each site were grouped together to generate a list of problems for each site. The three lists generated were examined to identify similar problems across the three sites. Consequently, 19 common areas of usability problems were identified, which suggested identifying 19 problem sub-themes. These 19 problem sub-themes suggested identifying six problem themes based on the type of problems identified. The six problem themes related to: navigation, design, content, internal search, ease of use and support for the Arabic language, and missing capabilities.

The 19 usability problems were then classified into two types based on their seriousness. The first type was *major problems* and related to mistakes/errors that a student made and was unable to recover from in order to complete the task on time. The user might or might not have realized his/her mistake/error. The second type related to *minor problems*, which included mistakes/errors that a student made but was able to recover from and complete the task, or other difficulties that were observed or indicated by users' comments while performing the tasks. Consequently, 12 major usability problems and seven minor usability problems were identified on the websites. Table 3 shows the 19 problem sub-themes, their themes, and the seriousness of each problem.

Table 3: Usability problem themes and sub-themes that students identified by observation, together with their seriousness.

Problem Theme	Problem Sub-theme	Seriousness of the Usability Problem
Navigation	Links were not obvious	Major
	Links not opening the destination pages (*e.g.*, it remained on the same page)	Minor
	Misleading links (*e.g.*, the link name did not match the content of the destination page)	Major
	Weak navigation support (*e.g.*, lack of navigational menu or links to other pages in the site)	Minor
	Broken links	Major
Design	Inappropriate choice of fonts (*e.g.*, small size)	Minor
	Inconsistency in the language of the interface (*e.g.*, links at the English interface opened pages that displayed Arabic content and vice versa)	Major
	Misleading images (*e.g.*, it did not have a link when it was suggested to users that it had one)	Minor
	Inappropriate page design (*e.g.*, long and cluttered pages)	Major

	Ineffective text format (*e.g.,* the information was not aligned correctly on the site's pages)	Minor
	Broken images	Minor
Content	No information regarding the type of a file that a link would open	Major
	Irrelevant content (*e.g.,* the content of a page was not clear to users)	Major
	Old content	Major
	Empty pages	Major
Internal Search	Ineffective internal search (*e.g.,* it did not work properly)	Major
Ease of Use and Support for the Arabic Language	Difficult interaction with a website	Major
	Not supporting the Arabic language	Major
Missing Capabilities	Missing functions/ information (*e.g.,* no internal search facility)	Minor

The following presents an explanation and examples regarding the major and minor usability problems that were identified on the websites. The 12 major usability problems related to:

1. *Links were not obvious*: this problem was identified on website 1 and related to links that were not situated in an obvious location on a page so they could be recognized by students. For example, the link required to change the language of the Home page from English (default) into Arabic was located at the very top right-hand corner of the Home page, as shown in Figure 1. It was observed that this link was not obvious for 20 (out of the 30) students. The observer helped the 20 students to find this link so that they were able to continue the other tasks. It was difficult to interact with the site for most of the students in the English language interface.

2. *Misleading links*: this related to the fact that the destination page, which was opened by a link, was not expected by students because the link name did not match the content of the destination page. This problem was found on websites 1 and 3. An example of such a link is the *Home Page* link which was located in the top menu of the Registration unit sub-site in the two websites. The students expected this link to open the Home Page of the university. However, it opened the Home Page of the sub-site (Registration unit sub-site).

3. *Broken links*: some broken links were identified on websites 1 and 2, which prevented the students from performing the required tasks successfully. An example of these links was the *Study Plans* link, which was located at the new student sub-site in website 2.

4. *Inconsistency in the language of the interface:* this problem was mainly related to the existence of links in the Arabic interface that opened pages with English content. This problem was identified on websites 1 and 2.

5. *Inappropriate page design:* this problem related to pages on the tested websites that did not clearly represent their content; it was found on all three websites. For example, the Self-Registration page in the Registration unit sub-site for website 1, which included the *Course Schedule* link, was very long and cluttered, as shown in Figure 2. It was observed that most of the students (26 out of 30) (Table 2) could not find the *Course Schedule* link on this page and therefore could not complete the required task successfully (Task 6).

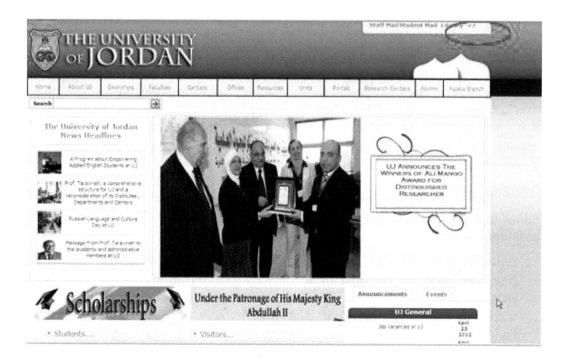

Figure 1: The Home page of website 1

6. *No information regarding the type of file that a link will open*: this problem was found on websites 1 and 2, and related to the fact that there was no information regarding the type of file (*e.g.*, PDF) that a link would open. For example, the *Calendar* link in the advertisements sub-site on website 2 opened the academic calendar of the university in PDF format. It was observed that the PDF file took a long time to open, which made most of the students think that there was a problem with the link. Most of the students stated qualitatively that there was no file to be opened and therefore, they did not complete the related task successfully (Task 1).

7. *Irrelevant content*: this problem related to the fact that some pages on the tested websites displayed an unclear message. This problem was found on all three of the tested websites (e.g., the Course Schedule page on website 3).

8. *Old content*: this problem related to the fact that the content of a page was out of date. This problem was found on website 2. The academic calendar in the Registration unit sub-site displayed old information: the calendar for the year 2010.

This problem was the main reason behind the failure to complete Task 1 successfully on website 2 by most of the students (26 out of 30) (Table 2).

Figure 2: The upper part of the Self-Registration page in the Registration unit sub-site for website 1

9. *Empty pages*: this problem related to the existence of some pages on website 2 that had empty content. Examples on these pages are: the Services page on the Registration sub-site, and the Clubs and Activities page on the Student Affairs sub-site.

10. *Ineffective internal search*: this problem related to the fact that the internal search function on all three websites did not work properly.

11. *Difficult interaction with a website*: this problem related to the fact that it was not easy to visit some pages on the three websites. For example, it was observed that it was difficult for the students to visit the Registration unit sub-site from the Home page of the three websites (Table 2).

12. *Not supporting the Arabic language*: this problem related to the fact that websites 1 and 2 did not support the Arabic language. For example, the Home page of website 2, including its main menu, was displayed only in the English language. Also, the faculties and departments sub-sites at these two universities did not display their content in the Arabic language; they were presented only in English. It was observed that this problem prevented most of the students from completing many of the required tasks successfully (*e.g.*, Tasks 6, 7 and 8 at website 1; Tasks 1, 3, 4, 5, 6, 7 and 8 at website 2).

The seven minor usability problems that were identified by the observation method related to:

1. *Links not opening the destination page*: this problem related to a link that did not work properly as expected by the students; it remained on the same page. For example, the *Student Gate* link, which was located on the Home page of website 1, had this problem.

2. *Weak navigation support*: this problem related to a page that did not have a navigational menu or links to other pages on the site. This problem was found on the Self Registration page at the Registration unit sub-site on website 1.

3. *Inappropriate choice of fonts*: this problem related to the use of an inappropriate font size (small size) at websites 1 and 3. For example, the observation showed that the font used for the *Arabic* link on the Home page of website 1, which was used to change the language of the interface from English into Arabic, was small from the viewpoint of the students (Figure 1).

4. *Misleading images*: this problem related to the existence of some images on website 1 which did not function as the students expected. For example, such images did not have a link while users expected them to have one (*e.g.*, the logo of the University at the header of the Graduate Studies sub-site).

5. *Ineffective text format*: this problem related to the existence of some pages on website 2 in which the information, figures and tables were not aligned correctly. Examples included these pages: the Financial Department unit sub-site and the Forms page on the Registration sub-site.

6. *Broken images*: this problem related to the existence of some images at the Clubs at the Student Affairs sub-site on website 2 which were broken.

7. *Missing functions/information*: this problem related to the fact that website 2 did not have some functions or capabilities. For example, it did not have an internal search facility at the Registration unit sub-site.

5.3 The Quantitative Data from the Post-Test Questionnaires

The analysis of the quantitative data from the post-test questionnaires showed that websites 1 and 2 had usability problems (Appendix 1). The results showed, however, that the students were satisfied with website 3; the Likert scores for all the statements of the post-test questionnaire for this site were more than 5. It is important to explain the reason behind the students' satisfaction with website 3, which was clearly identified by the observation. The reason was the support of website 3 for the Arabic language.

The negative statements with Likert score ratings of 1 to 3 (Appendix 1, statements 1, 3, 4, 7, 10, 11, 12, 19, and 25) identified six usability problems on websites 1 and 2. Each of these problem sub-themes were compared with the problem sub-themes that were identified by the observation method for agreement. Consequently, these statements were mapped to the identified problem themes and sub-themes. It was found that four of the six problems were also identified by the observation method; these related to: misleading links, old content, ineffective internal search, and difficult interaction with a website. However, two statements (Appendix 1, statements 7, 25) identified two new problem sub-themes, relating to poor structure and missing information, respectively. The poor structure problem suggested a new problem theme, which concerns architecture/ organization, while the missing information problem was mapped to the content problem themes. The new problems, as well as their descriptions, are shown in Table 4.

Table 4: New problem themes and sub-themes that were identified by the quantitative data of the post-test questionnaires, together with their descriptions.

Problem Theme	Problem Sub-theme
Content	Missing information (Adequate information about the departments of the university was not displayed)
Architecture/organization	Poor structure (complicated)

However, the results showed that the quantitative data obtained from the analysis of the post-test questionnaires revealed that this method was inaccurate and ineffective in identifying usability problems on university websites. The inaccuracy issue of this method was discovered by making a comparison between the results of this method and the results of the observation. It was found that, despite the fact that this method identified similar types of usability problems (problem sub-themes) that were also identified by the observation method, there were clear differences between the location of three (out of four) of the problems obtained using this method and the location of the usability problems that were identified by the observation method. Specifically:

1. The observation method identified misleading links as major problems on websites 1 and 3. However, the quantitative data of the post-test questionnaires identified this kind of problem on websites 1 and 2.

2. The observation method showed that the three websites had ineffective internal search problems as major problems. However, the post-test data of the questionnaires identified this problem only on websites 1 and 2.

3. The observation method identified difficulty interacting with the three websites as major problems, while the quantitative data of the post-test questionnaires identified this type of problems only on websites 1 and 2.

Regarding the inefficiency issue of the quantitative data obtained from the analysis of the post-test questionnaires, it was found that this method was unable to identify several usability problems on the tested websites. The post-test questionnaires included specific statements which related to potential usability problems on the tested websites, including: broken links, inappropriate font size, inappropriate page design, irrelevant content, and empty pages (Appendix 1, statements 5, 15, 17, 20, 21, 23, 24 and 25). However, it was found that the students rated these statements as either positive or neutral when most of these types of usability problem were identified by the observation method as major issues (Table 3).

5.4 The Qualitative Data from the Post-Test Questionnaires

The analysis of the qualitative data from the post-test questionnaires resulted in the identification of 16 usability problems. These problems were compared and then mapped to the appropriate problem themes and sub-themes identified by the previous two methods (observation, and the quantitative data from the satisfaction questionnaires). It was found that there were no matches between five problems and the identified problem sub-themes. Therefore, five new sub-themes were identified and mapped to four appropriate problem themes (navigation, design, architecture/ organization, and ease of use and support for the Arabic language).

Table 5: New problem themes and sub-themes that were identified by the qualitative data of the post-test questionnaires, together with their descriptions.

Problem Theme	Problem Sub-theme
Navigation	Orphan pages (pages that did not have any links)
Design	Unaesthetic design (unattractive interface)
	Inappropriate choice of colors (e.g. inappropriate combination of background and link colors)
Architecture/Organization	Deep architecture (the number of clicks to reach goals was more than 3)
Ease of Use and Support for the Arabic Language	Slow downloading of the site's pages

The unique identification of the five usability problems by the qualitative data obtained from the post-test questionnaires provided additional evidence regarding the inefficiency of the quantitative data obtained from the analysis of the post-test questionnaires. Despite the fact that there were five specific statements in the post-test questionnaire relating to the five new problems that were uniquely identified by the qualitative method (Appendix 1, statements 6, 8, 9, 13 and 16), the students did not rate these statements negatively and therefore did not identify these problems via the quantitative data.

Regarding the 11 usability problems which were also identified by the other previous methods, it was found that there were similarities between most of them (seven out of the 11) and the usability problems that were identified by the observation method in terms of their locations. Specifically:

- This method identified broken links on website 2, which was identified also as a major problem by the observation method.

- The students via this method qualitatively identified usability problems related to inappropriate choices of font on websites 1 and 3; this was also identified by the observation method.

- The students identified four other usability problems on the three websites relating to inappropriate page design, irrelevant content, ineffective internal search, and difficult interaction with the websites. These problems were also identified by the observation method as major problems on the three websites (Table 3).

- This method identified a lack of support for the Arabic language on websites 1 and 2, which was also identified by the observation method on those websites as a major problem.

However, it was found that there were differences between four (out of 11) of the usability problems that were identified by the qualitative data of the questionnaire method, and the usability problems that were identified, either by the observation or the quantitative data of the post-test questionnaire, in terms of their location. Specifically:

- This method identified misleading links on websites 2 and 3, while the observation method identified misleading links on websites 1 and 3. However, the quantitative data of the post-test questionnaire identified the misleading link problem on websites 1 and 2.

- The students via this method identified inconsistency in the language on websites of 2 and 3, while the observation method identified this problem on websites 1 and 2.

- The students qualitatively identified the problem of empty pages on websites 1 and 2, while the observation method identified this as a major problem only on website 2.

- The missing information problem was identified by this method on websites 1 and 2, while it was identified by the quantitative data of the post-test questionnaire only on website 2.

6. DISCUSSION

Researchers need to understand the usefulness or the contribution of the most common supplementary user testing methods (*e.g.*, observation, and using quantitative and qualitative data from post-test questionnaire) in identifying specific usability problems on a university website, in order to decide which method to use when evaluating such websites. This research has uniquely addressed a specific gap in the literature regarding illustrating the extent to which three supplementary user testing methods (observation, and using both quantitative and qualitative data from a satisfaction questionnaire) to complement each other in the evaluation of the usability of university websites. This was achieved by conducting a comparison among the results obtained by each of the three user testing methods, which uncovered the contribution or the value of each of the three methods in the identification of specific usability problems on such websites. Table 6 presents a comparison of the output of the three methods.

Table 6: Comparison of the output of the three methods.

Problem Theme	Problem Sub-Theme	Observation	Quantitative Data from the Post-test Questionnaire	Qualitative Data from the Post-test Questionnaire
Navigation	Links were not obvious	website 1	NA	NA
	Links not opening the destination pages	website 1	NA	NA
	Misleading links	websites 1 and 3	websites 1 and 2	websites 2 and 3
	Weak navigation support	website 1	NA	NA
	Broken links	websites 1 and 2	NA	website 2
	Orphan pages	NA	NA	websites 1 and 2
Design	Inappropriate choice of fonts	websites 1 and 3	NA	websites 1 and 3
	Inconsistency in the language of the interface	websites 1 and 2	NA	websites 2 and 3
	Misleading images	website 1	NA	
	Inappropriate page design	websites 1, 2 and 3	NA	websites 1, 2 and 3
	Ineffective text format	website 2	NA	NA
	Broken images	website 2	NA	NA
	Unaesthetic design	NA	NA	websites 1, 2 and 3
	Inappropriate choice of colors	NA	NA	websites 1, 2 and 3
Content	No information regarding the type of a file that a link will open	websites 1 and 2	NA	NA
	Irrelevant content	websites 1, 2 and 3	NA	websites 1, 2 and 3
	Old content	website 2	website 2	
	Empty page	website 2	NA	websites 1 and 2
	Missing information	NA	website 2	websites 1 and 2
Internal Search	Ineffective internal search	websites 1, 2 and 3	websites 1 and 2	websites 1, 2 and 3
Ease of Use and Support to Arabic Language	Difficult interaction with a website	websites 1, 2 and 3	websites 1 and 2	websites 1, 2 and 3
	Not supporting the Arabic language	websites 1 and 2	NA	websites 1 and 2
	Slow downloading of the site's page	NA	NA	websites 1, 2
Architecture/ organization	Poor structure	NA	website 2	NA
	Deep architecture	NA	NA	websites 1, 2
Missing Capabilities	Missing functions	website 2	NA	NA
NA: not applicable, which means that the method was not able to identify the problem.				

It is worth mentioning that Table 6 provides evidence regarding the fact that if just one method is employed to identify usability problems on university websites, it may result in costly developments that may be prove to be misguided. The following illustrates how each set of data provided by each method could be interpreted:

- The data obtained from the observation method provided clear indications that all three tested websites had usability problems. Furthermore, as explained earlier, the seriousness of the problems were also determined, which could facilitate giving higher priority to major problems while giving less priority to minor problems during the development of the websites. However, Table 2 shows that this method was unable to identify seven usability problems which were identified by the students using the other methods. These included: slow downloading of the site's pages, poor structure, deep architecture, missing information, inappropriate choice of colors, unaesthetic design, and orphan pages.

- The data obtained from the quantitative data from the post-test questionnaire provided indications that only websites 1 and 2 had a small number of usability problems. However, the location of these problems was not clear. This would require further efforts to be made by the developer in order to find out which usability problems to fix. Furthermore, the quantitative data obtained from the post-test questionnaire indicated that website 3 had no usability problems when in fact it had major usability problems (e.g. ineffective text format, difficulty interacting with the website), which were identified using the observation methods.

- The qualitative data obtained from the post-test questionnaire indicated that the three websites had usability problems and identified usability problems which were not identified by the other methods. However, Table 2 shows that this method was not able to identify specific major usability problems that were identified by the other methods (e.g. links were not obvious, there was no information regarding the type of file that a link would open)

Despite the fact that this research focused mainly on addressing a unique gap that was found in the literature regarding uncovering the role of three supplementary user testing methods in evaluating the usability of university websites, there was agreement between most of the results of this research and the results of earlier research, which employed a variety of user testing methods while evaluating the usability of university websites (Table 7). Such agreement highlighted common usability problems that were identified on various university websites from the viewpoint of students which should be taken into consideration when evaluating or developing such websites. Table 7 summarizes the common usability problems that were identified in earlier research which were also identified in this research.

Table 7: Common usability problems on university websites from students' viewpoints.

Usability Problem	Reference(s)
Inappropriate page design	Tüzün *et al.* (2013); Chaparro (2008); Alexander (2005); Hasan (2014)
Inappropriate font size	Tüzün *et al.* (2013)
Non-obvious links	Chaparro (2008)
Inappropriate organization of information on a site	Chaparro (2008)
Deep architecture	Alexander (2005)
Poor content (e.g. lack of clarity, long pages, insufficient details)	Alexander (2005); Kasli and Aucikurt (2008)
Ineffective internal search	Alexander (2005); Christoun *et al.* (2006)
Difficulty using PDF format documents	Alexander (2005)
Broken links	Alexander (2005)
Old information	Kasli and Aucikurt (2008)
Lack of internal search function	Kasli and Aucikurt (2008)
Lack of support for the Arabic language	Hasan (2014)
Difficulty finding information	Christoun *et al.* (2006)
Inconsistency (e.g. colors, fonts, design of the pages)	Hasan (2014)

The results of this research, which has made a contribution in terms of highlighting the usefulness of each of three user testing methods regarding their ability to identify usability problems on university websites, stress the usefulness of the observation method in identifying specific usability problems on such websites. This method was the most effective method compared to the other two in terms of the number of usability problems identified and the seriousness of the problems. This method identified 19 specific types of usability problem on university websites; 12 (out of the 19) were major usability problems which related to mistakes/errors that a student made from which he/she was unable to recover and complete the task on time. However, seven (out of the 19) were minor usability problems which included mistakes/errors that a student made but was able to recover from and complete the task, or other difficulties that were observed, or users' comments while performing the tasks. Section 5.2 summarizes the 19 specific usability problems, which related to six problem areas that were identified by this method. This method, however, could not identify problems related to seven areas: missing information, poor structure, orphan pages, unaesthetic design, inappropriate choice of colors, deep architecture, and slow downloading of the site's pages.

However, the results of this research showed that the quantitative data from the post-test questionnaires method was inaccurate and ineffective in identifying usability problems on university websites. These results were in agreement with the results provided by earlier research (Lencastre and Chaves, 2008) regarding shedding light on the inaccuracy of the questionnaire method. However, Lencastre and Chaves (2008) in their research employed only the questionnaire method in the evaluation of the usability of an educational website, while this research employed three user testing methods, and compared the results obtained from the analysis of the three methods. The results of this research suggest that the quantitative data from the post-test questionnaires was not effective or useful in pointing out specific usability problems on university websites.

The results of this research also showed that the quantitative data obtained from the post-test questionnaire method reflected the students' overall satisfaction with a site. This result agreed with the indications provided by researchers regarding the effectiveness of quantitative data in highlighting users' overall preferences with regard to a site (Holzinger, 2005; Nielsen, 1993). However, this research provided empirical evidence regarding the inability of quantitative data from the post-test questionnaire method to complement the other user testing methods in terms of identifying specific types of usability problem on university websites.

Conversely, the findings of this research suggested the usefulness of using open-ended questions in the post-test questionnaire to identify additional and specific usability problems on university websites, problems which could not be identified using the observation method. Furthermore, this research illustrated the types of specific usability problem that students could identify using this method after their interaction with a university website. Section 5.4 summarizes the five usability problems which were identified by this method; these were related to four main problem areas and were not identified by the observation. This research showed that qualitative data from the post-test questionnaire method have the ability to complement other user testing methods in terms of identifying additional specific usability problem on university websites, which could not be identified by the other methods.

The results of this research suggested that the observation method should be employed, followed by open-ended questions using a post-test questionnaire since they complemented each other and resulted in identifying a large and specific number of usability problems while evaluating the usability of university websites. Regarding collecting quantitative data using a post-test questionnaire, this research suggests using a small number of questions if the researcher(s) wishes to discover the overall preferences/satisfaction with a website.

7. CONCLUSIONS

This research has achieved its aim and illustrated the usefulness of three supplementary user testing methods (observation, and using both quantitative and qualitative data from satisfaction questionnaires) regarding their ability or inability to identify specific usability problems on university websites. This research confirms the complementary value of two user testing evaluation methods: observation and qualitative data from the post-test questionnaires; each is capable of identifying usability problems which the other is unlikely to identify. This research also provided empirical evidence regarding the inability of the quantitative data of the post-test questionnaire to complement the other methods and identify specific usability problems on university websites. A final Likert-style questionnaire provided at the end of the evaluation is likely to result in an overall impression of satisfaction with a site, but will not reveal the exact differences between the sites; most certainly it cannot be used alone to make design recommendations

This research has managerial and academic implications. *Managerial implications*: this research provides empirical evidence for the selected university websites regarding weak design issues on their websites. Also, it is expected to raise awareness among universities regarding how to investigate and improve the usability of their websites by clarifying explicitly the role of specific user testing methods in identifying usability problems. *Academic implications*: this paper presents an evaluation of the value/contribution of three user testing methods in the evaluation of the usability of university websites, and illustrates what kind of problems each method is capable or not capable of identifying. Also, it provides empirical evidence regarding the usefulness of these methods in the evaluation of the usability of university websites. The results of this research could contribute to the literature regarding the effectiveness of supplementary user testing methods in complementing each other while they are being used to evaluate the usability of websites.

However, this research has certain limitations. The sample used in this research was limited to students of only one university in Jordan. Also, other stakeholders of the selected university websites (e.g. faculty staff, employees, parents) were not taken into consideration while conducting the user testing methods. It is worth mentioning that, despite the fact that this research was conducted in Jordan, where the selected websites displayed Arabic content, it is likely that the results can be useful to other countries because many of the details concerning the specific usability problems may be experienced by users on other university websites in various countries. This was shown in the discussion section which presents an agreement between most of the results of this research and the results of earlier research; it, therefore, highlighted common usability problems that were identified on various university websites from the students´ viewpoint.

Acknowledgment:
This research was funded by the Deanship of Research and Graduate Studies in Zarqa University /Jordan.

REFERENCES

Alexander, D. (2005). How Usable are University Websites? A Report on a Study of the Prospective Student Experience. *Technical Report*. Monash University.

Alva, M., Martínez, A., Cueva, J.M., Sagástegui, C., and López, B. (2003). Comparison of Methods and Existing Tools for the Measurement of Usability in the Web. *In the Proceedings of the 3rd International Conference on Web Engineering (ICWE'03)*, Spain, Springer, 386-389.

Bidgoli, H. (2004). *The Internet Encyclopaedia*. John Wiley and Sons.

Brooke, J. (1996). SUS: A Quick and Dirty Usability Scale. In: P.W. Jordan, B. Thomas, B.A. Weerdmeester & I.L. McClelland (Eds.), *Usability Evaluation in Industry*. London: Taylor and Francis.

Chaparro, B. (2008). Usability Evaluation of a University Portal Website. *Usability News*, 10(2), 1-7.

Chin, J.P., Diehl, V.A. and Norman, K.L. (1988). Development of an Instrument Measuring User Satisfaction of the Human-Computer Interface. In: Soloway E, Frye D, Sheppard SB, editors. *In the Proceedings of the SIGCHI Conference on Human Factors in Computing Systems*; Washington, DC. New York, ACM Press, 213-221.

Christoun, S., Aubin, H., Hannon, C., and Wolk, R. (2006). Web Site Usability in Higher Education. *Information Systems Education Journal*, 4(110).

Doll, W.J. and Torkzadeh. G. (1988). The Measurement of End-user Computing Satisfaction. *MIS Quarterly*, 12(2), 259-274.

Dumas, J. S. and Redish, J. C. (1999). *A Practical Guide to Usability Testing*, Second Intellect Ltd, Rev Sub Edition.

Finstad, K., (2006). The System Usability Scale and Non-Native English Speakers. *Journal of Usability Studies*, 1(4), 185-188.

Goodwin, S. (2005). Using Screen Capture Software for Website Usability and Redesign Buy-in. *Library Hi Tech*, 23(4), 610-621.

Gray, W. and Salzman, C. (1998). Damaged Merchandise? A Review of Experiments that Compare Usability Evaluation Methods. *Human-Computer Interaction*, 13, 203-261.

Eduroute. [accessed 14.02.2011].

Harper, B., Slaughter, L., and Norman, K. (1997). Questionnaire Administration via the WWW: A Validation & Reliability Study for a User Satisfaction Questionnaire. In: Lobodzinski S, Tomek I, editors. *In the Proceedings of the World Conference on the WWW, Internet & Intranet*, Toronto, CA. Charlottesville (VA), AACE, 808-818.

Hasan, L. (2014). Evaluating the Usability of Educational Websites Based on Students' Preferences of Design Characteristics. *The International Arab Journal of e-Technology (IAJeT)*, 3(3), 179-193.

Hasan, L. (2013). Heuristic Evaluation of Three Jordanian University Websites. *Informatics in Education*, 12(2), 231–251.

Hasan, L., Morris, A., and Probets, S. (2012). A Comparison of Usability Evaluation Methods for Evaluating E-Commerce Websites. *Behaviour & Information Technology Journal*, 31(7), 707–737.

Holzinger, A. (2005). Usability Engineering Methods for Software Developers. *Communications of the ACM*, 48(1), 92-99.

ISO 9241-11. (1998). International Standard. First Edition, Ergonomic Requirements for Office Work with Visual Display Terminals (VDTs). Part11: Guidance on Usability.

Kasli, M. and Avcikurt, C. (2008). An Investigation to Evaluate the Websites of Tourism Departments of Universities in Turkey. *Journal of Hospitality, Leisure, Sport and Tourism Education*, 7(2), 77-92.

Kirakowski, J. and Corbett, M. (1993). SUMI: The Software Measurement Inventory. *British Journal of Education Technology*, (24), 210-212.

Kirakowski, J. (1995). The Software Usability Measurement Inventory: Background and Usage, in *Usability Evaluation in Industry*, Jordan, P., Thomas, B. and Weerdmeester, B. (eds.), Taylor & Frances, London.

Lazar, J. (2006). *Web Usability: A User-Centered Design Approach*. Pearson/Education Inc.

Lencastre J. and Chaves J. (2008). A Usability Evaluation of Educational Websites. *in the Proceedings of EADTU Conference*. France.

Lewis, J.R. (1995). IBM Computer Usability Satisfaction Questionnaires: Psychometric Evaluation and Instructions for Use. *International Journal of Human Computer Interaction*, 7(1), 57-78.

Mustafa, S. and Al-Zoua'bi, L. (2008). Usability of the Academic Websites of Jordan's Universities. *In the Proceedings of the International Arab Conference on Information Technology*. Tunisia.

Nielsen, J. (1993). *Usability Engineering*. London: Academic Press.

Nielsen, J. (2003). *Usability 101: Introduction to Usability*. Useit.com,

Nielsen, J. and Mack, R. L. (1994). (Eds.). *Usability Inspection Methods*, John Wiley & Sons. New York.

Nielsen, J. and Pernice, K. (2010). *Eyetracking Web Usability*. New Riders Press. ISBN 0-321-49836-4.

Rubin, J. (2008). *Handbook of Usability Testing: How to Plan. Design, and Conduct Effective Tests*. Wiley Publishing Inc.

Rogers, Y., Sharp, H., and Preece, J. (2011). *Interaction Design: Beyond Human-Computer Interaction*. Wiley. Third Edition.

Sauro, J., (2011). Measuring Usability with the System Usability Scale (SUS).

Stone, D., Jarrett, C., Woodroffe, M., and Minocha S. (2005). *User Interface Design and Evaluation*. The Open University. Morgan Kaufmann.

TechSmith. (2014).

Tullis, T. S. and Stetson, J. N. (2004). A Comparison of Questionnaires for Assessing Website Usability, *In the Proceedings of the Usability Professionals Association (UPA) 2004 Conference*, Minneapolis, USA.

Tüzün, H., Akinci, A., Kurtoğlu, M., Atal, D., and Pala, F. (2013). A Study on the Usability of a University Registrar's Office Website Through the Methods of Authentic

Tasks and Eyetracking. *The Turkish Online Journal of Educational Technology (TOJET)*, 12(2), 26-38.

Van den Haak, M. and de Jong, M. (2005). Analyzing the Interaction between Facilitator and Participants in Two Variants of the Think-Aloud Method. *In the Proceedings of IEEE International Professional Communication Conference*, 323-327.

Veenendall Van E. (1998). Questionnaire based Usability Testing. In: Unknown, editor. EURO & Y2K: The Industrial Impact. *In the Proceedings of the the European Software Quality Week*, Brussels, BE. San Francisco (CA): Software Research, Inc. 1-9.

WAMMI. (2014). [accessed 22.07.2014].

Appendix 1. Likert scores and standard deviation of the post-test questionnaires.

No.	Question	Website 1		Website 2		Website 3	
Navigation							
		Likert Score	STD	Likert Score	STD	Likert Score	STD
1	Moving around the website without getting lost was easy	3.96	1.57	2.66	3.99	5.9	6.16
2	It was easy to go to the home page from any sub page of the site	4.14	2.73	5.25	4.58	6.42	7.89
3	The site's internal search function was effective	3.21	4.63	3.23	3.40	5.10	3.93
4	Links are working properly and not misleading so that the user knows what to expect from the destination page	3.93	2.34	3.89	2.45	5.97	5.88
5	The site has no broken links	4.45	3.29	4.32	2.51	6.23	8.66
6	The site has no orphan (dead-end pages)	4.83	3.76	5	3.68	5.83	6.26
Architecture/organization							
7	The structure of the site (organization of the site's information) was clear	4.21	3.13	3.55	3.02	6.07	5.40
8	The architecture of the site was not too deep (the number of clicks to reach goals was not too large: e.g. it does not require clicking more than 3 links)	4.69	3.48	4.5	3.04	5.87	5.44
Ease of use and communication							
9	Quick downloading of the site's pages	4.31	1.98	4.77	2.51	5.97	6.68
10	Interaction with the website was easy	3.38	2.12	2.73	3.45	6.17	6.02
11	Finding the required information was easy	3.07	3.45	2.59	3.24	5.65	4.58
12	Generally, I was satisfied with the ease of use of the site	3	3.13	2.53	4.15	5.73	4.96
Design							
13	The site was attractive and appealing so that it impresses the potential student	4.66	2.85	4.3	2.93	5.37	3.95
14	The use of images was appropriate	4.41	3.73	4.86	2.97	5.4	3.35
15	The size of the text made the site easy to read	5.31	4.22	5.42	4.65	6.27	6.52
16	The choice of colors was appropriate	5.41	3.48	5.6	4.89	5.77	4.79
17	The design of the pages was appropriate	4.97	2.15	4.59	3.21	5.48	3.93
18	Page layout or style was consistent throughout the web site	4.79	2.54	4.59	2.37	5.53	4.61
Content							
19	The information presented on the site was up-to-date	5.87	6.60	3.2	4.19	6.6	9.18
20	The information on the site was clear and relevant to user needs	4.71	3.34	4.2	2.50	6.37	6.80
21	There were no 'under construction' pages	5.29	4.47	4.87	3.68	5.48	4.79
22	The information on the site was accurate	4.72	3.13	4.93	2.63	5.83	5.62
23	Adequate and clear information about the university was displayed	5.41	4.15	4.35	2.51	6.53	8.68
24	Adequate and clear information about the faculties was displayed	4.90	3.45	4.07	1.80	6.53	7.61
25	Adequate and clear information about the departments was displayed	4.46	2.99	3.87	1.80	6.42	7.52
STD: Standard Deviation							

Appendix 2: Mean time (in Seconds) for each task across the three

Task	Website 1		Website 2		Website 3	
	Mean	Std. Deviation	Mean	Std. Deviation	Mean	Std. Deviation
Task 1	138.3000	112.6952	159.3333	82.3664	79.8333	73.0716
Task 2	25.2000	22.7390	23.9667	30.6667	21.0333	20.9868
Task 3	130.5667	77.3758	96.5000	64.1640	111.5333	73.9211
Task 4	101.4667	85.0471	54.6000	51.7838	61.2333	65.2918
Task 5	101.5333	83.8104	50.4667	59.7464	69.5333	52.1951
Task 6	172.2000	75.7948	85.3667	56.2320	124.0333	74.8159
Task 7	154.1667	82.3508	123.6333	73.3666	93.4667	107.8475
Task 8	137.0333	66.6170	118.2000	54.9472	75.0000	38.1621

Appendix 3: Result of One-Way within-Subjects ANOVA test for each task among the three sites

Task	ANOVA Test (One-Way within-Subjects)
	Was there a statistically significant difference among Website1, 2 and 3
Task 1	Yes $F(2,87) = 6.152, p=.003$
Task 2	No $F(2, 87) = .217, p=.805$
Task 3	No $F(2, 87) = 1.685, p=.191$
Task 4	Yes $F(2, 87) = 4.083, p=.020$
Task 5	Yes $F(2, 87) = 4.500, p=.014$
Task 6	Yes $F(2, 87) = 11.743, p=.000$
Task 7	Yes $F(2, 87) = 3.484, p=.035$
Task 8	Yes $F(2, 87) = 10.213, p=.000$

8

NEW TIMES, NEW STRATEGIES: PROPOSAL FOR AN ADDITIONAL DIMENSION TO THE 4 P'S FOR E-COMMERCE DOT-COM

Maximiliano Gonetecki Oliveira
FAE Centro Universitário, Curitiba, Paraná, Brazil

Ana Maria Machado Toaldo
Federal University of Paraná, Curitiba, Paraná, Brazil

ABSTRACT

Proper marketing management is fundamental to any business endeavor, including dot-coms. However, to date, as identified in a review of the International Journal of Electronic Commerce (IJEC) production and the last 10 years of EnANPAD (EnANPAD is the annual Brazilian Academy of Management conference). There are no works on the applicability of the 4P's to e-commerce, a gap in the literature that this study proposes to fill. It uses a qualitative approach methodology, investigating several empirical studies about digital commerce, and comparing it with the mainstream strategic marketing literature. Inferences were developed, pushing further the theory boundaries of this field. Both the classical works as those from Borden (1964) and Mccarthy (1960) and many other contemporaries are evaluated. The present research utilizes these works as a source of information and data. Using a process of comparison with the marketing mix model, it searches for a possible lack of fit between the related empirical environments and such a model. The results identify several key variables in each of the P's related to security in electronic commerce. This dimension seems to be the key in shaping the perception of customer value, thus supporting its inclusion as a fifth dimension along with the 4P's.

Keywords: e-commerce, e-tailing, dot-com, electronic retail, marketing strategy, marketing mix.

1. INTRODUCTION

The structural reality of the new markets, driven by information technology, progressively imposes a need for adaptation by organizations into their relation to markets and stakeholders. Regarding this demand, Katsikeas, Robson and Hulbert (2004) and Roberts and Adams (2010) highlight Digital Marketing and emerging new technologies as themes of interest to marketers. The increasing role of e-business in an organization's net profit also promotes this trend (E-COMMERCE, 2009). EITO 2010

Address for correspondence / Endereço para correspondência

Maximiliano Gonetecki de Oliveira, Me., R. 24 de Maio, 135, Centro, Curitiba-PR, 80230-080, FAE Centro Universitário, max@magox.com.br

Ana Maria Machado Toaldo, Dr., Av. Lothario Meissner, 632, 2º andar, Jardim Botânico, Curitiba-PR, 80210-170, Universidade Federal do Paraná, anatoaldo@ufpr.br

estimated the value of the global Information Technology and Communication market to be €2.3 trillion (Euros) (EITO, 2010). The U.S. Department of Commerce Economics and Statistics Administration reported $3.371 billion in e-commerce in the U.S.A. in 2009, including both Business to Business (B2B) and Business to Consumer (B2C) transactions (E-STATS, 2011).

It is important to align academic interests with those of practitioners. Bharati and Tarasewich stated that "e-commerce as a research field is still in its infancy" (Bharati and Tarasewich, 2002) which suggests that a considerable knowledge gap still exists. Due to the significant growth of the Internet as a new stratum for business, marketers are required to achieve results in this environment. It presents a duality, since the fertile, but unique business environment requires specific tools and techniques, but still lacks a mature theoretical body. One of the underlying questions is whether it is plausible to assume the applicability of traditional marketing strategy methods in this new social-cultural-economic paradigm.

Stemming from this question, the marketing mix enters the spotlight. The works of Mccarthy in the sixties are still a consistent framework for marketers. But with the emergence of e-commerce as a powerful environment to do business, questions about its reliability were raised. Schultz, (1999), by analyzing the speech of Peter Sealey, a retired vice president of Coca-Cola, made the observation that the 'p' in promotion and 'p' in place would disappear, and that the obsolescence of marketing and communication would come only when consumers ceased to shop in brick and mortar stores. However, since the publication of his article, there have been great technological developments. Mobile phones with Internet access, free wireless networks, popular laptops, readers and countless other devices with browsers that before were accessible to only a select few are a reality for a large portion of the population. Despite these changes, traditional trade has not ended, and probably never will as long as we are relational beings, but it is undeniable that e-commerce has gained representative space as a business model.

In Brazil, the virtual world gains new followers every day, as shown by the level of mobile and Internet access as reported by Instituto Brasileiro de Geografia e Estatística – IBGE (2009) in the 2008 Supplement to the National Survey by Household Sampling (PNAD) about internet access and possession of cellular telephones for personal use. This study showed a clear trend of strong growth in internet use, including an increase of 75.3% between 2005 and 2008 for Brazilians over 10 years old, a total population of 56 million users. It seems beyond doubt that the 'virtual environment' has been consolidated.

Numbers aside, the virtual environment offers other interesting dynamics, such as a reduction in information asymmetry, connectivity between consumers and even the assumption of a market that is closer to perfection. Within this environment with its own rules, human creativity is gaining ground in terms of innovation and enterprise.

Organizations, business models, and the dot-com companies emerge based exclusively on the virtual environment, with the underlying concept of not having an extension into the offline world. In other words, they generally do not have a tangible structure for interacting directly with the consumer. Some of these enterprises even operate without the need for physical distribution of products; such as digital service providers, software developers and any vendors of intellectual capital. Regarding tangible products, it is possible to carry out only their distribution. Major retailers such as Amazon.com, e-Bay, Alibaba, and Submarino are examples of this type of company.

Due to this scenario, marketing professionals are facing a new situation triggered by the Internet and technology as a whole when performing their activities. While planning and analyzing marketing strategies, they face questions like: Should the pragmatic model of marketing mix, i.e., the 4 P's, be applied to dot-com businesses? Do all of its dimensions match the reality of e-commerce? Or is a new approach necessary?

Through the literature review of previous works that have mainly explored analysis of organizational performance in the virtual environment, this study aims to answer the above questions. Only empirical works published in major journals were adopted as raw material to improve the study's consistency. The theme of these papers addressed issues at e-commerce in a retail perspective. Adopting this base of information, the present research used the qualitative approach as a methodology to investigate such empirical conclusions, data, and present literature to evaluate the fit with the current marketing mix model. Within this approach, it was possible to reach a theoretical conclusion.

We searched scientific publications for any studies addressing the applicability of the marketing mix to e-commerce. Surprisingly, out of the last 10 EnANPAD conferences (EnANPAD is the annual Brazilian Academy of Management conference) and the entire production of the International Journal of Electronic Commerce (IJEC one of the most respected journal in the field of e-commerce) no work considered the topic. This paper's relevance is found in trying to answer if the existing theory is sufficient to meet the challenges of this new environment or if there is a need for a new conceptual perspective of the operational tactics of marketing strategy. Also considering that "academic research is not contributing enough to the development of technologically sophisticated marketing strategies" (Katsikeas, Robson and Hulbert, 2004, p.573], studying the applicability of traditional marketing techniques in virtual business can be fruitful for both companies and academics.

The understanding of best practices and correct frameworks to operate e-commerce business is mandatory for practitioners as well. Within the increasing relevance of virtual commerce in company portfolios and the massive adoption of mobile devices by consumers, competitiveness in the virtual world can be directly related to business success. This scenario impels marketers to acquire the necessary knowledge to take appropriate actions in their business.

Briefly, this paper presents a diagnosis of the marketing management paradigm from the perspective of dot-com businesses. It develops a compelling analysis that culminates in proposing an expansion of the marketing mix, offering a better structure for operating digital marketing strategies. This also opens the door for discussing the strategic marketing management methodology in greater depth, given an e-commerce perspective. We begin with a theoretical review of the marketing mix and then of e-consumers. This is followed by a transposition of the marketing mix into the virtual environment, with a proposal for adaptation. The article finishes with limitations to this current investigation and proposals for future research.

2. MARKETING MIX

Webster (1992)states that marketing strategy involves market segmentation (S), targeting (T) and positioning (P) of a company in a market, or simply STP. These settings are directly related to the level of strategic business units (SBU - Strategic Business Unit) and are part of the corporate strategy. Still, in each business unit there are tactical strategies, which are strategies that correspond to the marketing mix (4 P's). The same methodology is highlighted by Kotler (2009), where marketing management is described as a process that begins with research, followed by strategic definitions (STP), with further development of the four marketing mix elements (4P's) guided by initial results. Plans are then implemented and subject to control. This process formally uses the 4P's as facilitators of marketing strategy operationalization, representing a company's final outputs (Yanaze, 2006).

While STP addresses the direction that the company will take, the marketing mix is concerned with how to operationalize such a strategy. Each of the four dimensions must be carefully and jointly planned with the others and aligned with corporate strategy, Webster (1992). In all, the company must structure a web of interactions that are inherent to or necessary for its value proposition to make sense and, thus, to reach its goals with consumers.

Regarding value perceived by clients, Neal (2002) proposes an interesting breakdown involving the sum of the product (Product), channel (Placement), and brand (Promotion) benefits, while subtracting the cost (Price). Thus, formulating the product price while considering marketing, distribution and product features follows marketing strategy precepts aimed at delivering value to consumers, which is the final goal of marketing as stated by AMA (2013).

Briefly, the marketing mix can be viewed as an action plan that will operationalize company functions, so that it can be delivered upon its strategic plan and, consequently, achieve corporate objectives.

Product, Price, Placement and Promotion have been elements consolidated in the area literature since the mid-twentieth century. Even though the overall concept has been the target of numerous efforts by academics seeking to 'expand' or 'upgrade' its elements, they have remained consistent (Dominici, 2009). They have been used for more than 50 years as the ideal model in marketing management. However, there are two distinct fields concerned with studying the contemporary model. Both have compelling arguments, exposing an ambivalence that foreshadows the longevity of a heated debate. The so-called revisionists criticize McCarthy's model as too internally focused, which ignores the consumer (Dominici, 2009), and thus discounts the customer orientation from the current marketing paradigm (Webster, 1988). On the other hand, conservationists seek to adapt the model to the supposed new reality (Dominici, 2009).

Evaluating the applicability of the 4P's to today's organizations has become an obsession for many authors, with many criticizing that the "P's" focus is on the process and not on the consumer. In contrast, the 4P concept has an uncanny adaptability. Since each dimension's sub variables are not fully defined, they provide for a framework with multiple possibilities. The great power of "P's" rests in how they are not exhaustive but adaptive. This is probably why revisionists have difficulty introducing a new a paradigm.

When Borden (1964) developed the twelve elements that McCarthy (1960) would later rearrange into the four P's, he said: "The list of items I used in my classes and my work as a consultant cover the main areas of marketing activities that require a management decision [...] I understand that others may build a different list " (Borden, 1964, p. 9).

With this attitude, the forefather of what would become the marketing paradigm took an open position regarding the elements' construction, demonstrating the concept's inherent flexibility. This same point is raised by Grönroos (1994) when criticizing McCarthy's 4P's as rigid, not customer-focused and limiting Borden's initial idea about the marketing mix. This was probably why Borden had no intention of creating a fixed list. Even though this last discussion is important and needs to be mentioned, the central proposal of this article does not include debating the current marketing paradigm's conceptual sphere, but rather focuses on its operation within the virtual environment.

3. THE VIRTUAL CONSUMER

During the first decade of this century it became apparent that online consumers, despite being essentially the same as people who patronize traditional stores, demonstrate unexpected behavior, since they do not face the same restrictions in time, space or money (Torres, 2009). Online shopping uses electronic payments and does not require paper money, which is easier, especially when considering international transactions. Concurrently, a new phenomenon began with the so-called Web 2.0. In this scenario consumers have been empowered through a reduction in information asymmetry in the market. Today, all companies, both traditional and dot-com, are faced with a different context. In the 12 years following the Internet "bubble", e-commerce in the United States grew dramatically (Table 01).

Year	Volume in US$ (billions)	Growth
2000	27.763	
2001	34.930	25.81%
2002	45.212	29.44%
2003	58.157	28.63%
2004	74.175	27.54%
2005	92.804	25.11%
2006	114.912	23.82%
2007	138.145	20.22%
2008	142.281	2.99%
2009	145.214	2.06%

Table 1: B2C transactions in the U.S.A. (E-STATS, 2011)

It would be natural to assume that the Internet's commercial potential results in a market demand for technical guidance, but apparently researchers' interest in this area is still incipient, reflected in the small number of articles on the topic at EnANPAD conferences over the past 11 years (Table 02). Internationally, there are many papers devoted to e-commerce (Bharati and Tarasewich, 2002), many of which have been published in IJEC. However, there are apparently no articles anywhere in its history (1996 to 2011) that specifically address the theme of the marketing mix. Thus, the major components of the marketing mix do not seem to be getting the attention deserved by researchers.

Year	2001	2002	2003	2004	2005	2006	2007	2008	2009	2010	2011	Total
Number of Articles	4	5	6	4	6	4	5	9	9	7	8	68

Table 2: Number of Internet related publications at EnANPAD conferences

Source: Prepared by authors from ENANPADs publications from 2001 to 2011.

This context does not eliminate the market's need to operationalize these variables. This need could possibly motivate professionals who have personal experience with the development of digital marketing tactics to document their tacit knowledge. One example is the recent "Bible of Digital Marketing" (original in Portuguese: A Bíblia do Marketing Digital) (Torres, 2009), produced by a market professional and graduate school professor, who apparently used only his personal empirical experience to write the book. Other authors with a similar profile are Adolpho (2011), who authored "The 8P's of Digital Marketing" (original in Portuguese: Os 8P's do Marketing Digital), and Gabriel (2010) who authored "Marketing in the Digital Era" (original in Portuguese: Marketing na Era Digital). The last one is even considered a best seller. This interesting phenomenon is a reflection of marketing's early history, when early practitioners began documenting tacit knowledge that then aroused the interest of the academia (Bartels, 1988). There are initiatives to produce knowledge on Digital Marketing, but research on the topic is still incipient.

4. THE 4P'S

Several authors have suggested adding new variables to the Marketing Mix as used in traditional business models. Judd (1987) proposes the addition of People, while Kotler (1986) adds Formation of Public Opinion and Political Power. Booms and Bitner (1982) bring the perspective of services by adding Participants, Physical Evidence and Process. Finally, Baumgartner (1991) presents the most extensive model to date, the 15P's, adding: Politics, Public Relations, Probe, Partition, Prioritization, Profit, Plan, Performance, and Positive Implementations.

The list of attempts to modify the 4P's does not stop with these authors. Goldsmith (1999) adds an eighth 'P' of Personalization to Booms and Bitner's proposal (1982). Melewar and Saunders (2000) add Publications, considering the areaof Corporate Visual Identity Systems - CVIS.

Focusing exclusively on the digital market, "Cybermarketing", by Karsaklian (2001), apparently the first Brazilian publication dealing with this subject, dates from the turn of the century). This book examined the four P's of marketing within the online business model context proposing additions (Database and Dialogue). However, the "D's" were not embraced by the market. It is unknown whether any study has examined the ineffectiveness of Karsaklian's model, but a superficial assessment sheds light on its deficiencies.

A database system, from Karsaklian's viewpoint, is an important variable for companies, not consumers. Looking at business strategy, correct management of data in order to produce competitive information can represent a significant increase in strategic sustainability. However, this variable means little to the consumer since there is not a direct impact on the purchasing process, so from client perspective it has little value.

Dialogue is an important variable for consumers because it represents the ability to communicate with the company. However, it can and should be framed within the component "Place", as it relates to interface with consumers. Thus, it is not strong enough to be deployed as a new dimension.

Gabriel (2010) disagrees with the concept of Digital Marketing as a new field, having its own body of knowledge. Her perspective brings the assumption of the existence of only one type of Marketing, which should be applied to any business endeavor. She argues that principles and applications are the same as 4P's.

Adolpho (2011) suggests using an extended marketing mix: Research, Production, Planning, Publication, Promotion, Propagation, Precision and Customization. As this is a current proposal focused exclusively on the electronic market, it deserves a more detailed analysis. Out of the eight variables, promotion is the only one framed in the traditional model.

The research element refers to how well a company understands its clients. The author suggests that the company needs to gather information about its customers. This element should not be framed in the marketing mix since it is part of the Marketing Management process as defined by Kotler (2009).

Planning would be the customization of digital marketing for a certain company. This is equally untenable as a dimension, since the definition of the strategic process itself includes planning.

Propagation is related to social networking about a website in order to attract more users and generate a viral logic. Again, the author is referring to a good communication tactic. This will not impact the consumer buying process as defined in the marketing literature, so it does not represent an obstacle for the consumer.

Publication would fall within the domain of content management, paying attention to the search engines. This variable could be easily absorbed by the place dimension, which addresses the element of user interface.

Accuracy studies a site's performance indices, evaluating the number of hits, length of stay, etc. This element is in fact a management support tool, and does not have a place in the tactical framework of the Marketing Mix, as again, it doesn't impact directly in the consumer buying process as a barrier.

Production is the ability to generate internal and external content. Another element that can be characterized as a variable dimension in Promotion, as traditionally defined in the marketing mix.

Finally, the item customization, which is usually deemed as the Holy Grail of customer relationship, generates the ability to interact with individual customers in a more effective way. Despite being viewed as applicable to all of the 4P's, it is clearly not an element that inhibits the purchase process. That is, its use can improve users' experience, but its absence is not an impediment to the buying process.

Thus, Adolpho's proposal (2011) may have value for general management as a map for some relevant points, but it is a rudimentary attempt to supplant the traditional elements of the marketing mix in the Strategic Marketing level.

It is interesting to note that for all of the additional P's proposed, whether for digital or traditional market, these authors primarily take into account the organizational perspective; i.e., variables that are important to keep a company's status quo and competitiveness in the markets it serves. However, none of these additional variables has as direct impact on the buying process from a consumer perspective as traditional 4P's do. For example, if the store is inaccessible to the consumer, they will not complete the purchase process. Similarly, if the product does not meet their needs, the price is inconsistent, or the client is not aware of the existence of the offer, the purchase will be unlikely. It can be said that the 4P's represent variables that can become obstacles to the consumption process. This perspective is where all the other dimensions proposed so far lose their meaning as new elements of the Marketing Mix.Can the 4P's be used as a tool for Digital Marketing? This question leads to a more detailed assessment of factors related to the marketing mix.

Despite the youth of Digital Marketing as a discipline, many variables and characteristics have been studied by researchers and practitioners and can be highlighted. Each of the P's from the marketing mix can be defined from the digital perspective, based on variables highlighted in academic articles and contextualized by empirical observations whenever possible, in order to offer a critical overview of how it differs from the traditional context. The goal is not to form an exhaustive list, which is beyond the scope of this work, but to offer a guide, which can directly impact the development of Digital Marketing plans.

Price - consumers have enormous power in comparing prices and finding information, creating a tendency to eliminate the asymmetry of information; some even would argue that this is the principle of a perfect market (Kuttner, 1998). Bertrand's (1883) classical model of competition highlights product homogeneity, zero search costs and consumers that are perfectly informed about prices as factors characterizing an economy based purely on sale at the lowest price. However, Brynjolfsson and Smith (2000) point out that other factors also influence consumer choice, and highlight trust as an important element. There are Brazilian websites devoted to comparing prices, such as "Buscapé" and "Bomdefaro", which offer the service free of charge and display the price of products for sale in different shops on the Internet. In addition, consumers can access a vast amount of information on product characteristics. A traditional search that could take days in the real world, an effort that many consumers would not be willing to undertake, is simple and comfortable in the digital environment. However, analysis of this dimension should not be summed up using merely the economic logic of classical competition, as other variables ranging from each client's motivational particularities when performing a search to the subjective aspects that affect consumer behavior ultimately influence the price search process.

Place - with online shopping, switching stores only requires a few clicks. A customer can go virtually anywhere in the world, and is not limited by geography. Buyers do not face inconveniences, traffic, parking, queuing, or any other problematic characteristics found in the traditional buying process. However, customer satisfaction and their overall purchasing experience are important to attracting and retaining clients, and should be taken quite seriously, since online customers can more easily change stores. From a business perspective, another big change that the Internet has made possible is the strategy of offering rare, low demand, or micro-targeted products, since it allows access to specific consumers in a large scale, as related to the long-tail concept (Anderson, 2006).

An observer without much experience might infer that Place in e-commerce has the same function as in traditional commerce. This is a common error coming from inexperienced observers, believing that business products should be delivered solely by physical means. Although many virtual businesses offer products that need to be handled, there are others who do not. Some offers demand solely virtual distribution. This includes software development projects (web sites, engineering schematics, technical plans, etc.), pictures, music, advertising materials, remote computer maintenance services, publishing services and others.

Product – experience products have a lower probability of success in e-commerce than search products (Morgado, 2003). Products with extensive sensorial aspects that need to be handled, tested, and proven end up with a disproportionate disadvantage compared to traditional sales channels. This limitation does not exert much influence on functional products, which do not require great interaction with consumers seeking specific features, functions, attributes, or patterns that are relatively easily quantified. The challenge to understanding the perspective consumers have of products inserted in the digital environment might be one of the watersheds between success and failure of an e-commerce.

Promotion - communication on the Internet has a feature it shares with the Price element. It allows interaction and can be manipulated or customized by the user. Advertising obtains a whole new world of possibilities with different mechanics, which means a careful analysis of viability in order to adapt any work to the digital environment (Torres, 2009). In this channel there is a plethora of possibilities that can be exploited for digital communication that are only limited by available technological resources and marketers' imaginations. In developing Internet promotions, it is important to consider end user accessibility, since different devices can generate different experiences, not all necessarily satisfactory.

But what really defines the digital market? One of the first concepts that must be consolidated in a strategist's mind is that the planner is not just a company website, but the seller. "In the context of the Internet, the seller is replaced by a website" (Lohse and Spliller, 1998, cited in Jarvenpaa and Tractinsky, 1999).

This concept shows an important logic of e-commerce, since the point of interaction in a traditional store is the seller and in the virtual one the website. In other words, this interface should provide an experience and value as close as theoretically possible to that a client receives in a physical store. Many electronic stores invest in technology to try to maximize the customer experience through customization. Amazon.com uses sophisticated algorithms and data analysis to provide information and promotions for each visitor, based on their individual navigation, products of interest and other multidimensional analysis.

It could be said that the care that exists in traditional patterns of trade can be transferred in large part to a virtual store. However, regarding some characteristics of the marketing mix in the digital market, there are limitations. For example, the consumer will probably not have direct contact with a vendor, and in most cases will receive support that is not necessarily in real time. Most often, they will have to make self-service purchases where they cannot handle products, payments are electronic and there are delivery deadlines for receiving the goods. If there is a problem in a transaction, customers must use virtual channels to try to solve it or even return the product, probably at their own expense. Clearly in all these stages there is an inherent risk that is considered and assumed by the client.

In conclusion, the three goals of the first phase of marketing strategy advocated by Webster (1992) are: check market attractiveness in terms of consumer desires and needs and competitive offerings; promote customer orientation; and finally offer a value proposition consistent with the previous ones. In the author's view, it is possible to shift the focus from a transaction-oriented perspective to that of an ongoing relationship. These three values would be developed as part of strategy and operationalized through the marketing mix. Also in the virtual world, it is assumed that the four dimensions of the marketing mix individually preserve different aspects of a strategic composition that must be carefully studied to be attractive to consumers.

5. THE MARKETING MIX IN THE VIRTUAL ENVIRONMENT: ANALYSIS AND PROPOSITION

As discussed, the elements of the marketing mix have structures apparently applicable to Digital Marketing. The logic of dot-com stores follows primarily the same principles as traditional stores since they also demand a process for analyzing price, product, promotion and place, and the same marketing goal - delivering customer value. Supposedly the Marketing Mix should also be used to operationalize marketing strategy. On a more theoretical perspective, meta-analysis of the concepts already presented suggests that these aspects were defined due to relevance of generalized critical points to the significant majority of enterprises as a way of addressing the operationalization of Marketing Strategy. However, the virtual world presents new problems that must be considered. Among them, security stands out, identified as a key element in virtual shopping for generating the confidence needed to make the virtual buying process happen. (Akin and Singh, 2005, Barbosa et al., 2009, Benbasat and Kim, 2010, Cristóbal et al, 2011, Featherman and Pavlou, 2003, Jarvenpaa, Tractinsky, 1999, Johnston and Warkentin 2004, Kaur, 2005, Koyuncu and Lien, 2003, Kulbupar, 2005, Ling et al, 2011, Lohse, Bellman and Johnson, 2000, Monsuwé, Dellaert and Ruyter 2004, Nilash et al, 2011, Oliveira, 2007, Torres, 2009). Security is also relevant to other types of digital commerce, such as m-commerce or pervasive e-commerce, accomplished through various electronic devices such as cell phones, PDA's, tablets and mobile devices in general (Joubert and Belle, 2009).

In summary, it can be said that security concerns can directly or indirectly cause an inhibition to electronic shopping. In addition, each of the 4P's must be evaluated for e-commerce to outline the relevance of the security dimension to each.

Place - security is important to creating the environment of a stable store, which requires a good Information Technology infrastructure [Cristóbal, 2011, Ferreira, et al 2008, Kulbupar, 2005, Oliveira, 2007, Tung, Kun, 2011). Consumers need the serenity to navigate the website without worrying about any system "crashes" or "bugs". There is also a need for security involving the product being shipped as specified and received in perfect condition (Kovacs and Farias, 2001).

Product - consumers need to obtain what they examined and purchased in the online store. This represents the need to be sure that customers will receive what they choose, with appropriate specifications and expected performance and quality without unpleasant surprises (Barbosa, et al 2009, Featherman and Pavlou, 2003, Ferreira, et al 2008, Jarvenpaa and Tractinsky, 1999, Kaur, 2005, Kim and Benbasat, 2010, Kovacs and Farias, 2001, Monsuwé, Dellaert and Ruyter 2004) the subsequent consumption and disposal of products are also valued, just like traditional products sold in physical stores. This last point should be supported by electronic commerce whenever appropriate.

Price, perhaps the most easily "contextualizable" dimension, because of the importance of payment security. The virtual environment is known to be vulnerable due to the large number of frauds committed, so consumers are particularly sensitive to payment security (Barbosa, et al 2009, Benbasat and Kim, 2010, Kailani and Kumar, 2011, Kaur, 2005, Kovacs and Farias, 2001, Koyuncu and Lien, 2003, Ling et al, 2011, Monsuwé, Dellaert and Ruyter 2004).

Promotion - even cyber promotion has a security perspective. In the case of advertising, due to numerous phishing attempts to acquire information from Internet users by using spam e-mail, spyware or even cookies to track behavior; many anti-virus tools block sites in an attempt to protect consumers (Torres, 2009). More experienced Internet users distrust suspicious deals, which inhibits involvement due to the fear of being cheated, even if the opportunity is real. Additionally there are traditional viruses spread by email (such as worms), making safety also important to various forms of digital communications.

As noted, each of the P's has security-related elements. However, there are other variables linked to this dimension that are not necessarily steeped in the traditional marketing mix elements. Given the importance of Security in e-commerce, it is plausible to adde it to the model as a dimension of a Digital Marketing Mix, as a tool to guide managers in the implementation of Strategic Marketing.

Additionally, the inherent virtual nature and magnitude (in the sense of range) of e-commerce are incompatible with traditional dimensions, as they are ambiguous in terms of value and risk, especially when they comes from an exclusively online store. The media has widely publicized the various problems for virtual consumers. Some studies suggest that brand trust has the ability to minimize this effect (Hernandez, 2001), by increasing the perception of a consumer guarantee. This inherent risk is not a recently discovered feature, but it was identified at the end of the twentieth century as a major problem of buying electronics. Consumers who first contact a virtual store are uncertain if it is legitimate or not, whether it is a website created by a hacker in a remote region of the world or if it is a real company. This weakness inherent to virtuality demands legitimacy, and places great importance on security in e-commerce.

Security begins to reflect its importance empirically by the emergence of companies like Paypal, PagSeguro and e-Bit, which offer financial transactions through a to payment gateway on their websites. This symbolically conveys greater credibility to visitors and facilitates payment security. Projects like the Google '+1' button and antivirus tools like Norton Internet Security, Avast, Kaspersky, and Bitdefender, among others, are trying to create a community of secure websites by assigning scores that rate security and/or warnings that users can reference during navigation. However, this question remains open because it has not completely eliminated the possibility of fraud, which naturally leads consumers to keep a defensive posture. Similar fear is found when it comes to personal data and privacy (Rohm and Milne, 1998). In some countries like Brazil, this problem is compounded by a lack of any legal regulation involving the misuse of personal data, which in this case is not considered a crime punishable by imprisonment.

The importance of security in e-commerce has been highlighted by several studies as cited herein. These studies reveal that security is present in each of the four pillars of the e-commerce marketing mix perspective. Such a fact strengthens a critical view of this variable's relevance in the marketing mix pillars and also exposes a secondary role of security, as it is, for use in digital commerce.

In principle, the security issue does not invalidate the 4P's structure for use in digital marketing, since in each dimension it supposedly addresses key elements of tactical relevance for a virtual store's strategy. However, because of the 4P's structure they end up by being subdued to a key issue in e-commerce: the security variable. (as the 4P's are, the structure ends subduing a key issue in e-commerce: the security variable.)

Considering the elements of security within the traditional format of the Marketing Mix, in other words using the 4P's without modification, it assumes the use of conservationist logic (Dominici, 2009). This means the new variable would lose relevance in any analysis.

However the issue of security in the virtual environment goes beyond the four dimensions and has a higher level of tactical relevance as part of the value perceived by the customer impacting directly on the shopping analysis, representing a strong barrier to the buying process. Thus, without security, users are unlikely to make purchases. Like all 4P's, security is a critical variable of the consumer perspective that enables the buying process to be complete.

Again, recalling that customers usually pay close attention to security aspects when making online purchases, we suggest that this dimension should be represented as a variable in the equation of perceived value, because security improves the attractiveness of online stores from customers' perspectives, thus leveraging perceived value. The use of security as a guiding element can direct the creation of virtual stores with better service structures, more stable technological environments, more reliable logistic structures and processes, as well as more comprehensive customer support.

Furthermore, the inclusion of security in a store's value proposition needs to be assessed against marketing objectives in the pursuit, creation, development and delivery of customer value (Rust, Zeithmal and Lemon, 2001). Thus, the fact that Marketing Strategy aims to deliver value and Marketing Mix in turn operationalizes it deserves attention. The Digital Marketing Mix, ultimately, must be correctly aligned with the same strategic objective: maximizing value from the customer's perspective.

As already mentioned, the Marketing Mix operationalizes key elements that must be addressed, representing the dimensions that make a difference in practical application. They are critical factors for successful marketing. That said, one wonders whether it would be reasonable to consider if the 4P's alone are able to guide Digital Marketing management without underestimating the relevance of Security.

Without going into the conservationists or revisionist merits, the full effectiveness of this tool in e-commerce should continue to be as relevant as it has been in traditional marketing. Observing the Internet scenario and all the considerations made so far, it is clear that security is a crucial element due to its relevance in enabling effective electronic retailing, for being a variable that enters customer perceived value, for being present throughout the other P's, and also for being a strong barrier to electronic consumption.

It is logical that using traditional Marketing Mix elements in Digital Marketing requires the inclusion of a security variable. This implies a fifth dimension, or "S" of Security that would absorb all variables related to safety, presently divided among the other dimensions or simply ignored. The introduction of the fifth element is completely justified in view of the virtual environment, since it is a key dimension for success in e-commerce from a consumer perspective that must be correctly structured by practitioners.

According to Neal (2002), an offer's value is equal to the product's benefits (Product) + channel benefits (Square) + brand benefits (Promotion) - cost (price); i.e., the Marketing mix. At first glance, the delivery of value in the digital environment follows this principle. So for the Digital Marketing Mix to continue representing the final value from the customer perspective it needs an update that includes the Security value equation (Figure 01). In this equation the variable can assume a positive value when perceived by the customer, or negative in its absence.

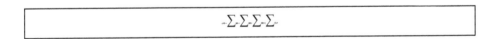

Figure 1 - Equation for calculation of Perceived Value in Digital Marketing based on Neal (2002). BP1 = Product Benefits; BP2 = Channel Benefits; BP3 = Brand Benefits; S = Perception of Safety; P = Price. Source: Prepared by the authors.

A highlighted Security analysis can create the necessary emphasis for managers to apply this element so that a company can deliver the best value to consumers. As an example, some of the aspects that need to be addressed in such a security dimension include:

- Infrastructure/Hardware: Assessing infrastructure issues involves the correct planning and installation of equipment that will operate the website in terms of hardware, supporting the system demand without a bottleneck in a way that the user experience is not compromised. Contingency plans and backup operations should also be part of them. SLA (Service Level Agreement) services and planning scalability for equipment are imperative for monitoring business growth over time.

- Checkout: This is a critical stage in the online buying process. Simplified signup, low system response time, payment stability and flexibility are essential in order to provide assurance to users, offering online or telephone support, personalizing the shopping experience, and obtaining security gateways and certifications. Systems can be strengthened by correctly prioritizing speed, consistency and third-party access to private information.

- Confidential Information: Customers' personal information must be internally controlled and properly managed, to prevent inadequate use or distribution by both employees and third parties with bad-intentions.

- Ambience: Development of partnerships with certifying companies, banks or credit card operators in order to create a better ambience for the virtual store, which signals greater website credibility.

- Ambience Exhibition: Preparing correct product exposure and description maximizes clients' comprehension, to result in a correct expectation of the product in terms of visual function and quality.

- Terms: The client must be concisely and objectively informed about their rights and risks in buying a product and what support is offered by the store after purchase and use.

- Delivery: Product delivery must be monitored to see that it corresponds to what is promoted on the website and that products are in perfect condition after shipping. This includes enabling client to monitor or be informed of delivery progress and evaluating the mechanisms supporting this process so that the buyer feels comfortable and secure with delivery.

- Stocks: Consistency of stock generates credibility with customers. Selling a product and then telling the customer it is under backorder creates uncertainty and dissatisfaction.

- Protection: Protecting the store from any cyber attacks that could affect its credibility or even generate a system crash is paramount, to prevent loss of earnings and value and creating a strong image to customers.

It is important to note that temporality becomes a powerful influencer for the validation of the "s" for security. The current technological, social and legal situation and customers' close scrutiny of security makes it an essential element for any online business. However, this does not necessarily imply that it will remain so in the future, since the cited variables can change, influencing the consumer perception of shopping over the Internet.

6. FINAL THOUGHTS

This study sought to offer a broad theoretical review of critical points related to the construction and subsequent success of Digital Marketing by assessing the applicability of the 4P's. As a result, a fifth dimension representing security aspects was identified that should be added to the marketing mix. This element is more important in client value assessment for virtual stores than brick and mortar stores, and an integral aspect of the purchasing process, making it a key element in the operationalization of Marketing Strategy. The direct applicability of the 4P's is not ideal for marketing managers of online stores, but the additional dimension called "Security" increases the effectiveness of the 4P model.

The real reason for the addition of the fifth dimension in the Digital Marketing Mix is to keep its efficacy as a managerial tool for this environment, because it is the primary guide for the practitioner in structuring digital marketing tactics. This proposition is grounded in the concept of the structural pillars for an endeavor, the absence or failure of which can prevent correct implementation of marketing strategy at the operational level. In Traditional Marketing, an error in one of the four pillars can cause the collapse of a venture; in Digital Marketing, an error in one of the five pillars can have the same effect. Also, proper analysis, planning and execution helps a company achieve success from a competitive perspective.

Expanding the Marketing Mix for e-commerce systematizes the main elements related to security of a virtual store. Such aspects went beyond the primary infrastructure logic to reach more functional aspects of the process, such as product delivery that is in accordance with the purchase order. This enhanced managerial tool provides practitioners with greater strength in planning and executing digital marketing strategy. Consequently there might be gains in operating income, total value proposition and in the longevity and success of the enterprise.

As the proposal was based only on a theoretical review, future studies might empirically assess the validity of the expanding the 4P's into 4PS. This would validate their effectiveness using practical results from market experiences in the management of electronic commerce. A qualitative study with prominent practitioners could generate support for the consolidation of the fifth element "S" as a critical factor in the operationalization of digital strategy.

Limitations of this study include its theoretical nature and that it focuses on analyzing only dot-com companies that operate exclusively on the Internet; it did not consider companies with a real representation in the offline world. Further works should also investigate the model with primary data, producing empirical conclusions. Once it is a theoretical study its assumptions must be taken within the limitations of such a format.

A conclusive research type should be addressed to evaluate the perspective of consumers about the proposed model. Marketing mix is a framework that deals with major issues which could affect the consumers motivation to reach a specific objective, thus it would be an important complement for this paper to investigate the impact of security over consumers buying decision process.

Another relevant point on the agenda in many academic circles is the validity of the current marketing mix and marketing paradigm in today's world. The marketing mix has not been evaluated within a more contemporary holistic perspective that includes certain subjective aspects. Thus, criticism about the internal focus of the marketing mix, as made by revisionists, could also be extended to the proposed 4ps model.

REFERENCES

Adolpho, C. (2011) Os 8 Ps do Marketing Digital - o Seu Guia Estratégico de Marketing Digital. Novatec, São Paulo.

American Marketing Association (2013). <www.marketingpower.com>

Anderson, C. (2006) *The Long Tail: Why the Future of Business Is Selling Less of More.* Hyperion Books, New York.

Akin, S.M.A. and Singh, R. (2005) *Building Consumer Trust: An Online Perspective.* Luleå University of Technology. (Thesis) Department of Business Administration and Social Sciences, Division of Industrial Marketing and e-Commerce, Luleå, Sweden.

Barbosa, M. L. A, Farias, S.A., Kovacs, M.H. and Souza A.G. (2009) Marketing virtual: Separando o joio do trigo- Os riscos inerentes e manipulados no e-commerce. *Revista Brasileira de Marketing*, 8(2).

Bartels, R. (1988) *The History of Marketing Thought.* Columbus, Publishing Horizons.

Baumgartner, J. (1991) Nonmarketing Professionals Need More than 4Ps, *Marketing News*, July 22, , p. 28.

Benbasat, I., and Kim, D. (2010) Designs for Effective Implementation of Trust Assurances in Internet Stores. *Comunications of the ACM*, 53 (2).

Bertrand, J. (1883) Book review of theorie mathematique de la richesse sociale and of recherches sur les principles mathematiques de la theorie des richesses, *Journal de Savants,* 67, pp. 499–508.

Bharati, P. and Tarasewich, P. (2002) Global Perceptions of Journals Publishing e-Commerce Research. *Communications of the ACM – The Adaptative Web*, 45 (9).

Booms, B.H. and M.I. Bitner. (1982) Marketing Strategies and Organisation Structures for Service Firms, in J. Donnelly and W. George (eds) *Marketing of Services*, Chicago, IL: American Marketing Association.

Borden, N.H. (1964) The Concept of the marketing mix. *Journal of Advertising Research*,2-7.

Brynjolfsson, E and Smith, M. D. (2000) Frictionless Commerce? A Comparison of Internet and Conventional Retailers. *Management Science,* 46 (4).

Cristóbal, E., Marimon, F., Daries, N. and Montagut, Y. (2011) Spanish E-Consumer Segmentation and Positioning in Virtual Supermarkets Sector. *International Journal of Marketing Studies,* 3(2), pp. 16-31.

Dominici, G. (2009) From Marketing mix to E-Marketing mix: a Literature Overview and Classification. *International Journal of Business and Management,* 4(9).

E-Commerce (2009) The Economist (http://www.economist.com/node/14298940).

EITO. 2010 (http://www.eito.com/pressinformation_20100303.htm).

E-Stats. (2011) U.S. Census Bureau, (http://www.census.gov/econ/estats/2009/2009reportfinal.pdf)

Featherman, M. S. and Pavlou, P. A. (2003) Predicting e-services adoption: a perceived risk facets perspective. *International Journal of Human-Computer Studies,* 59 (4).

Ferreira, L. B., Carvalho, H.C., Castro, D.M.F., Boccia, M.F. and Marinho, B.L. (2008) Quais os obstáculos à adoção do e-commerce pelos internautas? *Anais em meio eletrônico do XI Seminários em Administração*, USP, São Paulo, Agosto.

Gabriel, M (2010) *Marketing na Era Digital.* Martha Gabriel. São Paulo: Novatec, (2010).

Goldsmith, R. E. (1999) The personalised marketplace: Beyond the 4Ps. *Marketing Intelligence & Planning, 17*(4), pp. 178-178.

Grönroos, C. (1994) From the Marketing mix to Relationship Marketing: Toward a Paradigm Shift in Marketing. *Management Decision,* 32(2), pp. 4-20.

Hernandez, J.M.C. (2001) Brand Trust and Online Consumer Behavior. *XXV Encontro da ANPAD*, Campinas, São Paulo.

Instituto Brasileiro de Geografia e Estatística- IBGE (2009). De 2005 para 2008, acesso à Internet aumenta 75,3%, (http://saladeimprensa.ibge.gov.br/en/noticias).

Jarvenpaa, S. and Tractinsky, N. (1999) Consumer Trust in an Internet Store: A Cross-Cultural Validation. *Journal of Computer Mediated Communication,* 5 (2), pp. 1-35.

Johnston, A. C. and Warkentin, M. (2004) The Online Consumer Trust Construct: A Web Merchant Practitioner Perspective. *Southern Association for Information Systems: 2004 Proceedings*, (http://aisel.aisnet.org/sais2004/36).

Joubert, J. and Belle, J. V. (2009) The Importance of Trust and Risk in M-Commerce: A South African Perspective. *Pacific Asia Conference on Information Systems 2009 proceedings.* (paper 96).

Judd, V. (1987) Differentiate with the 5th P: People, *Industrial Marketing Management*, November.

Kailani, M.A. and Kumar, R. (2011) Investigating Uncertainty Avoidance and Perceived Risk for Impacting Internet Buying: A Study in Three National Cultures. *International Journal of Business and Management, 6(5),* , pp. 76-92.

Karsaklian, E. (2001) *Cybermarketing*. Editora Atlas, São Paulo.

Katsikeas, C. S., Robson, M. J. and Hulbert, J. M. (2004) In search of relevance and rigor for research in marketing. *Marketing Intelligence and Planning*, 22(5).

Kaur, K. (2005) Consumer Protection in e-Commerce in Malaysia: an Overview. *UNEAC Asia Papers*, (10).

Kim, D. and Benbasat, I. (2010) Designs for Effective Implementation of Trust Assurances in Internet Stores. *Comunications of the ACM*, 53 (2), fevereiro.

Kotler, P. (1986) Megamarketing, *Harvard Business Review*, March–April, pp. 117–24.

Kotler, P. (2009) *Marketing para o século XXI: como criar, conquistar e dominar mercados.* (1st ed.), Rio de Janeiro:Livraria Editouro.

Kovacs, M.H. and Farias, S.A. (2001) Comércio Eletrônico: Há Diferentes Dimensões de Riscos Percebidos entre os Usuários da Internet Que Compram e os Que Nunca Compraram por Este Meio? *XXV Encontro da ANPAD*, Campinas, São Paulo.

Koyuncu, C. and Lien, D. (2003) E-commerce and consumer's purchasing behaviour. *Applied Economics*, 35(6).

Kulbupar, T. (2005) *Consumer Trust in Thailand Online B2C Company.* (Thesis) Luleå University of Technology, Department of Business Administration and Social Sciences, Division of Industrial Marketing and e-Commerce, Luleå, Sweden.

Kuttner, R. (1998) The Net: A Market too Perfect for Profits. *BusinessWeek,* May, 10.

Ling, K.C., Daud D., Piew, T.H., Keoy, K.H. and Hassan, P. (2011) Perceived Risk, Perceived Technology, Online Trust for the Online Purchase Intention in Malaysia. *International Journal of Business and Management*, 6 (6), June.

Lohse, G.L., Bellman, S. and Johnson, E.J. (2000) Consumer Buying Behavior on the Internet: Findings from Panel Data. *Journal of Interactive Marketing*, 14 (1), pp. 15-29.

Mccarthy, E. J. (1960) *Basic Marketing: A managerial Approach*, Homewood, IL: Richard Irwin, Inc..

Melewar, T. C., and Saunders, J. (2000) Global corporate visual identity systems: Using an extended marketing mix. *European Journal of Marketing, 34*(5), pp. 538-550.

Monsuwé, T. P., Dellaert, B.G.C. and Ruyter, K. (2004) What drives consumers to shop online? A literature review. *International Journal of Service Industry Management*, 15 (1), pp. 102 -121.

Morgado, M.G. (2003) *Comportamento do consumidor online: perfil, uso da Internet e atitudes*. (Thesis) Doutorado em Administração, Fundação Getúlio Vargas, São Paulo, SP, Brasil.

Neal, W. D. (2002) Defending the Four Ps [Letter to the editor]. *Marketing Management,* 11 (6), 46.

Nilash, M., Fathian, M., Gholamian, M. R. and Ibrahim. O. B. (2011) Propose a Model for Customer Purchase Decision in B2C Websites Using Adaptative Neuro-Fuzzy Inference System. *International Journal of Business Research and Management, 2,* , pp. 1-18.

OLIVEIRA, E.C. (2007) *Custódia de Comportamento do consumidor: processo de decisão de compra de livros pela Internet*. (Thesis), Doutorado em Administração, Faculdade de Economia, Administração e Contabilidade da Universidade de São Paulo, São Paulo, Brasil.

ROBERTS, D. and Adams, R. (2010) Agenda development for marketing research: the user's voice. *International Journal of Market Research*, 52 (3), pp. 339-362.

Rohm, A.J. and Milne, G.R. (1998) Emerging marketing and policy issues in electronic commerce: attitudes and beliefs of Internet users. *Marketing and Public Policy Proceedings*, 8, , pp. 73-79.

Rust, R.T., Zeithmal, V., and Lemon, K.N. (2001) *O Valor do cliente (customer equity): o modelo que está reformulando a estratégia corporativa*. Porto Alegre: Bookman.

Schultz, D.E. (1999) Total Switch to e-marketing not likely in near future. *Marketing News*, 33 (21), p. 8.

Torres, C. (2009) *A Bíblia do Marketing Digital: Tudo o que você queria saber sobre marketing e publicidade na internet e não tinha a quem perguntar*. Editora Novatec, São Paulo.

Tung, F.C., Kun, S. Factors Affecting the Adoption of Online Travel Websites in Taiwan. *The Business Review, Cambridge*, 18 (1*),* (2011) p. 149.

WEBSTER, Jr., F. E. (1988) The Rediscover of the Marketing Concept. *Business Horizons*, 31 (3), pp. 29-39.

Webster, Jr., F. E. (1992) The Changing Role of Marketing in the Corporation. *Journal of Marketing*, 52, pp. 1-17.

Yanaze, M. H. (2006) *Gestão de Marketing e Comunicação*. São Paulo, Saraiva.

9

ROLE OF GIS, RFID AND HANDHELD COMPUTERS IN EMERGENCY MANAGEMENT: AN EXPLORATORY CASE STUDY ANALYSIS

Ashir Ahmed

Swinburne University of Technology, Australia

ABSTRACT

This paper underlines the task characteristics of the emergency management life cycle. Moreover, the characteristics of three ubiquitous technologies including RFID, handheld computers and GIS are discussed and further used as a criterion to evaluate their potential for emergency management tasks. Built on a rather loose interpretation of Task-technology Fit model, a conceptual model presented in this paper advocates that a technology that offers better features for task characteristics is more likely to be adopted in emergency management. Empirical findings presented in this paper reveal the significance of task characteristics and their role in evaluating the suitability of three ubiquitous technologies before their actual adoption in emergency management.

Keywords: Emergency management; RFID; Task-technology Fit Model; Ubiquitous Technologies

1.   INTRODUCTION

Mark Weiser (1991, p. 94) introduced the concept of ubiquitous technologies in 1991 by stating as:

> *"The most profound technologies are those that disappear. They weave themselves into the fabric of everyday life until they are indistinguishable from it".*

Since then, the world has witnessed rapid growth and eminent success in the adoption and diffusion of ubiquitous technologies in various disciplines including education, science, defence and public service (Chainey and Ratcliffe, 2005; Loebbecke and Palmer, 2006; Sara, 2003; Shannon, and Feied, and Smith, and Handler, and Gillam, 2006). Moreover, it is important to note that the use of emerging technologies that have unique characteristics is still not well understood (Sharma, and Citurs, and Konsynski, 2007). Therefore, to evaluate the performance of technologies before their actual adoption is still believed to be quite intricate (Davies and Gellersen, 2002).

Address for correspondence / Endereço para correspondência

Ashir Ahmed, PhD Lecturer, Department of Information Systems, Entrepreneurship and Logistics Faculty of Business & Law EN Building, Room 610a Swinburne University of Technology PO Box 218 John Street Hawthorn 3122 Victoria, Australia

This paper is built on the key concept of Task-technology Fit (TTF) model presented by Goodhue and Thomson. In their paper presented in MISQ in 1995, Goodhue and Thompson (1995, p. 216) described Task-Technology Fit as:

"[The] *degree to which a technology assists* [its users] *in performing his or her portfolio of tasks. More specifically, TTF is the correspondence between task requirements,* [users'] *abilities, and functionality of a technology".*

It is further argued that the better 'fit' between task and technology characteristics increases the likelihood of adoption of a technology in a particular domain (Goodhue and Thompson, 1995, p.216). Aligned with the above argument, this paper suggests that a better 'fit' between task characteristics of emergency management and technology characteristics of ubiquitous technologies increase the likelihood of successful adoption of these technologies in this domain. However, before examining the 'fit', it is commendable to address the task and technology characteristics. Therefore, the objectives of this paper are as follows:

a.   Identify task characteristics of emergency management, and

b.   Identify technology characteristics of RFID, handheld computers and GIS.

Overall, this paper is structured as follows: firstly, the paper addresses the task characteristics of emergency management and technology characteristics of RFID, Handheld computers and GIS. Next, the paper presents a conceptual model and then outlines the research methodology. Later on, the paper presents the research findings. The paper includes the justification of unplanned results generated from multiple case studies, and it ends with a discussion and conclusion.

2. TASK CHARACTERISTICS OF EMERGENCY MANAGEMENT

Emergency management life cycle is generally described as a series of various phases or stages such as preparedness, mitigation, response and recovery (Kimberly, 2003). Literature relevant to emergency management reported several models that describe various numbers of phases such as three phases (ADPC., 2000; Atmanand, 2003; Tuscaloosa., 2003), four (Kimberly, 2003; Turner, 1976), six (Toft and Reynolds, 1994), seven (Shaluf, Ahmadun, and Mustafa, 2003) or even eight (Kelly, 1999) phases which collectively form the emergency management life cycle. In depth analysis of these emergency management models reveals that they comprise of various individual tasks. For instance, a task such as 'information sharing' is performed in different phases of emergency management including preparedness, mitigation, response and recovery. Similarly, an individual phase may include more than one task. For instance, response phase may include such tasks as 'information sharing' and 'resource management'. In general, this paper agrees with the description of emergency management in terms of phases or stages. However, this paper advocates that the concept of phases does not facilitate the process of technological adoption. Furthermore, aligned with the recommendation of Goodhue and Thompson (1995, p. 216), this paper argues that the objective of adoption of a technological process is to facilitate a particular task and not a phase.

In order to identify the task characteristics of emergency management, this paper built on two streams of literature, including:

1-   Emergency management models – theoretical models suggesting various phases of the emergency management life cycle. The following section reports various tasks mentioned in these emergency management models.

2-   Emergency management studies – case studies discussing several tasks performed in real emergencies situations. Section below lists various tasks reported in various emergency management case studies.

2.1   Emergency Management Models

The following tasks are mentioned in various emergency management models:
- People/victim management (ADPC. (2000); Kelly, 1999; B. Richardson, 1994)
- Planning (Manitoba-Health-Disaster-Management., 2002; B. Richardson, 1994; I.M. Shaluf, and F.R. Ahmadun, and S. Mustapha, 2003)
- Information sharing (Manitoba-Health-Disaster-Management., 2002; B. Richardson, 1994)
- Immediate response to disaster (B. Richardson, 1994)
- Training (ADPC., 2000; Kimberly, 2003; Tuscaloosa., 2003)
- Communication (ADPC., 2000; Kimberly, 2003; Manitoba-Health-Disaster-Management., 2002)
- People and object management (ADPC., 2000; Kelly, 1999; Kimberly, 2003)
- Maintenance of inventories (ADPC., 2000; Atmanand, 2003)
- Conducting drills (ADPC., 2000; Atmanand, 2003; Tuscaloosa., 2003)
- Resource management (ADPC., 2000; Atmanand, 2003; Kelly, 1999; Tuscaloosa., 2003)
- Authentication (Toft and S. Reynolds, 1994; Turner, 1976)
- Detecting emergency signals (B. Richardson, 1994; I.M. Shaluf et al., 2003)
- Tagging/tracking (Kelly, 1999)

2.2   Emergency Management Studies

The following tasks are mentioned in various emergency management case studies:
- Resource management (Haddow, and Bullock, and Coppola, 2008; José, and Pérez, and Ukkusuri, and Wachtendorf, and Brown, 2007; E.L. Quarantelli, 1997; Tran, and Yousaf, and Wietfeld, 2010)
- Information management (Celik and Corbacioglu, 2010; José et al., 2007; E.L. Quarantelli, 1997; Tomasinia and Wassenhoveb, 2009; Tran et al., 2010; S. Zlatanova, and P. Oosterom, and E. Verbree, 2004a)
- Training (José et al., 2007; Wilks and Page, 2003)
- Automation (Carver and Turoff, 2007; Zlatanova et al., 2004a)
- Coordination and collaboration (Carver and Turoff, 2007; Celik and Corbacioglu, 2010)
- Authentication (Haddow et al., 2008; Tran et al., 2010)
- Tagging and Tracking (Carver and Turoff, 2007; Tomasinia and Wassenhoveb, 2009; Zlatanova et al., 2004a)

The above discussion presents a number of tasks that are performed in the emergency management life cycle. However the careful analysis of such tasks suggests that some tasks such as 'communication', 'resource management' and 'information management' are reported more than once across various phases of the emergency management life cycle. Similarly there are few tasks that are identical in nature such as 'resource management', 'people and object management'. It is also important to note that a number of tasks mentioned above are not relevant to the context of this research that is about the role of ubiquitous technologies in emergency management. In order to clearly understand the eminent tasks involved in the emergency management life cycle, it is wise to group similar tasks and form the key groups of tasks which can be used as 'task characteristics' of emergency management.

The relevant literature suggests that tasks have been categorized across three dimensions: (a) difficulty, (b) variety and (c) interdependence (W. Louis Fry and Slocum, 1984). However, the research related to technological adoption asks whether a significant difference exists between variety and difficulty (L. Dale Goodhue, 1995; Wells, and Sarker, and Urbaczewski, and Sarker, 2003). Nevertheless, the overall process of task analysis involves a hierarchical decomposition of autonomous tasks into lower-level sub-tasks (Hackos and Redish, 1998). The nature of an autonomous task dictates the degree of variety, difficulty and interdependence of a particular task (Wells et al., 2003). In contrast to decomposing tasks into sub-tasks based on the variety, difficulty and interdependence, sub-tasks can be grouped together to form major tasks based on their common attributes. Aligned with the above line of argument, this research agrees that emergency management tasks can be grouped into major tasks based on their common attributes. In addition, this research also carefully considers the recommendations of Wells et al. (2003) who argues that the overall classification of tasks is primarily based on the domain characteristics and context of that classification. Therefore, in context of technological adoption, this paper combines the emergency management tasks based on their commonalities and form the key task characteristics of emergency management.

Task – A: Authentication

In order to protect a system from an emergency or disaster - especially a man-made disaster - it is critical to protect that system from an unauthorized or illicit use. Toft and Reynolds (1994), Haddow et al (2008) and José et al.(2007) suggest that the following tasks should be performed for the safe, secure and authorized use of a system.

- Implementing authentication protocol
- Assigning privileges to the users
- Verification of access requests

Aligned with the above recommendations, this paper argues that the above mentioned tasks are critical for system security, and thus a technology that offers better support for these tasks is more likely to be adopted in emergency management. Moreover, this paper places the above mentioned tasks under a broader category of related tasks and calls it as 'authentication'. This task (authentication) assures that only valid users can interact with the system, which will eventually minimize the risks of various man-made disasters such as technological disasters and terrorist attacks. Use of technology for authentication refers to the process through which a pertinent technology is used to verify the identity of a user who wishes to access a system.

Task – b: Automation

Literature related to emergency management suggests that during emergencies, data is available from many sources and in huge quantities, but the actual problem arises in the processing of this data (Zlatanova et al., 2004a). During emergencies, unfavourable working conditions further complicate the required working performance from human operators. During hostile working environment of emergencies, a technology that can automate various procedures and ensure consistency is likely to be adopted successfully (M. Ibrahim Shaluf, and R. Fakharul Ahmadun, and Sa'Ari. Mustapha, 2003; S. Zlatanova, and P. Van. Oosterom, and E. Verbree, 2004b). Furthermore, the relevant literature has identified the following tasks which could be better performed with the help of a suitable technology (Carver and Turoff, 2007; B. Richardson, 1994; I.M. Shaluf et al., 2003; Zlatanova et al., 2004a). These tasks are:

- Identification of tasks which can be performed by control systems

- Automatic detection of inputs using sensors

- Automatic decision making based on received data- using artificial intelligence

Built on common attributes of the above mentioned tasks, this paper groups them into a broader category and calls it as 'automation'. In general, automation also refers to a process of using a control system, such as computers, to control machinery and processes and replacing human operators (2002).

Task – C: Tagging and Tracking

One of the most important and urgent problems at the emergency scene is the overwhelming number of victims that must be monitored, tracked and managed by each of the first responders or individuals (Barbara, 2008; Killeen, and Chan, and Buono, and Griswold, and Lenert, 2006; Bill Richardson, 1994; Tuscaloosa., 2003). In addition, the equipment deployed at the emergency scene needs to be managed appropriately. It is suggested that the whole process of managing humans and other objects during emergencies is composed of following tasks (ADPC., 2000; Kelly, 1999; Kimberly, 2003; B. Richardson, 1994):

- Marking or tagging of humans and objects

- Use these tags to track humans/objects

- Use these tags for objects management before, during, and after emergencies.

Aligned with the existing literature, this paper agrees that a technology that offers better features to conduct these tasks would be well accepted in emergency management. Based on the common attributes of the above tasks, this paper groups them into a broader category of 'tagging and tracking'. By definition, the purpose of tagging and tracking is to identify the target object in a group of similar objects, as well as to keep real-time information about its position. In the context of emergency management, people and object management are the main objectives of this task (Schulz, and Burgard, and Fox, and Cremers, 2001) and this paper identifies it as one of the key task characteristics of emergency management.

Task – d: Information Management

Wybo and Kowalski (1998) argue that the lack of inadequate and incomplete information is considered to be the main operational problem during emergency management. A study of recent emergencies shows that, at one or another level, information was available that could have prevented the emergency from happening (Chan, and Killeen, and Griswold, and Lenert, 2004; Kelly, 1999; Lee and Bui, 2000;

Mansouriana, and Rajabifardb, and Zoeja, and Williamson, 2006; Enrico L. Quarantelli, 1988; M. Ibrahim Shaluf et al., 2003; B. Toft and S. Reynolds, 1994). Further to the importance of 'information' in emergency management, the following are some of the tasks that are reported in the literature (Celik and Corbacioglu, 2010; José et al., 2007; Manitoba-Health-Disaster-Management., 2002; B. Richardson, 1994; Tran et al., 2010):

- Collection of information from various sources

- Broadcast warnings/alerts

- Building and maintaining information pools

- Communication with other agencies

Based on the common attributes in the above tasks, this paper segregates the above mentioned tasks into a broader category of 'information management'. This task refers to the collection and management of information from one or more sources, and its distribution to one or more audiences who have a stake in that information or a right to that information. In context of technological adoption, this paper advocates that, information management and communication play a vital role (Enrico and Quarantelli (1988)) and act as an important task characteristics of emergency management.

Four tasks characteristics including authentication, automation, tagging / tracking and information management are collectively referred as AATI in this paper.

3. UBIQUITOUS TECHNOLOGIES

According to Kumar and Chatterjee (Kumar and Chatterjee, 2005) ubiquitous technology is the trend towards increasingly ubiquitous, connected computing devices in the environment, a trend being brought about by a convergence of advanced electronic - and particularly, wireless-technologies and the Internet. Ubiquitous technology is pervasive in nature and unobtrusively embedded in the environment, completely connected, intuitive, effortlessly portable, and constantly available. Although there are several ubiquitous technologies available such as RFID, handheld computers, GIS, GPRS, wearable computers, smart homes and smart building, this paper focuses only on three technologies including RFID, handheld computers and GIS.

3.1   Radio Frequency Identification

RFID is a term coined for the use of short to medium range radio technology for the communication between two objects without any physical contact (Wang, and Chen, and Ong, and Liu, and Chuang, 2006). Objects on the two sides of the RFID link can be either stationary or moveable. A typical RFID system consists of (a) tag, (b) reader/interrogator, and (c) an antenna. When the reader sends out the electromagnetic signals to couple with the tag antenna, the tag gets electromagnetic energy from waves to power its circuits in the microchip. The microchip located inside the tag then sends back electromagnetic waves to the reader, and the reader receives and returns the waves and converts them into digital data. The data transmitted by the tag actually provides the data and information for the object, and the information can be processed in any information system or network connected to the reader (Xinping, and Yuk, and Sheung, 2007). Contactless and no line of sight communication are the key features of RFID.

Literary volumes of research are available on the application of RFID in various domains. Most significantly, this technology has been used in supply chain management, inventory control, asset management, retail, manufacturing, warehouse automation, security, defence, aerospace, road pricing, fashion, libraries, hospitals, telemedicine and farm management.

Further to the use of RFID in the above mentioned domains, Fry and Lenert (2005) proposed the use of RFID in hospitals during a disaster, such as a mass causality situation. An integrated RFID-equipped hardware-software system (MASCAL) was designed to enhance a hospital's resource management capabilities. The RFID-equipped system (MASCAL) was targeted at conducting the tasks related to patient management during an emergency with improved efficiency and better performance. The MASCAL system created an end-to-end environment for the management of casualties from a battlefield or catastrophic civilian event. The system utilizes positional information from wireless asset tags to reduce dependencies on manual processes, and it improves situational awareness during inherently chaotic events. Its potential value lies in providing visibility into the supply and demand workflows, augmented with select data that is considered helpful in making appropriate management decisions.

3.2 Handheld Computers

Handheld computer also referred to as personal digital assistants (PDAs). These are lightweight, compact computers that are literally held in one's hand or stored in a pocket (Lu, and Xiao, and Sears, and Jacko, 2005). These gadgets have developed increasing functionality, with decreasing size and weight. In addition to mobility and ubiquity, they offer high resolution colour displays and provide sufficient memory to store a large amount of data (Kho, and Henderson, and Dressler, and Kripalani, 2006). Latest handheld computers have larger screens, the ability to run multiple programs simultaneously, and natural handwriting recognition software. These devices allow users to access electronic mail and the internet remotely, creating virtually limitless access to the information.

During emergencies, the use of the Internet on these devices can provide useful information about emergencies and disasters to the public and first responders (Alfonso and Suzanne, 2008). Furthermore, such devices have the ability to enable responders to work well with others due to their ability to communicate quickly and share resources (Pine, 2007).Wireless technology ranges from doing simple tasks, such as communicating with first responders remotely, to more complex tasks such as collecting digital data efficiently and accurately (Troy, and Carson, and Vanderbeek, and Hutton, 2008).

3.3 Geographic Information System

GIS integrates hardware, software, and data for capturing, managing, analysing, and displaying all forms of geographically referenced information. It is a powerful tool for various organizations because it has the ability to capture the data by digitizing, scanning, digital imagery, or aerial photography. Databases associated with GIS applications can be used (a) to store the data, (b) to manipulate the data, (c) to form data queries and (d) to visualize the data (Gunes and Kovel, 2000).

GIS technology can play an important role in emergency management because it has the ability to enhance emergency management information systems by digitally capturing, storing, analysing and manipulating data (Senior and Copley, 2008). Because of its ability to gather, manipulate, query and display geographic information quickly and present it in an understandable format, GIS could be decisive for emergency management (Cutter, and Emrich, and Adams, and Huyck, and Eguchi, 2007). Table 1 summarizes some of the key characteristics of RFID, handheld computers and GIS.

Table 1: Characteristics of Ubiquitous Technologies

RFID	Handheld computers	GIS
Tracking, scanning, information management, automation (Michael and McCathie, 2005)	Data storage, transformation and transmission (Lu et al., 2005)	Digitally captures, stores, analyses and manipulates data (Senior and Copley, 2008)
Automatic non-line of sight scanning, labour reduction, enhanced visibility, item level tracking, robustness (2005)	Real-time data gathering, concurrent data transformation and instant data transmission (Kho et al., 2006)	Ability to gather, manipulate, query and display geographic information (Cutter et al., 2007).
Automation, object tracking, asset management, object management. (Xiao, and Shen, and Sun, and Cai, 2006)	Communication and information management (Pine, 2007)	Analytical modelling (2000)

4. CONCEPTUAL MODEL

The rationale for building a conceptual model on the theory of TTF is an argument that claims that *'there must be a good fit between the technology and the tasks it supports'* (Goodhue and Thompson, 1995). It also claims that 'good fit' between task and technology features brings performance improvements to its users. Built on the notion of *'task-technology fit'*, a conceptual model is presented that highlights the task characteristics of emergency management and technology characteristics of radio frequency identification, handheld computers and geographic information system and the 'fit' between task and technology characteristics.

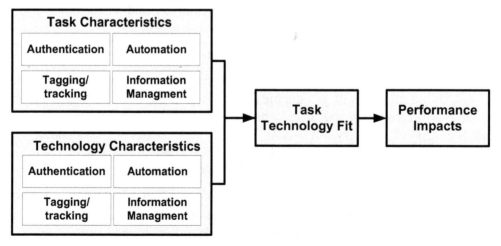

Figure 1: Conceptual Model based on TTF

Task Characteristics refer to the key tasks performed in the emergency management life cycle, such as authentication, automation, tagging/tracking, and information management (AATI). These tasks are derived from the relevant literature and then contextualized for this study. As discussed above, AATI are the key emergency management tasks which need to be performed by the use of any pertinent technology.

Technology Characteristics refer to the features of ubiquitous technologies that perform the task requirements of authentication, automation, tagging / tracking and information management. Once the task characteristics of emergency management are identified (as AATI in this study), the potential technology needs to be evaluated against such tasks.

Task-technology Fit refers to the degree by which task characteristics match with the technology characteristics. It also addresses the factors that influence the 'fit' between task and the characteristics of ubiquitous technologies.

Performance Impacts refer to the perceived impacts of technological adoption on the performance of emergency management operations.

This paper only examines the task and technology characteristics whereas discussion on TTF (factors) and performance impacts (mentioned in the conceptual model) is not under the scope of this paper.

5. RESARCH METHODOLY

By employing a conceptual study, four major tasks of emergency management are identified (as reported in the Section above). Moreover, multiple case study method is adopted to empirically validate the significance of those tasks. Five emergency management organizations are selected to participate in this research. Out of the total five cases, three are located in Australia, one in New Zealand and one in Switzerland. Although, five cases are too few to allow statistical validity, they do allow a large enough range to result in an acceptable theoretical replication. Moreover, many well-known case studies have used this number or fewer cases (Dick, 2002; Eisenhardt, 1989; Markus, 1983; Orlikowski, 1983). The cases selected for this research cover the variations in the evaluation process within the context of technological adoption in emergency management. The criteria for selecting the participating organizations were based on the fact that those organizations have already used or are willing to use any ubiquitous technology in emergency management. The selection criteria are imposed to achieve analytical generalization whereas statistical generalization is not targeted in this study. In relation to the triangulation of data, data was collected from multiple sources, including formal interviews, organizations' websites, email communication, telephone conversations, and other relevant documents (see Table 2 for more details). However, the case studies mainly rely on the formal in-depth interviews with the eight key participants from the selected cases (each case represented by a unique alphabet such as A, B, C, D and E). Primary data was collected from eight respondents including Director disaster operations (DDO), Executive Manager Disaster Operations (EMDO), Coordinator Emergency Management (CEM), Team Lead Spatial Systems (TLSS), Regional Director Emergency Management (RDEM), Director Emergency Management and Communication (DEMC), Senior Logistics Officer (SLO) and Logistic Officer (LO) representing five case organizations. Data collected from the other sources assists in further understanding and explaining the data from the formal interviews, providing a contextual richness to the collected data. With the consent of the participants of the case studies, all conversation held during an interview was recorded on a digital voice recorder. The recorded interviews were further transcribed in total and analysed by a pattern matching technique. The qualitative analysis tool called NViVo 8.0 was used for such a purpose.

Table 2: Overview of Supporting Documents

Case	Document Name	Abbre-viation	Accessi-bility	Overview
A	Critical Infrastructure Emergency Management Assurance Handbook	CIEMAH	Public	This handbook provides information for senior emergency risk managers dealing with critical infrastructure. The handbook complements and supports AS/NZS 4360: 1999 Risk Management and Emergency Management Australia's Emergency Risk Management Application Guide.
	Disaster Management Planning Guidelines	DMPG	Public	The aim of these guidelines is to provide a process for local governments to develop a local disaster management plan, and to understand the need for a consistent local government approach to disaster management planning.
	Emergency Risk Management	ERM	Public	The aim of emergency risk management (ERM) is to present a systematic process that produces a range of risk treatments that reduces the likelihood or consequences of disastrous events.
	Disaster Management Plan	DMP	Public	Disaster management plan outlines the potential hazards and risks that are evident in an area; steps to mitigate these potential risks; and an implementation strategy to enact should a hazard impact and cause a disaster.
	The Overview of Disaster Management Arrangements	DMA	Public	It is intended for this book to provide a high-level overview for anyone interested in disaster management arrangements in the State, including disaster managers, stakeholders and communities.
B	*None*			

C	Emergency Management Planning Guide	EMPG	Public	The aim of the emergency management planning guide is to assist local councils and communities to better assess and manage emergencies such as flood, storms and earthquakes, in order to reduce the consequences of disastrous events and to create safe and resilient communities.
	Response Plan for Victoria	RPV	Public	The purpose of this plan is to provide strategic guidance for effective emergency response to flood events. The plan also describes the roles and responsibilities of agencies and organizations that have a role in the floodplain management, forecasting of meteorological events, dissemination of information to the community and the role of minimizing the threat and impact to people, property and the environment.
	Emergency Management Discussion Paper	EMDP	Public	The emergency management discussion paper provides a range of suggested recommendations on how to address the challenges arising from changing demographics, community expectations and regulatory environments for emergency management.
D	Disaster Response and Contingency Planning Guide	DRCPG	Public	Disaster response and contingency planning is a management tool that helps to ensure organizational readiness and that adequate arrangements are made in anticipation of an emergency. Thoughtful execution of planning can help to ensure that the resource needs for any type or size of disaster, no matter where or when it strikes, are met quickly and effectively.
	Disaster Management Operational Strategy	DMOS	Public	The objective of the disaster management operational strategy is to strengthen disaster management tools and systems, analysis, planning, funding tools and cross-divisional integration practices to ensure most effective stewardship of donations so the organization can provide more disaster management services to more vulnerable people.
E	*None*			

6. EMPIRICAL EVIDENCES

In context of tasks involved in emergency management, the following discussion covers the empirical evidence collected from the participating case organizations. In response to an open-ended question about the task characteristics of emergency management, the interviewees from the participating case organizations identified several tasks in their discussions. Such tasks are identified by using NViVo 8.0 and are given below:

- **DDO–Case A** suggests (i) Train, teach and practice with individuals (ii) Facilitate communication and information flow (iii) Collect, collate, analyse and distribute information (iv) Maintain distribution lists and systems (v) Maintain information accuracy.

- **EMDO–Case A** suggests (i) Keep track of volunteers and equipment going out in emergencies (ii) Automated and quick distribution of information to the target audience (iii) Information dissemination; (iv) Training (v) Coordinate a state-level response to all hazards and recovery from any disaster (vi) Maintain and enhance equipment.

- **CEM–Case B** suggests (i) Drills; (ii) Asset management system (iii) Authentication (iv) Communication and sharing of information with other emergency management organizations (v) Resourcing and resource allocation.

- **TLSS–Case B** suggests (i) Keep records of things deploying to emergencies (ii) Keep up to date information about emergencies (iii) Incident management system (iv) Information sharing and dissemination.

- **RDEM–Case C** suggests (i) Respond to floods, earthquakes, tsunamis and rescues the victims (ii) Training (iii) Communication (iv) Access the system according to privileges granted.

- **DEMC–Case C** suggests (i) Managing incoming emergency related calls (ii) Issue emergency warnings (iii) Situational awareness (iv)Information dissemination (v) Resource management.

- **SLO–Case D** suggests (i) Development of global infrastructure and response capacities (ii) Field support (assessment and set-up of operations) (iii) Disaster response (iv) Disaster preparedness (v) Tagging and tracking of goods (vi) Management of emergency related information.

- **LD–Case E** suggests (i) Planning for emergency management (ii) Communication (iii) Authentication (iv) Use of an automated system that can replace humans or at least assists them during the emergencies (v) Track the goods through the system (vi) Inventory management.

In addition to the tasks identified by key informants, the participants of the case study were also invited to record their feedback on the significance of four tasks (such as AATI) suggested in this paper. Following discussion reports the feedback recorded from case study interviews along with the empirical findings on the significance of authentication, automation, tagging/tracking and information management.

6.1   Authentication: Empirical Findings

Empirical evidence related to authentication reveals that the interviewees from four out of five of the case study organizations supported this task as one of the key tasks in the emergency management life cycle. Only one case (that is, Case D) rated the significance of this task as 'moderate' in the emergency management life cycle. By analysing all the important facts related to this task, it was found that authentication is more critical during pre – (before) disaster or the planning phase than during or post – (after) the emergency. Table 3 depicts the significance of authentication in various stages of the emergency management life cycle.

Table 3: Significance of Authentication

Case	Key Informant	Before	During	After
A	DDO	X	-	-
	EMDO	X	X	X
B	CEM	X	X	X
	TLSS	X	X	X
C	RDEM	X	-	-
	DEMC	-	-	X
D	SLO	-	-	-
E	LD	X	-	-

Although, the findings given in Table 3 reflect the importance of authentication in various stages of emergency management, this research further processed the qualitative data gathered at the end of data collection phase and convert into quantitative results. This paper also supports the argument of Katharina and Sabine (2007), which states that the qualitative data can be converted into quantitative results for better understanding and for rigor empirical findings. Furthermore, Bazeley (2002) and Christina et al. (2002) also claimed that the mixed-method research has gained acceptability and becomes increasingly popular in empirical research.

Based on the above arguments, this paper calculated the relevance of the proposed tasks in emergency management. In order to do so, weighted average of such tasks is calculated based on the following formula (called, R1).

$$R1 = \text{Relevance} = \frac{\sum_{i=1}^{3} a_i x_i}{j \times k}$$

Where:

a_1 = Supported = 2

a_2 = Neutral = 1

a_3 = Not supported = 0

x_i = Number of case study participants for a particular response

j = Total number of case study participants

k = Maximum possible score for any response = 2

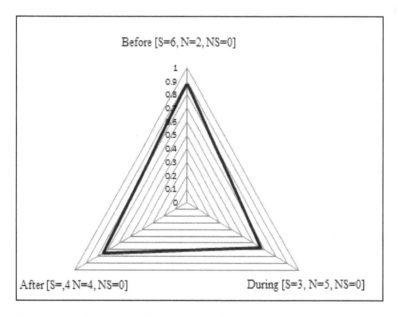

Figure 2: Relevance of Authentication

As depicted in Figure 2, authentication remains critical throughout the emergency management life cycle. In short, ensuring a rigorous authentication system could certainly minimize the likelihood of a potential emergency situation, such as terrorist attack.

In Figure 2 to 6, "S" represents the number of participants who supported an argument, "N" represents Neutral and "NS" represents Not Supported.

6.2 Automation: Empirical Findings

A key argument in support of this task is the fact that during emergencies, human performance does not remain consistent. Extreme climatic conditions and an unfavourable working environment are considered as major factors in creating this inconsistency. Therefore, control systems are highly desirable in emergency management, as they can perform consistently even in unfavourable working conditions. The empirical evidence shows that automation is more important during an emergency than it is before or after an emergency situation. Table 4 highlights the importance of automation at various stages of the emergency management.

Table 4: Significance of Automation

Case	Key Informant	Before	During	After
A	DDO	-	X	-
A	EMDO	-	X	-
B	CEM	-	X	-
B	TLSS	X	X	X
C	RDEM	X	X	X
C	DEMC	X	X	X
D	SLO	-	X	-
E	LD	-	X	-

It is important to note that all participants of this case study supported this task especially during emergencies. Key argument in favour of this task is the fact that humans are unable to work consistently and efficiently during unfavourable working conditions of emergencies. Thus, a technology that could assist humans during emergencies is very well supported.

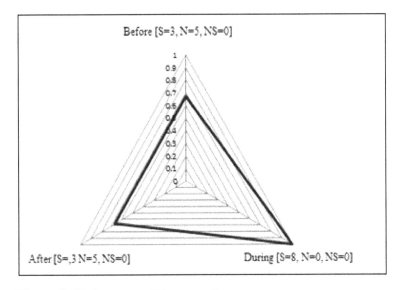

Figure 3: Relevance of Automation

6.3   Tagging/Tracking: Empirical Findings

It is interesting to note that, through the data collected from the key informants, this task remains critical throughout the emergency management life cycle. Table 5 and Figure 4 summarize the significance of this task and its relevance during various stages of emergency management.

Table 5: Significance of Tagging/Tracking

Case	Key Informant	Before	During	After
A	DDO	X	X	X
A	EMDO	X	X	X
B	CEM	X	X	X
B	TLSS	X	X	X
C	RDEM	-	X	X
C	DEMC	X	X	X
D	SLO	X	X	-
E	LD	X	X	X

Figure 4 summarizes the number of case study participants that supported the significance of tagging/tracking and the overall relevance of this task is also presented in Figure 4 below:

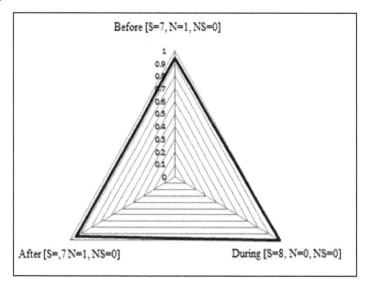

Figure 4: Relevance of tagging/tracking

Overall, this task consists of two sub-tasks: first, tagging of humans or other objects, and second, use of tags or marks for tracking them. During the case study interviews, tagging/tracking is reported as a very important task in emergency management with a special emphasize during an emergency and it was related to the better management of humans and objects in the emergency management life cycle.

6.4   Information Management: Empirical Findings

Information management is considered as the backbone of, and remains critical throughout the emergency management life cycle. It is a task that connects all the other tasks and operations together. Furthermore, the empirical evidence collected from the participating case organizations reveals that information management plays an important role throughout the emergency management life cycle. Table 6 highlights the significance of this task in various stages of the emergency management life cycle.

Table 6: Significance of Information Management

Case	Key Informant	Before	During	After
A	DDO	X	X	X
A	EMDO	X	X	X
B	CEM	X	X	X
B	TLSS	X	X	X
C	RDEM	X	X	X
C	DEMC	X	X	X
D	SLO	X	X	-
E	LD	X	X	X

In addition to the key informants, Figure 5 depicts the number of case study participants that supported information management as a key activity, along with its relevance in various stages of the emergency management life cycle.

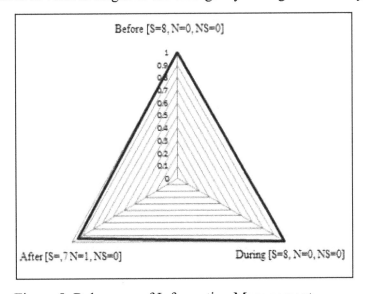

Figure 5: Relevance of Information Management

Data shown in figure 5 corroborates the initial claim made by this research. It is evident that information management is one of the most important tasks in emergency management and use of technology that can assist in conducting this task are more likely to be welcomed by the emergency management organizations.

7. RELEVANCE OF AATI

The above sections reported the empirical evidence collected from the participating case organizations and are further analysed and used to portray the significance of AATI before, during and after an emergency situation. Based on the number of participants who supported AATI, the overall relevance of each of the four tasks is calculated across the entire emergency management life cycle and is shown in Figure 6 below:

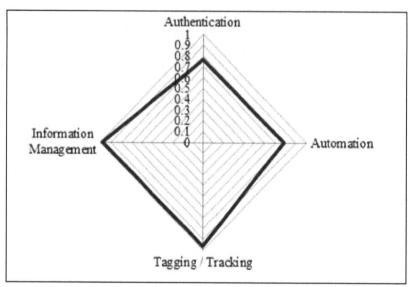

Figure 6: Relevance of AATI

The empirical findings reported in Figure 6 reveals that in the context of technological adoption, information management is the most important task requirement. After this, tagging/tracking is considered as the next most important task; automation is considered as of moderate importance and authentication as the least important task in emergency management.

8. JUSTIFICATION OF OTHER TASKS

In addition to the support of AATI as key characteristics of emergency management, representative from first three cases (that is, case A, B and C) suggested that 'training' is another important task of the emergency management process (see Table 7 below). In order to understand the importance of training in emergency management, it is worthy to understand what 'training' actually means.

According to the definition at:

http://www.businessdictionary.com/definition/training.html, training can be described as:

"Organized activity aimed at imparting information and/or instructions to improve the recipient's performance or to help him/her attain a required level of knowledge or skill".

In addition to the definition of training, Perry and Lindell (2003) described the role of training in the emergency management process. According to them, education and drills are key components of pre-emergency phase. Education in emergency management covers the preparation of emergency plans and involves communication amongst several emergency management personnel and organizations. On the other hand, drills can be viewed as the settings where problems are expected and conflicts can be resolved. These are the exercises that are performed in settings similar to actual emergency situations. Thus, the training process represents two aspects: (a) the transfer of information; and (b) drills/exercises/ simulations. During the interviews, it was perceived that the word 'training' was used to refer to both aspects (transfer of information and drills). During the interviews, it was perceived that the word 'training' was used to refer to both aspects ('transfer of information' and 'drills').

The following is a discussion of the two aspects of training and their associations with AATI in the perspective of technological use in emergency management.

Training as Transfer of Information: Training can be conducted in order to transfer information (knowledge). It also involves the management of information by the trainer as well as by the recipient. This aspect of training is generally used for emergency planning (Perry and Lindell, 2003). It ensures that the required information is available at the time of emergency. Furthermore, this aspect of training bridges the communication gap between several emergency management individuals and agencies that are working during emergencies. The role of technology in this aspect of training is to facilitate the process of the proper distribution and management of information. Thus, this aspect has already been covered under the broad category of information management and, then, this aspect of training did not satisfy the requirements to be considered an independent activity of emergency management.

Training as 'Drill' / 'Exercise' / 'Simulation': The other aspect of training covers the activities ('drills' / 'exercises' / 'simulations') that are performed in settings similar to a real emergency situation. This includes the simultaneous and comprehensive test of emergency plans, staffing levels, procedures, facilities, equipment and materials (Perry and Lindell, 2003).

According to Simpson (2002), there are a few differences between emergency management drill and the real emergency, such as:

- Drills/exercises are planned whereas most of the emergencies are unexpected;

- Drill/exercises are performed on a smaller scale as compared to real emergencies;

Unlike real emergencies, drills/exercises are performed under a controlled environment.

Other than the above-mentioned differences, comprehensive drills / exercises are the same as real emergencies; therefore, they go through all the phases and conduct all the activities (regardless of the scale) of the emergency management life cycle.

Based on the above discussion, it is evident that this aspect (drills / exercises) of training does not need to be declared an independent activity as all its requirements can be placed under the existing emergency management activities of authentication, automation, tagging/tracking and information management.

Although this research agrees that training is an important activity of emergency management, from the perspective of technological adoption in emergency management, all the underlying functions of the training process are covered under the broader categories of AATI.

9. DISCUSSION AND CONCLUSION

The early sections of this paper provided a comprehensive discussion on important emergency management studies. In addition to the discussion presented above, this paper agrees with the existing body of literature on the description of emergency management in terms of several phases or stages.

However, in the context of technological adoption, this research also highlights the following shortcomings in the existing literature (see Section 2 for more details):

- Existing emergency management models lack in uniformity in a number of the phases used to represent the emergency management life cycle.

- The concept of 'phases' or 'stages' of the emergency management process does not assist in evaluating the feasibility of technology for emergency management.

- Technology is used to perform a particular task, such as tracking of objects, information dissemination and authentication, not to perform a particular phase.

Thus, in order to overcome the above shortcomings, this paper identified the task characteristics of the emergency management process. Overall, these tasks are not only supported in the relevant literature (see Section 1) but their significance is also verified by the participants of multiple case studies (see Section 5). These tasks are further used as task characteristics in the conceptual model that has its roots in TTF (see Section 4). It is anticipated that the conceptual model presented in this paper could be used as a criterion to evaluate the potential of ubiquitous technologies before their actual deployment in emergency management. As a result of the above discussion, this paper concludes that: (i) from the perspective of technological adoption authentication, automation, tagging / tracking and information are the key tasks of the emergency management life cycle (ii) from the perspective of the adoption of ubiquitous technologies, information management and tagging / tracking are the most important tasks. Authentication is next in terms of importance and automation is the least important task (iii) the potential of a technology should be evaluated against its ability to perform the task characteristics (AATI) of emergency management and (iv) a technology that better supports the task characteristics could serve well in emergency management.

Table 7: Empirical Findings on the Significance of AATI

Case	Task Characteristics of Emergency Management												AATI as Key tasks in Emergency Management			Other tasks in Emergency Management
	Authentication			Automation			Tagging /tracking			Information Management						
	S	N	NS	S	N	NS	S	N	NS	S	N	NS	S	N	NS	
A	✓			✓			✓			✓			✓			Training
B	✓				✓		✓			✓			✓			Drills/ training
C	✓			✓			✓			✓			✓			Training
D		✓			✓		✓			✓			✓			None
E	✓			✓			✓			✓			✓			None

Legend: S: Supported, N: Neutral, NS: Not Supported

REFERENCES

ADPC. (2000). Community Based Disaster Management (CBDM): Trainers Guide Module 4: Disaster Management. *Asian Disaster Preparedness Center (ADPC) Bangkok, Thailand.*

Alfonso, G.-H., and Suzanne, S. (2008). Crisis Communications Management on the Web: How Internet-Based Technologies are Changing the Way Public Relations Professionals Handle Business Crises. *Journal of Contingencies and Crisis Management, 16*(3), 143-153. doi: 10.1111/j.1468-5973.2008.00543.x

Atmanand. (2003). Insurance and Disaster Management: The Indian Context. *Disaster Prevention and Management, 12*(4), 286-304.

Barbara, L. P. (2008). Identifying and Tracking Disaster Victims: State-of-the-Art Technology Review. *The Journal of Health Promotion and Maintenance, 31*(1), 23-34. doi: 10.1097/01.FCH.0000304065.40571.3b

Bazeley, P. (2002, April 10). *Issues in Mixing Qualitative and Quantitative Approaches to Research.* Paper presented at the 1st International Conference - Qualitative Research in Marketing and Management, University of Economics and Business Administration, Vienna.

Carver, L., and Turoff, M. (2007). Human-computer interaction: the human and computer as a team in emergency management information systems. *Communications of the ACM - Emergency response information systems: emerging trends and technologies, 50*(3).

Celik, S., and Corbacioglu, S. (2010). Role of information in collective action in dynamic disaster environments. *Disasters, 34*(1), 18. doi: 10.1111/j.0361-3666.2009.01118.x

Chainey, S., and Ratcliffe, J. (2005). *GIS and Crime Mapping*. Chichester, UK: John Wiley and Sons.

Chan, C. T., Killeen, J., Griswold, W., and Lenert, L. (2004). Information Technology and Emergency Medical Care During Disasters. *Academic Emergency Medicine, 11*(11), 1229-1236.

Christina, M. G., and Greg, J. D. (2002). *Lessons Learned: Integrating Qualitative and Quantitative Methods in the Study of the Family*. Duke University. Durham.

Cutter, S. L., Emrich, C. T., Adams, B. J., Huyck, C. K., and Eguchi, R. T. (2007). *New information technologies in emergency management'*. Washington, DC.: International City/County Management Association.

Davies, N., and Gellersen, H.-W. (2002). Beyond Prototypes: Challenges in Deploying Ubiquitous Systems. *IEEE Pervasive Computing, 1*(1), 26 - 35.

Fry, A. E., and Lenert, A. L. (2005). *MASCAL: RFID Tracking of Patients, Staff and Equipment to Enhance Hospital Response to Mass Casualty Events*. Paper presented at the AMIA Annual Symposium Proceedings, Washington, D.C.

Fry, W. L., and Slocum, W. J. (1984). Technology, Structure, and Workgroup Effectiveness: A Test of a Contingency Model. The Academy of Management Journal. *The Academy of Management Journal, 27*(2), 221-246.

Goodhue, L. D. (1995). Understanding User Evaluations of Information Systems *Management Science, 41*(12), 1827-1844

Goodhue, L. D., and Thompson, L. R. (1995). Task-Technology Fit and Individual Performance. *MIS Quarterly, 19*(2), 213-236.

Gunes, A. E., and Kovel, J. B. (2000). Using GIS in Emergency Management Operations. *Urban Planing and Developement, 126*(3), 136-149

Hackos, J. T., and Redish, J. C. (1998). *User and Task Analysis for Interface Design*. New York: Wiley Computer Publishing.

Haddow, D. G., Bullock, A. J., and Coppola, P. D. (2008). *Introduction to Emergency Management*. Burlington, USA: Elsevier.

Johnson, R. (2000). GIS Technology for Disasters and Emergency Management *An ESRI White Pape*. New York, USA: ESRI.

José, H.-V., Pérez, N., Ukkusuri, S., Wachtendorf, T., and Brown, B. (2007). Emergency Logistics Issues Affecting the Response to Katrina: A Synthesis and Preliminary Suggestions for Improvement *Transportation Research Record: Journal of the Transportation Research Board, 2022*, 76-82. doi: 10.3141/2022-09

Katharina, S., and Sabine, K. (2007). From Words to Numbers: How to Transform Qualitative Data into Meaningful Quantitative Results. *Schmalenbach Business Review, 59*. http://ssrn.com/abstract=960677

Kelly, C. (1999). Simplifying Disasters: Developing a Model for Complex Non-Linear Events *Australian Journal of Emergency Management, 14*(1), 25-27.

Kho, A., Henderson, L. E., Dressler, D. D., and Kripalani, S. (2006). Use of Handheld Computers in Medical Education. *Journal of General Internal Medicine, 21*(5), 531-537. doi: 10.1111/j.1525-1497.2006.00444.x

Killeen, P. J., Chan, C. T., Buono, C., Griswold, G. W., and Lenert, A. L. (2006). *A Wireless First Responder Handheld Device for Rapid Triage, Patient Assessment and Documentation during Mass Casualty Incidents.* Paper presented at the AMIA 2006 Symposium Proceedings, Washington, DC.

Kimberly, C. (2003). Disaster preparedness in Virginia Hospital Center-Arlington after Sept 11, 2001. *Disaster Management and Response, 1*(3), 80-86.

Kumar, R., and Chatterjee, R. (2005). *Shaping Ubiquity for the Developing World.* Paper presented at the International Telecommunications Union (ITU) Workshop on Ubiquitous Network Societies, Geneva, Switzerland.

Lee, J., and Bui, T. (2000, January 4-7). *A Template-based Methodology for Disaster Management Information Systems.* Paper presented at the 33rd Hawaii International Conference on System Sciences Hawaii.

Loebbecke, C., and Palmer, J. (2006). RFID's Potential in the Fashion Industry: A Case Analysis.

Lu, Y.-C., Xiao, Y., Sears, A., and Jacko, J. A. (2005). A review and a framework of handheld computer adoption in healthcare. *International Journal of Medical Informatics, 74*(5), 409-422. doi: 10.1016/j.ijmedinf.2005.03.001

Manitoba-Health-Disaster-Management. (2002). Disaster Management Model for the Health Sector: Guideline for Program Development.

Mansouriana, A., Rajabifardb, A., Zoeja, M. J. V., and Williamson, I. (2006). Using SDI and Web-Based System to Facilitate Disaster Management. *Computers & Geosciences 32 (2006) 303–315, 32*(3), 303-315 doi: 10.1016/j.cageo.2005.06.017

Michael, K., and McCathie, L. (2005, July 11-13). *The Pros and Cons of RFID in Supply Chain Management.* Paper presented at the International Conference on Mobile Business (ICMB'05) 2005 Sydney, Australia.

Perry, W. R., and Lindell, K. M. (2003). Preparedness for Emergency Response: Guidelines for the Emergency Planning Process. *Disasters, 27* (4), 336-560.

Pine, C. J. (2007). *Technology in Emergency Management.* Hoboken, NJ: John Wiley and Sons.

Quarantelli, E. L. (1988). Disaster Crisis Management: A Summary of Research Findings *Journal of Management Studies, 25*(4), 373-385.

Quarantelli, E. L. (1997). Ten Criteria for Evaluating the Management of Community Disasters. *Disasters, 21*(1), 1-56.

Richardson, B. (1994). Socio-Technical Disasters: Profile and Prevalence. *Disaster Prevention and Management, 3*(4), 41 - 69. doi: 10.1108/09653569410076766

Richardson, B. (1994). Socio-Technical Disasters: Profile and Prevalence. *Disaster Prevention and Management, 3*(4), 41-69.

Sara, M. L. (2003). GIS and health care. *Annual Review of Public Health, 24,* 25-42. doi: 10.1146/annurev.publhealth.24.012902.141012

Schulz, D., Burgard, W., Fox, D., and Cremers, B. A. (2001, December 8-14). *Tracking Multiple Moving Objects with a Mobile Robot* Paper presented at the IEEE Computer Society Conference on Computer Vision and Pattern Recognition (CVPR'01) Hawaii, USA.

Senior, A., and Copley, R. (2008). Developing a new system for recording and managing information during an emergency to aid decision making. *Journal of Business Continuity and Emergency Planning., 2*(3), 267-280.

Shaluf, I. M., Ahmadun, F. R., and Mustapha, S. (2003). Technological Disaster's Criteria and Models. *Disaster Prevention and Management, 12*(4), 305-311.

Shaluf, M. I., Ahmadun, R. F., and Mustapha, S. A. (2003). Technological Disaster's Criteria and Models. *Disaster Prevention and Management, 12*(4), 305-311.

Shannon, T., Feied, C., Smith, M., Handler, J., and Gillam, M. (2006). Wireless handheld computers and voluntary utilization of computerized prescribing systems in the emergency department. *The Journal of Emergency Medicine, 31*(3), 309-315.

Sharma, A., Citurs, A., and Konsynski, B. (2007, January 7-10). *Strategic and Institutional Perspectives in the Adoption and Early Integration of Radio Frequency Identification (RFID)*. Paper presented at the Proceedings of the 40th Hawaii International Conference on System Sciences - 2007, Hawaii, USA

Sheridan, B. T. (2002). *Humans and Automation: System Design and Research Issues* New York, USA: John Wiley & Sons, Inc. .

Simpson, M. D. (2002). Earthquake Drills and Simulations in Community-based Training and Preparedness Programmes. *Disasters, 26*(1), 55-69.

Toft, and Reynolds, S. (1994). Learning from Disasters. *Butterworth-Heinemann*.

Toft, B., and Reynolds, S. (1994). *Learning from Disasters*. Oxford: Butterworth-Heinemann.

Tomasinia, R. M., and Wassenhoveb, L. N. V. (2009). From preparedness to partnerships: case study research on humanitarian logistics. *International Transactions in Operational Research, 16*(5), 549-559.

Tran, T., Yousaf , F. Z., and Wietfeld, C. (2010). RFID Based Secure Mobile Communication Framework for Emergency Response Management *IEEE Wireless Communications and Networking Conference (WCNC)* (pp. 1-6). Sydney, NSW.

Troy, D. A., Carson, A., Vanderbeek, J., and Hutton, A. (2008). Enhancing community-based disaster preparedness with information technology. *Disasters, 32*(1), 149-165. doi: 10.1111/j.1467-7717.2007.01032.x

Turner, B. A. (1976). The Organizational and Interorganizational Development of Disasters. *Administrative Science Quarterly, 21*(3), 378-397.

Tuscaloosa. (2003). Tuscaloosa County Emergency Management Cycle.   Retrieved June 4, 2007, from http://www.tuscoema.org/cycle.html

Wang, S., Chen, W., Ong, C., Liu, L., and Chuang, Y. (2006). RFID Application in Hospitals: A Case Study on a Demonstration RFID Project in a Taiwan Hospital. *Volume: 8, On page(s): 184a- 184a.*

Weiser, M. (1991). The computer for the 21st century. . *Scientific American, 265*(3), 94-104.

Wells, D. J., Sarker, S., Urbaczewski, A., and Sarker, S. (2003, January, 6-9). *Studying Customer Evaluations of Electronic Commerce Applications: A Review and Adaptation of the Task-Technology Fit Perspective.* Paper presented at the Proceedings of the 36th Hawaii International Conference on System Sciences Hawaii, USA.

Wilks, J., and Page, S. (2003). *Managing Tourist Health and Safety in the New Millennium.* Oxford: Elsevier.

Wybo, L. J., and Kowalski, M. K. (1998). Command Centers and Emergency Management Support. *Safety Science, 30*(1-2), 131-138. doi: 10.1016/S0925-7535(98)00041-1

Xiao, Y., Shen, X., Sun, B., and Cai, L. (2006). Security and Privacy in RFID and Applications in Telemedicine. *IEEE Communications Magazine, 44,* 64-72.

Xinping, S., Yuk, C. P., and Sheung, Y. M. (2007). *Theoretical Foundations and Strategies for RFID Adoption in Supply Chain Management Context*: Global Logistics.

Zlatanova, S., Oosterom, P., and Verbree, E. (2004a). *3D Technology for Improving Disaster Management: Geo-DBMS and Positioning.* Paper presented at the XXth ISPRS congress.

Zlatanova, S., Oosterom, P. V., and Verbree, E. (2004b). *3D Technology for Improving Disaster Management: Geo-DBMS and Positioning.* Paper presented at the XXth ISPRS congress.

10

THE IMPACT OF E-TICKETING TECHNIQUE ON CUSTOMER SATISFACTION: AN EMPIRICAL ANALYSIS

Mazen Kamal Qteishat
Haitham Hmoud Alshibly
Mohammad Atwah Al-ma'aitah
Albalqa Applied University, Amman, Jordan

ABSTRACT

Recently, internet technology is considered to be the most used information and communication technology by organizations: it can ease the process of transactions and reinforce the relation between companies and customers. This investigation empirically examines the impact of e-ticketing technique on customer satisfaction; a convenience sample of Jordanian airline passengers that had booked flights in the last 12 months through companies offering e-ticketing services was acquired. The findings indicate that customer satisfaction with e-ticketing services was influenced by all of the independent variables measured (Data security, Customer and Technical Support, and User-Friendliness) were noted to have significant impact on customer satisfaction with e-ticketing services.

Keywords: E-ticketing, Customer Technical Support, Infrastructure, Security, User-Friendliness

1. INTRODUCTION

The popularity of Internet technology has increased substantially over the course of the last several years (Lopez-Bonilla & Lopez-Bonilla, 2013). As a result, organizations have worked diligently to develop new methods for interfacing with customers. Central to this process has been the development of e-tickets (Borthick & Kiger, 2003). As noted by Tripathi, Reddy, Madria, Mohanty and Ghosh (2009), e-tickets can be used by a wide range of organizations to provide services including coupons for e-shopping, to tickets for entrance into a concert or sporting event.

Address for correspondence / Endereço para correspondência

Mazen Kamal Qteishat, Assistant Professor, Department of Business, Albalqa Applied University, P.O. Box 1705, Amman 11118, Jordan, E-mail:mazenqteishat@hotmail.com

Haitham Hmoud Alshibly, Associate Professor, Department of Business, Albalqa Applied University, P.O. Box, Amman 11118, Jordan,E-mail:mazenqteishat@hotmail.com

Mohammad Atwah Al-ma'aitah,Assistant Professor, Department of MIS, Albalqa Applied University, P.O. Box, Amman 11118, Jordan, E-mail:Z_maytah@yahoo.com

Although it is not fair to argue that e-tickets have become ubiquitous, it is evident that the proliferation of e-tickets represents a change in the way that traditional ticket purchasing occurs (Bukhari, Ghoneim, Dennis & Jamjoom, 2013). E-tickets appear to offer a number of advantages to organizations, including lower costs and increased operational efficiency (Boyer, Hallowell & Roth, 2002). As such, it is projected that the use of e-tickets will only continue to increase over time (Bukhari, et al., 2013).

Even though e-ticketing services appear to be the future of operations for many organizations seeking to streamline operations and improve customer service, research regarding e-ticketing and e-service indicates that these processes have not been without their challenges (Hallowell, 2001). Curbera, et al. (2002) contend that e-ticketing services, much like many internet and mobile applications, developed in an ad hoc manner. This has created a situation in which the function and utilization of e-tickets has not been actively integrated into the strategy of the organization (Curbera, et al., 2002). Other scholars examining the adoption of e-ticketing contend that a host of cognitive variables impact consumer decision-making, leading positive or negative perceptions regarding e-ticketing as a principle method for acquiring service within an organization (Sulaiman, Ng & Mohezar, 2008).

In addition, the cognitive elements of e-ticketing have become such an important issue of concern for organizations in recent years as efforts to expand e-ticketing progress (Lopez-Bonilla & Lopez-Bonilla, 2013). Specifically, the issue of customer satisfaction in e-ticketing has become a central issue of focus, prompting organizations to investigate the specific variables that shape customer outcomes when choosing e-ticketing options (Wei & Ozok, 2005). Using this as a foundation for investigation, the current research utilizes customer satisfaction as the dependent variable to assess what specific independent variables (customer technical support, infrastructure, data security and/or user-friendliness) shape customer satisfaction in decision-making when it comes to purchasing an e-ticket. By correlating independent variables with customer satisfaction, it will be possible to acquire a deeper understanding of how customer satisfaction is developed when it comes to e-ticket purchasing and use by consumers.

2. LITERATURE REVIEW

A review of the literature examining the definitions of e-ticketing that have been reported demonstrates efforts to explicate the full spectrum of e-ticketing for both the consumer and the organization. For instance, Alfawaer, Awni and Al-Zoubi (2011) define an e-ticket as "a paperless electronic document used for ticketing travelers, mainly in the commercial airline industry" (p. 848). Sorooshian, Onn and Yeen (2013) further define e-ticketing as "a procedure of keeping record of sales, usage tracking and accounting for a passenger's transport with no requirement for a paper 'value document'" (p. 63). This definition clearly indicates that the e-ticket includes more than just a paperless document for the passenger: rather the e-ticket represents an extensive architecture within the organization that provides a wealth of information about the consumer.

The definitions of e-tickets and e-ticketing provided in the literature clearly suggest that e-ticketing has a host of implications. Lubeck, Wittmann and Battistella (2012) are able to examine these issues by tracing the evolution of e-tickets and efforts by the organization to improve efficiency in ticketing operations. According to these authors, e-tickets have evolved to address concerns associated with "inefficiency in information management and control of operations" (p. 18). E-tickets, as noted by Lubeck and co-workers, require the creation of a comprehensive technological platform that controls almost every aspect of the customer relationship within the organization. As such, the roots of e-ticketing go much further than the interface with the customer.

3. THEORETICAL FRAMEWORK

Customer satisfaction with e-ticketing services was selected as the dependent variable for this investigation. A review of the literature regarding customer satisfaction with e-ticketing indicates that satisfaction has been measured through two components: customer satisfaction and customer retention. Patterns of loyalty in e-ticketing and e-service have been reviewed by Chang, Wang and Yang (2009). These authors argue that patterns of customer satisfaction in e-service are similar to those that develop in face-to-face transactions and interactions. Specifically, these authors assert that: "When perceived value is low, the customer will be inclined to switch to competing businesses in order to increase perceived value, thus contributing to a decline in loyalty" (p. 424). Satisfaction develops over time as a response to the way in which customers are treated by the organization.

In the context of e-ticketing, satisfaction is thus influenced by a wide range of variables focused on the quality of service provided to the customer. Bernardo, Llach, Marimon and Alonso-Almeida (2013) illustrate this point by noting the loyalty in e-services is shaped by services provided to customers before and after a sale, as well as the general environment in which the transaction takes place. If the environment meets customer expectations for security and support, loyalty with the customer will often be established, leading to the ability of the organization to retain the customer over the long-term. Thus, loyalty and customer retention are integrally related when it comes to the development of e-services (Enzmann & Schneider, 2005).

The relationship between loyalty and customer retention for e-services and e-ticketing appears to stem from commitment, trust, involvement of the organization, and the perceived value of the service provided (Chen, 2012). As such, companies offering e-ticketing services must carefully consider elements of customer support and service to build strong relationships with consumers. Noor and Azila (2012) argue that in order to achieve this outcome, companies offering any type of e-service must be able to build comprehensive relationships with customers. This insight effectively supports what Kolsaker, et al. (2004) note about the need for customer support and service in e-ticketing. Even though many organizations believe that customer service and support is not needed with e-ticketing, in actuality there is a definitive impetus to develop customer service and support that targets customer needs for e-ticketing to ensure the development of commitment and trust leading to increased loyalty and customer retention.

3.1 E-ticketing factors influencing customer satisfaction

Critical review of the literature suggests that E-ticketing Technique factors such as Customer Technical Support, Infrastructure, Security and User-Friendliness work together to shape the relationship with customer satisfactions.

3.1.1 Customer Technical Support

Evaluation of the factors which contribute to customer adoption of e-ticketing clearly indicates that customer and technical support are critical issues of concern (Buhalis, 2004). Lau, Kwek and Tan (2011) assert that customer perceptions of service quality will play a significant role in shaping decision-making for the individual to utilize e-ticketing services. As argued by these authors, customer perception influenced by the level of support provided to the customer, especially when problems arise in e-ticketing service. Sureshkumar and Palanivelu (2011) delve further into this issue arguing that perceptions of the customer regarding customer service have direct ramifications for customer behavior. If the customer believes that the organization will provide customer service and support through the purchase of e-tickets, customers will be more likely to purchase these products (Sureshkumar & Palanivelu, 2011).

Furthermore, the true impact of customer perceptions regarding customer service and technical support is illustrated by Haewoon (2007) who contends that many airlines have alienated customers as a result of a failure to provide customer support in e-ticketing services. Viewing e-ticketing as a panacea for reducing costs and increasing efficiency in operations, Haewoon argues that airlines quickly adopted e-ticketing without establishing protocols for customer and technical support. Research regarding this issue suggests that while many companies employing e-ticketing believe that this service should preclude the need for extensive customer service - thus reducing costs - in actuality, this is not the case (Kolsaker, Lee-Kelley & Choy, 2004). Kolsaker and co-workers report that many organizations have found that the implementation of e-ticketing often requires the development of targeted customer service practices that address specific customer needs related to e-ticketing and e-service. Without these supports in place, customers will view the e-ticketing process as cumbersome and will not gravitate to e-service to meet their needs (Kolsaker, et al., 2004).

3.1.2 Infrastructure

Infrastructure to support e-ticketing operations may also play a role in developing customer satisfaction for these services. As noted in the introduction of this investigation, e-ticketing services typically developed in an ad hoc manner within the organization (Curbera, et al., 2002). As a result, e-ticketing was not initially integrated with other operations, leading to problems when customers required additional service or support (Curbera, et al., 2002). Jakubauskas (2006) considers these issues, noting that e-ticketing systems have undergone notable changes since their inception. In order to ensure effective and efficient use of e-tickets, Jakubauskas maintains that organizations have had to establish network architectures to support e-ticketing services. These infrastructures have been essential to creating a comprehensive system that simultaneously addresses customer needs while creating the supports needed to streamline operations within the organization (Jakubauskas, 2006). Without the infrastructure to support e-ticketing, organizations would not be able to utilize these services to achieve cost reductions and enhanced customer satisfaction.

Moreover, the importance of infrastructure in the development of e-ticketing systems is further reviewed by Zambon, Etalle, Wieringa and Hartel (2011) who note the myriad of ways in which infrastructure impacts both customer and organizational outcomes. With regard to the implications of e-ticketing infrastructure for customers, Zambon and co-workers note the importance of availability and accuracy in service. The infrastructure used by the organization will have implications for the ability of the customer to use the system and to ensure accuracy when purchasing a ticket. For organizations, infrastructure can provide business continuity and offer the ability to minimize risks and improve operational functionality (Zambon, et al., 2011). Thus, when developing e-ticketing services, infrastructure issues must be carefully considered.

3.1.3 Data Security

Data security is also an issue of concern impacting consumer behavior and decision-making with regard to e-ticketing. Mut-Puigserver, Payeras-Capellà, Ferrer-Gomila, Vives-Guasch and Castellà-Roca (2012) consider the security concerns associated with e-ticketing, noting that security breaches remain a significant barrier for the adoption of e-ticketing services in many transportation organizations and agencies. The scope and extent of security issues related to e-ticketing is highlighted by Mut-Puigserver and co-workers who argue that "the use of ET systems enables various privacy abuses both in real-time and retrospect since the anonymity of users is not always guaranteed and, therefore, users can be traced and their profiles of usual movements can be created" (p. 926).

Smith and Smith (2012) further examine security issues that can arise in the use of e-ticketing services. As acknowledged by these authors, security issues have been reported with e-tickets as a result of efforts on the part of organizations to integrate e-services with other customer relationship management (CRM) programs. CRM programs have long been part of operations to track customer preferences and behaviors. The integration of e-ticketing with these systems has resulted in significant security issues utilization of CRM systems in this capacity has been shown to compromise these infrastructures (Smith & Smith, 2012). This problem appears to relate back to the ad hoc nature in which e-ticketing services have been established within the organization (Curbera, et al., 2002).

Security issues in online services including e-ticketing have been noted to be a significant problem for many consumers (Zhang, Prybutok & Huang, 2006). Yang and Jun (2008) argue that if customers perceive problems with security in e-services, they will be less likely to make purchases via the internet. Perceptions of security impact the level of trust for the consumer (Yang & Jun, 2008). If trust is not present in the relationship between the customer and the e-service provider, there is less likelihood that the consumer will conduct business with the organization (Yang & Jun, 2008). Zhang and co-workers further argue that security issues affect customer satisfaction with e-services, making it necessary for organizations to ensure that customer data is protected.

3.1.4 User Friendliness

E-ticketing services must also be user-friendly for the customer. Dekkers and Rietveld (2007) consider the issue of user-friendliness, noting that customers, depending on their willingness to use mobile technology, will view this issue differently. Specifically, these researchers examined the use of e-ticketing systems in the public transportation system of the Netherlands. Tracking usage patterns and customer preferences, Dekkers and Rietveld found that e-ticketing services were convenient for regular and semi-regular customers using the transportation system. These individuals found the e-ticketing system easy to use and navigate. For less regular users, the system was viewed as difficult to utilize, resulting in a decline of e-ticket use among this group.

Lei, Quintero and Pierre (2009) further review usage patterns of e-ticketing systems examining those that are integrated and those that require two different processes for use: authentication and payment. Analysis provided by these authors indicates that integrated e-ticketing systems that require fewer steps for customers were typically utilized more frequently, suggesting the need to streamline these systems in order to increase customer adoption. In short, system interfaces will influence customer adoption of e-ticketing to some degree. However, as reported by Dekkers and Rietveld (2007), user characteristics, including technological capabilities and frequency of system use, will also impact outcomes. According to the previous literature research, model-1 was developed and applied as the theoretical framework for understanding the impact of e-ticketing techniques as (independent variable) on customer satisfaction (dependant variable).

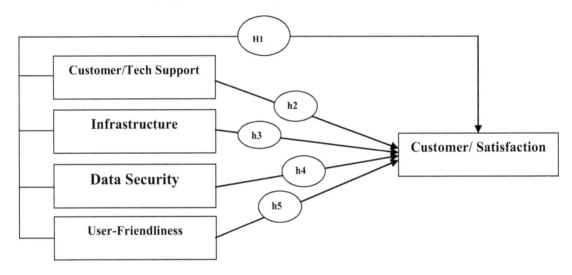

Model-1: e-ticketing technique on customer satisfaction

4. MAIN RESEARCH QUESTION

To what extent does the proposed model, and in particular the role of components: Customer Technical Support, Infrastructure, Security and User-Friendliness play in Customer Satisfaction?

4.1 Sub-research Questions

- Is there a significant effect of e-ticketing factors (customer/technical support) on customer satisfaction?
- Is there a significant effect of e-ticketing factors (infrastructure) on customer satisfaction?
- Is there a significant effect of e-ticketing factors (Data Security) on customer satisfaction?

Is there a significant effect of e-ticketing factors (User-Friendliness) on customer satisfaction?

5. THE RESEARCH METHODOLOGY

Population and Sample

The population for this investigation was drawn from a local group of airline customers that had utilized airline services that offer e-ticketing in the last 12 months. Customer names and addresses were obtained from marketing information collected by airlines. Customers on the list had agreed to have their personal information shared for marketing purposes. A total of 250 surveys were mailed to potential respondents for the survey. Of these surveys, 177 were completed and returned for a 71 percent response rate. Although respondents were initially identified for mailing of the surveys, return responses did not include any identifying information about the customer ensuring the ability of the researcher to protect the anonymity of respondents.

Table I: Demographic Characteristics

Percent	Frequency	Characteristics
		Gender
53.1	94	Male
46.9	83	Female
		Age
4.5	8	LESS THAN 20
70.1	124	29-20
15.2	27	30-39
10.2	18	40 AND OVER
		Education
7.8	14	HIGH SCHOOL
4.5	8	DEPLOMA
81.8	145	BA
5.9	10	POST GRADUTE
		Computer Literacy
89.8	159	Yes
10.2	18	No
		Internet Accessibility (Home)
75.7	134	Yes
24.3	43	No

In terms of demographic composition of the respondents Table 1 shows that, 53.1 percent (n = 94) were male with the remaining 46.9 percent (n = 83) female. Additionally, 4.5 percent (n = 8) of the respondents were under the age of 20, 70.1 percent (n = 124) were between the ages of 20 and 29, 15.32 percent were between the ages of 30 and 39 (n = 27), and 10.2 percent were over the age of 40 (n = 18). Of those returning surveys, 7.8 percent (n = 14) had some high school education while 4.5 Percent (n = 8) had a high school diploma, 81.8 percent had a Bachelors Degree (n = 145), and 5.9 percent had a post-graduate degree (n = 10). A majority of respondents reported computer literacy (89.9 percent, n = 159) and internet accessibility in the home (75.7 percent, n = 134).

5.2 Data Collection and Analysis

For the purpose of this investigation, reliability coefficients of scales (Cronbach's Alpha), multiple regression modeling and simple regression was used to evaluate the relationships between variables. The questionnaire used for the research was designed based on an analysis of the empirical literature - see table-2. Pilot-testing was utilized on a small sample of airline passengers that had used e-ticketing services in the past three months. Based on the feedback provided by these participants, the questions were revised. Components of e-ticketing on customer satisfaction were measured using a 5-point Likert scale with 5 = strongly agree and 1 = strongly disagree. Respondents were asked to evaluate their reaction to each of the assessments, identifying areas for agreement and disagreement.

The reliability for the instrument was established using Cronbach's alpha, which is a measure of the internal consistency of the instrument. Cronbach's alpha estimates the true score variance captured by the items in the scale by comparing the sum of the item variance with the variance of the sum of the scale (Hill & Lewicki, 2006, p. 461). A Cronbach's alpha result of 0.70 or higher is generally considered to show adequate reliability for instruments used to gather psychometric data (Dunn-Ranking, 2004, p. 118). The analysis of the data with Cronbach's alpha indicated that the instrument was reliable for each of the five scales: customer and technical support, infrastructure, data security, user-friendliness and customer satisfaction. Table 2 shows Cronbach's alpha for the instrument scales.

Table II: Reliability coefficients of scales (Cronbach's Alpha)

Scales	Questionnaire instrument	Cronbach Alpha	N. of Items
Customer Technical Support	1. E-ticketing provides good personal sales assistance by e-mail or SMS. 2. E-ticketing provides FAQ (frequently asked questions and answers) links to the relevant information. 3. E-ticketing technical support terms and conditions of sales are easy to find through the web. 4. E-ticketing provides an easy access to the company's policy for shipping and handling of their products. 5. E-ticketing provides full details of pricing and taxes for product and service.	0.791	5
Infrastructure	6. E-ticketing infrastructure allows information to be readily accessible to you. 7. E-ticketing Infrastructure helps new users with an easy access to all applications. 8. E-ticketing Infrastructure can be integrated with other e-things. 9. E-ticketing Infrastructure flexibly adjusts to new job demands 10. E-ticketing Infrastructure provides sufficient information. 11. I'm satisfied with the accuracy that E-ticketing website provides.	0.837	6
Data security	12. E-ticketing Websites check online customers' identity for security purposes 13. E-ticketing websites ensure that information about electronic transactions is protected from being altered or destroyed. 14. I felt secure in providing personal information for purchasing airline tickets online 15. Airline companies have adequate website security features. 16. Airline companies protect my privacy when purchasing tickets online. 17. Airline companies websites provide high protection on my credit card information	0.866	6
User-Friendliness	18. I find it easy to get E-ticketing Websites to do what I want them to do 19. It is easy for me to become skilful at using E-ticketing Websites. 20. Using E-ticketing Websites enables me to accomplish my purchasing. 21. I find E-ticketing Websites easy to use. 22. Learning to operate E-ticketing Websites is easy for me.	0.877	5
Customer Satisfaction	23. Overall, as a customer, are you satisfied with this website? 24. How effective is this websites in supporting your purchase from your perspective as a customer? 25. How satisfied are you with the technical quality of these websites? 26. How satisfied are you with the information provided through these websites? 27. How satisfied are you with the quality of the service available through these websites? 28. How satisfied are you with the way these websites adjust to your particular needs?	0.901	6

Scoring for the questionnaire included an overall review of the total scores for all independent variables (customer and technical support, infrastructure, data security and user-friendliness). Data is provided by Table 2 which supports the main hypothesis:

H1: Is there a significant effect of e-ticketing factors on customer satisfaction?

Table III: E-Ticketing Technique and Customer Satisfaction

E-Ticketing Factors	B	Beta	t-value	Sig	R^2	Adjusted R^2	F	Sig	hypothesis
E-Ticketing Factors	.637	.712	13.409	.000	.763	.577	121.2	.000	Accepted

To answer the main research question "to what extent does the proposed model, and in particular the role of components: Customer Technical Support, Infrastructure, Security and User-Friendliness, play in Customer Satisfaction?" Multiple linear regression analysis was used to explore the impact of the independent variables (customer and technical support, infrastructure, data security and user-friendliness) on the dependent variable customer satisfaction. The total R^2 value includes a unique results support and accepting hypotheses H1 with ($R^2 = .763$) shown in Table 3, which indicates that the hypothesis was accepted.

The remainder of the tables (Tables 4, 5, 6 and 7) focus on the sub-hypotheses examining each of the independent variables separately using simple linear regression to understand their influence on the dependent variable: customer satisfaction.

h2: Is there a significant effect of e-ticketing factors (customer technical support) on customer satisfaction?

Table IV: Customer Tech Support and Customer Satisfaction

E-Ticketing Factors	B	Beta	t-value	Sig	R 2	Adjusted R2	F	Sig	hypothesis
Customer Tech Support	.431	.474	7.125	.000	.474	.220	50.76	.000	Accepted

The results from the single linear regression analysis as shown in Table 4 provide support for accepting hypotheses h2. The coefficient of determination ($R^2 = .758$) indicates that a strong effect exists between Customers/Tech Support and Customer Satisfaction.

h3: Is there a significant effect of e-ticketing factors (infrastructure) on customer satisfaction?

TableV: Infrastructure and Customer Satisfaction

E-Ticketing Factors	B	Beta	t-value	Sig	R 2	Adjusted R2	F	Sig	hypothesis
Infrastructure	.486	.553	8.789	.000	.306	.302	77.2	.000	Accepted

The results from the single linear regression, as shown in Table 5, provide support for accepting hypotheses h3 by showing that there is a positive correlation between the independent variable of Infrastructure and the dependent variable of Customer Satisfaction, which indicates that Infrastructure accounts for a larger amount of the variance in customer satisfaction with R = .306.

h4: Is there a significant effect of e-ticketing factors (data security) on customer satisfaction?

TableVI: Data Security and Customer Satisfaction

E-Ticketing Factors	B	Beta	t-value	Sig	R 2	Adjusted R2	F	Sig	hypothesis

Data Security	.637	.712	13.409	.000	.507	.504	179.8	.000	Accepted

The results from the single linear regression, as shown in Table 5, provide support for accepting hypotheses h4 by showing that there is a positive correlation between the independent variable of data security and the dependent variable of Customer Satisfaction, which indicates that Infrastructure accounts for a larger amount of the variance in customer satisfaction with R = .507.

h5: Is there a significant effect of e-ticketing factors (user-friendliness) on customer satisfaction?

Table VII: Customer Satisfaction and Data Security

E-Ticketing Factors	B	Beta	t-value	Sig	R 2	Adjusted R2	F	Sig	hypothesis
User-Friendliness	.487	.665	11.792	.000	.443	.440	139.056	.000	Accepted

The results from the single linear regression, as shown in Table 6, provide support for accepting hypotheses h5 by showing that there is a positive correlation between the independent variable of user-friendliness and the dependent variable of Customer Satisfaction, which indicates that Infrastructure accounts for a larger amount of the variance in customer satisfaction with R^2 = .443.

6.   RESULTS AND DISCUSSION

Model testing is necessary to address the main research question of the study, which is: To what extent does the proposed model, and in particular the role of components: Customer/Technical Support, Infrastructure, Security and User-Friendliness play in Customer Satisfaction? Examining the adjusted R^2 value (0.763) for the main hypothesis (Table 3), it is evident that the four independent variables evaluated in this investigation account for over 76 percent of the variance in customer satisfaction with e-ticketing. Statistical analysis using a significance level of $p < 0.05$ employed when looking at each independent variable separately supports the significance of each variable in the development of customer satisfaction as it relates to e-ticketing. Thus, the research supports the inclusion of customer and technical support, infrastructure, data security and user-friendliness as integral components of e-ticketing services to ensure that customer satisfaction is achieved.

Based on the data obtained for this investigation, it becomes evident that there is an impetus for organizations using e-ticketing services to carefully consider each of the independent variables noted in a comprehensive platform for e-ticketing. Each of the variables contributes significantly to the development of customer satisfaction. However, it is evident that data security, customer and technical support, and user-friendliness represent the most significant variables for consideration. Infrastructure is clearly important but may not be as evident to the customer utilizing an e-ticketing system. Infrastructure for e-ticketing appears to support the other functions of security, customer service, and user-friendliness (Zambon, et al., 2011; Jakubauskas, 2006).

The results in conjunction with the literature reviewed on the topic suggest that the development of an integrated system is thus imperative for the success of e-ticketing systems. When information technology architecture is developed and integrated as part of the organization's system for customer service, the end result is a fully functioning system that can provide elements of data security, customer and technical support as well as user-friendliness (Curbera, et al., 2002). As in the literature, the need for creating a comprehensive and integrated infrastructure for the development of e-ticketing systems is emphasized (Curbera, et al., 2002).

7. IMPLICATIONS

The implications of the research lie in the recognition of the need for organizations to consider a wide range of variables when developing e-ticketing services for customers. Although ad hoc systems have been widely used in the past, it is evident that in order to achieve high levels of customer satisfaction, integrated systems that offer a number of different supports for the end user are needed (Curbera, et al., 2002). When developing e-ticketing services, organizations must be aware of the need for: customer service (Sureshkumar & Palanivelu, 2011), data security (Mut-Puigserver, et al., 2012), and the development of systems that are easy to use from the point of view of the customer (Lei, et al., 2009). The development of user-friendliness in e-ticketing can be tricky and may require the organization to garner an integral understanding of its customer base (Dekkers & Rietveld, 2007).

The implications of this research are quite significant as they require the organization to comprehensively and holistically develop and implement e-ticketing services. By addressing e-ticketing in this manner, organizations will be able to effectively cover most of the pertinent concerns that will impact customer satisfaction with e-ticketing. Although the process is one that will require the organization to engage in more extensive planning and development for e-ticketing, it is also one that should improve the ability of the organization to establish effective and efficient e-ticketing services without the need for continual change and improvement to the systems over time.

8. CONCLUSION

Customer satisfaction in e-ticketing is a complex phenomenon that is shaped by a wide range of variables including customer technical support, infrastructure, data security and user-friendliness. Understanding these issues is critical for organizations to create e-ticketing systems that initially meet customer needs and generate a high level of satisfaction. E-ticketing systems that meet these requirements will provide the organization with satisfied customers who will express their satisfaction through loyalty and by remaining with the organization over the long-term. High levels of customer retention will form the foundation to maintaining the organization's bottom line. Although creating e-ticketing systems that achieve customer satisfaction is a significant undertaking for the organization, addressing the key issues noted in this investigation should facilitate the ability of the organization to create an e-ticket system that allows for building customer satisfaction, loyalty and retention.

REFERENCES

Alfawaer, Z.M., Awni, M., & Al-Zoubi, S. (2011). Mobile e-ticketing reservation system for Amman International Stadium in Jordan. *International Journal of Academic Research, 3*(1), 848-852.

Bernardo, M., Llach, J., Marimon, F., & Alonso-Almeida, M.M. (2013). The balance of the impact of quality and recovery on satisfaction: The case of e-travel. *Total Quality Management & Business Excellence, 24*(11/12), 1390-1404.

Borthick, A.F., & Kiger, J.E. (2003). Designing audit procedures when evidence is electronic: The case of e-ticket travel revenue. *Issues in Accounting Education, 18*(3), 275-290.

Boyer, K.K., Hallowell, R., & Roth, A.V. (2002). E-services: Operating strategy—A case study and a method for analyzing operational benefits. *Journal of Operations Management, 20*, 175-188.

Buhalis, D. (2004). eAirlines: Strategic and tactical use of ICTs in the airline industry. *Information & Management, 41*(7), 805-825.

Bukhari, S.M.F., Ghoneim, A., Dennis, C., & Jamjoom, B. (2013). The antecedents of travellers' e-satisfaction and intention to buy airline tickets online: A conceptual model. *Journal of Enterprise Information Management, 26*(6), 624-641.

Chang, H.H., Wang, Y., & Yang, W. (2009). The impact of e-service quality, customer satisfaction and loyalty on e-marketing: Moderating effect of perceived value. *Total Quality Management & Business Excellence, 20*(4), 423-443.

Chen, S. (2012). The customer satisfaction-loyalty relation in an interactive e-service setting: The mediators. *Journal of Retailing & Consumer Services, 19*(2), 202-210.

Curbera, F., Duftler, M., Khalaf, W., Nagy, W., Mukhi, N., & Weerawarana, S. (2002). Unraveling the web services web: An introduction to SOAP, WSDL and UDDI. *IEEE Internet Computing, 3*(4), 86-93.

Dekkers, J., & Rietveld, P. (2007). Electronic ticketing in public transport: A field study in a rural area. Journal of Intelligence Transportation Systems, 11(2), 69-78.

Dunn-Rankin, P., 2004. Scaling methods. Lawrence Erlbaum.

Enzmann, M., & Schneider, M. (2005). Improving customer retention in e-commerce through a secure and privacy-enhanced loyalty system. Information Systems *Frontiers, 7*(4/5), 359-370.

Haewoon, Y. (2007). Airlines' futures. *Journal of Revenue & Pricing Management, 6*(4), 309-311.

Hallowell, R. (2000). Scalability: The paradox of human resources in e-commerce. *International Journal of Service Industry Management, 12*(1), 34-43.

Hill, T. & Lewicki, P., 2006. Statistics: methods and applications: a comprehensive reference for science, industry, and data mining. StatSoft, Inc.

Jakubauskas, G. (2006). Improvement of urban passenger transport ticketing systems by deploying intelligence transport system. *Transport, 21*(4), 252-259.

Kolsaker, A., Lee-Kelley, L., & Choy, P.C. (2004). The reluctant Hong Kong consumer: Purchasing travel online. *International Journal of Consumer Studies, 28*(2), 295-304.

Lau, T., Kwek, C., & Tan, H. (2011). Airline e-ticketing service: How e-service quality and customer satisfaction impacted purchase intention. *International Business Management, 5*(4), 200-208.

Lei, T., Quintero, A., & Pierre, S. (2009). Mobile services access and payment through reusable tickets. *Computer Communications, 32*(4), 602-610.

Lopez-Bonilla, J.M., & Lopez-Bonilla, L.M. (2013). Self-service technology versus traditional service: Examining cognitive factors in the purchase of the airline ticket. *Journal of Travel & Tourism Marketing, 30*(5), 497-513.

Lubeck, T.M., Wittmann, M.L., & Battistella, L.F. (2012). Electronic ticketing system as a process of innovation. *Journal of Technology Management & Innovation, 7*(1), 17-29.

Mut-Puigserver, M., Payeras-Capellà, M.M., Ferrer-Gomila, J., Vives-Guasch, A., & Castellà-Roca, J. (2012). A survey of electronic ticketing applied to transport. *Computers & Security, 31*(8), 925-939.

Noor, M., & Azila, N. (2012). Trust and commitment: Do they influence e-customer relationship performance? *International Journal of Electronic Commerce Studies, 3*(2), 281-295.

Smith, A.A., & Smith, S.D. (2012). CRM and identity theft issues associated with e-ticketing of sports and entertainment. *Electronic Government: An International Journal, 9*(1), 1-26.

Sorooshian, S., Onn, C.W., & Yeen, C.W. (2013). Malaysian-based analysis on e-service. *International Journal of Academic Research, 5*(4), 62-64.

Sulaiman, A., Ng, J., & Mohezar, S. (2008). E-ticketing as a new way of buying tickets: Malaysian perceptions. *Journal of Social Science, 17*(2), 149-157.

Sureshkumar, D., & Palanivelu, P. (2011). Perceptions of value: E-CRM features. *SCMS Journal of Indian Management, 8*(2), 106-111.

Tripathi, A., Reddy, S.K., Madria, S., Mohanty, H., & Ghosh, R.K. (2009). Algorithms for validating e-tickets in mobile computing environment. *Information Sciences, 197*(11), 1678-1693.

Wei, J., & Ozok, A. (2005). Development of a web-based mobile airline ticketing model with usability features. *Industrial Management & Data Systems, 105*(9), 1261-1277.

Yang, Z., & Jun, M. (2008). Consumer perception of e-service quality: From internet purchaser to non-purchaser perspectives. *Journal of Business Strategies, 25*(2), 59-84.

Zambon, E., Etalle, S., Wieringa, R., & Hartel, P. (2011). Model-based qualitative risk assessment for availability of IT infrastructures. *Software & Systems Modeling, 10*(4), 533-580.

Zhang, X., Prybutok, V., & Huang, A. (2006). An empirical study of factors affecting e-service satisfaction. *Human Systems Management, 25*(4), 279-291.

11

AUTOMATED TEXT CLUSTERING OF NEWSPAPER AND SCIENTIFIC TEXTS IN BRAZILIAN PORTUGUESE: ANALYSIS AND COMPARISON OF METHODS

Alexandre Ribeiro Afonso
Cláudio Gottschalg Duque
University of Brasília (Universidade de Brasília–UnB), Brasília, DF, Brazil

ABSTRACT

This article reports the findings of an empirical study about Automated Text Clustering applied to scientific articles and newspaper texts in Brazilian Portuguese, the objective was to find the most effective computational method able to cluster the input of texts in their original groups. The study covered four experiments, each experiment had four procedures: 1. *Corpus Selections* (a set of texts is selected for clustering), 2. *Word Class Selections* (Nouns, Verbs and Adjectives are chosen from each text by using specific algorithms), 3. *Filtering Algorithms* (a set of terms is selected from the results of the preview stage, a semantic weight is also inserted for each term and an index is generated for each text), 4. *Clustering Algorithms* (the clustering algorithms Simple K-Means, sIB and EM are applied to the indexes). After those procedures, clustering correctness and clustering time statistical results were collected. The sIB clustering algorithm is the best choice for both scientific and newspaper corpus, under the condition that the sIB clustering algorithm asks for the number of clusters as input before running (for the newspaper corpus, 68.9% correctness in 1 minute and for the scientific corpus, 77.8% correctness in 1 minute). The EM clustering algorithm additionally guesses the number of clusters without user intervention, but its best case is less than 53% correctness. Considering the experiments carried out, the results of human text classification and automated clustering are distant; it was also observed that the clustering correctness results vary according to the number of input texts and their topics.

Keywords: Text Mining; Text Clustering; Natural Language Processing; Brazilian Portuguese; Effectiveness.

Address for correspondence / Endereço para correspondência

Alexandre Ribeiro Afonso is doctoral-degree student in the Information Science program (Faculdade de Ciência da Informação – FCI), University of Brasília (Universidade de Brasília–UnB), Brasília - DF, Brazil. E-mail: rafonso.alex@gmail.com

Cláudio Gottschalg Duque works as professor and researcher in the Information Science program (Faculdade de Ciência da Informação – FCI), University of Brasília (Universidade de Brasília–UnB), Brasília - DF, Brazil. Campus Universitário Darcy Ribeiro, Faculdade de Ciência da Informação,Edifício da Biblioteca Central, Entrada Leste, Brasília, DF- Brazil. CEP: 70.919-970. E-mail: klaussherzog@gmail.com

1. INTRODUCTION

Automated text clustering systems have been developed and tested as an experimental and scientific activity. The purpose of text classification automation is to be as effective as humans when classifying texts in knowledge fields. A previous effective automatic clustering over a set of documents contributes to an effective automatic or manual information retrieval.

The main difference between clustering and categorization systems is that the clustering systems do not utilize any formal knowledge (like ontologies or thesauri) for training previously the system; instead, it works as an unsupervised learning system (Manning at al., 2008).

An automatic text clustering process could be divided in four main stages: *Corpus Selection, Word Class Selections, Filtering Algorithms* and *Clustering Algorithms*; during the experiments, we applied different procedures for each stage described to find the best combination of procedures which produced correct textual clustering by consuming less time, both for newspapers and scientific texts in Brazilian Portuguese.

Clustering Algorithms have been developed for general use, for all languages, but they have been tested mainly for English, and many studies about text clustering, using corpora in English as input, have been described over the last decade. However, different natural languages could produce different levels of correctness in clustering results, since each natural language has specific structures and properties (such as morphological and syntax peculiarities) with different levels of complexity in their use (number of repetitions of words in newspaper texts, number of synonyms, use of idiomatic expressions, and terminologies).

Some authors have described the impact of the linguistic characteristics over classification and information retrieval systems. For example, Rossel and Velupillai (2005) investigated the impact of using phrases in the vector space model for clustering documents in Swedish in different ways. Stefanowski and Weiss (2003) consider the problem of web search results clustering in the Polish language, supporting their analysis with results acquired from an experimental system named *Carrot*. Basic, Berecek and Cvitas (2005) argue that text processing algorithms and systems in English and other world languages are well developed, which is not the case with Croatian language, they affirm that the quality of input data strongly influences clustering and classification results.

Another fact *very important* to be noted is that the format (news or scientific) and the content (History, Geography, Pharmacy, etc.) of the corpus could produce different results for clustering experiments. This verification was performed during our second experiment.

All these cultural and linguistic particularities and the evident studies about the impact of the language over information retrieval systems make us to think about the scientific and newspaper communication in Brazil as having particular features. When analyzing the results of a clustering process, specifically for texts written in Brazilian

Portuguese, we can identify the best and not best procedures for each clustering stage, also observing their advantages and failures. Considering this observation, in future works, new procedures for text clustering can be proposed.

The goal of our study was to verify whether an automated clustering process could create the correct clusters for two text corpuses: a scientific corpus having five knowledge fields (Pharmacy, Physical Education, Linguistics, Geography, and History) and a newspaper corpus having five knowledge fields (Human Sciences, Biological Sciences, Social Sciences, Religion and Thought, Exact Sciences). Therefore, we had two corpuses already classified by humans and we wanted to measure the effectiveness of the clustering process (clustering correctness and clustering time) by using the human classification as reference for correctness. Then, using a statistical method, we searched for the combinations of clustering stages that produced the best clustering correctness values and the shortest clustering time values.

Through the following sections, we describe in detail each experiment stage (*corpus selections*, *word class selections*, *filtering algorithms,* and *clustering algorithms*), the procedures for each stage, the statistical methods adopted for clustering correctness and time measurement, statistical analysis, and results.

2. TEXT CLUSTERING IN BRAZILIAN PORTUGUESE: LITERATURE REVIEW

2.1 Text clustering approaches

In this article, we focus on a non-hierarchical text clustering method as opposed to hierarchical text clustering approach. Non-hierarchical text clustering is applied when the goal is to produce text clusters which do not fit in a specific knowledge hierarchy; it means that each text is only inside a specific cluster, a text would not be grouped in two or more clusters at the same time (Markov & Larose, 2007). When a hierarchy is necessary to organize the texts, the hierarchical approach is able to group, for example, two related clusters inside a major cluster such as taxonomy. Some scientific fields like Medicine are structured in low level sub-fields and a hierarchical approach could be well applied. But, when the user needs to group the documents in major scientific areas (for example, Geography, Linguistics, Pharmacy, etc.), a non-hierarchical clustering method would be better applied because the fields do not have a high level of related terminological characteristics, or the fields/areas are independent.

2.2 Non-hierarchical text clustering in Brazilian Portuguese

Our interest is to study the effect of the well-known text clustering technology (specifically, non-hierarchical text clustering methods) over a Brazilian digital repository where the texts are written in Brazilian Portuguese. Many possibilities for the four levels of a clustering experiment (*corpus selections*, *word class selections*, *filtering algorithms,* and *clustering algorithms*) were not tested yet for this language; so we execute new clustering experiments testing new corpora formats, filtering algorithms and using the well-known clustering algorithms.

The three articles described below (Maia & Souza, 2010), (DaSilva et. al, 2004), and (Seno & Nunes, 2008) are closely related to our work. They test and evaluate the effectiveness of traditional non-hierarchic text clustering algorithms by using scientific and newspaper corpora in Brazilian Portuguese.

The study reported by Maia and Souza (2010) is the most similar to our study. The study is about Automatic Text Categorization and Automatic Text Clustering in Brazilian Portuguese. The study regarding clustering methods aimed to compare the use of noun phrases and single terms as text representations for Simple K-Means clustering algorithm, trying to find the best linguistic representation. The researchers analyzed the effectiveness of the Simple K-Means clustering algorithm when clustering a corpus with 50 scientific texts about subareas of Information Science. The corpus was divided into 5 Information Science subareas (Historical and Epistemological Studies about Information; Knowledge Organization and Information Representation; Information Propagation, Mediation and Usability; Politics, Ethics and Information Economy; Management of Information Units) and the researchers aimed to evaluate the results from Simple K-Means when clustering texts indexed by noun phrases or terms. The manuscript also describes the same process for a newspaper corpus having 160 texts of 4 newspaper sections (informatics, tourism, world, vehicles). About the best clustering results, Maia and Souza (2010) describe 44% of clustering correctness using single terms from the scientific corpus, and 81% of clustering correctness using noun phrases from the newspaper corpus. They concluded that the use of noun phases is not better than the use of single terms as a representation for clustering tasks, since the correctness rate for noun phases and terms has an approximated percentage number, but the use of noun phases consumed a longer time. About the difference between text clustering and text categorization, considering the best results for correctness, they observed 8 percentage points difference between automatic text clustering and automatic text categorization for the scientific corpus, and 10 percentage points difference for the newspaper corpus, the text categorization process got the best values.

A related study for Brazilian Portuguese was performed by DaSilva et al. (2004). The researchers propose and evaluate the use of linguistic information in the preprocessing phase of text mining tasks (categorization and clustering). They present several experiments comparing their proposal for selection of terms based on linguistic knowledge with usual techniques applied in the field. The results show that *part of speech information* (in this paper, we use the term *word classes*) is useful for the preprocessing phase of text categorization and clustering, as an alternative for stop words and stemming.

We could also cite the study of Seno and Nunes (2008) as a related work. The paper presents some experiments on detecting and clustering similar sentences of texts in Brazilian Portuguese. They propose an evaluation framework based on an incremental and unsupervised clustering method which is combined with statistical similarity metrics to measure the semantic distance between sentences. Experiments show that this method is robust even to treat small data sets. It has achieved 86% and 93% of F-measure and Purity, respectively, and 0.037 of Entropy for the best case.

3. AUTOMATED TEXT CLUSTERING: DESCRIPTION OF THE EXPERIMENTS' STAGES

Our study was performed by analyzing the statistical results from four text clustering experiments. The four experiments had the same architecture; it means the four experiments are composed by the same sequential stages. In this section, we describe the possibilities for the four sequential stages: *Corpus Selections*, *Word Class Selections*, *Filtering Algorithms,* and *Clustering Algorithms*.

Corpus Selections: We chose two textual databases to extract the newspaper and the scientific corpus. The scientific corpus was taken from five scientific journals published by the digital library of Federal University of Goiás (UFG) in Brazil. We got the articles from five scientific fields (Pharmacy, Physical Education, Linguistics, Geography, and History). The text choices from the scientific digital library were a random process.

The newspaper corpus was taken from the "Lácio-Web Textual Database" described by Aluísio and Almeida (2006). It is produced by NILC (Núcleo Interinstitucional de Linguística Computacional), a Computational Linguistics research group in Brazil. The texts from Lácio-Web database are classified in five areas (Human Sciences, Biological Sciences, Social Sciences, Religion and Thought, Exact Sciences). Lácio-Web stores texts from newspapers that are currently active in Brazil. The text choices from the textual database were a random process.

The content of the newspaper texts was not modified after corpus selection, but a text partition was executed for the scientific corpus after corpus selection. Since the scientific texts are larger texts, we took from each scientific text: title, abstract, keywords, and the first page/column of the introduction; the first page was selected since it was observed that in scientific texts the introduction, generally, fills no more than one or two pages/columns (considering the scientific fields analyzed), this choice permits to keep a small set of terms but considering the content of the introduction. An initial conjecture was that the terms which identify the topic are more frequent in these first parts of the scientific text, this verification is part of the experiments done.

Although some texts from the Lácio-Web Database can be classified in more than one area, we did not permit text replicas in our corpus. When a text was found inside two or more clusters in our corpus, it was replaced by another one, but the text chosen could still be replicated by many clusters in Lácio-Web database. The original topics of the scientific articles are chosen according to the scope descriptions of the journals in their web pages (there is a section "Foco e Escopo" for each journal which describes the topics of interest). The scientific database is found at (http://www.revistas.ufg.br/) and the newspaper Lácio-Web database can be found at (http://www.nilc.icmc.usp.br/lacioweb/).

Both formats (newspaper and scientific texts) have public access and they are commonly found in libraries, and since our goal was to evaluate the current technology over digital libraries, we decided to test these specific text formats. We worked with at most five knowledge areas for each format during the experiments; if we chose more than five knowledge areas it would create a very large study for a single research. Another reason for this number is that we divided the original set of texts in two corpuses (having three and five knowledge areas) to verify whether, when the number of knowledge areas and the number of texts increase, the clustering effectiveness decreases. The criterion for choosing the knowledge areas to construct the corpora is the approximation of the knowledge areas and their distances; it means we decided to choose two areas inserted in the same major area (e.g. History and Geography) and other two areas not directly related (e.g. Physical Education and Linguistics) and one more area was chosen randomly. The same criterion was set for the newspaper texts (Social Sciences and *Religion and Thought*) and (Human Sciences and Biological Sciences).

The two sets of data produced after this manual processes were the experiment corpora that follow the original human classifications from the two databases.

Word Class Selections: We first applied (for each text from both corpuses) a POS-Tagger algorithm (Part-of-Speech tagger); it inserts tags (word class tags like Noun, Verb, Adverb, Adjective, etc.) to every word inside a text. The POS-Tagger used is trained by the researchers of the NILC institute, as described by Aires (2000), the MXPOST Tagger application (Ratnaparkhi, 1996) was used to produce this Brazilian Portuguese Tagger. This POS-Tagger was chosen because the taggers for (Nouns, Adjectives and Verbs) are inserted, and the tagger does not differentiate the hierarchies of the nouns, it also was trained by using a Brazilian Portuguese corpus. Moreover, the tagger was developed and tested by natural language processing specialists from NILC.

After applying the POS-Tagger algorithm for each text of the corpus and selecting Nouns, Verbs and Adjectives, we applied a stemming algorithm for each tagged text. The stemming process was performed by using an application developed by NILC; it is described by Caldas (2001). The stemmer follows Porter's algorithm and works for Brazilian Portuguese by identifying the stem of words by incrementally removing their suffix/termination. After tagging and stemming, each text from the scientific and newspaper corpus is represented only by their stems and their tags (only Nouns, Verbs and Adjectives). This stemmer was chosen because it was developed specifically for Brazilian Portuguese, and it was developed by natural language processing specialists from NILC.

Filtering Algorithms: In this experiment stage, we applied some algorithms for creating a text index for each text. The index must contain the main stems from the previous *word class selections* stage and it has to represent the text by holding its semantic meaning. So, the index produced by this stage is a reduced set of stems also having a semantic weight for each stem. The semantic weight algorithm executes a mathematical function that returns the stem's semantic weight according to its semantic importance inside the text and the entire corpus. For the four experiments, we applied the mathematical function *IDF* (Inverse Document Frequency)-Transform (Markov & Larose, 2007):

$$IDF\text{-}T = fij*log \text{ (number of documents/number of documents with stem i)} \text{ (I)}$$

fij is the frequency of the stem *i* in document *j*. The *Weka* toolkit is a free software for data mining and text mining tasks, and we used *Weka* software to apply the *IDF-T*.

After inserting a semantic weight (*IDF-T*) for each stem of each text, we can apply one of three procedures for stem selections. The first procedure is to use the same set of stems returned by the *word class selections* stage without intervention. It means the index produced by the *filtering algorithms* stage is simply the set of stems selected during the *word class selections*: (nouns), (nouns, verbs), (nouns, adjectives), (verb, adjectives), (nouns, adjectives, verbs), or (nouns, adjectives, verbs - without tags) with their *IDF-T* semantic weights. The second filter procedure possible is to use an intelligent algorithm based on the *Genetic Search* Metaheuristic (Goldberg, 1989) combined with *Correlation-based Feature Subset Selection* (it is named cfsSubSetEval by *Weka*) for selecting the stems, both implemented by *Weka*. The third option is to filter the set of stems coming from the *word class selections* stage by using a frequency filter algorithm; this frequency filter algorithm selects the stems according to the stems' frequencies adopted by the researcher, for example if the researcher chose (frequency: 2) only the stems having at least two occurrences inside the corpus could be selected to the output index. These filtering procedures for selecting terms were chosen since they work over different paradigms (no specific filtering, an intelligent filtering, or a frequency filtering), the objective was to verify the impact of each one during the clustering experiments.

The indexes produced during this stage represent the input texts as a set of selected terms (text indexes) and they are clustered by the clustering algorithms during the next stage.

Clustering Algorithms: The clustering algorithms are executed in this final stage. Since the clustering algorithms do not receive any extra knowledge (like a hint for the topics or vocabulary) about the texts to be classified, it only works on the texts' content, and the clustering algorithms must preview the topic for each cluster, or even the number of clusters. A few clustering algorithms such as SKM (Simple K-Means) described by Manning and Schütze (1999), and sIB (Sequential Information Bottleneck) described by Slonin et al. (2002), are algorithms that ask for the number of clusters from the user. Other algorithms such as EM (Expectation Maximization) (Manning & Schütze, 1999), Evolutionary Searches (Jones at al., 1995), or Neural Networks Architectures (Kohonen, 1997), (Kohonen, 1998) can try to guess the number of clusters and the topic for each cluster, but guessing the number of clusters is a more difficult algorithmic task. Each clustering algorithm may find a different result, since they could apply different mathematical strategies and heuristics to compare the texts (represented by indexes) when clustering. Algorithms can use formal knowledge of the language (as grammar structures or textual features) when executing a clustering process, therefore natural languages having a high level of scientific description would get better results for text clustering.

The Data Mining toolkit *Weka* already has the three clustering algorithms we chose for the experiments (EM, SKM, and sIB), so we decided to use this tool again for the *clustering algorithms* stage of the experiments. Many options of running can be chosen before starting the algorithm execution; we can choose an iteration number, the number of groups for clustering, and other restrictive alternatives for each algorithm. The three algorithms we tested make linear and excluding clusters, which means they are non-hierarchical.

After describing each stage, we can set a final architecture for the experiments, the figure below shows the final model adopted for the four experiments performed. The *evaluation methods* for measurement are described in the next section.

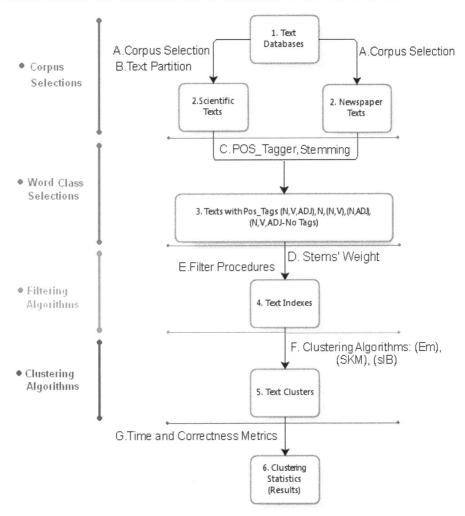

Figure 1: Experiment Stages and measurement

4. EVALUATION METHODS

4.1 Clustering correctness metrics

The usual metrics for clustering correctness are F-measure, Percentage Values of Correctness, Purity and Entropy. The usual metrics evaluate clustering algorithms' performance and the quality of the resulting clusters. F-Measure has been applied to measure the quality of the entire clustering process, while Purity and Entropy are used to measure the quality of the resulting clusters, and Percentage Values of Correctness is applied to measure the errors of the clustering results considering a human classification as reference, Percentage Values of Correctness returns the exact number of clustering errors from each cluster.

Song and Park (2006) only applied F-Measure, Seno and Nunes (2008) uses three metrics (F-measure, Purity and Entropy), and Maia and Souza (2010) uses Percentage Values of Correctness as metric, we notice the choice of each metric depends on the objectives of the experiment. Our decision was to use Percentage Values of Correctness as metric, since we wanted to compare the clustering results returned by the clustering algorithms and the previous human classification, the exact number of clustering mistakes from each experiment was necessary to choose the best clustering experiment. We also used an additional metric for measuring the number of deviated clusters, a Deviation Number (DN) which identifies the exact number of clusters created more than the expected number of clusters or less than the expected number of clusters. This metric value (DN) is calculated only for the EM algorithm since only this clustering algorithm guesses the number of clusters when executing a clustering process.

We realized that these two values (Percentage Values of Correctness and a Deviation Number - DN) are more informative than using a single statistical value about the distribution of the documents over the clusters created, as returned by (F-measure, Purity and Entropy metrics); the results of the two metrics described is more informative (for this specific set of experiments) then the usual averages since they return two different exact numbers and not a single average from a clustering result.

The result analysis is performed according to *Weka* outputs. For each clustering algorithm execution, *Weka* provides the output of n clusters (0 to n-1) and m texts classified (0 to m-1) for each cluster. We can see the clustering results through the result window as Cartesian Coordinates (x, y) and colors for each cluster. The next figure 2 below shows the result for the sIB algorithm execution for 3 clusters:

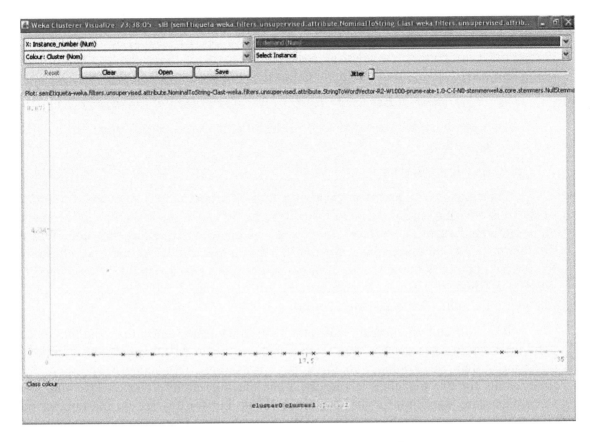

Figure 2: *Weka* image for sIB clustering algorithm output

The x-axis holds the number of the document; this sample experiment has 36 text documents. By our configuration, we know that the 0-11 numbers represent the documents about cluster 1 (for example, Pharmacy); numbers 12-23 represent cluster 2 (for example, Physical Education) and cluster 3 (for example, Linguistics) is represented by numbers 24-35.

The y-axis holds the corpus items (in this case, stems), and the symbol "*" indicates both a document (0-35) and a Boolean value (true or false) for a stem on the y-axis. If the document has the stem shown on the y-axis then the symbol "*" is aligned according to the y-axis. The color of the symbol "*" indicates the cluster where the document is found. Each cluster produced by the sIB, EM or SKM algorithm execution will get a specific color.

The percentage values of correctness are calculated by analyzing the results displayed by figure 2, it shows us a *Weka* experiment result using the sIB algorithm, for 3 clusters (Pharmacy, Physical Education, and Linguistics), with 12 documents queued for each area (0 to 35), as shown by the x-axis. Each color represents a cluster generated by the system (sIB asks the user for the number of clusters to be generated). Cluster 0 is blue, cluster 1 is red, and cluster 2 is green. We consider the last 12 elements as green, with 7 mistakes; the 12 elements in the middle are blue, having 2 mistakes; and the 12 elements at the beginning are red, with 6 mistakes. The error summation is 15, so the experiment correctness percentage is 58.3% of correct classifications. We apply this calculus to all the experiments performed.

For a clustering experiment using the EM algorithm we use two metrics: we check whether the number of clusters generated by the EM algorithm execution is correct or, if not correct, we calculate a deviation number (DN) given by the absolute value function (it always returns a number equal or greater than zero):

$$DN = (\,|\,Number\ of\ Expected\ Clusters\ \text{-}\ Number\ of\ Output\ Clusters\,|\,)\ (II)$$

Then we calculate the percentage values of correctness as described for the sIB and SKM algorithms.

4.2 Clustering time metrics

The time unit chosen for clustering time measurement is minutes, since the executions are long, and they could take from seconds to hours to complete. Minutes are an intermediate metric, and for this reason, we decided to use this time unit. When the time taken by an execution is broken, like 2 minutes and 35 seconds, we chose to extend the number to the next unit of minutes, but if the past seconds are less than 30, we round down to the nearest minute unit. For example, 2 min 29 sec. becomes 2 minutes, but 2 min. 30 sec. becomes 3 min.

It is difficult to measure and compare exact time, since the computational conditions could vary even when the machine architecture, hardware configuration, operating system, and compiler are the same. For example, let's suppose we expect the time results for two machines having the same machine architecture and running the same clustering algorithm for the same experiment, but for any reason the number of processes running on machine one is greater than machine two. As a consequence the time results will have different values when clustering is finished, since machine one needs to control more processes than machine two. For this reason, the time values we got here are just an approximation under a few specific conditions.

For these experiments, we use a machine having a Pentium Dual Core T4500 Intel processor. It has 2 GB Main Memory; the Operating System is Microsoft Windows XP Professional 2002 SP 3; the *Weka* version is 3.6.3; and the Java Development Kit (JDK) installed is jdk1.6.0_04.

We took notes only for the time consumed by *Weka* to build the clusters. It means we just measured the time taken by the *clustering algorithms* stage: SKM, sIB, and EM clustering algorithms.

5. RESEARCH QUESTIONS

Question 1: Considering the four experiments performed, and their different configurations for the four stages, what is the experiment which produces best results (the one that produces the best clustering correctness value and consumes less time) having a **scientific corpus** as input?

Question 2: Considering the four experiments performed, and their different configurations for the four stages, what is the experiment which produces best results (the one that produces the best clustering correctness value and consumes less time) having a **newspaper corpus** as input?

6. EXPERIMENTS' DESCRIPTION AND RESULTS

6.1 Experiment 1

6.1.1 Configurations of the experiment 1A (newspaper corpus)

Corpus Selection: Newspaper texts from Lácio-Web corpus, related to Biological Sciences, Exact Sciences, and Human Sciences. 15 texts from each area. Total: 45 texts.

Word Class Selections: We experimented different sets of word tags (4 options kept the word class tags and 1 option did not use the tags): (nouns), (nouns, verbs), (nouns, adjectives), (nouns, adjectives, verbs), (nouns, adjectives, verbs - without the tags).

Filtering Algorithms: 2 options: A *Weka* intelligent filter named *Genetic Search* with the method for evaluating stems named cfsSubSetEval. We kept the default values for (GeneticSearch/ cfsSubSetEval). Another try with no filter. The formula for Lexical Item Weights was only *IDF-T*.

Clustering Algorithms : EM, SKM and sIB algorithms.

Notice there are 30 executions for each possible combination above (5 Sets of Tags * 2 Filters Procedures * 3 Clustering Algorithms).

6.1.2 Configurations of the experiment 1B (scientific corpus)

Corpus Selection: Scientific Journals from UFG Digital Library from 3 different journals, about Pharmacy, Physical Education, and Linguistics. 12 papers from each journal. Total: 36 texts.

Word Class Selections: We tried many different sets of tags (4 options kept the word class tags and 1 option without the tags): (nouns), (nouns, verbs), (nouns, adjectives), (nouns, adjectives, verbs), (nouns, adjectives, verbs - without the tags).

Filtering Algorithms: 2 options: A *Weka* intelligent filter named *Genetic Search* with the method for evaluating stems named cfsSubSetEval. We kept the default values for (GeneticSearch/ cfsSubSetEval). Another try with no filter. The formula for Lexical Item Weights was only *IDF-T*.

Clustering Algorithms : EM, SKM and sIB algorithms.

Notice there are 30 executions for each possible combination above (5 Sets of Tags * 2 Filters Procedures * 3 Clustering Algorithms).

For both Experiments 1A and 1B, the result having the best value of correctness for each clustering algorithm is chosen as the best (only one combination for each algorithm is chosen).

6.2 Experiment 2

Experiment 2 aimed to verify the clustering correctness percentage when we inserted more input texts and clusters; a more diverse corpus was compiled. We verified how the percentage correctness error rate increases when adding more textual elements.

For this experiment, we only tested the combinations that reached the best values for Experiments 1A and 1B, since we wanted to verify whether the best values of clustering correctness would be kept from the experiments 1A and 1B, and how much additional time it would consume. It means we redid the experiments 1A and 1B, but having 5 knowledge areas and 5 clusters and choosing new documents for the five knowledge areas.

6.2.1 Configurations of the experiment 2A (newspaper corpus)

For Experiment 2A, which works with newspaper texts, we added two additional sets: Social Sciences, and *Religion and Thought* texts (15 additional texts for each area). The set of POS-Tags and filters were the same from the best values obtained during Experiment 1A. Therefore, the algorithms had to produce 5 clusters instead of 3 clusters, and the total number of texts was 75 texts for the newspaper corpus.

6.2.2 Configurations of the experiment 2B (scientific corpus)

For Experiment 2B, which works with scientific texts, we added History and Geography texts (12 additional texts for each area). The set of POS-Tag and filters were the same from the best values gotten during Experiment 1B. Therefore, the algorithms had to produce 5 clusters instead of 3 clusters, and the total number of texts was 60 texts for the scientific corpus.

The total number of executions for this experiment is 6: (1 filter * 3 algorithms * 1 tag set) = 3 executions for each corpus.

6.3 Experiment 3

This experiment verified the effect of taking the Nouns out of the text indexes. Our goal was to check the importance of the Nouns for text clustering. If the importance of the Nouns for clustering is high, their absence will produce poorer clusters. We again modified a few features from Experiment 1. For this experiment, two corpuses were used as before, a newspaper corpus, the same from Experiment 1A, and a scientific corpus, the same from Experiment 1B.

From Experiment 1A and 1B, all the configurations described were kept, except the POS-Tags. Here we only used the tag set: (Verb, Adj); so we kept the configurations for *corpus selections, filter algorithms, clustering algorithms* but this time we tested only Verbs and Adjectives as tags for the stage *word class selections*.

The total number of executions for this experiment is 12 (2 filters * 3 algorithms * 1 tag set) = 6 executions for each corpus. The result having the best value of correctness for each clustering algorithm was chosen as the best.

6.4 Experiment 4

This experiment used another kind of filtering procedure for the *filter algorithms* stage, so we tried a filter based on stem frequencies. It means that instead of using the text indexes produced during Experiment 1, this time we selected the main stems from the texts to be clustered according to their frequency inside the corpus. The goal was to verify whether the filter's variation causes a notable effect over clustering performance (correctness and time).

We tried different frequencies 2, 3, 4, 5 for each term of the corpus for this new filter, since we were trying to find the best one. During these executions we only chose two sets of tags: (Nouns) and (Nouns, Verbs, Adjectives – without tags) for the *Word Class Selections* stage. These word classes were chosen since, initially, we had the hypothesis that (Nouns) were the best alternative to identify a topic from a text, and the set (Nouns, Verbs, Adjectives - without tags) has been applied to many works for text mining, indexing, and clustering. We performed these new tests for the newspaper corpus (Experiment 4A) and also for the scientific corpus (Experiment 4B).

When we specify we tried different frequencies 2, 3, 4, 5 for the experiment, it means that we only considered stems having frequency 2, 3, 4, or 5 inside the entire corpus for each execution test.

The number of execution tests for each corpus was ((4 possible frequencies for filtering * 3 clustering algorithms * 2 tag sets) = 24 possibilities), or 48 executions considering both newspaper and scientific corpus. The result having the best value of correctness for each clustering algorithm was chosen as the best.

7. EXPERIMENTAL ANALYSIS AND RESEARCH ANSWERS

The three pairs of charts below summarize the best results of clustering correctness and time achievement for experiments *(1-4)A* (newspaper corpus) and *(1-4)B* (scientific corpus), which we described in the last section. In the first graphic pair, we use a percentage notation "%" for clustering correctness, in the second pair a time notation in minutes. The last pair of charts shows the deviation numbers (DN) for the EM algorithm. The blue charts are about *Experiments A* (newspaper corpus) and red graphics about *Experiments B* (scientific corpus). Notice the results are always only for the last experiment stage (*Clustering Algorithm*ms), so the results for time and correctness are always from the sIB, SKM and EM algorithms.

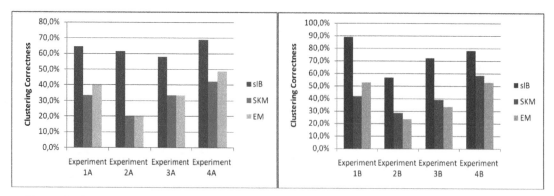

Figure 3: Two charts show the clustering correctness values gotten by each algorithm for each experiment (1-4) described. Percentage values of correctness on y-axis and the experiment name on x-axis.

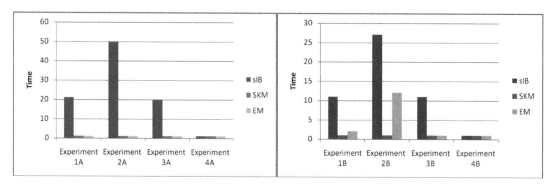

Figure 4: Two charts show the time consumed by each algorithm.

Time in minutes on y-axis and the experiment name on x-axis.

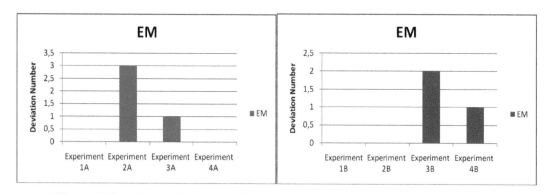

Figure 5: Two charts show the *Deviation Number* (DN) only for the EM algorithm.

Units of deviation on y-axis and the experiment name on x-axis.

Question 1 - Notable patterns about the scientific corpus (experiments: 1B, 2B, 3B and 4B – red graphics)

Best stages' combination for the scientific corpus considering correctness and time: 77.8% correctness in 1 minute by the fourth experiment.

Configuration for the best result (considering the best rate of correctness and less time):

Corpus selections: A corpus having three not related topics, Pharmacy, Linguistics and Physical Education.

Word class selections: (Nouns + Verbs + Adjectives - No Tags).

Filtering algorithms: (Frequency Filter: Frequency 5).

Clustering algorithm: sIB.

Question 2 - Notable patterns about the newspaper corpus (experiments: 1A, 2A, 3A and 4A – blue chart)

Best stages' combination for the newspaper corpus considering correctness and time: 68.9% correctness in 1 minute by the fourth experiment.

Configuration for the best result (considering the best rate of correctness and less time):

Corpus selections: A corpus having three not related topics, Biological Sciences, Exact Sciences, and Human Sciences.

Word class selections: (Nouns)

Filtering algorithms: (Frequency Filter: Frequency 3)

Clustering algorithm: sIB

For the newspaper experiments, we must observe that a few texts selected for tests can be found inside two or more groups from the Lácio-Web Database. The corpus for Experiments 1, 3, and 4 has 31.1% of the texts previously classified inside more than one group. The corpus for Experiment 2 has 9.3% of the texts previously classified inside more than one group.

8. CONCLUSION

This study tried to determine certain performance patterns when executing automated text clustering. We verified whether the best results found for automated text clustering and human text classification are approximated, we chose a realistic, experimental, and statistical point of view for finding clustering correctness and time values. Many works on this topic can be found for the English language, but we could not find many works for Brazilian Portuguese, so this was the motivation for our research.

The first problem about evaluation of text clusters produced by a clustering algorithm is the concept of correctness: what is correct clustering? Or, what is a good cluster? Is the best clustering process the one that got the best time, or the best grouping or both? We accepted the predefined classified databases used as having correct classification, and they were produced by humans, so this classification follows a specific criterion, but is this specific criterion the best one? What is the best choice to the user: a system able to find the correct number of clusters having a low rate of clustering correctness, or having a high rate of clustering correctness over additional clusters? We can see the problem of evaluating text clustering is something relative, and the concept of correctness and quality for clustering depends on one's expectations. During this study, we chose a specific criterion for evaluation as we described during the experiments' description.

It was noticed that there is a combinatorial property for this kind of investigation, and the combinatorial choices are broad, with many different trees of possible investigation for the experiment stages: *corpus selections*, *word class selections*, *filtering algorithms,* and *clustering algorithms*. So we decided to investigate a few trees and specific branches for these trees, using the current linguistic tools available for Brazilian Portuguese. We see the possible investigations are very broad, and simple details during the stages of the experiments can produce very different results. Although we did 126 clustering tests during the four experiments, we investigated only a small part of the possibilities, under some exact conditions. So many attempts can still be performed.

Considering the results, regularity can be observed between the newspaper and the scientific experiments: the sIB algorithm always got the best clustering correctness values for both corpuses. We can notice the rate of clustering correctness for newspaper experiments is equal to or lower than the values obtained for the scientific corpus for all tests, except for Experiments sIB-2A, EM-3A, and EM-4A. One possible reason for this best result is the scientific vocabulary, since it is formal and rich, and it uses specific language which gives better clues for clustering algorithms.

Although we have gotten a reasonable result for the tuple (scientific texts, frequency filter, Nouns + Verbs + Adjectives - without tags, sIB algorithm) as described, the sIB algorithm asks for the number of clusters to be created and, in most cases, the user does not know the nature of the texts and topics or even the number of clusters; moreover sIB algorithm got a reasonable result only when producing three clusters for the scientific corpus. Some algorithms (like the EM algorithm) try to find the number of cluster and their terminological features, but EM does not yet have a high level of correctness, and much work must be done in this way to improve the results.

The second experiment (which works with five clusters) got a very worse result. We can see from Experiments 1 and 2 (figure 3) that the differential values of clustering correctness between the columns (Experiment 1A and Experiment 2A), for each clustering algorithm, have lower values than the differential values between the columns (Experiment 1B and Experiment 2B) for each clustering algorithm. Perhaps it happens because of the scientific corpus chosen, since we added History and Geography texts for the new Experiment, 2B. So, we suspect that these two scientific fields have a similar vocabulary, which would cause an algorithmic clustering confusion over these two clusters, or that the two fields do not have a very formal or technical vocabulary powerful enough for clear text discrimination in relation to the other fields. Therefore, this fact opens a new hypothesis for the higher percentage difference between the columns (Experiment 1B and Experiment 2B).

Something important to observe is the fact that texts have a multi-classification nature and according to Ranganathan (1967), a textual topic could be analyzed from many different viewpoints (classes and facets). Even though works and studies about automatic text classification and clustering have been using a deterministic classification (each document inside only one group), a more realistic classification should permit a document to be inserted into more than one group, at least for some knowledge fields from the newspaper corpus. We realized that scientific texts are better classified using a deterministic approach than newspaper texts, since most of time a formal vocabulary is present for each scientific field. This formal language could not always be identified for newspaper texts, so an experimental possibility is to redo the tests considering a multi-clustering possibility for each text, but we should also consider that a multi-clustering approach could generate difficult searching and maintenance for documents, at least for databases having many clusters and having the same document inside many clusters.

Without getting a semantic or pragmatic level of analysis it would be hard to produce a good and practical clustering near to human classification. Therefore, we believe that general linguistic tools are important for clustering success. A Wordnet database (Fellbaum, 1998) for Brazilian Portuguese and other general language descriptions would play a very important role in acceptable clustering, at least for informative newspaper texts.

The evolution of the algorithms, scientific natural language descriptions and Bibliometrics is a key for text clustering improvement.

REFERENCES

Aires, R. V. X. (2000). *Implementação, Adaptação, Combinação e Avaliação de Etiquetadores para o Português do Brasil. [Implementation, Adaptation, Combination and Evaluation of Brasilian Portuguese Taggers.]* Unpublished MsC Thesis. Universidade de São Paulo, São Paulo, Brazil.

Aluísio S. M., & Almeida G. M. B. (2006). O que é e como se constrói um corpus? Lições aprendidas na compilação de vários corpora para pesquisa lingüística. [What is a corpus and how to build a corpus? Lessons learned during the compilation of various corpora for linguistic research.] *Calidoscópio*, **4**(3), 155-177.

Basic, B. D., Berecek B., & Cvitas A. (2005). Mining textual data in Croatian, in *Proceedings of the 28th International Conference, MIPRO 2005,* Business Intelligence Systems. (pp. 61–66).

Bezerra, G. B., Barra, T. V., Ferreira, H. M., & Von Zuben, F. J. (2006). A hierarchical immune-inspired approach for text clustering. *Selected papers based on the presentations at the 2006 conference on Information Processing and Management of Uncertainty,* IMPU, Paris, France. (pp. 131-142).

Biderman, M. T. C. (2001). O Português Brasileiro e o Português Europeu : Identidade e contrastes. [The Brazilian Portuguese and European Portuguese: Identity and contrasts.] *Revue belge de philologie et d'histoire,* **79** (3), 963-975.

Caldas Junior, J., Imamura, C.Y.M., & Rezende, S.O. (2001). Avaliação de um Algoritmo de Stemming para a Língua Portuguesa. [Evaluation of a Stemming Algorithm for Portuguese Language.] *The Proceedings of the 2nd Congress of Logic Applied to Technology,* São Paulo, Brazil. (pp. 267-274). São Paulo, Brazil: SENAC/Plêiade.

Camargo, Y. B. L. (2007). *Abordagem lingüística na classificação de textos em português. [A linguistic approach to the classification of texts in Portuguese.]* Unpublished MsC Thesis. COPPE - Universidade Federal do Rio de Janeiro, Rio de Janeiro, Brazil.

DaSilva, C. F., Vieira, R., Osório, F. S., & Quaresma, P. (2004). Mining Linguistically Interpreted Texts. In *Proceedings of the 5th International Workshop on Linguistically Interpreted Corpora.*

Fellbaum, C. (1998). *WordNet. An electronic lexical database.* Cambridge, MA: MIT Press.

Furlanetto, M. M. (2008). Neological Formations in Brazilian Portuguese: a Discursive View. *Fórum Lingüístico,* **5** (2), 1-22, Florianópolis, Brazil.

Goldberg D. E. (1989). *Genetic Algorithms in Search, Optimization and Machine Learning.* Addison-Wesley.

Hall M. A. (1998). *Correlation-based Feature Subset Selection for Machine Learning.* Hamilton, New Zealand. (University of Waikato Ph.D. dissertation).

IBGE (2000). *Brasil: 500 anos de povoamento [Brazil: 500 years of settlement].* Rio de janeiro: IBGE.

Jones, G., Robertson, A. M., Santimetvirul, C., & Willett, P. (1995). Non-hierarchic document clustering using a genetic algorithm. *Information Research,* **1**(1), Retrieved 15 April, 2012 from http://InformationR.net/ir/1-1/paper1.html.

Hammouda, K. M., & Kamel. M. S. (2004). Efficient phrase-based document indexing for web document clustering. *IEEE Transactions on Knowledge and Data Engineering,* **16**(10), 1279–1296.

Kohonen, T. (1997). *Self-Organizing Maps.* 2nd ed., Berlin: Springer-Verlag.

Kohonen, T. (1998). Self-Organization of Very Large Document Collections: State of the Art. *Proceedings of ICANN98, the 8th International Conference on Artificial Neural Networks,* Skövde, Sweden, 2-4 September, 1998, **8**(1), 65-74: Springer.

Maia, L. C., & Souza, R. R. (2010). Uso de sintagmas nominais na classificação automática de documentos eletrônicos. [The use of noun phrases in automatic classification of electronic documents.] *Perspect. Ciênc. Inf.*, **15**(1), 154-172.

Manning, C. D, Raghavan, P., & Schütze, H. (2008). *Introduction to Information Retrieval.* Cambridge, New York, Melbourne, Madrid, Cape Town, Singapore, São Paulo, Delhi: Cambridge University Press.

Manning, C. D., & Schütze, H. (1999). *Foundations of Statistical Natural Language Processing.* Cambridge, Massachusetts: The MIT Press.

Markov, Z., & Larose D. T. (2007). *Data Mining the Web: Uncovering Patterns in Web Content, Structure and Usage.* Hoboken, New Jersey: John Wiley ; Sons, Inc.

Palmeira, E., & Freitas, F. (2007). Ontologias detalhadas e classificação de texto: uma união promissora. [Detailed ontologies and text classification: a promising union.] *ENIA 2007: VI Encontro Nacional de Inteligência Artificial.* Rio de Janeiro, Brazil, July, 03-06, 2007. Rio de Janeiro: Instituto Militar de Engenharia.

Ranganathan, S. R. (1967). *Prolegomena to Library Classification.* London: Asia Publishing House.

Ratnaparkhi, A. (1996). A Maximum Entropy Model for Part-of-Speech Tagging. *Proceedings of the First Empirical Methods in NLP Conference.* University of Pennsylvania, May 17-18, 1996. (pp. 133-142).

Reis, João José (2000). Presença Negra: conflitos e encontros. In Brasil: 500 anos de povoamento [Black Presence: conflicts and encounters]. Rio de Janeiro: IBGE, 2000. pp: 91.

Rossel, M., & Velupillai, S. (2005). The Impact of Phrases in Document Clustering for Swedish. *Proceedings of the 15th NODALIDA conference,* NoDaLiDa 2005, Joensuu, Finland. (pp.173-179).

Seno, E. R. M., & Nunes, M. D. V. (2008). Some Experiments on Clustering Similar Sentences of Texts in Portuguese. In Teixeira, A., StrubeDeLima, V. L., CaldasDeOliveira, L., Quaresma, P. (Eds.), *Lecture Notes in Artificial Intelligence, Vol. 5190. 8th International Conference on Computational Processing of the Portuguese Language,* PROPOR 2008, Aveiro, Portugal, September 08-10, 2008. (pp. 133-142). Berlin, Germany: Springer-Verlag.

Silva. A. S. (2006). Sociolinguística cognitiva e o estudo da convergência/divergência entre o Português Europeu e o Português Brasileiro. [Cognitive Sociolinguistics and the study of convergence / divergence between European Portuguese and Brazilian Portuguese.] *Veredas :Revista de Estudos Lingüísticos,* **10** (2006): Universidade Federal de Juiz de Fora.

Slonin, N., Friedman N., & Tishby, N. (2002). Unsupervised document classification using sequential information maximization. *Proceedings of the 25th International ACM*

SIGIR Conference on Research and Development in Information Retrieval, Tampere, Finland, August 11-15, 2002. (pp. 129-136). New York: ACM Press.

Song W., & Park S. C. (2006). Genetic Algorithm-based Text Clustering Technique. In Licheng Jiao, Lipo Wang, Xinbo Gao, Jing Liu, Feng Wu (Eds.), *Lecture Notes in Computer Science, Vol. 4221. Advances in Natural Computation, Second International Conference*, ICNC 2006, Xi'an, China, September 24-28, 2006. (pp. 779-782). Berlin: Springer-Verlag.

Stefanowski, J., & Weiss, D. (2003). Web search results clustering in Polish: experimental evaluation of Carrot. Advances in Soft Computing, Intelligent Information Processing and Web Mining, *Proceedings of the International IIS: IIPWM'03 Conference*, Zakopane, Poland, vol. 579 (14). (pp. 209-22).

Viera, A.F.G., & Virgil, J. (2007). Uma revisão dos algoritmos de radicalização em língua portuguesa. [A review of stemming algorithms for Portuguese Language.] *Information Research*, **12**(3), paper 315. Retrieved 15 April, 2012 from http://InformationR.net/ir/12-3/paper315.html.

Witten I. H., & Frank E. (2005). *Data Mining: Practical Machine Learning Tools and Techniques, 2º Ed.* Amsterdam, Boston, Heidelberg, London, New York, Oxford, Paris, San Diego, San Francisco, Singapure, Sydney, Tokyo: Elsevier.

12

ANALISYS OF IT OUTSOURCING CONTRACTS AT THE TCU (FEDERAL COURT OF ACCOUNTS) AND OF THE LEGISLATION THAT GOVERNS THESE CONTRACTS IN THE BRAZILIAN FEDERAL PUBLIC ADMINISTRATION

Graziela Ferreira Guarda
Edgard Costa Oliveira
Rafael Timóteo de Sousa Júnior
University of Brasília – UnB, Federal District, Brazil

ABSTRACT

Information technology (IT) outsourcing has for a long time been a major trend in business and government. Accountability of IT outsourcing contracts in the public administration is recognized as an important factor contributing to government transparency and public services quality, given the legislation governing these contracts and the amount of related expenditures. Considering the trend towards open government data publishing, including data on outsourcing contracts, there is an interesting opportunity for citizens to participate in the open auditing of these contracts as a means to assess the good application of public resources. In this study we explore this possibility by analyzing open data published by the Brazilian Federal Court of Accounts (TCU is its acronym in Portuguese), an interesting case since this agency has a paramount role in auditing the whole Brazilian Federal Public Administration. To this end, we gathered open data from the TCU regarding all outsourced IT services contracts maintained by the agency during the years 2000-2013. This data is analyzed to verify, from an external point of view, the related duration and values, identifying diferences between the predicted and actual amounts spent and evaluating the administration of such contracts regarding legislation. This analysis is based on a detailed survey of the relevant legislation as well as the verification of original contract terms and their addendums. As a result, we observed substantial differences in the amount spent on execution with respect to those predicted in the original contracts. Also, we identified the utilization of special justifications prescribed by law to sustain the extension of some contracts. Given these results, it is possible that IT outsourcing is not necessarily proved to be the best solution for the public sector problems regarding the lack of skilled personnel, which implies the need to assess the cost-benefit of maintaining these contracts. Also, it is possible that the existing legislation needs development in order to provide more flexibility to outsourcing contract management.

Keywords: IT Services, IT Governance, IT Outsourcing Contracts, Open Social Auditing, Brazilian Federal Public Administration, Brazilian Federal Court of Accounts (TCU).

Address for correspondence / Endereço para correspondência

Graziela Ferreira Guarda, Mestre em Engenharia Elétrica, Rua 34 norte lote 04 apto 208 - Águas Claras - DF, Universidade de Brasília - UnB, E-mail: grazielafg@yahoo.com

Edgard Costa Oliveira, Doutor em Ciências da Informação, Área Especial de Indústria Projeção A - UnB Gama - Setor Leste, Caixa-postal: 8114 - DF, Universidade de Brasília - UnB, E-mail: ecosta@unb.br

Rafael Timóteo de Sousa Júnior, Doutor em Processamento de Sinais e Telecomunicações, Campus Universitário Darcy Ribeiro, FT, ENE, Laboratório de Engenharia de Redes – Asa Norte - DF, Universidade de Brasília - UnB, E-mail: desousa@unb.br

1. INTRODUCTION

The activity of information technology (IT) outsourcing[1] has had significant growth rates within the IT service segment[2], a trend that is valid both for the Brazilian and global markets (Hendry, 1997).

In Brazil, Public Administration is one of the main contractors of outsourced IT services, thus contributing to the strengthening of this growth rate. Decisions to adopt such contracts are in line with Decree-Law No. 200/67, Art. 10 §7°, which mandates that administration should focus its efforts on management activities and not on operational tasks. In addition, Decree 2.271/97 established that computer-related activities should preferably be contracted to third parties. However, some authors who have examined the hiring of IT services by the public sector reported performance problems due to lack of formalization of the hiring process, lack of knowledge about this process and shortcomings in its implementation (Barbosa, Junqueira, Laia and Faria, 2006; Cardoso, 2000 and Cardoso, 2006).

Thus, the process of hiring of IT services needs to be more efficient, requiring extensive planning to guide investment and to ensure the desired benefits to the business processes. This planning should permeate the entire organization, providing IT alingment to the direction and goals of the organization. Consequently, all procurement of IT goods and services should have as a major goal to support one or more strategic objectives, detailing the intended benefits and evaluation indicators as well as specific goals to be achieved (Cruz, 2008).

Accountability of IT outsourcing contracts in public administration is recognized as an important factor contributing to government transparency and public services quality, given the legislation governing these contracts and the amount of related expenditures. Considering the trend towards open government data publishing[3], including data on outsourcing contracts, there is an interesting opportunity for citizens to participate in the open auditing of these contracts as a means to assess the good application of public resources. In this study we explore this possibility by analyzing open data published by the Brazilian Federal Court of Accounts (TCU is its acronym in Portuguese), an interesting case since this agency has a paramount role in auditing the whole Brazilian Federal Public Administration.

This methodology is nearly analogue to a black box software testing and validation approach (Howden, 1980) where external indicators are collected and analyzed so as to verify conformance to requirements. This approach presents interests that allow the evaluation of the effects of the whole organizational functioning, abstracting its internal structure and constituents, though this imposes limitations to the approach since it does not assess internal motivations and constraints. It is also noteworthy that this approach is adequate for an open social verification of governement data as there is more independence between the observer and the object

---

[1] IT outsourcing is defined as hiring an external organization to provide specialized IT services. This occurs when the contractor does not want to use its internal resources to operate and/or implement its own IT sector.

[2] The IT industry can be roughly divided into three main segments: (i) hardware; (ii) software; and (iii) IT services. In the IT services segment, the different categories or types of services include: (i) outsourcing; (ii) advice; (iii) integration and development; (iv) support and training. The outsourcing services can in turn be subdivided into: (i) outsourcing of software applications (development and maintenance); (ii) outsourcing of IT infrastructure management (machines, servers), and (iii) outsourcing processes highly dependent on IT business, such as purchasing, human resources, among others.

[3] Brazil is a founder member of the Open Government Partnership, a multilateral initiative that aims to secure concrete commitments from governments to promote transparency, empower citizens, fight corruption, and harness new technologies to strengthen governance (http://www.opengovpartnership.org/about).

of interest. Alternative approaches such as this were foreseen by (Broadbent and Guthrie, 1992).

Moreover, the chosen methodology reflects a commitment of this paper to contribute to the social control of public services, an idea that has been gaining thrust in Brazil in recent years, contemporary to the maturing of the Brazilian democracy (Schomer, 2012). It is an important attitude towards transparency of public services in Brazil, and the TCU openly provides information on its IT contracts, since it is one of the most important institutions to control the use of public resources (Speck, 1999) and has a significant performance and effectiveness auditing role combined with the release of recommendations for improving the performance of public federal agencies (Robinson, 2007), being an exemplary organization for these agencies.

This paper, which constitutes an extendend version of (Guarda, Oliveira and de Sousa, 2014), comprises a literature review addressing the concepts of outsourcing and IT outsourcing within public administration. Also, a survey of the TCU expenses on IT outsourcing is presented covering contracts for the period 2000 to 2013. The ensuing analysis using the gathered data was divided into two stages, since the years 2000-2011 refer to concluded contracts, while the years 2009-2013 refer to contracts still in progress.

1.1. GOALS

The central goal is to analyze all contracts related to IT outsourcing through the years 2000 to 2013 by the TCU, in order to observe contratct durations and values. The gathered data is then used to identify differences between planned and actual duration and spending values, as well as to analise the management of these contracts in light of the related legislation and public regulations.

1.2. MOTIVATION

Until 2008, the Brazilian Federal Public Administration has lacked a unified standard to regulate the process of hiring IT services or resources, such as the purchase of hardware and software, and the procurement of computing and/or information services.

In april 2008, the Brazilian Ministry of Planning, Budget and Management (MPOG is its acronym in Portuguese) published a normative instruction (NI) for the purpose of disciplining the hiring of services, whether continuously or not, by member agencies of the General Service System (SISG). This regulatory document, formally NI SLTI/MPOG No. 02/08, presented rules and guidelines for hiring services in public administration, adopting the expression "hiring services" in a generic sense, indeed applying the regulations to all types of services contracted by government.

Then, in addition to NI 02/08, in May 2008 the MPOG published NI SLTI/MPOG No. 04/08, which provides instructions specifically for the hiring process of IT services by directfederal public administration. On November 16th, 2010, NI 04/08 was replaced by NI SLTI/MPOG 04/10,, which entered into force on January 2nd, 2011, establishes the necessary IT service hiring phases: planning for procurement, vendor selection and contract management.

In addition to NI 04, with nearly concomitant new rules , the TCU has reiterated and further developed the theme, producing a new and challenging legal framework for government IT managers. These facts demanded the development of new professional skills, which are still lacking in most public bodies, as the TCU itself has come to this conclusion in its audits since then. This new legal framework causes significant impacts on public bodies, requiring special care for its adoption by top managers, in view of the restrictions related to public budget, existing staff, operational situation and government strategic planning.

Considering this legislation , it is an interesting research subject to take into account the challenging problems faced by the Federal Public Administration with respect to IT outsourcing. It is important to assess spending on the outsourcing of IT services in this context, especially considering that the government has invested in hiring personnel specifically assigned to and trained for performing public procurement.

1.3. RESEARCH PROBLEM

According to (Hendry, 1997), the services sector has been one of the fastest growing in Brazil and around the world in recent decades. Apart from its positive and negative points, outsourcing has become a reality in Brazilian companies and organizations, and especially in public service, where it has been used increasingly in recent years. Therefore the development of this research was performed to identify wether the practiced IT outsourcing contract management contributes to the quality of public spending, given that IT outsourcing involves a significant amount of public resources.

Thus, in this study the analysis of all contracts held by the TCU during the years 2000 to 2013 also has the intention to verify if the option for IT outsourcing has been financially and managerially appropriate to public service, considering that an alternative solution was to maintain those services in the hands of public employees.

One of the main problems identified in Brazilian public administration, with respect to outsourcing, is that the government has already identifyied items for improvement, but has not keep an adequate pace for developing actions to enable the required improvement. These problems were identified by the TCU itself in various public agencies, resulting in a TCU recommendation for MPOG to publish a specific standard for IT service hiring, which was consolidated in NI 04/08 and later in NI 04/10.

Thus, it is motivating to make a detailed analysis of the advantages and disadvantages of outsourcing IT services in public administration, so this study aims to contribute to the body of knowledge on this subject, particularly by verifying whether the process of hiring these IT services has been effective for the public administration.

1.4. METHODOLOGY

This section specifies the materials used to develop the study, and presents the methodology used for analysis and results interpretation.

1.4.1 MATERIALS

The materials used throughout the development of this work include the follwing:

- Current Brazilian legislation on hiring IT in Public Administration;
- IT Contracts data regarding the years 2000-2013 and addenda published by the TCU.

These documents are available as open data published by the MPOG and the TCU in their respectives web portals.

1.4.2 RESEARCH STAGES

Theoretical Review: The first stage of the work consisted in a literature review about the main issues addressed in this study. This phase proved to be of paramount importance in order to elucidate some of the basic concepts related to the topic of IT outsourcing in the Federal Public Service, and other related topics.

Survey and Choice of the TCU Contracts: a number of 35 contracts were chosen to be objects of analysis. The sources of data were contracts and addendum terms available on the TCU web portal regarding the provision of IT services. Contracts solely aimed at purchasing or leasing of computer equipment and software licenses were excluded from the data set. The chosen contracts were separated into a set for the analysis of finalized contracts (2000-2011) and a set for contracts in progress (2009-2013), giving way to the following lists:

- Concluded: 56-2000; 57-2000; 78-2001; 84-2001; 85-2001; 86-2001; 48-2003; 04-2004; 09-2005; 17-2006; 25-2006; 05-2007; 06-2007; 08-2007; 37-2007; 53-2007; 59-2007; 67-2007; 39-2008; 53-2008; 61-2008; 57-2009 e 34-2011.

- In Progress: 08-2009; 01-2010; 17-2010; 24-2010; 33-2011; 61-2011; 69-2011; 13-2012; 52-2012; 02-2013; 11-2013 e 20-2013.

Compilation of Information: The information gathered was compiled in the following separate tables:

- Concluded Contracts – table that contains relevant information of 23 finished contracts between 2000 and 2011;

- Contracts in Progress – table that contains relevant information of 12 ongoing contracts between 2009 and 2013;

- Summary of Concluded Contracts – table showing the amount and percentage of actual spending related to all IT services contractors during the period 2000 to 2011;

- Summary of Contracts in Progress – table showing the amount and percentage of actual spending related to all IT services contractors during the period 2009 to 2013;

- Highest Contract Values in the sampling period (13 years) – table intended to identify companies and classify by value their related IT Outsourcing contracts with the TCU (Indeed this table shows data regarding a single company).

2. LITERATURE REVIEW

2.1. CONCEPTS RELATED TO OUTSOURCING

Outsourcing, in what seems to be its broadest sense, means the purchase of any product or service from another company. In general, companies outsource products and services that they can not or will not produce for themselves (Turban, McLean & Wetherbe, 2004). Thus, outsourcing is a management approach that delegates to an external agent the operational responsibility for processes or services hitherto performed in the organization. As outsourcing has different approaches, it is important to understand the concepts of some authors before assessing which model fits best in a given organization.

Although there are several contradictions among researchers on the definition of outsourcing, the evolution of this practice led to a richer theoretical background of the phenomenon (Hätönen and Eriksson, 2009). The classic form of outsourcing can be defined as a management process based on transferring support activities to third parties - establishing a partnership with them so that the company concentrates only on tasks directly linked to the business in which it operates (Guarda, 2008).

There are authors arguing that outsourcing is the transfer of functions and services to third parties (Foina, 2001) or that business process outsourcing is the transfer of all activities that are not part of the company core competency (Beal, 2005). These authors also state that outsourcing has emerged in order to reduce costs, increase business productivity, and increase the quality and productivity of services, even if these factors are not always met.

Notwithstanding these factors, outsourcing requires a transformation in organizations, forcing them to concentrate their energies on their primary value-added business activity, thus better results are created to favor the effectiveness and optimization of management. According to (Queiroz, 1998), the quality resulting from outsourcing is linked with the specialty of the partners, as the more experience the third party has in relation to its service, the better the efficiency and effectiveness in the practice.

2.2. OUTSOURCING IN INFORMATION TECHNOLOGY (IT)

Outsourcing IT services has been increasingly common in the organizational context, especially in the public sector, since these services are now almost indispensable in any field and many organizations prefer to outsource IT (to specialized companies) while focusing their management on core activities, thus building more confidence in being ahead of their competitors and obtaining better profits.

According to (Earl, 1998) IT outsourcing is motivated by the need to cut costs and reduce staff. Also IT outsourcing has been defined as an organization's strategy to maintain control over deadlines and quality of service (Leite, 1997). For (Araújo, 2008), the reason why companies outsource the IT area is related to the amazing and rapid advances in this technology field, so it is easier to be more productive by outsourcing these services to specialized companies that keep pace with these advances.

2.3 ADVANTAGES AND DRAWBACKS OF IT OUTSOURCING

IT Outsourcing main advantages are related to the provision of various multidisciplinary professionals to solve the problem of the contracting organization, resulting in cost reduction, concentration of activities, adequate skills, labor savings and the elimination of routine activities. In general, the expected IT outsourcing benefits are (Hätönen and Eriksson, 2009):

- Financially: cost reduction, stability of capital outflows with periodic payments for services;

- Technically: improvement of the quality of IT services, gaining access to new technologies; and,

- Strategically: Focusing on core business, time to market, and the possibility of attracting skilled professionals to the job.

According to (Laudon, 2004), outsourcing advantages include to reduce or to control IT costs, while producing information systems even when internal resources are not available or are disabled. In this regard, (Leite, 1997) argues that IT outsourcing allows the company to have access to experts on the subject while still focusing on IT considering business priorities.

On the other hand, IT outsourcing drawbacks include problems of contract termination, loss of activities control, excessive bureaucracy, loss of professional experiences and conflicts of interest (Dias, 2000). This author further states that the lack of internal management for IT services implies the loss of knowledge which is given to third parties, hindering services continuity if the ousourcing company is no more available. An interesting drawback example is documented by the TCU in its Judgment No. 1.521/03-Plenary Session showing that excessive IT outsourcing in the federal public administration resulted in the loss of business intelligence.

Table 2.1 highlights the main IT outsourcing advantages according to (Leite, 1997) and (Vidal, 1993), as well as the main drawbacks to outsource the provision of IT services according to (Laudon and Laudon, 2004), an author who states that, despite the benefits resulting from outsourcing services, not all organizations benefit from this process, which, if not properly understood and managed, can cause serious problems for contractors.

In light of the findings by the authors referenced above, many IT outsourcing risks exist for the Brazilian Federal Public Administration, including major non-conformities to contractual statements and non-use of the delivered services, especially by means of information systems. The lack of contract management and supervision processes can result in getting services that do not always meet the goals set. In some cases it is observed that failures come from the specifications for outsourcing procurement, a step before hiring suppliers. If the rules for the provision of services are not well specified and do not provide administrative sanctions in case of non-compliance, outsourcing risks increase considerably.

Table 2.1 – *IT Outsourcing Advantages and Drawbacks.*

	Advantages	Drawbacks
1	Unconcern with the process of providing supplies.	Lack of training / qualification of the third party.
2	High level of services, with increased user satisfaction.	Difficulties by the third party to understanding the contractor business.
3	Technical Flexibility.	Loss of control over quality, costs and deadlines.
4	Objectivity of cost-benefit analysis for new projects.	Internal resistance of the technical staff and users in regard to outsourced professionals.
5	Expenditure forecast.	Culture differences of the outsourced services in regard to company standards.
6	Transfer of responsibility regarding the operation of information systems.	Poorly planned goals.
7	-	Labor claims.
8	-	Leakage of confidential information.
9	-	Increase in costs and difficulties in bidding processes since the volume of expenses at the end of a contract are hardly the same as originally planned.

Given these potential problems, (Foina, 2001) proposes the following precautions regarding IT outsourcing:

- Clearly define in the contract the area of operation for the third company;

- Establish metrics for managing the quality of services;

- Set a minimum number of monthly hours to be developed by the service provider.

2.4. IT OUTSOURCING IN THE BRAZILIAN FEDERAL PUBLIC ADMINISTRATION

Currently, most IT services in the Brazilian Federal Public Administration are provided under outsourcing contracts, since this is the management model adopted based on the assertion that the core objective is the proper functioning of the public administration while IT services comprise support objectives.

The paper by (Ramos, 2001) states that outsourcing has been used especially at the federal level to hire services related to support activities or complementary to core activities, these ones being defined as strategic since they can not be assigned to third parties in full as this would jeopardize public safety and interest.

In public companies and agencies, the outsourcing of IT has been considered a way to improve the services provided by the State, following exemplary experiences from the private sector. To (Willcocks, 1994) the government embraced the idea based on the fact that, in some, cases private companies could obtain better performance performing some government functions, thus outsourcing IT services were envisioned to improve government processes.

2.5. THE BRAZILIAN FEDERAL LAW REGARDING OUTSOURCING

A considerable set of laws and regulations govern the procurement of IT services and goods for the Brazilian Federal Public Administration. This section summarizes the key pieces of this corpus, using Table 2.2 to arrange the instruments in the order of time. This compilation, illustrating the evolution of the law from 1991 to

2010, includes the official instrument name and number, its publication date, a brief description and comments on the instrument objectives and legal obligations related to outsourcing, including relationships with other instruments.

Table 2.2 – *Brazilian federal legal instruments used in hiring IT services and goods.*

	Instrument	Publication Date	Description	Comments on Objectives and Relation with Outsourcing
1	Law No. 8.248/1991	23/10/1991	Provides the capacity and competitiveness of the IT and automation industry, and makes other provisions.	Defines in Article 8 what common automation and data processing goods and services are.
2	Law No. 8.666/1993	21/06/1993	Regulates article. 37, item XXI, of the Federal Constitution, establishing rules for biddings and contracts by the Public Administration and makes other provisions.	Establishes rules for biddings and contracts to be performed by the Public Administration. Defines in Article 22 the procedure for bidding and in Article 24 the cases in which the bidding is dispensable.
3	Decree No. 1.048/1993	21/01/1994	Regulates the Information and IT Resource Management System of the Federal Public Administration.	Regulates the Information and IT Resources System (SISP), which is responsible for planning, coordination, organization, operation, control and monitoring of IT resources. Defines in Article 2 the goals of the SISP.
4	Decree No. 2.271/1997	07/07/1997	Regulates the procurement of services by the Federal Public Administration, direct, autonomous agencies and foundations and makes other provisions.	Defines which activities may be subject to hiring via bidding. States in its Article 1 that incidental, instrumental activities, or those complementary to matters that constitute the area of legal competence of the organ, may be subject to indirect execution. Its Article 3 states that the object of the contract must be explicitly defined in the bidding announcement.
5	Decree No. 3.555/2000	08/08/2000	Establishes the rules for the public bidding processes in the form of auctions for the procurement of common goods and services.	Constitutes a complement to Law No. 8.666/1993 (item 2 in this table). Its Article 5 states that auctions do not apply to engineering works and services nor to real estate leasing and sales.
6	Decree No. 3.931/2001	19/09/2001	Regulates the Prices Registration System which is governed by article 15 of Law No. 8.666/1993 (item 2 in this table), and makes other provisions.	Defines the Prices Registration System (SRP) which is a set of procedures for the formal recording of prices in relation to the provision of common services and the procurement of goods. Defines in its Article 2 when the SRP should be used.

	Instrument	Publication Date	Description	Comments on Objectives and Relation with Outsourcing
7	Law No. 10.520/2002	17/07/2002	Establishes, on the realm of the Union, States, Federal District and Municipalities, in accordance with article 37, item XXI, of the Federal Constitution, the bidding method by auctions for the procurement of common goods and services, and makes other provisions.	Modifies the Law No. 8.666/1993 (item 2 in this table), including electronic auctions as a bidding method. Complements this Law items 5 and 6, establishing that the process may be held by means of electronic auctions for the purchase of common goods and services. Defines in its Article 11 that the procurement and purchasing of common goods and hiring of services must be made using the SRP (item 6 in this table).
8	Law No. 11.077/2004	30/12/2004	Modifies Law No. 8248/1991 (item 1 in this table), Law No. 8237/1991, and Law No. 10.176/2001, providing the capacity and competitiveness of the IT and automation industry, and makes other provisions.	Modifies Law No. 8248/1991 and supplements Decree No. 3.555/2000 (item 5 in this table), regulating the capacity and competitiveness of the IT and automation industry. Recommends the use of electronic bidding for procurements defined by Law.
9	Decree No. 5.450/2005	31/05/2005	Regulates electronic auctions for the purchase of common goods and services, and makes other provisions.	Convalidates the Decree No. 3.555/2000 (item 5 in this table), and determines that the electronic auctions should be mandatory in the procurement of common goods and services as highlights its Article 4.
10	Decree No. 5.504/2005	05/08/2005	Establishes the requirement for using the public auction, preferably in its electronic form, by public and private entities, for the procurement of common goods and services performed as a consequence of voluntary public funds transfers from the Federal Government[4].	Reinforces the Decree No. 5.450/2005(item 9 in this table). Expands the mandatory use of electronic auctions for public and private entities for the procurement of common goods and services due to voluntary public funds transfers from the Federal Government.
11	IN No. 02 MPOG/SLTI	30/04/2008	Provides rules and guidelines for the procurement of services, continued or not.	Complements the instruments defined in items 2, 4, and 7 in this table. Controls rules and guidelines for hiring services continued or not.

---

[4] Transfer of resources from the Federal Government to another government level, as financial assistance, cooperation, or help, which is not a result of a constitutional or legal requirement, or destined to the public federal healthcare system.

	Instrument	Publication Date	Description	Comments on Objectives and Relation with Outsourcing
12	Ordinance No. 11 MPOG/SLTI	30/12/2008	Defines the General Information Technology Strategy (EGTI) for the Federal Public Administration.	Complements the instrument described in item 11 of this table and enforces compliance with the instrument described in Item 3. Lays the foundation for transitioning from the current state of the Federal Government IT environments. The EGTI aims to define a set of improvements and is the foundation for a governance model for the renowned Information Technology Resources Administration System (SISP), serving as contextualization between the parties to reach maturity.
13	Decree No. 7.063/2010	13/01/2010	Approves the Regimental Structure and the Demonstrative Table on Commission and Gratified Functions of the Ministry of Planning, Budget and Management, and makes other provisions.	Complements the instrument described in item 3 of this table.
14	Decree No. 7.174/2010	12/05/2010	Regulates the procurement of IT and automation goods and services by the Federal Public Administration, direct or indirect agencies, foundations instituted and maintained by the Government and other organizations under the direct or indirect control of the Union.	Complements the instruments described in items 1, 2 and 7 in this table and modifies the instrument in item 5. Highlights in its Article 2 that the acquisition of IT goods and services should be preceded by the procurement planning, including basic design or reference specifications containing the object to be hired.
15	IN No. 04 MPOG/SLTI	16/11/2010	Provides the process of hiring IT solutions by members of the SISP of the Federal Executive Branch agencies.	Revokes the instruments defined in items 3 and 11 of this table and builds upon the instrument in item 14. Reorganizes the topics and steps that must be completed for the hiring of IT solutions within SISP.

Table 2.2 is aimed at summarizing how outsourcing rules have developed over the last decade, given law modifications and the creation of new perspectives. In this context, it is noteworthy the inclusion of the electronic bidding method for the acquisition of common goods and services. Before that inclusion, the bids for the purchase of goods or hiring IT services used competitive bidding.

According to Decree 3.555/00, public auctions constitute the category by which the competition for providing common goods or services is made in public sessions, by means of written pricing proposals and verbal bids, giving way to a decision in which the winning bidder will necessarily be the one that offers the lowest price. Thus, in Brazil, materials or services procurement occurs through public bidding processes (auctions) held by the government, either in-person or electronic auctions.

There is evidence that electronic auctions represent a substantial evolution in public hiring of services because it entails considerable gains in economy, transparency, competitiveness, and control of the process as a whole (Santanna, 2007). The advantages of using this bidding category include savings in time and cost. Regarding time, the typical deadline for the traditional competitive bidding is 45 days while the auction category is 15 days, which represents a reduction of one third of the time for completion of the process, due to fewer bureaucratic obstacles. In relation to cost, the auctioneer has the opportunity to negotiate in real time the values with the bidders, so that the amount spent on bids tend to be smaller, resulting in potential savings for the Public Administration.

3. RESULTS AND DISCUSSION

This section aims to compile the published data and then analyze IT outsourcing contracts by the TCU convering the years 2000-2013, including the analysis of contracts already finalized (2000 to 2011) and contracts still in progress (2009 to 2013).

The actual expenses are calculated by adding the initial values to the values given in each addendum. The results are grouped into the following tables: Table 3.1 – Concluded Contracts – 2000 to 2011; Table 3.2 – Contracts in Progress – 2009 to 2013; Table 3.3 – Summary of Concluded Contracts – 2001 to 2011; Table 3.4 – Summary of Contracts in Progress – 2009 to 2013.

Table 3.1 – *Concluded Contracts – 2001 to 2011.*

Contract 56-2000-DF				
Category: **Competition**			Status: **Concluded Contract**	Company: **CTIS**
	Value:	%↑	Date:	Rationale:
Initial Value:	517.704,00	-	14/11/00	Hiring services to design, implement and deploy the system for Electronic Collection of Statement of Accounts.
Total Value:	517.704,00			
Contract 57-2000-DF				
Category: **Unenforceability of Bid**			Status: **Concluded Contract**	Company: **LINK DATE**
	Value:	%↑	Date:	Rationale:
Initial Value:	31.200,00	-	20/11/00	Hiring a company specializing in IT, to perform maintenance for the "Automation System of Inventory" software, related to Equity and Warehouse modules.
Total Value:	31.200,00			
Contract 78-2001-DF				
Category: **Competition**			Status: **Concluded Contract**	Company: **FÓTON**
	Value:	%↑	Date:	Rationale:
Initial Value:	364.320,00	-	31/12/01	Hiring systems development consultancy, based on the systems development methodology Rational Unified Process - RUP or a similar methodology, based on the Unified Process - UP, as specified in the Annexes of the Call.
Addendum 1	364.320,00	100.0	31/12/04	Extension until 31.12.2003.
Addendum 2	364.320,00	100.0	31/12/04	Extension of the Term of the Contract until

				31/12/04.
Addendum 3	486.712,92	133.5	31/12/04	Renegotiation of prices in the Contract.
Total Value:	1.579.672,92			

Contract 84-2001-DF

Category: **Competition**			Status: **Concluded Contract**		Company: **CTIS**
	Value:	%↑	Date:	Rationale:	
Initial Value:	4.215.577,50	-	31/12/01	Development and implementation of information systems, corrective and adaptative maintenance and documentation based on the methodology Rational Unified Process - RUP.	
Total Value:	4.215.577,50				

Contract 85-2001-DF

Category: **Competition**			Status: **Concluded Contract**		Company: **CTIS**
	Value:	%↑	Date:	Rationale:	
Initial Value:	1.623.072,00	-	31/12/01	Development of information systems currently in operation at the TCU. The service warranty is 36 months, according to clause 16.	
Addendum 1:	81.153,60	5.0	30/12/03	Promote growth of 5% to the value of the original contract.	
Addendum 2:	1.704.225,60	105.0	31/12/04	Extends until December 31st, 2003 the validity of the original contract.	
Addendum 3:	-		31/12/04	Changes the First and Fourth Clauses of the Contract.	
Addendum 4:	1.704.225,60	105.0	31/12/04	Extension of the term until December 31st, 2004.	
Addendum 5:	245.578,90	15.1	31/12/04	Renegotiation of the contract value.	
Addendum 6:	1.949.804,50	120.1	31/12/05	Extension of contract validity until 31/12/05.	
Addendum 7:	1.949.804,50	120.0	31/12/06	Extension of validity.	
Total Value:	9.257.864,70				

Contract 86-2001-DF

Category: **Competition**			Status: **Concluded Contract**		Company: **CTIS**
	Value:	%↑	Date:	Rationale:	
Initial Value:	1.099.460,60	-	27/12/01	Provision of support services to computer services users - remote and local support.	
Addendum 1:	1.170.380,60	106.5	27/12/03	Extension of Contract until 27.12.2003 and to promote a 6.4505% increase of the initial contract value.	
Addendum 2:	1.170.380,60	106.5	27/12/04	Extension of the term of the contract until 27/12/04.	
Addendum 3:	112.841,16	10.3	27/12/04	Renegotiation of contract prices.	
Addendum 4:	1.284.170,04	116.8	27/12/05	Extension of validity.	
Addendum 5:	1.284.170,04	116.8	27/12/06	Extension of validity.	
Addendum 6:	1.284.170,04	116.8	27/12/07	Exceptional extension of the contract validity until 27/12/07.	
Total Value:	7.405.573,08				

Contract 48-2003-DF

Category: **Exemption of Bid**			Status: **Concluded Contract**		Company: **SERPRO**
	Value:	%↑	Date:	Rationale:	
Initial Value:	336.000,00		01/07/03	Provision of information and IT services for continuous online access to the CPF and CNPJ registry data.	

	Value:	%↑	Date:	Rationale:
Addendum 1:	54.000,00	16.1	01/07/07	Increase of 16.07%.
Total Value:	390.000,00			

Contract 4-2004-DF				
Category: **In-person Auction**		Status: **Concluded Contract**		Company: **CAST**

	Value:	%↑	Date:	Rationale:
Initial Value:	83.040,00	-	10/02/04	Hiring of technical support services and software versions update.
Addendum 1:	83.040,00	100.0	10/02/06	Sixth clause- On the Validity and Effectiveness.
Addendum 2:	83.040,00	100.0	10/02/07	Extension of the term until 10/02/07.
Addendum 3:	83.040,00	100.0	10/02/08	Extension of the term until 10/02/07.
Total Value:	332.160,00			

Contract 9-2005-DF				
Category: **Competition**		Status: **Concluded Contract**		Company: **SOFTTEK**

	Value:	%↑	Date:	Rationale:
Initial Value:	447.760,00	-	11/04/05	Supply, installation and configuration of a software integrated solution for support, upgrade and remote assistance services, and training for the construction and administration of an extract, transform and load data service (Extract, Transform and Load - ETL).
Addendum 1:	88.560,00	19.8	06/06/07	Extension of the term.
Addendum 2:	88.560,00	19.8	06/06/08	Extension of the term of Contract No. 09/2005 entered into force between the parties on 11/04/05, corresponding to the item 1.1 of the seventh clause.
Addendum 3:	88.560,00	19.8	06/06/09	Extension of CT n° 09-05.
Addendum 4:	88.560,00	19.8	06/06/10	Extension of the Term of the Contract 09/05.
Total Value:	802.000,00			

Contract 17-2006-DF				
Category: **Unenforceability of Bid**		Status: **Concluded Contract**		Company: **LINK DATE**

	Value:	%↑	Date:	Rationale:
Initial Value:	15.600,00	-	01/04/06	Hiring maintainance for the "Automation System of Inventory" software, related to Equity and Warehouse modules. Posted on 23/03/06.
Total Value:	15.600,00			

Contract 25-2006-DF				
Category: **Exemption of Bid**		Status: **Concluded Contract**		Company: **SERPRO**

	Value:	%↑	Date:	Rationale:
Initial Value:	12.500.000,00	-	31/05/06	Provision of data extraction and transmission services from SIAFI and SIASG services, as well as services for the production of a data warehousing solution named Intelligence and Support System for the External Control (SÍNTESE).
Addendum 1:	-	NA	30/11/08	Amendment of terms and deletion of items.
Total Value:	12.500.000,00			

Contract 5-2007-DF				
Category: **Electronic Auction**		Status: **Concluded Contract**		Company: **HEPTA**

	Value:	%↑	Date:	Rationale:
Initial Value:	119.000,00	-	13/03/07	Provision of technical support services to

				products pertaining to the Microsoft platform integrating the computing infrastructure of the TCU.
Total Value:	119.000,00			

Contract 6-2007-DF

Category: **Electronic Auction**			Status: **Concluded Contract**	Company: **UNIMIX**
	Value:	%↑	Date:	Rationale:
Initial Value:	194.190,00	-	13/03/07	Provision of technical support services to products pertaining to the Oracle platform integrating the computing infrastructure of the TCU.
Addendum 1:	194.190,00	100.0	13/03/09	Extension of contract validity until 13/03/09.
Total Value:	388.380,00			

Contract 8-2007-DF

Category: **Electronic Auction**			Status: **Concluded Contract**	Company: **CAST**
	Value:	%↑	Date:	Rationale:
Initial Value:	45.840,00	-	13/03/07	Providing technical support services for OLAP Business Objects solutions integrating the computing infrastructure of the TCU.
Addendum 1:	45.840,00	100.0	13/03/09	Extension of Contract 08/07.
Addendum 2:	45.840,00	100.0	13/03/10	Extension of the term of the Contract Signed on 13/03/2007 between the parties for the provision of technical support to computer services.
Addendum 3:	45.840,00	100.0	13/03/11	Extension of the term of the Contract until 13/03/11.
Addendum 4:	45.840,00	100.0	13/03/12	Extension of validity of the CT 08/07.
Total Value:	229.200,00			

Contract 37-2007-DF

Category: **Exemption of Bid**			Status: **Concluded Contract**	Company: **SERPRO**
	Value:	%↑	Date:	Rationale:
Initial Value:	42.840,00	-	01/06/07	Provision of Data Processing services for the Tape 50 aggregate values all over Brazil.
Addendum 1:	42.840,00	100,.0	01/06/09	Extension of contract validity until 01/06/09.
Addendum 2:	42.840,00	100.0	01/06/10	Extension of the term of the Contract until 01/06/10.
Addendum 3:	42.840,00	100.0	01/06/11	Extension of the term of the Contract n° 37/07.
Total Value:	171.360,00			

Contract 53-2007-DF

Category: **Exemption of Bid**			Status: **Concluded Contract**	Company: **SERPRO**
	Value:	%↑	Date:	Rationale:
Initial Value:	322.000,00	-	03/09/07	Provision of information and IT services (queries to CNPJ and CPF).
Total Value:	322.000,00			

Contract 59-2007-DF

Category: **In-person Auction**			Status: **Concluded Contract**	Company: **DG10**
	Value:	%↑	Date:	Rationale:
Initial Value:	241.400,00	-	16/10/07	Provision of specialized IT technical services, including planning, development, implementation and execution of the operation

				and monitoring of the Information Technology environment. Note: The closure of the Montana activities occurred on 24/10/07 and the Data Graphics company started delivering services on 25/10/07.
Total Value:	241.400,00			

Contract 67-2007-DF

Category: **Electronic Auction**			Status: **Concluded Contract**		Company: **CTIS**

	Value:	%↑	Date:	Rationale:
Initial Value:	1.945.000,00	-	28/12/07	Provision of specialized technical IT services, including planning, development, implementation and execution of remote and onsite technical support activities to Information Technology clients within the TCU.
Addendum 1:	101.724,69	5.2	28/12/08	Increase of 12.81% in the value of services, with a temporary and a permanent instalment.
Addendum 2:	2.194.121,64	112.8	28/12/09	Extension of the term until 28/12/09.
Addendum 3:	0,01	0.0	28/12/09	Suspension of software and information systems services - item 3 of "remote support services".
Addendum 4:	141.864,76	7.3	28/12/09	Renegotiation of contract values that, in the period from 01/05/2008 to 31/07/09, changes from R$ 181.843,47 to R$ 188.129,52 and, after 01/08/08, changes from R$ 181.843,47 to R$ 189.107,64.
Addendum 5:	567.322,92	29.2	28/03/10	Extension of the term of the Contract until 28/03/10.
Addendum 6:	378.215,28	19.5	28/05/10	Extension of the term of the Contract n° 67/07.
Addendum 7:	109.009,95	5.6	28/05/10	Renegotiation of prices in the Contract n° 67/07.
Total Value:	5.437.259,25			

Contract 39-2008-DF

Category: **Exemption of Bid**			Status: **Concluded Contract**		Company: **SERPRO**

	Value:	%↑	Date:	Rationale:
Initial Value:	488.254,35	-	18/08/08	Provision of information and IT services, consolidated in the delivery of data drawn from the Registry of Individuals – CPF, the National Registry of Legal Entities - CNPJ and Individual Income Tax - IRPF, pertaining to the Secretariat of the Federal Revenue of Brazil, by means of special calculations on databases localized in the Federal data Processing Service SERPRO.
Addendum 1:	-	NA	18/02/11	Deletion/modification of items of the basic design.
Total Value:	488.254,35			

Contract 53-2008-DF

Category: **Electronic Auction**			Status: **Concluded Contract**		Company: **DG10**

	Value:	%↑	Date:	Rationale:
Initial Value:	157.289,34	-	17/10/08	Provision of specialized IT technical services, including planning, development, implementation and execution of the operation and monitoring of the information technology environment.
Total Value:	157.289,34			

Contract 61-2008-DF					
Category: **Electronic Auction**			Status: **Concluded Contract**		Company: **REDECOM**
	Value:	%↑	Date:	Rationale:	
Initial Value:	172.800,00	-	02/12/08	Provision of technical support services for network solutions.	
Addendum 1:	172.800,00	100,0	01/12/10	Extending the term of Contract No. 61/08 signed between the parties on 01/12/2008, according to the terms in its Fifth Clause.	
Addendum 2:	172.800,00	100,0	01/12/11	Extension of the term until 01/12/11.	
Addendum 3:	172.800,00	100,0	01/12/12	Extension of the CT 61/08.	
Total Value:	691.200,00				

Contract 57-2009-DF					
Category: **Electronic Auction**			Status: **Concluded Contract**		Company: **REDECOM**
	Value:	%↑	Date:	Rationale:	
Initial Value:	51.194,00	-	30/12/09	Provision of upgrade and technical support services for the IBM Tivoli Storage Manager backup solution, as specified in Annex I - Terms of Reference of the Electronic Auction Bid No. 71/09.	
Total Value:	51.194,00				

Contract 34-2011-DF					
Category: **Electronic Auction**			Status: **Concluded Contract**		Company: **AMÉRICA**
	Value:	%↑	Date:	Rationale:	
Initial Value:	2.854.491,00	-	21/12/11	The provision of data storage solutions, including training, installation and configuration services, additionaly to onsite technical support to the products during the warranty period. ATA - SRP.	
Total Value:	2.854.491,00				

For the composition of Table 3.1, the 'Value' rows as well as the 'Date' and 'Rationale' columns were all gathered from the querying of Contracts and Addendum terms, available on the TCU web portal at https://contas.tcu.gov.br/contrata/ConsultaPublica?opcao=resultado.

To calculations for the '%↑' column consist of percentage increases in amounts spent within the listed Contracts.

The 'Total Value' represents the sum of the values in column 'Value' for Contracts where Addendum terms were found.

Table 3.2 – *Contracts in Progress – 2009 to 2013.*

Contract 8-2009-DF					
Category: **Electronic Auction**			Status: **Contract in Progress**		Company: **DG10**
	Value:	%↑	Date:	Rationale:	
Initial Value:	325.850,00	-	15/04/09	Provision of specialized technical IT services, including planning, development, implementation and execution of the operation and monitoring of the Information Technology environment of TCU.	
Addendum 1:	325.850,00	100.0	14/04/11	Extension of the term until 14/04/11.	

Addendum 2:	2.319,43	0.7	14/04/11	Renegotiation of prices of the Contract signed between the parties on 14/04/09.
Addendum 3:	326.159,19	100.1	14/04/12	Extension of the term of the Contract 08/09.
Addendum 4:	49.435,92	15.2	14/04/12	Adding one more monitoring and operation round (from 0 to 6 hours) to contract n° 08/09.
Addendum 5:	0,01	0.0	14/04/12	Modification of official and commercial name.
Addendum 6:	421.556,29	129.4	14/04/13	Extension of the term and modification of the sixth clause.
Addendum 7:	452.220,84	138.8	14/04/14	Extension of the CT 08/09.
Total Value:	1.903.391,68			

Contract 1-2010-DF

Category: **Electronic Auction**			Status: **Contract in Progress**		Company: **HEPTA**

	Value:	%↑	Date:	Rationale:
Initial Value:	240.876,00	-	21/01/10	Provision of technical support services to Microsoft products integrating the computing infrastructure of the TCU, under contract by unit price, under the contract unit price for Microsoft products services, including preventive and reactive support, as specified by the Electronic Auction Notice # 73/09.
Addendum 1:	240.876,00	100.0	21/01/12	Extension of the term until 20/01/12.
Addendum 2:	254.450,40	105.6	21/01/13	Extension of the term of the contract n° 1/10.
Addendum 3:	254.450,40	105.6	21/01/14	Extension of the term of 21/01/2013 to 01/20/14.
Total Value:	990.652,80			

Contract 17-2010-DF

Category: **Electronic Auction**			Status: **Contract in Progress**		Company: **CTIS**

	Value:	%↑	Date:	Rationale:
Initial Value:	3.224.000,00	-	31/05/10	Execution of specialized technical services in the field of information technology for the organization, development, implementation and ongoing execution of remote and local technical support to users of information technology solutions, including performing regular routines, guidance and clarification of questions and receiving, recording, analysis, diagnosis and care of user requests.
Addendum 1:	3.224.000,00	100.0	28/05/12	Extension of validity for CT 17/10.
Addendum 2:	3.224.000,00	100.0	28/05/13	Extension of the term until 28/05/13.
Addendum 3:	357.166,71	11.1	28/05/13	Renegotiation of prices in the contract n° 17/10.
Addendum 4:	3.545.208,35	110.0	28/05/14	Extension of technical services for organization, development, implementation and ongoing execution of remote and local technical support, for users of IT solutions.
Addendum 5:	104.088,79	3.2	28/05/14	Review and Renegotiation of prices for contract n° 17/2010.
Total Value:	13.678.463,85			

Contract 24-2011-DF

Category: **Exemption of Bid**			Status: **Contract in Progress**		Company: **SERPRO**

	Value:	%↑	Date:	Rationale:
Initial Value:	151.207,87	-	23/05/11	Provision of information and IT services, for data extracted from the CPF, CNPJ and IRPF systems, of the Secretariat of the Federal Revenue of Brazil, by special calculation in databases located in SERPRO.

	Value:	%↑	Date:	Rationale:
Total Value:	151.207,87			

Contract 33-2011-DF

Category: **Exemption of Bid**			Status: **Contract in Progress**	Company: **SERPRO**
	Value:	%↑	Date:	Rationale:
Initial Value:	56.133,24		02/07/11	Provision of Data Processing services for Tape 50 added values.
Addendum 1:	56.133,24	100.0	01/07/13	Extension of the term of the contract n° 33/11.
Addendum 2:	56.133,24	100.0	01/07/14	Extension of the term of the contract n° 33/11.
Total Value:	168.399,72			

Contract 61-2011-DF

Category: **Exemption of Bid**			Status: **Contract in Progress**	Company: **SERPRO**
	Value:	%↑	Date:	Rationale:
Initial Value:	300.034,56	-	01/11/11	Provision of information and IT services.
Total Value:	300.034,56			

Contract 69-2011-DF

Category: **Electronic Auction**			Status: **Contract in Progress**	Company: **AMÉRICA**
	Value:	%↑	Date:	Rationale:
Initial Value:	2.232.691,36	-	28/12/11	Provision of data storage solutions, including training, installation and configuration services, and onsite technical support to products during the warranty period.
Addendum 1:	-	NA	13/10/12	Extension of the term specified in Item 1 of 5th Clause of contract n° 69/11, signed by the parties on 28/12/11.
Addendum 2:	-	NA	27/12/12	Extension of the term provided in Item 1 of 5th Clause of contract n° 69/11.
Total Value:	2.232.691,36			

Contract 13-2012-DF

Category: **Electronic Auction**			Status: **Contract in Progress**	Company: **TECNISYS**
	Value:	%↑	Date:	Rationale:
Initial Value:	209.000,00	-	08/05/12	Provision of onsite technical support to software (item 1 - Red Hat Enterprise Linux Server and Item 2 - JBoss Enterprise Application Platform).
Addendum 1:	209.000,00	100,0	07/05/14	Extension of the validity and amendment to fifth clause of contract n° 13/12.
Total Value:	428.000,00			

Contract 52-2012-DF

Category: **Electronic Auction**			Status: **Contract in Progress**	Company: **AÇÃO**
	Value:	%↑	Date:	Rationale:
Initial Value:	295.000,00	-	28/12/12	Provision of onsite technical support to VMware products, with an estimated employment of 1.000 credits, to be consumed on demand, under contract by unit price.
Total Value:	295.000,00			

Contract 2-2013-DF

Category: **Electronic Auction**			Status: **Contract in Progress**	Company: **AÇÃO**
	Value:	%↑	Date:	Rationale:
Initial Value:	605.000,00	-	10/04/13	Provision of management software for the virtualized environment, official training and implementation service the management

				solution.	
Total Value:	605.000,00				

Contract 11-2013-DF

Category: **Electronic Auction**			Status: **Contract in Progress**		Company: **AÇÃO**
	Value:	%↑	Date:	Rationale:	
Initial Value:	559.000,00	-	30/04/13	Provision of management software for the virtualized servers in the headquarters and state branches, including the execdution of official training and the implementation service of the management solution.	
Total Value:	559.000,00				

Contract 20-2013-DF

Category: **Electronic Auction**			Status: **Contract in Progress**		Company: **CAST**
	Value:	%↑	Date:	Rationale:	
Initial Value:	2.869.980,00	-	20/05/13	Provision of onsite and remote information systems development, maintenance and testing, under contract by unit price, as specified in the Annexes of the Electronic Auction Notice n° 16/13.	
Total Value:	2.869.980,00				

For the composition of Table 3.2, the same rules explained for Table 3.1 were applied, also on data gathered from the querying of Contracts and Addendum terms, available on the TCU web portal at https://contas.tcu.gov.br/contrata/ConsultaPublica?opcao=resultado.

The consolidation of data from Tables 3.1 and 3.2 results in Tables 3.3 and 3.4 which show values regarding the original contracts and addendums for the provision of IT services during the period 2000-2013, as well as the percentage increase ratio of total value to initial value for all contracts.

Table 3.3 – Summary of Concluded Contracts – 2000 to 2011

Contract	Company	Bid Category	Initial Value	Sum of Addendums	Total Value	↑%
56-2000	CTIS	Competition	517.704,00	-	517.704,00	0.00
57-2000	Link Date	Unenforceability	31.200,00	-	31.200,00	0.00
78-2001	Fóton	Competition	364.320,00	1.215.352,92	1.579.672,92	333.59
84-2001	CTIS	Competition	4.215.577,50	-	4.215.577,50	0.00
85-2001	CTIS	Competition	1.623.072,00	7.634.792,70	9.257.864,70	470.39
86-2001	CTIS	Competition	1.099.460,60	6.306.112,42	7.405.573,08	573.56
48-2003	SERPRO	Exemption	336.000,00	54.000,00	390.000,00	16.07
04-2004	Cast	In-person Auction	83.040,00	249.120,00	332.160,00	300.00
09-2005	Softtek	Competition	447.760,00	354.240,00	802.000,00	79.11
17-2006	Link Date	Unenforceability	15.600,00	-	15.600,00	0.00
25-2006	SERPRO	Exemption	12.500.000,00	-	12.500.000,00	0.00
05-2007	Hepta	Electronic Auction	119.000,00	-	119.000,00	0.00
06-2007	Unimix	Electronic Auction	194.190,00	194.190,00	388.380,00	100.00
08-2007	CAST	Electronic Auction	45.840,00	183.360,00	229.200,00	400.00
37-2007	SERPRO	Exemption	42.840,00	128.520,00	171.360,00	300.00
53-2007	SERPRO	Exemption	322.000,00	-	322.000,00	0.00
59-2007	DG-10	In-person Auction	241.400,00	-	241.400,00	0.00
67-2007	CTIS	Electronic Auction	1.945.000,00	3.492.259,25	5.437.259,25	179.55
39-2008	SERPRO	Exemption	488.254,35	-	488.254,35	0.00
53-2008	DG-10	Electronic Auction	157.289,34	-	157.289,34	0.00

61-2008	Redecom	Electronic Auction	172.800,00	518.400,00	691.200,00	300.00
57-2009	Redecom	Electronic Auction	51.194,00	-	51.194,00	0.00
34-2011	América	Electronic Auction	2.854.491,00	-	2.854.491,00	0.00
		∑ =	27.868.032,79	∑ =	48.198.380,14	57.82

Table 3.4 – *Summary of Contracts in Progress– 2009 to 2013*

Contract	Company	Bid Category	Initial Value	Sum of Addendums	Total Value	↑%
08-2009	DG-10	Electronic Auction	325.850,00	1.577.541,68	1.903.391,68	484.13
01-2010	Hepta	Electronic Auction	240.876,00	749.776,80	990.652,80	311.27
17-2010	CTIS	Electronic Auction	3.224.000,00	10.454.463,85	13.678.463,85	324.27
24-2011	SERPRO	Exemption	151.207,87	-	151.207,87	0.00
33-2011	SERPRO	Exemption	56.133,24	112.266,48	168.399,72	200.00
61-2011	SERPRO	Exemption	300.034,56	-	300.034,56	0.00
69-2011	América	Electronic Auction	2.232.691,36	-	2.232.691,36	0.00
13-2012	Tecnisys	Electronic Auction	209.000,00	209.000,00	428.000,00	100.00
52-2012	Ação	Electronic Auction	295.000,00	-	295.000,00	0.00
02-2013	Ação	Electronic Auction	605.000,00	-	605.000,00	0.00
11-2013	Ação	Electronic Auction	559.000,00	-	559.000,00	0.00
20-2013	CAST	Electronic Auction	2.869.980,00	-	2.869.980,00	0.00
		∑ =	8.198.793,03	∑ =	24.181.821,84	33.90

In Table 3.3, observing each percentage increase in the ratio of final contract value to the initial value (↑%), there are significant increases in a number of contracts with a maximum 573.56% increase. The results also show that the sum of initial contract values between 2000 and 2011 is R$ 27.868.032,79 and that with addendums these values were increased to R$ 48.198.380,14, which represents a total increase of 57.82% during the analyzed period.

In Table 3.4, observing each percentual increase in the ratio of final contract value to initial value (↑%), there are significant increases in a number of contracts with a maximum 484.13% increase. The results also show that the sum of initial contract values between 2009 and 2013 is R$ 8.198.793,03 and that with addendums these values were increased to R$ 24.181.821,84, which represents a total increase of 33.90% during the analyzed period.

These results indicate that the estimated values for the hiring of IT services are far below the amounts actually spent in the end. Since the Law says that a contract may be valid for a period of 60 months, it means that the best practice is to estimate the expenditures for the possible 5-year contract duration, considering that in practice the contract usually continues until the last possible deadline. This also indicates that maybe hiring IT outsourcing is strategic enough to justify longer contracts.

Another important aspect of the results are the real contract characteristics that differ from legislation governing the hiring of IT services by the public administration. For instance, Article 65 item II §1° of Law 8.666/93 defines that in case of procurement of services, the allowed percentage additions or reductions in addendums is up to 25% of the initial contract value. Also, Article 65 item II §2° instructs that no increase or reduction may exceed the limits established in the previous paragraph, except reductions resulting from an agreement between the contractors (terms stated by Law n° 9.648/1998). The present analysis observes that added addendum values are above the percentage allowed by law in different contracts, the highest ones being the following:

- Concluded contract 78-2001: in addendum 3 a value of R$ 486.712,92 represents an increase of 133.5% compared to the initial value of the contract;

- Contract in Progress 08-2009: in addendum 7 a value of R$ 452.220,84 represents an increase of 138.8% compared to the initial value of the contract.

This is a contract management difficulty imposed by Law as a means to preventively restrain fraud. Notwithstanding this fact, maybe the observed contract modifications in this case seem to indicate the need to develop the Law, since there is evidence that some IT outsourcing contracts would benefit if they were signed for longer periods. Also, considering new IT services provison modes, such as Cloud Computing (Mell and Grance, 2011), continuous or periodic payment per service should be allowed instead of fixed period contracts.

Finally, another observation is that a single company (CTIS) has got the highest values in the TCU IT outsorcing contracts, with its 6 contracts in a total of 35 analyzed contracts, as shown in Table 3.5. Considering that the sum of concluded contracts, R$ 48.198.380,14 and contracts in progress, R$ 24.181.821,84, totals RS 72.380.201,98, the observation is that the company earned 55.97% of the total amount spent by the TCU for outsorced IT services during the 13 years of the sampling period. So, a single company is bound to more than 50% of the values employed in IT outsourcing with its 6 contracts in a total number of 35 contracts (17,14%).

Table 3.5 – *Highest Contract Values in the sampling period (2000-2013).*

Company	Contract	Status	Total Value R$
CTIS	56-2000	Concluded	517.704,00
CTIS	84-2001	Concluded	4.215.577,50
CTIS	85-2001	Concluded	9.257.864,70
CTIS	86-2001	Concluded	7.405.573,08
CTIS	67-2007	Concluded	5.437.259,25
CTIS	17-2010	In Progress	13.678.463,85
		Total R$	40.512.422,28

This concentration on one provider gives way to an undesirable side effect that, by signing the successive contracts, the provider becomes expert in the object and in the client, thus becoming the most able to win the following bids on the same object.

4. FINAL CONSIDERATIONS

Long-term IT services planning is a necessary process for good IT governance. This exploratory study shows that there still are some issues to be dealt with in this process, specifically in regard to IT outsorcing planning. Although there is much talk in related cost savings, some discussion is lacking regarding necessary adaptations of outsourcing practices to existing conditions in the Brazilian public sector, in the light of Law and regulations. This study shows indicators that the Government still needs to mature its IT long-term planning, given that IT outsourcing has been broadly adopted for fundamental services by public bodies, although the respective contract management processes are characterized by difficulties regarding modifications in values, duration and specifications, as observed in this paper case study.

In Brazil there is an extensive set of Laws and regulations applied to IT contracts, whose evolution was summarized in the literature review in this study. The modifications in legal instruments over recent years make it clear that the Government has been developing and maturing in some issues, specialy the bidding categories that eased the acquisition of IT goods and services bound to a Federal Adminsitration IT spending that exceeds six billion dollars per year, according to data from the Integrated Financial Management System (SIAFI) and the Department of Coordination and Governance of State Owned Enterprises (DEST).

The improvement of procurement rules as well as the consolidation of related knowledge contributed to the reduction of risks, given that hiring IT services imply in high investments. Also this enables to verify whether management practices are really efficient, considering that the correct application of IT resources is part of good management and promotes the protection of critical information, helping organizations achieve their institutional goals. The improvements in this area also depend on strengthening management skills and qualification of people and processes within the agencies that use outsourced IT services. Another concern is that, considering some of the related contract values, possibly there are situations favoring the utilization of public employees for provision of some IT services in place of outsourced personnel. Independent of the adopted solution, it seems that either way requires investments in management policies, indicators and metrics for managing quality of service, and the adequate binding from IT services to overall government goals.

In which respects this paper methodology, although it has the interest of preserving the independence between de object and the observer, the chosen approach for this study shows some limitations since the object of study is considered under a black box verification method and the analysis is based solely on external indicators, although there surely are internal motivations and constraints that have been determinant for IT outsourcing contract management decisions regarding the duration and financial extensions of contracts.

It is also important to point out that the data used in this study is public and published by the source agency itself, as all analyzed information was taken from the TCU website. Thus, the information is delivered to the population openly, which is indeed positive in regard of the Public Administration transparency. It would be yet more useful if these publications were in the form of linked open government data, including data sets and related ontology, such as those concerning the Brazilian Federal Budget (Silva, Sousa, Veiga, Martins, Exposto and Mendonca, 2104). By proposing an effective analytic approach in this context, the present paper methodology contributes to empowering citizens to use these open data sets for exercising the necessary social control on government activities.

ACKNOWLEDGEMENTS

The authors wish to thank the Brazilian research and innovation agencies CNPQ, CAPES and FINEP, as well as the Brazilian Ministry of Planning, Budget and Management, for their support to this work.

REFERENCES

Araújo, L. C. G. Organização, sistemas e métodos e as tecnologias de gestão organizacional: 2nd Ed. São Paulo: Atlas, 2008.

Barbosa, A. F.; Junqueira, A. R. B; Laia, M. M.; Faria, F. I. Governança de TIC e Contratos no setor público. In: CATI - Congresso Anual de Tecnologia da Informação, 2006, Escola de administração de Empresas de São Paulo da Fundação Getulio Vargas

(FGV-EAESP), São Paulo, 2006. Available in: <http://www.fgvsp.br/cati/artigos/pdf/T00241.pdf>. Access on: 07/31/2009.

Beal, A. Segurança da Informação - Príncipios e Melhores Práticas para a Proteção dos Ativos de Informação nas Organizações. 1st Ed. São Paulo: Atlas, 2005.

Boas práticas em segurança da informação. 3rd Ed. Brasília: TCU, 2008.

Broadbent, J.; Guthrie, J. Changes in the Public Sector: A Review of Recent "Alternative" Accounting Research, Accounting, Auditing & Accountability Journal, Vol. 5 Iss 2 pp, 1992. Available at http://dx.doi.org/10.1108/09513579210011835. Access on: 11/03/2014.

Cardoso, H. M. Diagnóstico da Terceirização da Engenharia de software na Gerência de Unidade de Aplicações em Administração, Controle e Finanças da Prodabel - UFS-PB. Specialization Monography. Belo Horizonte, Pontifícia Universidade Católica de Minas Gerais, 2000. Available in: <http://www.pbh.gov.br/prodabel/cde/publicacoes/2000/cardoso2_2000.pdf>. Access on: 07/31/2009.

Cardoso, G. S. Processo de aquisição de produtos e serviços de software para administração pública do Estado de Minas Gerais. Master Thesis. Belo Horizonte, Universidade Federal de Minas Gerais, 2006. Available in: <http://dspace.lcc.ufmg.br/dspace/bitstream/1843/RVMR-6TJQEU/1/giselesilvacardoso.pdf>. Access on: 07/31/2009.

Cruz, C. S. Governança de TI e conformidade legal no setor público: um quadro referencial normativo para a contratação de serviços de TI. Master Thesis. Brasília, Universidade Católica de Brasília, 2008. Available in: <http://www.bdtd.ucb.br/tede/tde_arquivos/3/TDE-2008-11-25T123713Z-687/Publico/Texto CompletoCruz - 2008.pdf>. Access on: 08/25/2010.

Dias, C. Segurança e Auditoria da Tecnologia da Informação. 1st Ed. Rio de Janeiro: Axcel Books, 2000.

Decreto n° 1.048, de 21 de janeiro de 1994. Dispõe sobre o Sistema de Administração dos Recursos de Informação e Informática da Administração Pública Federal. Available in http://www.planalto.gov.br/ccivil_03/decreto/1990-1994/D1048.htm. Access on 05/07/2009.

Decreto n° 2.271, de 07 de julho de 1997. Dispõe sobre a contratação de serviços pela Administração Pública Federal direta, autárquica e fundacional e dá outras providências. Available in http://www.planalto.gov.br/ccivil_03/decreto/D2271.htm. Access on 05/07/2009.

Decreto n° 3.555, de 08 de agosto de 2000. Aprova o Regulamento para a Modality de licitação denominada pregão, para aquisição de bens e serviços comuns. Available in http://www.planalto.gov.br/ccivil/decreto/D3555.htm. Access on 05/07/2009.

Decreto n° 3.931, de 19 de setembro de 2001. Regulamenta o Sistema de Registro de Preços previstos no art. 15 da lei n° 8.666, de 21 de junho de 1993, e dá outras providências. Available in http://www.planalto.gov.br/CCIVIL/decreto/2001/D3931htm.htm. Access on 05/07/2009.

Decreto n° 5.450, de 31 de maio de 2005. Regulamenta o pregão, na forma eletrônica, para aquisição de bens e serviços comuns, e dá outras providências. Available in http://www.planalto.gov.br/ccivil/_Ato2004-2006/2005. Access on 05/07/2009.

Decreto n° 5.504, de 05 de agosto de 2005. Regulamenta o pregão, na forma eletrônica, para aquisição de bens e serviços comuns, e dá outras providências.

Available in http://www.planalto.gov.br/ccivil/_Ato2004-2006/2005/Decreto/D5504.htm. Access on 05/07/2009.

Decreto n° 7.063/2010, de 13/01/2010. Aprova a estrutura regimental e o quadro demonstrativo dos cargos em comissão e das funções gratificadas do ministério do planejamento, orçamento e gestão, e dá outras providências. Available in http://www.planalto.gov.br/ccivil_03/_Ato2007-2010/2010/Decreto/D7063.htm. Access on 11/20/2010.

Decreto n° 7.174/2010, de 12/05/2010. Regulamenta a contratação de bens e serviços de informática e automação pela administração pública federal, direta ou indireta, pelas fundações instituídas ou mantidas pelo Poder Público e pelas demais organizações sob o controle direto ou indireto da União. Available in: http://www.planalto.gov.br/Ccivil_03/_Ato2007-2010/2010/Decreto/D7174.htm#art14. Access on 11/20/2010.

Earl, M. Deve-se Terceirizar a Informática? HSM Management. São Paulo, v. 1, n. 6, p. 126-132, Jan/Feb 1998.

Foina, P. R. Tecnologia de Informação, Planejamento e Gestão. 1st Ed. São Paulo: Atlas, 2001.

Guarda, G. F.; Terceirização Estratégica de Tecnologia da Informação no Serviço Público Federal: Um estudo. Specialization Monografy, Electrical Engineering Department – University of Brasília, 2008.

Guarda, G. F.; Oliveira, E. C.; De Sousa JR, R. T. Analysis of Contracts of IT Outsourcing Services in TCU and the Legislation Governing these Contracts in the Federal Public Administration. In: Proceedings of the 11th International Conference on Information Systems and Technology Management CONTECSI, 2014.

Hätönen, J.; Eriksson, T. 30+ years of research and practice of outsourcing – Exploring the past and anticipating the future, Journal of International Management, Volume 15, Issue 2, June 2009.

Hendry, J. O custo oculto da terceirização. HSM Management, São Paulo, v. 0, n. 2, p. 82-90, May/June 1997.

Howden, W. E., "Functional Program Testing," Software Engineering, IEEE Transactions on , vol.SE-6, no.2, pp.162,169, March 1980.

Instrução Normativa n°. 02/2008 SLTI/MPOG. Available in http://www.comprasnet.gov.br/legislacao/in/in02_30042008.htm. Access on 01/10/2009.

Instrução Normativa n°. 04/2010 SLTI/MPOG. Disponível no DOU de 16/11/2010 (n° 218, Seção 1, pág. 69). Access on 12/10/2010.

Laudon, K. C.; Laudon, J. P. Sistemas de informação Gerencial: Administrando a empresa digital. 5th Ed. São Paulo: Pearson Prentice Hall, 2004.

Lei n° 8.248, 23 de outubro de 1991. Dispõe sobre a capacitação e competitividade do setor de informática e automação, e dá outras providências. Available in http://www.planalto.gov.br/ccivil/Leis/L8248.htm. Access on 05/07/2009.

Lei n°. 8.666, de 21 de junho de 1993. Regulamenta o art. 37, inciso XXI, da Constituição Federal, institui normas para licitações e Contratos da Administração Pública e dá outras providências. Available in http://www.planalto.gov.br/ccivil_03/LEIS/L8666cons.htm. Access on 05/07/2009.

Lei n°. 10.520, de 17 de julho de 2002. Institui, no âmbito da União, Estados, Distrito Federal e Municípios, nos termos do art. 37, inciso XXI, da Constituição Federal, Modality de licitação denominada pregão, para aquisição de bens e serviços comuns, e dá outras providências. Available in http://www.planalto.gov.br/ccivil/leis/2002/L10520.htm. Access on 05/07/2009.

Lei nº. 11.077, de 30 de dezembro de 2004. Altera a Lei nº. 8.248, de 23 de outubro de 1991, a Lei nº. 8.237, de 30 de dezembro de 1991, e a Lei nº. 10.176, de 11 de janeiro de 2001, dispondo sobre a capacitação e competitividade do setor de informática e automação e dá outras providências. Available in http://www.planalto.gov.br/ccivil/_Ato2004-2006/2004/Lei/L11077.htm. Access on 05/07/2009.

Leite, J. C. Terceirização em informática no Brasil. RAE – Revista de administração de empresas. São Paulo, 1997. Available in: http://www.rae.com.br/rae/index.cfm. Access on 03/10/2009.

Mell, P. and Grance, T. The NIST Definition of Cloud Computing. NIST Special Publication 800-145, September 2011.

Portaria nº. 11 SLTI, de 30 de dezembro de 2008. Define a Estratégia-Geral de Tecnologia da Informação para a Administração Pública Federal. Available in http://www010.Dateprev.gov.br/sislex/paginas/72/MPS-CSI/2009/2.htm. Access on 05/07/2009.

Queiroz, C. A. R. S. Manual de Terceirização. 10th Ed. São Paulo: STS, 1998.

Ramos, D. M. O. Terceirização na administração pública. São Paulo: Ltr, 2001.

Robinson, M. Performance Budgeting: Linking Funding and Results. International Monetary Fund, Oct 17, 2007.

Santanna, R. Electronic Procurement Allow for Inspection By Society. OECD Global Forum on Governance: Modernising Government: strategies & tools for change. Rio de Janeiro – Brazil, 2007. Available in http://www.oecd.org/site/govgfg/39612372.pdf. Access on 12/11/2014.

Schomer, P. C.; Nunes, J. T.; Moraes, R. L. Accountability, social control and co-production of public goods: the action of twenty Brazilian social observatories aimed at citizenship and fiscal education (in Portuguese). Publicações da Escola da AGU. Year IV, number 18, may-june 2012.

Silva, D. A. ; Sousa JR, R. T. ; Veiga, C. E. L. ; Martins, V. A. ; Exposto, E. N. ; Mendonca, F. L. L. A Extensão da Ontologia do Orçamento Federal com uma Classe de Geolocalização permite a Consideração de Indicadores de Desenvolvimento Humano nas Decisões da Política Orçamentária Brasileira. In: Actas de la 9ª Conferencia Ibérica de Sistemas y Tecnologías de Información, v. 1. p. 47-52. Lisboa: AISTI, 2014.

Speck, B. W. The Federal Court of Audit in Brazil Institutional Arrangements and its Role in Preventing Fraud and Abuse of Public Resources. 9th International Anti-Corruption Conference, 10-15 October 1999.

Turban, E.; Mclean, E.; Wetherbe, J.; Tecnologia da informação para gestão. Porto Alegre: Bookman, 2004.

Vidal, A. G. Terceirização: A arma empresarial. São Paulo: Érica, 1993.

Willcocks, L. *Managing Information Systems in U. K.* Public Administration: Issues and Prospects. Public Administration. [S.L.]: Spring 1994.

13

PROPOSITION OF AN ALUMNI PORTAL BASED ON BENCHMARKING AND INNOVATIVE PROCESS

PROPOSIÇÃO DE UM PORTAL DE EGRESSO (ALUMNI) BASEADO EM BENCHMARKING E PROCESSO INOVADOR

Gislaine Cristina dos Santos Teixeira
Emerson Antonio Maccari
UNINOVE - Nove de Julho University, São Paulo, SP, Brazil

ABSTRACT

A common concern in institutions of higher education is to keep its former students involved with academic activities. It is a consensus that one of the most valuable assets of universities is their alumni, given that their accomplishments ensure more exposure for the university. In recent years, universities have encouraged a movement toward the establishment of alumni associations, as they provide networking opportunities and contact between the university and the alumni or among the alumni. An association that seeks membership and participation of its alumni should invest in the development of an attractive portal. In this sense, this research aims to analyze the portal of alumni associations of well-ranked universities, using a benchmarking process and a creative technique called SCAMPER. We also present a portal prototype that meets the current needs of the market.

Keywords: Alumni, Alumni Association, Benchmarking, SCAMPER

RESUMO

Uma preocupação comum em Instituições de Ensino Superior (IES) é manter o aluno formado ligado às atividades acadêmicas, pois é consenso que um dos ativos mais valiosos das universidades é o seu egresso (*alumni*), já que suas ações práticas garantem mais visibilidade à universidade. Nos últimos anos, percebe-se um movimento das IES no sentido de incentivar a criação de associações de *alumni*, pois elas propiciam oportunidades de *networking* e manutenção do contato entre IES e *alumni* ou *alumni* entre si. Uma associação que busque adesão e participação de seus *alumni* deve investir no desenvolvimento de portal atrativo, contemplando informações que despertem o interesse do público-alvo. Esta pesquisa se propõe a

* Fast Track – 11th CONTECSI International Conference on Information Systems and Technology Management

Address for correspondence / Endereço para correspondência

Gislaine Cristina dos Santos Teixeira, Mestranda do Programa de Mestrado Profissional em Administração - Gestão de Projetos da Universidade Nove de Julho - UNINOVE

Emerson Antonio Maccari, Doutor em Administração pela Universidade de São Paulo - FEA/USP. Diretor do Programa de Pós-Graduação em Administração - PPGA da Universidade Nove de Julho - UNINOVE.

analisar o portal de associações de *alumni* de universidades bem avaliadas, por meio de *benchmarking* e de um processo inovador denominado SCAMPER. Ao final, apresenta-se a um protótipo de portal de egresso que atenda as atuais necessidades do mercado.

Palavras-chave: Egresso, Associação de Egressos, *Alumni*, *Benchmarking*, SCAMPER

1. INTRODUCTION

Globalization and advances in information technology have transformed the traditional business models in networks of relationships, so much so that the way people think and relate to one another is currently affected by the creative use of the media and information provision. Technology plays an important role by providing opportunities to develop resources and networking services that benefit both the company and its stakeholders (Kandampully, 2003). In addition, the new technology of the Internet offers innovative and effective ways to connect customers and companies, creating new sources of strategic positioning (Hax & Wilde II, 2002).

Primo (1997) states that the Internet revolutionized human communication as it allows the interactive exchange of information, synchronous or asynchronous, without physical proximity. The author also highlights that virtual communities, created by the technological society, are based on intellectual proximity and favor relationships, approaching people with common interests, and allow data sharing, regardless of geographical position, physical contact or time.

Among other purposes, virtual communities are used for entertainment, business, and education. Examples of the use of these communities include corporate portals, libraries, teaching/learning portals, alumni associations, among others. This type of virtual space allows people to extend contact beyond physical proximity or ordinary time.

In terms of promoting extended contact in the educational field, a common concern is to keep alumni connected to their educational institutions, given that it is a consensus that the alumni are some of the most valuable assets of universities. The effective contribution of education to the society is observed based on the alumni's experiences during the university course, proving the university name. Chia, Jonesa, and Grandhama (2012) state that alumni are people who represent the university in the real world.

Alumnus, plural alumni, is the term used to designate a graduated student (former student) of a university. The term originates from the Latin verb *"alere"*, which means to nurture, develop and maintain (Wikipedia, 2013). For Barnard (2007), a grouping of alumni has great potential to contribute financially, socially and strategically to enhance credibility of an educational institution that aspires to thrive in a rapidly changing and competitive market. The author adds that an integrated network of relationships could give the institution the opportunity to create a win-win situation.

In the United States and Europe, the culture of maintaining a link between alumni and educational institutions is stronger, but in Brazil, only in recent years, there has been a movement for the creation of alumni associations. This movement is more evident in some Brazilian business schools, which, with this kind of association, seek to consolidate the relationship between alumni and the educational institution.

However, the lack of updated data of alumni hinders the effective development of an alumni association. Existing associations are thinking of ways to increase the rapprochement with the alumni, such as the creation of specific areas to favor the relationship with the alumni, in order to transcend the mere dissemination of employment opportunities (Arcoverde, 2013).

Cunha *et al.* (2007) state that the alumni show no interest in keeping their data up-to-date even on the *Lattes* platform (database of résumés, research groups and institutions maintained by the Conselho Nacional de Desenvolvimento Científico e Tecnológico – CNPq – in Brazil), which gathers data from Brazilian researchers. The authors also emphasize that there is a clear lack of communication between the alumnus and the advisor and with the program/course as a whole. The lack of data updating can be tied to disinterest or ignorance of the alumnus about the potential of an alumni association to promote a professional network, academic and even personal relationships.

One of the ways to consolidate the relationship between alumni and educational institutions is to create a virtual and interactive portal to provide useful information to the alumni to help extend the contact between the alumni and the university to beyond the period of course completion, regardless of geographic location or time. For an educational institution that aims to create an alumni association and deploy an online attractive portal, it is important to analyze how the best Brazilian educational institutions ranked by the Coordenação de Aperfeiçoamento de Pessoal de Nível Superior [CAPES], and international ones, classified in rankings, create their portals. For Porter (1996), companies have to compare themselves with rivals to obtain greater efficiency and continuously evolve; therefore, the development of a portal based on benchmarking has a greater chance of success.

More important than creating something completely new or seeking an unprecedented response to common problems is to create new possibilities or solutions using different sets of knowledge that may result from experiences or from search processes (Tidd, Bessant, & Pavitt, 2008). In this sense, creative and innovative processes can favor the creation of an attractive portal for the alumni that allows them to keep contact with the university and their colleagues.

Considering the difficulties related to the relationship between the alumni and universities and the variety of features that can aggregate or pollute an online portal of an alumni association, it is necessary to plan the project properly in order to obtain better results. Thus, this study seeks to answer the following question: analyzing the online portals of alumni of high-ranking associations, what characteristics should be considered to create a new attractive portal?

In order to minimize the efforts spent in developing a portal of an alumni association, we propose to study the composition of online portals of alumni associations of high-ranking business schools in Brazil and in the world. We also propose, based on the creative technique called SCAMPER, a prototype portal of an alumni association that encourages the construction of a network of relationships among alumni and institutions of higher education.

It is expected that the literature review serve as a basis for the planning and proposal of an online portal of an alumni association, contributing to academic reflections on this subject and, in practical terms, collaborating with educational projects benefiting the alumni and educational institutions. The methodology used in this study involves qualitative research based on a literature review and a proposal of plans to solve organizational problems that have been diagnosed.

In addition to this section, this article includes other four sections, namely bibliographical review about alumni associations, social networks and innovative processes, methodology, analysis of the results with a proposal for a portal and the conclusion.

2. BIBLIOGRAPHICAL REVIEW

According to Teixeira, Maccari and Kniess (2012), in the scientific literature, studies related to educational projects focus on aspects that transcend administrative operations, such as training and teaching practices, program quality, social inclusion, legal regulation models, among others, with no reference in the specific literature for smaller projects that emerge from the difficulties of everyday operations. In this sense, the theoretical framework of this study is focused on alumni associations, social networks and innovative processes with emphasis on the creative technique SCAMPER.

2.1.   ALUMNI ASSOCIATIONS AND SOCIAL NETWORKS

For the Council for Advancement and Support of Education (2005), the relationship programs for the alumni and educational institutions aim to build and strengthen long-term relationships and facilitate communication between both. For the institution, the alumnus is a representative who helps preserve its history and traditions, ensuring the future of the organization. The council also posits some principles that could help the professionals that work closely with alumni to strengthen ties:

I. Provide a wide range of communication devices, including electronic mail.

II. Involve all the institution staff in the engagement of students.

III. Ensure that the mission, objective and programs of the alumni association are consistent with the objectives of the educational institution.

IV. Inform students and alumni about the institutional mission, objectives and programs of the association.

V. Obtain feedback from alumni to align services with existing and emerging needs. Involve them to think of ideas and have opinions in any planning process to define or modify the mission of the association.

VI. Ensure that the personal data provided by the alumni are treated professionally and confidentially.

VII. Encourage the alumni to support and participate in programs, services and events of the association.

Also about the role of this type of professional, Brant and Regan (2002) state that they are in the connections business and through these connections they promote the advancement of the institution, but it is often difficult to measure the impact of the work, requiring additional effort to asses and quantify the points of contact with the alumni. The authors add that benchmarking, regarding the alumni relationships and universities, has historically been difficult, since this type of program reflects unique histories, cultures, customs, structures and environments of their campuses in a way that every institution seems to want to introduce something different.

There is a great potential to raise funds from the alumni, in addition to the large capacity to build a network of knowledge that can be shared, providing lifelong learning, making a difference in the way the institution is perceived by potential external and internal clients, and even by competitors. Therefore, it is vital for an educational institution to establish and maintain a good relationship with its students and alumni by involving them in the decision-making process and building a relationship network, contributing to the global advancement of the institution. However, this requires the establishment of an open and direct channel of communication with students to ensure that relevant information can be continuously disseminated (Barnard, 2007).

Studies on alumni associations show that there are several challenges related to their implementation, success or even interest in this type of organization. For Barnard (2007), keeping valuable relationships with the alumni is a challenge, but the dissemination of information on online portals of alumni associations is even more challenging, because it is necessary to provide information generic enough to be understood and customized enough to generate interest in the target audience.

Newman and Petrosko (2011) clarify that there are few published studies on the registering of alumni to associations, most research in this area examines indicators related to donations. The authors have determined that the experiences the students undergo after graduation have an impact on the motivation to become a member of the association and, therefore, the work of professionals of these associations can help improve the alumni's perceptions, reflecting on the increase in the number of members. The results indicate that the alumni more likely to become members of the association are those who: (a) were donors, (b) had a phone number stored in the files, (c) are relatively older, (d) had positive experiences while students, (e) have a positive perception of the alumni association, (f) were more often involved with the university and (g) were acquainted with other members of the association.

For Chia *et al.* (2012), a major challenge to promote the relationship between alumni and universities is to improve mentoring between the alumni and current students. For the authors, incorporating social network features and data mining to the alumni system can favor the orientation.

According to Brant and Regan (2002), there are two stages to be followed by associations to increase alumni commitment:

I.   Strive to know the alumnus or increase the knowledge about him/her by obtaining a comprehensive profile involving their names, addresses, telephone numbers and e-mails.

II. Learn how the alumni are involved with the institution. The commitment can take many forms such as the use of e-mails to keep in contact with the institution, participation in annual events, credit cards, volunteering or traveling programs. An aggressive way to promote the interaction would be the hosting of events and services through the site, the release of regional bulletins or the cross-promotion of events.

Still about the dissemination of information, Barnard (2007) highlights that we should be concerned with the message content and with the channel used to disseminate it to reach the audience.

Amidst the various challenges listed, there are other concerns related to the operation of an online portal and especially how this portal should be designed to become attractive enough to draw interest when compared with many other social media to which, possibly, the alumnus is already linked.

Chia *et al.* (2012) claim that social networks are a powerful tool for people to meet and interact based on common interests and also that data mining can be used to understand the social interactions in order to increase the effectiveness of the services provided. The activity of a social network can be described as the act of sharing business or social relationships with the purpose of exploring the needs, interests or common goals. Relationship networks have been facilitated by the development of technology in a way that people can interact with each other, sharing ideas, discussing their personal or professional lives, without the need of traveling.

According to Chia *et al.* (2012), data from alumni networks can be used to enhance mentoring programs, to develop online networking and above all, they could be key components of maintaining students and strengthening university programs. The authors clarify that initially alumni networks emerged as regional groups to raise funds, however, they gained importance for their potential to promote the name of the university, which benefits the career of all the alumni as well as current students.

In recent years, the development of the Internet and social networks have led the alumni associations to undergo major changes. The existing systems are usually developed to facilitate networking between students and their institutions of higher education, but students, for many reasons, do not use most of the current systems significantly, for example: the systems are static, they provide information only about the university through one-way communication, and they have little room for future activities and interaction between the members. In addition, traditionally, these systems are only available for the alumni and do not identify the current students or professors as potential users. Therefore, it is important for universities to find modern ways to develop networks for their alumni, in order to increase the interactions between the various categories of people associated with the university. The authors propose separated fields for general, personal and professional information and interaction (Chia *et al.*, 2012).

The little use of existing systems require reorganization or re-engineering of the existing alumni portals. Innovation is necessary in light of new demands, otherwise this important relationship tool will run the risk of becoming useless.

2.2.   INNOVATIVE PROCESSES AND CREATIVE TECHNIQUES

The concept of innovation is in continuous evolution and can take different forms, depending on their dimensions, frequency, processing and outputs. Many studies on the subject have been developed and, currently, the criteria to classify innovation and environments to ensure the development of innovation are increasingly clear (Cagnazzo, Taticchi, & Botarelli, 2008).

For Tidd *et al.* (2008), Joseph Schumpeter is considered the creator of the subject. He describes innovation and creative destruction associated with the theory of economic innovation. However, for this research, the most suitable line of thought is described by the authors as incremental innovation, because although innovation sometimes involves a discontinuous change starting from something completely new, most of the time the products are not new to the world and innovation can be understood as creating new possibilities through the combination of different sets of knowledge in response to an articulated or latent need. The knowledge can be previously based on own experiences or result from the search process of technology, market or competitors' actions.

According to Khandwalla (2006), one must keep in mind the principles of creativity to be innovative. In addition, it is necessary to consider three common features in most innovations: they are performed amidst uncertainties, they have economic implications and a political dimension that makes the management of innovations a challenge. The challenge can be minimized using management tools and an organizational design that allows a continuous flow of innovations at all levels and functions. The author adds that creativity does not necessarily originate within the organization, often the idea comes from an external environment. This study introduces 16 management tools to stimulate innovation and, among the tools designed to stimulate intelligence enhancement are: creative research, creative experiences, creative benchmarking and reverse brainstorming. Two of these techniques are especially considered in this research.

I. Creative research: it refers to studies that request information that is rarely collected and the data is used in an innovative way.

II. Creative benchmarking: it seeks a standard of excellence, even though the standards come from an external environment. The data produced is used to reflect on new ways to fill gaps.

Corroborating the subject, Hidalgo and Albors (2008) highlight that innovation does not mean using cutting-edge technology; on the contrary, it is more a way of thinking and finding creative solutions within the company instead of it being a matter of technology. The authors present several techniques of management innovations, among the techniques available on the market, the study selected those that meet the following parameters: systematic and standardized methods that have an application; methods aimed at improving competitiveness of enterprises having knowledge as the greatest benefit; methods that have free access. SCAMPER and benchmarking are among the cited techniques that develop creativity and improve processes. Such techniques and methods support the innovation process, helping companies to meet the new challenges of the market.

Still on this subject, Santos (2012, p. 2) highlights that it is important to use creative processes to stimulate the production of ideas, to produce new combinations, to obtain unexpected, original and useful answers and, thus, to generate innovation for information systems and the way they are used. Creativity techniques aim to help change the mental state of the people and stimulate their creativity, helping in the generation of ideas for the reformulation of problems. Among the various techniques, the author highlights the focus techniques, that is, those that help focus on the issues, avoiding the dispersion caused by random techniques. Examples of these techniques include SCAMPER, Ideabox, Phoenix.

According to Michalko (2006), SCAMPER is a checklist of ideas stimulated by issues. The first issues were suggested by Alex Osborn, professor of creativity, and later transformed into mnemonics by Bob Eberle:

S – Substitute something
C – Combine with something else
A – Adapt something
M – Modify or magnify
P – Put to other uses
E – Eliminate something
R – Rearrange or revert something

According to Serrat (2010), the SCAMPER technique uses a set of directed questions to solve a problem (or find an opportunity). The aim is to generate creative ideas to specific problems or indicate creative ways to improve a current process or procedure. The technique is also recognized as a learning tool that promotes awareness, unity, fluency, flexibility and originality. Stimulation arises from questions that would not be normally formulated and answered otherwise. Santos (2012) adds that the SCAMPER technique is particularly suitable to examine the possible transformations to be applied to a product or process and, perceive the problem from different perspectives, enabling approaches of the "outside-the-box" thought.

The use of the SCAMPER technique to redefine a process or product is made from a checklist of questions, exemplified in Figure 1:

Figure 1: Examples of questions in the checklist of the SCAMPER technique

Transformations	Typical Questions
S – Substitute	What can I replace to improve? What happens if I change X to Y? How can I replace the place, time, materials or people?
C – Combine	What materials, features, processes, people, products or components can we combine within the problem area? Where can I create synergy with other products/processes or areas?
A – Adapt	What other products/processes are similar to our problem? What could we change in order to adapt them to our problem?
M – Modify or Magnify or Minimize	How can we change the product/process entirely? Can the product/process be improved making it stronger, bigger, more exaggerated or more frequent? Can the product/process be improved making it smaller, lighter, shorter, less important or less frequent?
P – Put to other uses	What other products/processes could do what we want? How can we reuse other products/processes that are happening?
E – Eliminate	What would happen if we removed a part of the product/process? What would happen if we removed everything? How can we achieve the same objective, if we were not able to do it this way?
R – Rearrange or Revert	What if we revert the process? What if we do step B before step A? What if A becomes the last step and Z becomes the first? What if we perform the two steps together?

SOURCE: (SANTOS, 2012, P.102)

3. METHODOLOGY

This study uses as research strategy the proposition of plans and programs based on a literature review about alumni associations, social networks and innovative processes. Data collection involved research on documentary sites and social networks of alumni associations for a basis of benchmarking and implementation of the SCAMPER technique. Therefore, based on this sequence, we propose a portal prototype of an alumni association in order to achieve maximum membership provided by the appropriate approach and planning.

Following the recommendations of Marconi and Lakatos (2010), we started the study from a bibliographical review, which involved surveying the theoretical framework about the topics. The purpose of this step is to place the researcher in direct contact with everything that was published about a particular subject. The bibliographical review serves as a first step to identify how the problem is addressed by the literature, the works that have already been carried out and the prevailing opinions on the matter. The second step allows for establishing an initial theoretical model of reference. Martins and Theophilo (2009) corroborate this view by stating that the literature review is a strategy required to conduct any scientific research, once it is aimed at the construction of a theoretical platform of the subject.

Also according to Martins and Theophilo (2009), the proposition of plans and programs is a strategy that provides solutions to organizational problems already diagnosed, sought, by means of empirical-analytical research, a study on the viability of alternative plans for the solution of problems. The author should, preferably, propose the use of models in practical situations, valuing ingenuity and creativity as the adjustments of the theoretical model to a specific situation. As for data collection, the documentary research seeks unedited material, and can be a source of data and auxiliary information that subsidizes a better understanding of the findings.

In the first phase, we defined the guiding questions of the literature review that served as support for the analysis of the results and subsequent proposal of a prototype.

The second phase involved choosing the units of benchmarking analysis. According to Melo, Carpinetti and Silva (2000), benchmarking is a powerful instrument of improvement that seeks to achieve competitive advantage through learning from best practices in the industry, leading to better performance. Among the possible classifications of benchmarking, the present study uses the functional/generic approach, because it identifies best practices in any type of organization that has established a reputation for excellence in a specific area. The authors also state that, in general, the benchmarking process involves five basic steps: determining the object of benchmarking, identifying partners, collecting and analyzing data, establishing goals, implementing actions and monitoring results.

Brazilian educational institutions were selected based on the triennial evaluation comparative worksheets from CAPES (2010) in the field of Business Management, Accounting and Tourism. We decided to analyze the portals of alumni associations of the institutions that had the highest scores (6 and 7) in academic programs, which culminated in four institutions: Federal University of Rio Grande do Sul (UFRGS), University of São Paulo (USP), Getulio Vargas Foundation – São Paulo (FGV-SP) and Federal University of Minas Gerais (UFMG). International institutions were selected from the Global Ranking MBA 2013 published by the Financial Times newspaper (2013), the first three of the ranking are: Harvard Business School, Stanford Graduate School of Business and University of Pennsylvania – Wharton.

The third and last phase included the discussion of the authors based on the SCAMPER technique to propose a prototype of an alumni portal.

4. ANALYSIS OF RESULTS

The analysis of the results is composed of three stages, namely benchmarking results that considered the points in common and the particularities of the portals of the institutions selected, application of the SCAMPER technique to propose an innovative portal and finally the prototype design.

4.1. BENCHMARKING OF ALUMNI PORTALS

As defined in the methodology, we proceeded to the stage of benchmarking completion. The study evaluated 18 items, usually displayed in the portals of alumni associations. Seven universities, four in Brazil and three in the United States, had their portals examined based on these items, the percentage of positive response, that is, the items are disclosed in the portals (Table 1).

Table 1: Items evaluated in the portals of alumni associations

Items evaluated in the portals of alumni associations			National Institutions	International Institutions
Dissemination of data related to the association:	1	History	75%	33%
	2	Mission	50%	0%
	3	Vision	50%	0%
	4	Values	25%	0%
	5	Objectives	100%	100%
	6	Target audience	100%	100%
	7	Benefits	75%	100%
	8	Partnerships	75%	0%
	9	Online form for membership	100%	100%
	10	Number of associates	0%	100%
	11	Has pages on social networks	50%	100%
Dissemination of data related to services or features:	12	Ways of alumni interaction	75%	100%
	13	Special projects of the association	50%	100%
	14	Periodicals, journals or bulletins	0%	100%
	15	News related to or written by alumni	25%	100%
	16	Professional opportunities	50%	100%
	17	Statute and guidelines of the association	25%	33%
	18	Restricted area (access with login and password)	75%	100%

Source: Elaborated by the authors

The objective, through the analysis of the frequency of disclosure items, was to understand the importance of each item for higher education institutions nationally and internationally, having as evidence the fact that they have a space in the portal to disseminate such information. The answers were analyzed separately, because international institutions have their consolidated associations while in Brazil, they are still seeking space.

The analysis in Table 1 shows that the portals of international institutions are similar because of the 18 items examined, 12 are present in 100% of the universities (5-7, 9-16 and 18). The other four do not appear in any of them (2-4 and 8) and only two items are found in only one institution (1 and 17). In the national institutions, the display of items varies, only three of them occur in 100% of the institutions (5, 6 and 9), and these same three items are displayed in all international institutions. Still about the national institutions of higher education, only one item does not appear in any of them (14).

The results in Table 1 indicate the market practice of the selected institutions, but they can also give rise to trends regarding the use of best practices to achieve superior performance. In addition, a more specific analysis of some items corroborates largely with the development of a portal for alumni.

Regarding item 6, target audience, 100% of the institutions have established alumni associations involving students of all levels of higher education with no specific association for undergraduates or graduates.

About item 7 (Table 2), benefits, it was found that national institutions do not disclose them. Only one national institution cites virtual library access and has a program of discounts on products or services, while 100% of international institutions allow access to the virtual library and databases and offer discount programs for alumni.

Table 2: Benefits of alumni associations

Benefits of alumni associations	National Institutions	International Institutions
Events	75%	33%
Dissemination of professional opportunities	50%	100%
Discount on products or services	25%	100%
Access to the virtual library	25%	100%
Discount on other courses	0%	33%
Free courses	0%	33%
Access to periodicals of the institution	0%	66%
Access to the fitness center of the institution	0%	66%
Travel programs	0%	66%
Access to the chapel of the institution	0%	33%

Source: Elaborated by the authors

Concerning item 9, online form for membership, it was found that 100% of the institutions request registration validation of the alumni. International institutions use the alumni ID number, while the national institutions request data on the year of completion and course name, to manually search in the files and subsequent approval.

With respect to item 11, pages on social networks, it was found that all international institutions have at least two pages on social media, while only two national institutions of higher education have pages on social media. The distribution is shown in Table 3.

Table 3: Pages on social network

Social network	National Institutions	International Institutions
Facebook	50%	100%
LinkedIn	50%	66%
Twitter	25%	100%
Flickr	25%	33%

Source: Elaborated by the authors

Regarding ways of interaction (item 12), the prevalence is of encounters at annual events. Only one national institution does not disseminate events. International institutions offer virtual environments for discussion of topics of common interest (virtual communities) as well as links to lectures and virtual courses (learning environment).

The special projects (item 13) involve volunteering, diversity groups or mentoring and are more common in international institutions.

About item 15, only one national institution releases news, while 100% of the international institutions disseminate news and matters related to alumni.

Regarding the features of the restricted area (item 18), Table 4 shows that 100% of international institutions provide access to the profile of their members and to employment vacancies, but the events are usually available in the public area of the site.

Table 4: Features of the restricted area

Restricted Area	National Institutions	International Institutions
Profile of the alumni members	25%	100%
Professional opportunities	50%	100%
Timetable of events	25%	33%
Library and database	0%	33%
Discussion forum	0%	33%
Story reports	0%	33%
News	0%	33%

Source: Elaborated by the authors

This study does not encompass the analysis of the strategy or the operation of alumni associations; still, some data about the functioning of associations have emerged from empirical observation and deserve to be reported in order to assist academic managers in the design of the portal (Table 5).

Table 5: Items of the analysis of the strategy observed in alumni associations

Items of the analysis of the strategy	National Institutions	International Institutions
The institution name is cited by the association	100%	100%
The word alumni is cited by the association	50%	100%
Compulsory contribution (registration and annual fees)	25%	33%
Accepts donations	No information	100%

Source: Elaborated by the authors

The data interpretation makes one believe that the term alumni is not as publicized in Brazil, as well as the culture of accepting donations, present in 100% of the international institutions. The culture of maintaining a link between the alumni and the university in Brazil does not follow the same pace of the international institutions, which could be a hindrance to deploy an association, however, it poses as a business opportunity as observed with the success of the international entities.

The analysis of the portals allows for the identification of particularities and findings that may assist in the innovative process, among which we highlight:

I. National Institutions

a) The social network Facebook was used for massive dissemination of the first alumni meeting, which featured the presentation of alumni who have become major executives.

b) Provision of an electronic form for the donation of missing books in the university library.

c) An area named Nostalgia for the alumni to write their stories.

d) All information is available in the restricted area of the site. In the public area, only two videos are offered on YouTube. One is a welcome video and the other features the importance of being a member of the institutions community.

e) Because email addresses were stored only from 2007 onwards, stakeholders who graduated before this period and wish to join the association have to update their files in an online form.

II. International Institutions

a) Provision of an online form for financial donation to innovative projects of the institution.

b) Clubs throughout the country for local interactions among alumni geographically near.

c) A lifelong email address connected to the institution.

d) Event photos for sale at cost price.

e) Online form for feedback about the site.

f) Disclosure of some statistics about alumni: programs, the alumni's gender, location, type of participation in the association and types of employment.

g) Permission for visitors to register to the site to have access to some restricted areas.

h) Displays suggestions for reading books written by alumni.

i) A lifelong email addresses managed by Google. It includes the following features at no charge to the alumni: POP and IMAP email, 25 GB of storage, Google Calendar and Google Docs.

j) Disclosure of data of alumni classes in the space "find my class", some classes have unique pages on social media sites such as Facebook, LinkedIn or Twitter.

k) Lectures around the world, with differentiated prices for the alumni.

l) It offers related institutions dedicated to facilitating relations between future students, current students and alumni.

Online stores to sell products, such as t-shirts and souvenirs.

4.2.   THE USE OF THE SCAMPER TECHNIQUE

In order to create new opportunities from the combination of different sets of information in response to the need to create an attractive alumni portal, the authors discussed the checklist of questions using the SCAMPER technique and found business opportunities, as described in Figure 2.

Figure 2: The use of the SCAMPER technique to develop an alumni portal

S – Substitute	• Substitute traditional features with Google apps for education. • Replace the disclosure of events for a page on the social media Facebook.
C – Combine	• Combine the alumni portal with the Alumni Monitoring System to ensure that the data is always up to date. • Invite alumni of *stricto sensu* graduate programs in Business Management or even alumni from other fields as visitors, in order to increase the networking base. • Perform annual meetings combined with scientific events at the university to enhance membership due to the convergent interests.

A – Adapt	• Adapt the LinkedIn profile to the profile of the alumni portal using a plug-in that updates automatically.
M – Modify or Magnify or Diminish	• Change the training area to area of interest, in this case, all dissemination of events or studies will be customized according to interest and not only to the field of study. • Allow the dissemination of professional opportunities not only through companies, but also through the alumni. • Include space for dissemination of research or developing studies linking them to the area of interest.
P – Put to other uses	• Disseminate in the space "Events", symposia or scientific congresses held by entities other than the university. Currently, each student or alumnus is responsible for identifying scientific events by themselves and in different channels. • Disseminate corporate events in the area, even if they do not occur in institutions of higher education.
E – Eliminate	• Remove documentary information, such as history, mission, and vision to avoid polluting the site.
R – Rearrange or Revert	• Register all students and alumni and email them a login and a password rather than request registration. • Create space for reporting of personal stories or articles on topics of interest and communicate them by email when new stories are published, not depending only on the alumni's initiative to check on news on the portal.

Source: Elaborated by the authors

Understanding innovation as the action of finding creative solutions, the answers obtained from the checklist of questions help educational institutions to deal differently with the challenges concerning alumni participation in alumni associations.

4.3. PROPOSITION OF AN ALUMNI PORTAL PROTOTYPE

Based on the benchmarking result and the use of the SCAMPER technique, the authors suggested an alumni portal prototype to serve the interests of the target audience and at the same time innovate what is already practiced in the market, in order to increase membership and alumni participation.

Figure 3 suggests the design of the public area of the portal. Aiming to increase the number of accesses by both the alumni and visitors, the menus "The Association", "News" and "Events" do not require a login or password for access. In addition, there is a pre-restricted area available to registered visitors, where they can register vacancies and have access to the journals of the institutions of higher education. The objective of this area is to increase the database for possible dissemination. Three other menus are presented: "Alumni Restricted Area", "Contact us" and shortcut to "Social Network".

Figure 3: Prototype of an Alumni Portal – Public Area

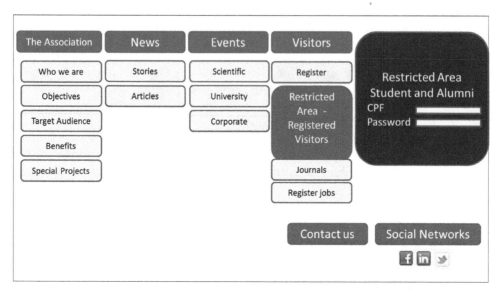

Source: Elaborated by the authors

Figure 4 illustrates that the area restricted to current students and alumni of the educational institution include the following features: "Google Apps" for e-mail and other benefits; "Virtual Community" for discussions on topics of common interest; "Research in development" for registration or consultation of areas of interest; "Follow-up of Alumni" for the university to follow the professional and academic career of its alumni; "Virtual Library" to access databases; "Consultation Profile" localizable from class, courses or area of interest; "Profile" imported from LinkedIn with the option for editing and finally "Professional Opportunities" to register and consult employment opportunities.

Figure 4: Prototype of an Alumni Portal – Restricted Area

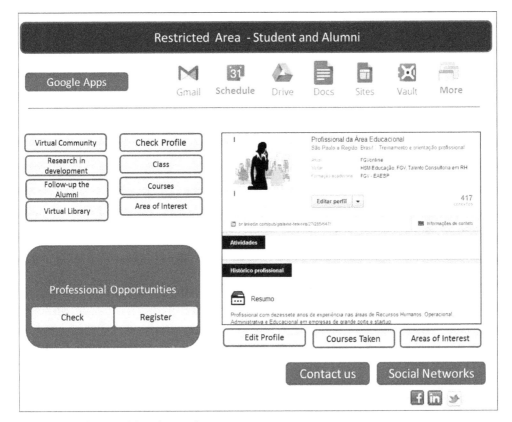

Source: Elaborated by the authors

This is a study based on creative technique, whose aim is to obtain the largest number of possible ideas, meaning that not all the ideas that have emerged will be implemented, because their implementation requires a complementary study on the technical and operational feasibility.

5. CONCLUSIONS

Admittedly, the alumni are some of the most valuable assets of the institutions of higher educations, because from their actions, the university's name is evidenced in the society. Thus, the more extended the contact between the institution and its alumni, the greater opportunities for feedback and knowledge development. An alumni portal facilitates the promotion of research, the exchange of experience, in addition to providing personal, professional and academic networking.

In view of the spread of Internet use, managers need to consider it as an important tool in their business strategy. The Internet is widespread for synchronous or asynchronous meetings regardless of time or geographic location, however, the amount of information that it offers can be confusing and users may use their time unduly. In this sense, a portal of relationships should have at its core the following premise: to be attractive and reach the target audience. It should consider the content for the target audience you want to reach, targeting the information for this purpose; otherwise, it runs the risk of having an alumni portal so generic that does not interest the institution or the target audience.

An alumni association portal should be designed to attract the alumni to the institution's current activities, a fact that hardly occurs when the student completes the course and no longer has the obligation to be physically involved in academic activities. It is necessary to consider that the alumni have their practical actions affected by experiences during the university course and that it transcends the issuing of the diploma. It is important that the relationships between students/institutions or students/students perpetuate beyond the course completion, as they contribute to the personal, professional and academic careers of the alumni from the networking generated. A portal of an alumni association should be intuitive and interesting in order to assist in enhancing the sense of belonging of the alumni to the educational institution.

The innovations arising from this study combine frequent elements at renowned educational institutions with demands of the target audience. Main innovations encompass the inclusion not only of the alumni, but also the current students to the alumni portal, therefore, the link with the university is strengthened from the beginning with a tendency to bolster the bond between the students (current and alumni) and the educational institution. The portal should also include all students of the programs regardless of the student's initiative to register and use the LinkedIn profile, which is a current networking tool and already used by most students and alumni. All innovations seek to establish a portal of an alumni association that facilitates interaction and information sharing about issues that transcend academic graduation, greatly contributing to the development of society.

A limiting factor of the study refers to the absence of a study on the operational and technical feasibility for the development of the alumni portal; therefore, the prototype is just a reference, with no purpose to be deterministic. Further studies could involve a bibliographical review and action research to support the development of the portal, or even with the strategic and cultural aspects of the alumni association.

REFERENCES

Arcoverde, L. (24 de Outubro de 2013). *Valor Econômico*. Acesso em 24 de Outubro de 2013, disponível em Valor Econômico:

Barnard, Z. (2007). UJDigispace. *Online Community Portals for Enhanced Alumni Networking,* Tese de Doutorado, University of Johannesburg. Johannesburg, South Africa.

Brant, K. E., & Regan, P. J. (Fevereiro de 2002). *The Spectrum of Alumni Involvement.* Acesso em 29 de Outubro de 2013, disponível em University at Albany :

Cagnazzo, L., Taticchi, P., & Botarelli, M. (2008). A literature review on innovation management tools. *Revista de Administração da UFSM, 1(3)*, 316-330.

CAPES. (2010). *Coordenação de Aperfeiçoamento de Pessoal de Nível Superior.* Acesso em 27 de Maio de 2013, disponível em Planilhas comparativas da Avaliação

Trienal 2010

Chia, H., Jonesa, E. L., & Grandhama, L. P. (2012). Enhancing Mentoring between Alumni and Students via Smart Alumni System. *Procedia Computer Science*, 1390-1399.

Council for Advancement and Support of Education. (Março de 2005). *Principles of Practice for Alumni Relations Professionals at Educational Institutions*. Acesso em 24 de Outubro de 2013, disponível em Case - Council for Advancement and Support of Education

Cunha, I. C., Freitas, M. A., Yázigi, L., Junior, L. K., Pietro, M. S., Poz, M. E., et al. (set./dez. de 2007). Construindo Instrumentos de Avaliação para os Cursos de Pós-Graduação Lato Sensu da Unifesp: relato de experiência. *Estudos em Avaliação Educacional*, pp. 29-40.

Financial Times. (2013). *Business Educacion*. Acesso em 15 de Outubro de 2013, disponível em Financial Times

Hax, A. C., & Wilde II, D. L. (Setembro de 2002). The Delta Model - Toward a Unified Framework of Strategy. *Working Paper*.

Hidalgo, A., & Albors, J. (2008). Innovation management techniques and tools: a review from theory and practice. *R&d Management, 38(2)*, 113-127.

Kandampully, J. (2003). B2B relationships and networks in the Internet age. *Management Decision, Vl. 41(5)*, 443-451.

Khandwalla, P. N. (2006). Tools for Enhancing Innovativeness in Enterprises. *VIKALPA, 31(1)*, 1-16.

Marconi, M. d., & Lakatos, E. M. (2010). *Fundamentos de Metotologia Científica*. São Paulo: Atlas.

Martins, G. d., & Theóphilo, C. R. (2009). *Metodologia da Investigação Científica para Ciências Sociais Aplicadas*. São Paulo: Atlas.

Melo, A. M., Carpinetti, L. C., & Silva, W. T. (2000). Proposta de Metodologia para Identificação de Objeto de Estudo de Benchmarking. *ENEGEP*.

Michalko, M. (2006). *Thinkertoys - A Handbook of Creative-Thinking Techniques*. Berkeley: Ten Speed Press.

Newman, M. D., & Petrosko, J. M. (25 de January de 2011). Predictors of Alumni Association Membership. *Research in Higher Education*, pp. 52:738–759.

Porter, M. E. (1996). What is Strategy? *Harvard Business Review*, 61-78.

Primo, A. F. (1997). A emergência das comunidades virtuais. *Intercom 1997 - XX Congresso Brasileiro de Ciências da Comunicação*, (pp. 1-17). Santos.

Santos, V. M. (Janeiro de 2012). *Criatividade e Inovação no Processo de Planeamento de Sistemas de Informação,* Tese de Doutorado, Universidade do Minho Escola de Engenharia. Minho, Portugal.

Serrat, O. (2010). *The SCAMPER Technique*. Acesso em 29 de Outubro de 2013, disponível em DigitalCommons@ILR - Cornell University ILR School

Teixeira, G. C., Maccari, E. A., & Kniess, C. T. (jul./dez. de 2012). Impactos do uso de técnicas de gerenciamento de projetos na realização de um evento educacional. *Revista de Gestão e Secretariado - GeSec*, pp. 67-86.

Tidd, J., Bessant, J., & Pavitt, K. (2008). *Gestão da Inovação*. Porto Alegre: Bookman.

Wikipedia. (Outubro de 2013). *Wikipedia*. Acesso em 22 de Outubro de 2013, disponível em Wikipedia

14

THE CASE OF INCA´S NATIONAL TUMOR BANK MANAGEMENT SYSTEM IN BRAZIL

Antonio Augusto Gonçalves
Instituto Nacional de Câncer - INCA (Brazilian National Cancer Institute), Rio de Janeiro, RJ, Brazil

Claudio Pitassi
Valter Moreno de Assis Jr.
Faculdades Ibmec do Rio de Janeiro, Rio de Janeiro, RJ, Brazil

ABSTRACT

Information Technologies can provide the basis for new directions in cancer research, supplying tools that identify subtle but important signs from the analysis of clinical, behavioral, environmental and genetic data. The purpose of this paper is to describe and analyze the system developed for managing Banco Nacional de Tumores (SISBNT) – National Tumor Bank System – highlighting its role in the technological innovation of Instituto Nacional do Câncer (INCA) – Brazilian National Cancer Institute. It is a qualitative empirical theoretical paper, descriptive and exploratory in nature, based on the single case study method and on participant observation. The results show the importance of good practices in information management for the full operation of a biobank in a research-oriented pharmaceutical company. There is also evidence that the implementation of SISBNT has contributed to the improvement of cancer treatment quality and to the support of efforts towards the organization of the integration of clinical, translational and basic research. The non-use of data mining techniques for the identification of molecular patterns and structures associated with the different types of cancer undergoing study at INCA seems to occur due to the early stage of Bioinformatics and translational research, as well as the National Tumor Bank, in the institution.

Address for correspondence / Endereço para correspondência

Antonio Augusto Gonçalves, Doctor´s Degree in Production Engineering from the Universidade Federal do Rio de Janeiro UFRJ, 2004. The INCA´s Head of the Information Technology Division and Assistant Professor at the Professional Administration Master´s Degree Course from the Universidade Estácio de Sá do Rio de Janeiro. Address: Rua do Rezende 195, sala 304, Centro - Rio de Janeiro, CEP: 20230-092

Claudio Pitassi, Doctor´s Degree in Administration from Pontifícia Universidade Católica do Rio de Janeiro, PUC-Rio, 2004, Address: Assistant Professor and Researcher at Faculdades Ibmec do Rio de Janeiro. Faculdades Ibmec-RJ Mestrado em Administração Mater´s Degree in Administration Address: Av. Presidente Wilson, 118 – CEP. 20030-020 - Centro - Rio de Janeiro – RJ

Valter Moreno de Assis Jr., PhD in Business Administration from the University of Michigan, 2001, Assistant Professor and Researcher at Faculdades Ibmec do Rio de Janeiro. Faculdades Ibmec-RJ Mestrado em Administração Mater´s Degree in Administration Address: Av. Presidente Wilson, 118 – CEP. 20030-020 - Centro - Rio de Janeiro – RJ

Keywords: Information and Communication Technologies (ICT); Biobank; Health Management; Technological Innovation; Biopharmaceutical.

1. INTRODUCTION

According to the World Health Organization, 2014, one out of eight deaths in the world is caused by cancer. In Brazil, there is a complex scenario in cancer treatment. The occurrences and rates of death have been growing, around 576,000 cases every year: they are particularly high when it comes to prostate cancer in men and breast cancer in women. Research has found that waiting lines for treatment and diagnosis have become commonplace in many regions of the country, resulting in patients being diagnosed at advanced stages of the disease.

According to the Rede Brasileira de Pesquisas sobre o Câncer – Brazilian Cancer Research Network – cancer is a disease caused by the buildup of genetic and epigenetic modifications in the genome of a normal cell. Such modifications result from errors that occur during DNA replication and exposure to mutagenic agents and agents in the cell metabolism. In addition, according to the Brazilian Cancer Research Network, *"the identification of the modified genes in tumor cells which are directly related to tumorigenesis has been the main focus of cancer genetics research over the last 30 years."*

Promptness in referring patients to proper therapeutic procedures, with a short waiting time, is essential to increase survival rates, improve quality of life and the chance of being cured. Being diagnosed early is one of the most critical success factors: it is, therefore, essential to create organizational mechanisms that simplify the access to pertinent information and to health care services in order to reduce the fragmentation of the services and to speed up diagnosis time and beginning of cancer treatment.

In the Brazilian context, Instituto Nacional do Câncer (INCA) – Brazilian National Cancer Institute – is the federal agency in charge of setting and implementing assistance, education and cancer prevention policies, with a specific coordination team based in the city of Rio de Janeiro. Ever since 1997, INCA has made huge changes in its organization, with the aim of transforming its Research Center (RC) into a Technological Development Center (TDC) that is capable of leading Brazilian efforts towards the development of drugs in the oncology therapeutic class. From this background of change, Information and Communication Technologies (ICTs) have played a relevant role in supporting R&D activities.

The Rede de Atenção Oncológica (RAO) - Oncologic Attention Network - is the main vehicle through which the Brazilian National Cancer Institute (INCA) bases its national integration plan on. Its purpose is to establish a partnership between organizations responsible for research and services in the cancer area. This network translates into a cooperation environment with the aim of joining doctors, administrators and society segments that represent patients. Its goals are the following: i) to make the access to information and knowledge easy on all spheres – doctors, hospital administrators and patients; ii) to create a community for the practice of research and treatment; iii) to develop a friendly environment and easy access to relevant information to support clinical and administrative decision-making processes.

Cancer-related research is a long, complex and high-risk process and involves a myriad of organizations (Goldblatt & Lee, 2010). Brazil still does not have a suitable public structure for the storage of tumor samples used in different cancer research lines. Hence, the creation of a biobank and of an IT architecture that provides easy information access is critical in order to speed up research projects and reduce the fragmentation of the databases used. According to the World Health Organization (2009), the biobank represents an organized collection of human biological material and associated information, collected prospectively and specifically stored for research purposes, in accordance with recommendations and technical, ethical and pre-defined operational standards.

This reality highlighted the need to establish policies that aim to create a national bank of tumor samples (National Tumor Bank). The first step towards it was the investment in the development of technological infrastructure. One important decision was the implementation of a system that could support the network of organizations involved in the collection and processing of normal and tumor tissue samples, blood and clinical data of the most relevant tumors in Brazil, becoming a necessary tool for the advancement of research at INCA.

Studies show that there is a big potential for theoretical and empirical research on the use of Information Science and IS Management to support cancer treatment and prevention (Clauser, Wagner, Aiello Bowles, Tuzzio, & Greene, 2011; Krysiak-Baltyn et al., 2014; O'Brien M., Kaluzny D., & Sheps G., 2014; Peterson, Bensadoun, Lalla, & McGuire, 2011; Pitassi, Gonçalves & Moreno, 2013).

This study broadens scientific knowledge in these areas, in an attempt to answer the following research question: how can modern information and communication technologies contribute to the management of technological innovation in health care, in particular in a biopharmaceutical company, which operates in an oncology therapeutic class? In this sense, the specific purpose of this paper is to describe and analyze the system developed for the management of Banco Nacional de Tumores (SISBNT) – National Tumor Bank System - highlighting its role in basic, translational and clinical research at INCA (Brazilian National Cancer Institute) in Brazil.

2. THEORETICAL FRAMEWORK

As shown by Pronovost and Goeschel (2010), most countries have been facing serious problems in healthcare, arising from: i) the increase in the demand for healthcare due to the growth in the number of elderly citizens with chronic diseases; ii) higher demand for accessibility to extra hospital care which ensures efficiency, equality and individualization of healthcare; iii) limitation of financial resources; iv) difficulty recruiting and retaining personnel. Medical resources, such as specialized personnel, hospital beds and state-of-the-art equipment, are usually costly, which results in a huge budgetary pressure. These challenges help to transform highly complex services, such as cancer treatment, into high relevance areas for the organizations that operate therein (Goldblat & Lee, 2010).

Healthcare organizations have generated massive amounts of data distributed on hospital information systems, patient electronic records, administrative systems, etc (Côrtes & Côrtes, 2011). However, most of this effort has proven unfruitful, as this information is hardly ever effectively used in decision-making processes (Abidi, 1999). According to this reality, there is a need to create an environment in healthcare organizations that makes it easy to transform all this raw information into knowledge (Barbosa et al., 2009). Therefore, as determined by Wickramasinghe (2000), researchers, doctors, nurses and other professionals in healthcare can be referred to as sophisticated knowledge workers.

They have the means of production, specialists' skills and training obtained throughout the years of formal learning and education, using this experience in clinical decision-making processes and treatment of diseases. Knowledge management in healthcare organizations can be defined as a combination of concepts and techniques to make it easy to create, indentify, acquire, develop, disseminate and use intellectual capital (O'Leary, 1998), whose creation and dissemination take place by means of multidisciplinary teams (Fried et al, 1998).

It is important to highlight that cancer patient services are inherently multidisciplinary, involving the primary care doctor, the pathologist, the oncologist and the surgeon (O'Brien M. et al., 2014; Peterson et al., 2011). The quality of these services has been affected by the limited number of qualified oncology professionals and by the reduced number of research professional networks specialized in complex scientific disciplines that involve cancer treatment (Rastogi, Hildesheim & Sinha, 2004; Lenoir, 1998). The use of information technology can contribute significantly to the improvement of healthcare (Abraham, Nishihara, & Akiyama, 2011; Bardhan & Thouin, 2013; Côrtes & Côrtes, 2011). For instance, Galligioni, Berloffa and Caffo (2009) describe their experiences in the development and use of electronic records of medical oncology patients to support research in this area. These records have been designed carefully in order to integrate the spectrum of cancer information and to allow it to be shared between researchers, stressing the importance of the use of Information and Communication Technologies (ICTs).

Despite such reports as the one by Galligioni et al. (2009), the implementation of Information Systems (IS) has basically scratched the surface of possibilities and the potential of applying Information Science to healthcare (Wallace, 2007), especially in the context of developing countries (Turan & Palvia, 2014). Such authors as Catanho, Miranda and Degrave (2007) and Wallace (2007) suggest that basic research using information and communication technologies can provide resources for new directions in clinical sciences. In the context of cancer treatment, Bash et al. (2004) present three fundamental lines of work. The first line has its focus on state-of-the-art clinical medicine, which can include therapies based on evidence and sophisticated and personalized studies on the nature of the patients' tumor and its biological characteristics. The second line regards the systemic approach of the patients' care and needs (physical, psychosocial, functional and spiritual). The third line regards the use of Information and Communication Technologies that support clinical medicine geared towards patients and their care.

As far as the first line is concerned, cell and molecular-related studies generated a large number of data related to genetic mapping and protein structures, turning Biology into a "mathematical" science and, increasingly, based on information (Lenoir, 1998). Researchers in Pharmacogenomics and Pharmacoepidemiology need this and other types of information in order to understand why patients respond differently to the treatment with certain drugs, both regarding adverse effects and efficiency in the treatment (Kim & Gilbertson, 2007). It is noticed, however, the importance of modern information technologies to provide the collection, management and processing of such data in an efficient and efficacious fashion. In general, their introduction in cancer research and treatment institutions means opportunities for the development and adoption of organizational innovations.

According to the Oslo Manual - The Organization for Economic Co-operation and Development (1997), technological innovations comprehend the implementation of technologically new products and processes, and meaningful technological improvements in products and processes. At the organizational level, innovation "[...] implies combining different types and parts of knowledge and transforming them into useful products and services" (Figueiredo, 2009, p.31). In the biopharmaceutical industry, technological innovation, characterized by the systematic discovery of new drugs or of new uses for the drugs already on the market, depends on the mastering and integration of various scientific disciplines, such as Molecular Biology, Fine Chemicals, Computer Science, Information Science, Physics, Optics, and Mechanical Engineering, among others (Pitassi, Moreno & Gonçalves, 2014). Therefore, the discovery of new drugs depends on the technological capability built by the organization in a variety of areas (Moreira & Pitassi, 2013). Given these characteristics, the pharmaceutical industry was one of the trailblazers in adopting open innovation models (Hughes & Wareham, 2010). Traditional linear and vertical models of innovation, such as the Innovation Funnel (Cooper, 1993), reflect a concern on the part of the companies regarding the "false positive", in view of the magnitude of the investments usually made in the development of new products (Chesbrough, 2006). In the current technical productive paradigm, due to the risks and costs involved, innovation is established as an interdepartmental and inter-organizational process (Bell & Figueiredo, 2012). Therefore, open innovation models are currently predominant in organizations, including Brazilian organizations, which seek to dynamize in-flows and outflows of knowledge and technology (Pitassi, 2014).

Biopharmaceutical organizations, which focus their research on the oncology therapeutic class, have resorted to (with the purpose of creating more new drug production opportunities) translational research, which guides research from "the bench to the bedside", as a mechanism to promote the integration between advancements resulting from basic research and clinical trials (Goldblat & Lee, 2010). According to Chiaroni, Chiesa and Frattini (2008), basic research in biopharmaceuticals is done at three essential stages: i) identification of the disease genetic base; ii) identification of the compound for the treatment of the disease; iii) pre-clinical tests. As for cancer, basic research is necessary for the advancement of knowledge on genetic mutation causes that lead to the different stages of the disease (Goldblat & Lee, 2010).

Studies on the possible causes of the poor performance of the information sent out by DNA then gave rise to the research in: Genomics, which analyzes genetic sequencing, aiming to quantify the gene expression in cells; **Proteomics**, which carries out experiments to identify the structure of proteins and their functions in living organisms; **molecular dynamics**, which simulates the physical movement of atoms and molecules (Lenoir 1998).

In general, a clinical trial or clinical study is defined by Good Clinical Practice (GCP) as "*any investigation in human subjects intended to discover or verify the clinical, pharmacological, and/or other pharmacodynamic effects of an investigational product(s), and/or to identify any adverse reactions to an investigational product(s), and/or to study absorption, distribution, metabolism, and excretion of an investigational product(s) with the object of ascertaining its safety and/or efficacy. In* the cancer studies, basic research in Molecular Biology is essential for the identification of new drugs and the *a priori* assessment of their positive and negative effects on the treatment of the disease. The development of this type of research is considerably driven forward by the availability of biological samples (Goebell & Morente, 2010). In this sense, biobanks have been developed in many countries with tumor samples (Specimen Central, 2014).

According to the World Health Organization (2009), a biobank is an organized collection of human biological material and associated information, collected prospectively and stored for research-related purposes in accordance with recommendations or pre-defined operational, ethical and technical standards. The challenges to establish, develop and sustain biobanks with the required size and scope for clinical studies are highlighted in the literature (McQueen et al., 2014).

The contribution of comprehensive and structured biobanks, as determined by good information management practices, is seen as a condition for the advancement of translational research on cancer, owing to the difficulty perceiving standards from the variety of causes and manifestations of the disease (Goebell & Morente, 2010). Thus, it is necessary to stress the importance of the standardization of processes for the integrity of the stored samples (Malm et al., 2013), as well as the potential for the use of data-mining techniques in translational research (Krysiak-Baltyn et al., 2014).

3. METHODOLOGY

The empirical theoretical study described in this paper is a field research, with a qualitative approach, descriptive and exploratory in nature (Vergara, 2005). It is descriptive as it shows the motivations for the implementation and main functionalities of Banco Nacional de Tumores (SISBNT) – National Tumor Bank System. It is exploratory as it seeks to analyze the contribution that SISBNT makes towards the integration between clinical, translational and basic research, a process that is still at an early stage in Brazilian pharmaceutical companies.

The study adopts the single case study method (Yin, 1994), having semi-structured interviews and participant observation as the main ways of data collection (Checkland, 1991). The case study, to the extent it takes dimensions of time and space into account (Yin, 1994), has proven to be a suitable methodological tool for the analysis of a phenomenon whose development occurred concomitantly to the huge structural changes that had taken place at INCA as of the second half of the 1990s.

The choice of emblematic cases is a suitable scientific procedure due to the opportunity to understand specific dynamics; therefore, they can teach important lessons to organizations with the same mission statement or organizational objectives (Yin, 1994). Choosing INCA as a single case owes to the fact that the organization is the most qualified in Brazil to perform all the translational research stages in the oncology therapeutic class and to the efforts of incorporating ICTs made by the institute over the last years.

The research analysis unit consisted of organizational units involved in the development and use of the National Tumor Bank (NTB), herein seen as components of a broad information system, supported by equipment and computer technologies. The focus of data collection and analysis was on the role of SISBNT in the management of the information generated at the biobank and applied to basic, translational and clinical research activities.

Field data collection took place by two different methods. One of the authors of this paper was a member of INCA´s Information Technology Division when this research was being done, working on the development and implementation of the organization's IT strategy. As such, he could closely monitor the development and implementation of SISBNT, interacting with the various actors and technological artifacts involved. In addition to the data obtained from the documents related to this process, the researcher´s own perceptions were used as an input for the analysis of the investigated phenomena herein.

Consequently, the first method of data collection - participant observation, - performed by him was selected (Argyris, Putnam & Smith, 1985): this method is justified because it was intrinsically associated to the implementation of the Banco Nacional de Tumores (SISBNT) – National Tumor Bank System.

In the second data collection method, the researchers conducted five semi-structured interviews with the persons in charge of the implementation of SISBNT in the area of Information and Communication Technologies and with five representatives of the areas of the Research Center (users of the system) including the manager of the SISBNT. The interviews had been conducted over the first six months of 2011, based on a script with open questions, and structured from the literature review used in the research. Its main purpose was the collection of evidence regarding the role that SISBNT had been developing in basic, translational and clinical research in oncology.

The choice of the interviewed subjects was intentional, made from the identification of the key actors in the process of the implementation of the National Tumor Bank. The fact that one of the researchers was in charge of INCA´s ICT contributed not only to the identification of these subjects, but also to the scheduling and quality of the interviews. All the interviews were conducted on the premises of INCA and recorded with the consent of the interviewees. All the answers were transcribed for later analysis.

The data collected was treated by the thematic or categorical content analysis method, triangulating the frequency in which terms and ideas present in the recorded answers occurred, with the observations and data obtained by the aforementioned researcher, in light of the concepts and constructs selected in the literature (Bardin, 1998). This researcher´s experience in the implementation of SISBNT was also important to the interpretation of the interviewees´ cognitive activity.

It is important to highlight the limitations of this method, given the subjectivity inherent to the interpretation of the researchers´ accounts during data analysis. In order to reduce this problem, the researchers´ interpretations, emerging at the data analysis stage, were sent to the interviewees for later corrections. However, no correction requests were received by the team.

4. THE CASE OF INCA´S NATIONAL TUMOR BANK

INCA is an organization from the Health Ministry, responsible for the development of activities and their coordination for the prevention and control of cancer in Brazil. INCA's hospital units are located in the City of Rio de Janeiro, integrating the Sistema Único de Saúde (SUS) – Unified Health System – and offer a full treatment to people with cancer. Patients with mobility issues, or without clinical conditions to attend outpatient appointments, are visited regularly at their homes by interdisciplinary teams.   Today, INCA is a landmark institution in Latin America when it comes to clinical trials for oncology therapeutic class. INCA is an active member of the Rede Brasileira de Pesquisas sobre o Câncer – Brazilian Cancer Research Network – whose strategy is the unification of basic, translational and clinical research on the disease. INCA is also a member of the Rede Nacional de Pesquisa Clínica em Hospitais de Ensino - National Clinical Research Network in School Hospitals – whose purpose is to be an institutional model in clinical studies, based on the best research practices, aimed at the Sistema Único de Saúde (SUS) – Unified Health System. Currently, the network is composed of 20 units associated with university institutions, serving all Brazilian regions, with the purpose of incorporating regional research vocations into development practices, in a decentralized management perspective.

4.1 The Banco Nacional de Tumores (SISBNT) – National Tumor Bank System

Over the last few years, INCA has been investing significantly in the implementation of an IT architecture that integrates the organization's main processes and departments and that provides the exchange of information and cooperation between the institute, clinics and laboratories, distributed in its hospital units.

Over the last ten years, the focus of the IT corporate unit has been on the management systems and medical assistance systems, seeking to standardize equipment and software and to unify access codes (single registration). In 2005, INCA developed a project with the purpose of establishing a network for collection and processing of normal and tumor tissue samples, blood and clinical data of the most relevant tumors in Brazil (in relation to their frequency and morbidity). This network is composed of cancer university medical centers and hospitals, including INCA's hospitals, totaling 20 centers in the five geographic regions of the country.

The centers were chosen based on their potential to recruit patients and on the availability of trained personnel for diagnosis, sample collection and data processing. It is important to highlight the fact that such activities are performed in accordance with protocols defined by INCA for collection, identification, storage and transference of samples obtained by the members of the network to the institute's Research Center.

The National Tumor and DNA Bank lies central in the aforementioned project, created with the purpose of supporting studies in the area of markers in diagnosis and therapy, in significant samples of the Brazilian population. INCA's National Tumor Bank consists of a biobank, with the clinical history data of patients who donated their samples to the institute, and of a physical repository for the cells obtained from such samples, in order to carry out clinical trials, and for use in basic research projects. Its development allows the standardization and computerization of the sample collection procedures, clinical data records and monitoring of patients for prospective studies, which may be used as a model for routine hospital conduct.

The Banco Nacional de Tumores (SISBNT) – National Tumor Bank System – is an information system developed by INCA's corporate IT department, in order to support the National Tumor Bank, depending on the demand of the institution's

Research Centre. As it can be seen in Figure 1, the process that SISBNT supports consists of six stages and involves professionals from such areas as Pathology, Surgery and Laboratory.

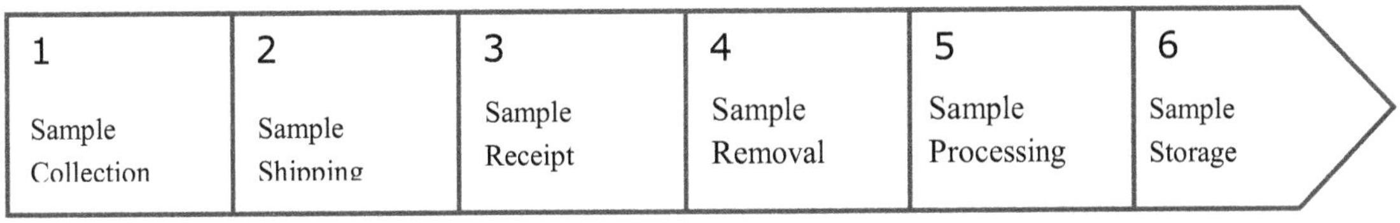

1	2	3	4	5	6
Sample Collection	Sample Shipping	Sample Receipt	Sample Removal	Sample Processing	Sample Storage

Figure 1 – National Tumor Bank´s Workflow Process

Source: by the authors

The National Tumor Bank team's internal workflow process is initiated with the signature of the informed consent document, in which the patient authorizes the collection of their tissue and blood samples during the surgical procedure they are undergoing. Collection procedure is performed directly in the operating theater of the National Tumor Bank´s associated hospitals. In the hospitals, there is a computer where the technician in charge of registering samples can perform a patient search by means of three different options: patients´ registration, number of the informed consent document, or number of the examination done on the pathological anatomy system, which is integrated to the Banco Nacional de Tumores (SISBNT) – National Tumor Bank System.

The technician in charge inputs the date and time of the collection (automatically entered with current date and time, but with the possibility of changing them in cases of previous date and time entry on the system). The system enables the sample-adding function where the user can add tissue samples and/or fluids to the same collection. For every new sample, the technician in charge inputs the class type (tissue or fluid) and fills out the fields with the characteristics of the sample, listed in Chart 1. Figure 2 shows the screen of the Banco Nacional de Tumores (SISBNT) – National Tumor Bank System - with which the technician interacts at this stage of the process.

Tissue Class Type Characteristic	Fluid Class Type Characteristics
Type of receiver (tube or microscope slide)	Type of receiver (tube or microscope slide)
Part region (A, B, C...)	Subclass
Subclass	Topography
Pathological state	Type of procedure
Type of procedure	Information on blood transfusion

Tissue Class Type Characteristic	Fluid Class Type Characteristics
Topography	Information on chemotherapy
Side	Information on anticoagulant
Type of preservation	Time of the collection
Observation	Type of preservation
	Volume

Chart 1: Characteristics of the Sample Type per Class

Source: by the authors

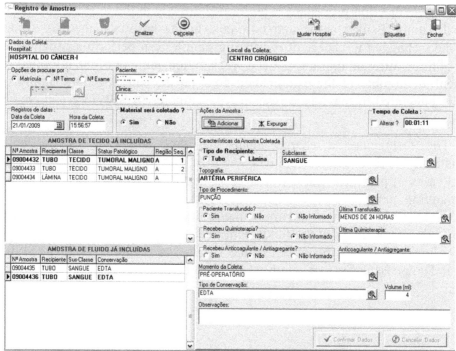

Figure 2 – Sample Collection

At the end of the sample collection, the technician generates a report containing information on the samples they entered on the system. This report is sent to the National Tumor Bank, together with the receiver of the collected samples. After receipt, the condition of the sample is defined; it can be *removed* (the sample is removed from the bank due to quality issues) or *processed,* which develops one of the following conditions: *restrict use* (sample restricted for the National Tumor Bank's use only), *available* (sample available for research*), unavailable* (sample unavailable for research), *depleted* (sample that originated secondary components), and *reserved* (reserved for some research).

The National Tumor Bank´s storage process is initiated by the barcode reading of the primary sample, from which their secondary components are extracted. According to the class and type of preservation of the primary sample, other types of secondary components are obtained, such as: serum, DNA, RNA, proteins, plasma, total leukocytes, mononuclear cells, layers, manipulated tissue and supernatant fluids.

In order to store a sample, the system needs to provide a map with the available positions in the National Tumor Bank´s physical storage where they can be stored (Figure 3). The technician in charge informs which batch (it is possible to choose one among all the batches received and not stored, according to the Banco Nacional de Tumores (SISBNT) – National Tumor Bank System), chooses the samples to be positioned and performs their allocation on the system.

The samples are allocated the first free positions in a receiver, complying with the criterion established for the storage conditions (for instance, blood can only be stored in the –80° freezer and marrow bone, in the –40° one). After the end of the allocation entered on SISBNT, a report is automatically generated, informing the technician in charge where each sample is going to be stored physically.

The Banco Nacional de Tumores (SISBNT) – National Tumor Bank System – also has a search tool that finds the receivers on the system, as well as their storage tree, as seen in Figure 3. It is possible to navigate through its boxes and positions and select one of them in order to obtain a summary of the information on the sample therein stored.

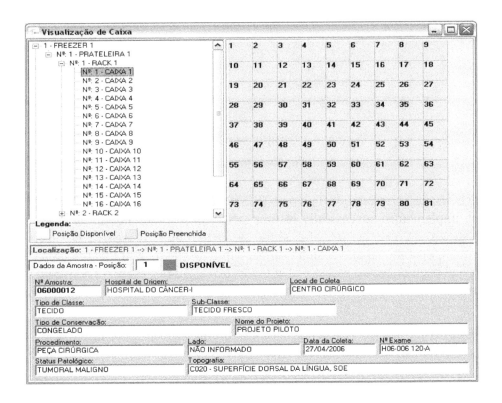

Figure 3 – Storage Map

In addition to the information on the samples, made available by the search in the freezer, the system also provides a sample search by code or donor. By using the sample code or donor's registration, the technician in charge is able to obtain all the information on the sample, as well as the characteristics of their collection, pathological anatomy, clinical laboratory and storage. Figure 4 shows the screen related to this type of search.

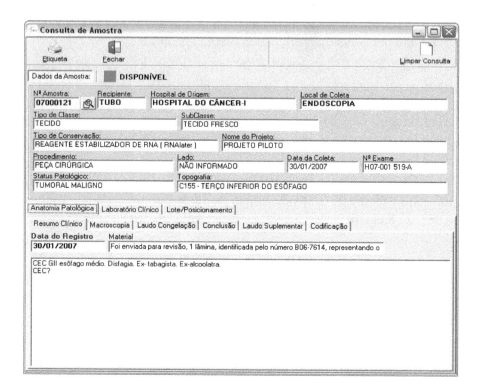

Figure 4 – Sample search by code or donor

The Banco Nacional de Tumores (SISBNT) – National Tumor Bank System – has been implemented successfully in four different hospitals in Rio de Janeiro. The system shows an average of 500 searches, made by 237 registered users with management, operational and search profiles. Up until the date of this research, 26.363 samples had been collected and stored at the National Tumor Bank. In addition, 19.721 informed consent documents had been signed and 19.401 clinical questionnaires had been answered.

Due to the nature of storing data and the need to protect the privacy of the patients, the Banco Nacional de Tumores (SISBNT) – National Tumor Bank System cannot be accessed directly by INCA's researchers. It has its own team for the management of the system, which is also responsible for providing the information requested in the experiments. In fact, in order for the researchers to have data available to their project, they first need to sign the terms and conditions at INCA's ethics committee. Therefore, the National Tumor Bank can be regarded as the facility for the institute's basic, translational and clinical research.

4.2 The Banco Nacional de Tumores (SISBNT) – National Tumor Bank System – and INCA´s Innovation Management

There was a consensus on INCA´s executive board of directors towards the fact that the institute needed to focus its strategic actions on the advancement of cancer knowledge in Brazil. Aligned with this consensus, the role of R&D has taken shape since the middle of the last decade, seeking to transform INCA´s Research Center into a Technological Development Center. Among all the initiatives regarded as critical for research to move on to the next level, the National Tumor Bank stands out in the eyes of the interviewees. Figure 5 shows the central role that the National Tumor Bank may play in INCA´s scientific research if the efforts towards the development of new compounds continue to advance in the institution.

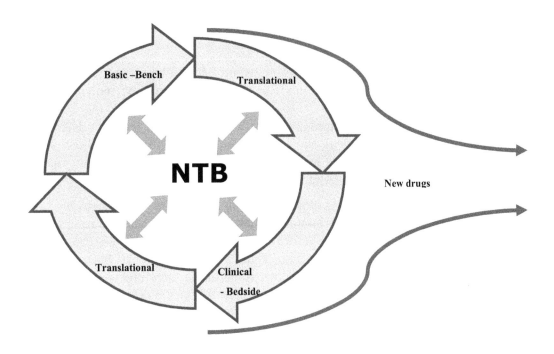

Figure 5 – The role played by the National Tumor Bank in INCA´s research

Source: by the authors

The National Tumor Bank was considered by the research coordination team as one of the milestones in the change of direction of the R&D strategies and policies at the institute, which is in line with the importance, highlighted in the literature, of creating and managing biobanks that support research in life sciences (McQueen et al, 2010). It was seen as an innovation, a structuring project for the research field, which initiated its automation process with a biobank that relied on an infrastructure for micro dissection and arrays of tissues and DNA, up to the point of implementing the Banco Nacional de Tumores (SISBNT) – National Tumor Bank System.

Thus, there was a clear strategic purpose behind the development and implementation of the National Tumor Bank system, which was aligned with the view, as far as innovation is concerned, predominant at that time at INCA's executive level. This high level of congruence was a determinant for the project to be supported by the institute's top management, making it a priority at the institution. It is confirmed in this research the idea that the commitment of the main stakeholders of the organization and a strong organizational leadership are highly necessary to the success of the implementation of information systems in healthcare organizations (Cresswell & Sheikh, 2013; Gruber, Cummings, LeBlanc, & Smith, 2009).

Currently, INCA is a landmark institution in Latin America when it comes to clinical trials for stages 1, 2 and 3 of oncology therapeutic class. Around 80% of INCA's clinical studies are sponsored by major global pharmaceutical companies, which use these clinical studies in multicenter tests of new drugs or for new uses for already existing active principles. The remaining 20% of the studies is requested by INCA's own researchers or by the Rede Nacional de Pesquisa Clínica - National Clinical Research Network.

INCA's basic research areas involve experiments focused on the identification of the genetic base of the disease and on the identification of molecules for the treatment of various cancer types. Five years ago, together with the experiments performed in physical laboratories, INCA, reflecting the change in the R&D profile under development, structured its Bioinformatics and Computational Biology, which carry out *in silico* analyses of the date generated in experiments in Genomics, Proteomics, molecular modeling and virtual screening.

The creation of a translational research laboratory was seen by INCA's managers as an essential step towards the effective integration of basic research where Bioinformatics is found - and clinical trials focused on drug projects, contributing to reducing the academic characteristic that INCA's research used to have a short time ago. As a rule, translational research is described in the literature as a link or a linear integration process of basic research into clinical trials (Goldblat & Lee, 2010). At INCA, as seen in Figure 5, the manager of the translational research laboratory manager understands that his projects are going to play an increasingly interactive role.

In line with this perspective, some projects carried out at INCA stemmed from problems observed in clinical practice, giving rise to research questions, whose answers made it necessary to resort to basic research in order to develop the hypothesis, retesting it in the translational or clinical context. The cells stored at the National Tumor Bank lie central in the clinical and retro alignment process, whose moving around is managed by the Banco Nacional de Tumores (SISBNT) – National Tumor Bank System.

The Research Center managers understood that INCA was qualifying itself, based on the new process and systems of Information and Communication Technologies, on the ongoing efforts for the construction of an institutional/legal landmark cancer research in order to support the network of Brazilian researchers (many of them in the academic community who do not have resources to advance their research towards pre-clinical and clinical study stages). Herein, SISBNT plays a critical role by providing objective conditions for this research to advance up to the point it reaches higher complexity stages that involve a higher need for resources, such as stage 1, 2 and 3 pre-clinical and clinical tests.

It is possible to see the important role of leaderships at the institute regarding the integration of the different areas of the organization, with the support of systems that would interconnect, improve and speed up relevant information flows between these areas. As a matter of fact, efforts to integrate and bring together the various sectors within the organization and its ICTs are usually seen as critical for the successful implementation of computational systems in the area of healthcare (Cresswell & Sheikh, 2013; Gagnon et al., 2010). Actually, it seemed that a consensus existed between the various actors involved in the process of adoption of the Banco Nacional de Tumores (SISBNT) – National Tumor Bank System.

This consensus related to the need for development and implementation of a system that properly supported the joint efforts of cancer care providers and researchers. Thus, the investigated case provides additional empirical support to how important it is for users to understand the potential benefits arising from technology and the effective commitment to the project (Yarbrough & Smith, 2007; Yusof, Stergioulas, & Zugic, 2007).

The role played by the Information Technology Division (ITD) in the design and implementation of SISBNT showed evidence that good practices in information management can contribute to the consolidation of the biobank in biopharmaceutical organizations, which adopt translational research in the oncology therapeutic class, as highlighted by Goebell & Morente (2010). The ability of the ITD team, in particular its manager, to discuss with the various stakeholders of the project, to understand their expectations and to define an IT solution that respected autonomy needs of the various areas - and at the same time, that promoted its integration - was essential for the success of the initiative.

As frequently cited in the literature (Cresswell & Sheikh, 2013; Gagnon et al., 2010; Yarbrough & Smith, 2007), the good relationship between the areas involved in the adoption of the new system was critical for the alignment of roles, responsibilities, activities information flows and functionalities inserted into the scope of the Banco Nacional de Tumores (SISBNT) – National Tumor Bank System. As highlighted by Yusof et al. (2007), "technological, human and organizational factors are equally important [to the success of IT adoption in healthcare organizations], as well as the alignment between them".

At the end of data collection, it was noticed that although the connection between the different research areas of the Research Center was still fragmented, the basic research areas, both in physical laboratories and in Computational Biology, already performed experiments proposed by translational research and they were assessed in clinical trials. Data from SISBNT were already used in basic bench research, in some translational research laboratory projects and in clinical trials.

In part, due to the fact that the *in silico* research still did not focus on the national drug program, the experiments in Bioinformatics had not accessed the data from SISBNT until the end of 2013, although this area had declared its intention to do so shortly. Among the initiatives that contributed for this to happen were the increase in the number of stored samples at SISBNT and the emergence of powerful tools of genetic sequencing and High Performance Computing, acquired in October 2001 and June 2012.

It is worthy of mentioning, however, that as Bioinformatics and translational research, and the National Tumor Bank itself, had been recently created in the institution - the adoption of techniques or data mining tools highlighted in the literature - with a focus on the recognition of standards, structures and rules (Krysiak-Baltyn et al, 2014), was not evident at INCA by the time this study was conducted.

5. CONCLUSIONS

In response to the previously defined research question, the analysis of INCA´s Banco Nacional de Tumores (SISBNT) – National Tumor Bank System illustrates how a biobank with the support of modern information and communication technologies can contribute to the improvement of scientific research in oncology therapeutic class. The benefits of such an innovation are immediately reflected in the improvement of the access to useful knowledge and in the increase of operational efficiency in R&D management. Other benefits are reflected as an increased focus on patients' expectations and their satisfaction, as well as on improvements in transference and dissemination of knowledge.

It is clear in the analysis of the evidence that the implementation of such an initiative demanded, before anything else, that the involved managers clearly understand the process of use of this information and the meaning of the initiative for the repositioning of INCA as an oncology innovation center. It was also confirmed that SISBNT represented an important innovation in the institute´s IT area, which meant a paradigm shift at INCA´s Research Center. Such an innovation contributed to, according to the interviewees´ own answers, positioning INCA as the only Brazilian organization that boasts technical conditions to perform all the stages of research focused on the development of new drugs in oncology therapeutic class. It was also clear that the Banco Nacional de Tumores (SISBNT) – National Tumor Bank System - is regarded by researchers as a critical tool, not only due to the relevance that the data contains, but also due to the fact it was developed in compliance with good practices from Information Science. This fact keeps the organization from resorting to database and technological platforms, which are unsuitable to the objectives of knowledge management, and to the integration of the technological co-development process, as these practices seem to be commonplace in R&D areas, which do not boast a suitable IT support.

The explanatory nature of this research imposes some limitations to the scope of the aforementioned conclusions. First, there is no intention to exhaust the discussion about the contributions to a biobank in cancer technological innovation, in particular regarding the organizational mechanisms and processes, which are necessary to its development and management. In addition, as one of the authors of this research is the person in charge of the implementation of SISBNT, the subjectivity in the treatment of the answers given cannot be ruled out. At last, the context of this research, INCA, a public organization associated with the Health Ministry of Brazil, imposes restrictions on the generalization of results for other private companies and for other countries.

Despite the aforementioned limitations, this research contributed to theory and practice as it highlights the importance of bringing together of IT and R&D in cancer research, as seen in the case of INCA´s Banco Nacional de Tumores (SISBNT) – National Tumor Bank System. From this finding, a question for further research is raised: what organizational mechanisms and processes can contribute to a better integration of IT into basic, translational and clinical research? Lastly, it is understood that R&D and IT managers of Brazilian biopharmaceutical companies can use the case herein described in order to learn important lessons that aim to improve their innovation efforts.

REFERENCES

Abidi, S.S.R. (1999). Healthcare knowledge management through building and operationalizing healthcare enterprise memory. In: *Medical informatics in Europe (MIE'99)*, Amsterdam: IOS Press.

Abraham, C., Nishihara, E., & Akiyama, M. (2011). Transforming healthcare with information technology in Japan: A review of policy, people, and progress. International *Journal of Medical Informatics*, 80(3), 157–170.

Argyris, C., Putnam, R. & Smith, D.M. (1985). *Action science*: action science concepts, methods and skills for research and intervention. Nova York: Jossey Bass.

Barbosa J.G.P., Gonçalves A.A., Simonetti V., & Leitão A.R. (2009). A proposed architecture for implementing a knowledge management system in the Brazilian National Cancer Institute. *Brazilian Administration Review-BAR,* 6 (3), pp.246-262.

Bardhan, I. R., & Thouin, M. F. (2013). Health information technology and its impact on the quality and cost of healthcare delivery. *Decision Support Systems*, 55(2), 438–449.

Bardin L. (1979). *Análise de conteúdo*. Lisboa: Edições 70.

Bash, E. M., Thaler, H.T., Shi, W., Yakren, S., & Schrag, D. (2004). Use of information resources by patients with cancer and their companions. *Cancer*, 100 (11), pp.2476–2483.

Bell, M., & Figueiredo, P.N (2012). Building innovative capabilities in latecomer emerging market firms: some key issues. In: Amann, E., & Cantwell, J (orgs). *Innovative firms in emerging market countries*. New York and London. 1ed. Oxford: Oxford University Press, 1, pp. 24-109.

Catanho M., Miranda A.B., & Degrave, W. (2007). Comparando genomas: bancos de dados e ferramentas computacionais para a análise comparativa de genomas procarióticos. *Revista Eletrônica de Comunicação, Informação & Inovação*, 1 (2), pp.335-58.

Checkland, P. B. (1991). From framework through experience to learning: The essential nature of action research. In: Eds. Nissen, H., Klein, H. K, & Hirschheim, R. A. *Information Systems Research: Contemporary Approaches and Emergent Traditions*. Amsterdam: North-Holland, pp.397-403.

Chiaroni, D., Chiesa V., & Frattini F. (2008). Patterns of collaboration along the Bio-Pharmaceutical innovation process. *Journal of Business Chemistry*, 5 (1), pp.7-22.

Clauser, S. B., Wagner, E. H., Aiello Bowles, E. J., Tuzzio, L., & Greene, S. M. (2011). Improving modern cancer care through information technology. *American Journal of Preventive Medicine*, 40(5 Suppl 2), S198–207.

Cooper, R. (1993). *Winning at new products*: accelerating the process from idea to launch. Cambridge: Perseus Books.

Côrtes, P.L., & Côrtes, E.G. de P. (2011). Hospital information systems: a study of electronic patient records. *Journal of Information Systems and Technology Management - JISTEM*, 8 (1), pp.131-154.

Cresswell, K., & Sheikh, A. (2013). Organizational issues in the implementation and adoption of health information technology innovations: an interpretative review. *International Journal of Medical Informatics*, 82(5), e73–86.

Figueiredo, P.N. (2009). *Gestão da inovação*: conceitos, métricas e experiências de empresas no Brasil. Rio de Janeiro: LTC.

Fried, B.J., Leatt, P., Deber, R., & Wilson, E. (1998). Multidisciplinary teams in health care: lessons from oncology and renal teams. *Healthcare Management Forum*, 4, pp.28-34.

Gagnon, M. P., Pluye, P., Desmartis, M., Car, J., Pagliari, C., Labrecque, M., ... Légaré, F. (2010). A systematic review of interventions promoting clinical information retrieval technology (CIRT) adoption by healthcare professionals. *Int. J. Med. Inf.*, 79, 669.

Galligioni, E., Berloffa, F., & Caffo, O. (2009). Development and daily use of an electronic oncological patient record for the total management of cancer patients: 7 years' experience. *Annals of Oncology*, 20 (2), pp.349-52.

Goebell, P.J. & Morente, M.M. (2010). New concepts of biobanks - strategic chance for uro-oncology. *Urologic Oncology,* 28, pp.449-457.

Goldblatt E.M., & Lee, W-H. (2010). From bench to bedside: the growing use of translational research in cancer medicine. *American Journal of Translational Research*, 2 (1), pp.1-18.

Gruber, D., Cummings, G., LeBlanc, L., & Smith, D. (2009). Factors influencing outcomes of clinical information systems implementation: a systematic review. *Comput. Inform. Nurs.*, 27(151).

Hagen, J.B. (2000). The origins of Bioinformatics. *Nature Reviews Genetics*, 1 (3), pp. 231-236.

Hughes, B., & Wareham J. (2010). Knowledge arbitrage in global pharma: a synthetic view of absorptive capacity and open innovation. *R&D Management*, 40(3), pp.324-343.

INCA (2014). Instituto Nacional do Câncer. *Estimativa 2014, Incidência de Câncer no Brasil.*

Kim, S., & Gilbertson, J. (2007). Information requirements of cancer center researchers focusing on human biological samples and associated data. *Information Processing & Management*, 43, pp.1383–1401.

Krysiak-Baltyn, K., et al. (2014). Compass: a hybrid method for clinical and biobank data mining. *Journal of Biomedical Informatics, 47,* pp.160–170.

Lenoir, T. (1998). Shaping biomedicine as an information science. In: Bowden, M.E., Hahn T.B., & Willians R.V. (eds). *Proceedings of the 1998 Conference on the History and Heritage of Science Information Systems*. ASIS Monograph Series. Medford, NJ: Information Today, pp. 27-45.

Macmullen, W. J., & Denn, S. (2005). Information problems in molecular biology and Bioinformatics. *Journal of the American Society for Information Science and Technology – JASIST*, 56 (5), pp.447-456.

Malm, J. et al. (2013). Developments in biobanking workflow standardization providing sample integrity and stability. *Journal of Proteomics*, 95, pp.38-45.

McQueen, M.J. (2014) The challenge of establishing, growing and sustaining a large biobank: a personal perspective. *Clinical Biochemistry,* 47, pp.239-244.

Ministério da Saúde, Departamento de Ciência e Tecnologia, Secretaria de Ciências, Tecnologia e Insumos Estratégicos. (2009). *Diretrizes nacionais para biorrepositórios e biobancos de materiais humanos em pesquisa. Revista de Saúde Pública* [online], 43 (5), pp.898-899.

O'Brien M., D., Kaluzny D., A., & Sheps G., C. (2014). The Role of a Public-Private Partnership: Translating Science to Improve Cancer Care in the Community. *Journal of Healthcare Management,* 59(1), 17–29.

O'leary, D. (1998). Knowledge management systems: converting and connecting. *IEEE- Intelligent Systems*, 13 (3), pp.30-33.

Organização Mundial da Saúde (2014), World Cancer Report, *International Agency for Research on Cancer*. IARC, ISBN 978928320429 .

Organização para a Cooperação e Desenvolvimento Econômico. (2007). Manual de Oslo - Diretrizes para a coleta e interpretação de dados sobre Inovação. 3ª ed., Tradução   FINEP,   2007.

Ouzounis, C.A., & Valencia, A. (2003). Early Bioinformatics: the birth of a discipline - a personal view. *Bioinformatics*, 19 (17), pp.2176-2190.

Peterson, D. E., Bensadoun, R.-J., Lalla, R. V, & McGuire, D. B. (2011). Supportive care treatment guidelines: value, limitations, and opportunities. *Seminars in Oncology*, 38(3), 367–73.

Pitassi, C (2014). Inovação aberta nas estratégias competitivas das empresas brasileiras. REBRAE. *Revista Brasileira de Estratégia (Eletrônica)*, v. 1, pp. 18-36.

Pitassi, C., Moreno, V. de A. Jr., & Gonçalves A.A. (2014). Fatores que influenciam a adoção de ferramentas TICs nos experimentos de Bioinformática de organizações biofarmacêuticas: um estudo de caso no Instituto Nacional do Câncer. *Revista Ciência e Saúde Coletiva,* 19(1), pp.257-268,

Pronovost, P. J., & Goeschel, C. A. (2010). Viewing healthcare delivery as science: Challenges, benefits, and policy implications. *Health Services Research*, 45, pp.1508–1522.

Rastogi, T., Hildesheim, A., & Sinha, R. (2004). Opportunities for cancer epidemiology in developing countries. *Naure Reviews Cancer*, 4, pp.909-917.

RBPC. (n.d.). *Rede Brasileira de Pesquisas sobre o Câncer.*

Specimen Central. (2014). *Global Directory of Biobanks, Tissue Banks and Biorepositories.*

Turan, A. H., & Palvia, P. C. (2014). Critical information technology issues in Turkish healthcare. *Information & Management*, 51(1), 57–68.

Vergara, S.C. (2005). *Projetos e relatórios de pesquisa em administração*, 6ª edição. São Paulo: Atlas.

Wallace, P.J. (2007). Reshaping cancer learning through the use of health information technology. *Health Affairs* (Project Hope), 26 (2), pp.169-177.

Wickramasinghe, N. (2000). IS/IT as a tool to achieve goal alignment in the health care industry. *International Journal of Healthcare Technology and Management*, 2 (1), pp.163-180.

Yarbrough, A. K., & Smith, T. B. (2007). Technology acceptance among physicians: a new take on TAM. *Med. Care Res. Rev.*, 64, 650.

Yin, R.K. (1994). *Case study research: Design and methods*. London: SAGE Publications.

Yusof, M. M., Stergioulas, L., & Zugic, J. (2007). Health information systems adoption: findings from a systematic review. *Stud. Health Technol. Inform.*, 129(262).

Permissions

The contributors of this book come from diverse backgrounds, making this book a truly international effort. This book will bring forth new frontiers with its revolutionizing research information and detailed analysis of the nascent developments around the world.

We would like to thank all the contributing authors for lending their expertise to make the book truly unique. They have played a crucial role in the development of this book. Without their invaluable contributions this book wouldn't have been possible. They have made vital efforts to compile up to date information on the varied aspects of this subject to make this book a valuable addition to the collection of many professionals and students.

This book was conceptualized with the vision of imparting up-to-date information and advanced data in this field. To ensure the same, a matchless editorial board was set up. Every individual on the board went through rigorous rounds of assessment to prove their worth. After which they invested a large part of their time researching and compiling the most relevant data for our readers.

The editorial board has been involved in producing this book since its inception. They have spent rigorous hours researching and exploring the diverse topics which have resulted in the successful publishing of this book. They have passed on their knowledge of decades through this book. To expedite this challenging task, the publisher supported the team at every step. A small team of assistant editors was also appointed to further simplify the editing procedure and attain best results for the readers.

Apart from the editorial board, the designing team has also invested a significant amount of their time in understanding the subject and creating the most relevant covers. They scrutinized every image to scout for the most suitable representation of the subject and create an appropriate cover for the book.

The publishing team has been an ardent support to the editorial, designing and production team. Their endless efforts to recruit the best for this project, has resulted in the accomplishment of this book. They are a veteran in the field of academics and their pool of knowledge is as vast as their experience in printing. Their expertise and guidance has proved useful at every step. Their uncompromising quality standards have made this book an exceptional effort. Their encouragement from time to time has been an inspiration for everyone.

The publisher and the editorial board hope that this book will prove to be a valuable piece of knowledge for researchers, students, practitioners and scholars across the globe.

List of Contributors

Josimeire Pessoa de Queiroz
Centro Universitário da FEI, São Paulo, SP, Brazil

Braulio Oliveira
Centro Universitário da FEI, São Paulo, SP, Brazil

Frederico Wergne de Castro Araújo Filho
Integrated Center of Manufacture and Technology –
National Service of Industrial Learning – DR, Salvador,
Bahia – Brazil

X. L. Travassos
Integrated Center of Manufacture and Technology –
National Service of Industrial Learning – DR, Salvador,
Bahia – Brazil

Paulo S. Figueiredo
Integrated Center of Manufacture and Technology –
National Service of Industrial Learning – DR, Salvador,
Bahia – Brazil

Mohammad Kamel Alomari
College of Business and Economics, Qatar University,
Doha, Qatar

Adriano Olímpio Tonelli
Instituto Federal de Educação, Ciência e Tecnologia de
Minas Gerais, Formiga, MG, Brasil

Paulo Henrique de Souza Bermejo
Universidade Federal de Lavras, Lavras/MG, Brasil

André Luiz Zambalde
Universidade Federal de Lavras, Lavras/MG, Brasil

Jose Melchor Medina-Quintero
Universidad Autonoma de Tamaulipas, Tamaulipas,
México

Alberto Mora
Universidad Autonoma de Tamaulipas, Tamaulipas,
México

Demian Abrego
Universidad Autonoma de Tamaulipas, Tamaulipas,
México

Danielle Lombardi
Villanova University, Pennsylvania, United States, USA

Rebecca Bloch
Fairfield University, Connecticut, United States, USA

Miklos Vasarhelyi
Rutgers University, New Jersey, Unites States, USA

Layla Hasan
Department of Computer Information Systems, Zarqa
University, Jordan

Maximiliano Gonetecki Oliveira
FAE Centro Universitário, Curitiba, Paraná, Brazil

Ana Maria Machado Toaldo
Federal University of Paraná, Curitiba, Paraná, Brazil

Ashir Ahmed
Swinburne University of Technology, Australia

Mazen Kamal Qteishat
Albalqa Applied University, Amman, Jordan

Haitham Hmoud Alshibly
Albalqa Applied University, Amman, Jordan

Mohammad Atwah Al-ma'aitah
Albalqa Applied University, Amman, Jordan

Alexandre Ribeiro Afonso
University of Brasília (Universidade de Brasília–UnB),
Brasília, DF, Brazil

Cláudio Gottschalg Duque
University of Brasília (Universidade de Brasília–UnB),
Brasília, DF, Brazil

Graziela Ferreira Guarda
University of Brasília – UnB, Federal District, Brazil

Edgard Costa Oliveira
University of Brasília – UnB, Federal District, Brazil

Rafael Timóteo de Sousa Júnior
University of Brasília – UnB, Federal District, Brazil

Gislaine Cristina dos Santos Teixeira
UNINOVE - Nove de Julho University, São Paulo, SP,
Brazil

Emerson Antonio Maccari
UNINOVE - Nove de Julho University, São Paulo, SP,
Brazil

Antonio Augusto Gonçalves
Instituto Nacional de Câncer - INCA (Brazilian National
Cancer Institute), Rio de Janeiro, RJ, Brazil

Claudio Pitassi
Instituto Nacional de Câncer - INCA (Brazilian National Cancer Institute), Rio de Janeiro, RJ, Brazil

Valter Moreno de Assis Jr.
Faculdades Ibmec do Rio de Janeiro, Rio de Janeiro, RJ, Brazil